ONE HUNDRED
TWENTIETH-CENTURY
PHILOSOPHERS

ONE HUNDRED
TWENTIETH-CENTURY
PHILOSOPHERS

Edited by
Stuart Brown
Diané Collinson
Robert Wilkinson

London and New York

First published 1998
by Routledge
11 New Fetter Lane, London EC4P 4EE
29 West 35th Street, New York, NY 10001

Typeset in Times by Routledge
Printed and bound in Great Britain by Page Bros (Norwich) Ltd

British Library Cataloguing in Publication Data
A catalogue record for this book is available from the British Library

Library of Congress Cataloging-in-Publication Data
One hundred twentieth-century philosophers / edited by Stuart Brown,
Diané Collinson, Robert Wilkinson.
p.   cm.
Includes biographical references.
(pbk.: alk paper)
1. Philosophers–Biography. 2. Philosophy, Modern–20th century.
I. Brown, Stuart C. II. Collinson, Diané
III. Wilkinson, Robert
B804.055   1988
190′.9′04–dc21   97–30846
[B]   CIP
ISBN 0-415-17996-3

CONTENTS

NOTES ON CONTRIBUTORS

Bredin, Hugh
Senior Lecturer in Scholastic Philosophy,
Queen's University, Belfast.

Brown, Stuart
Professor of Philosophy, Open University.

Bunnin, Nicholas
Fellow, University of Essex, and Director,
Philosophy Project, Centre for Modern
Chinese Studies, University of Oxford.

Cadwallader, Eva
Professor of Philosophy, Westminster
College, Pennsylvania.

Carr, Indira Mahalingam
Senior Lecturer in Law, University of Exeter,
Special Lecturer in Philosophy, University of
Nottingham, Director of Exeter University
Centre for Legal Interdisciplinary
Development (EUCLID)

Chant, Colin
Lecturer in History of Science and
Technology, Open University.

Colinson, Diané
Senior Lecturer in Philosophy,
Open University.

Davey, Nicholas
Lecturer in History and Theory of Art,
University College Llandalb.

Edwards, Jim
Senior Lecturer in Philosophy,
University of Glasgow.

Ellis, Anthony
Professor of Philosophy, Virginia
Commonwealth University.

Everitt, Nicholas
Lecturer in Philosophy, School of Economic
and Social Studies, University of East Anglia.

Fulford, K. W. M.
Professor of Philosophy and Mental Health,
University of Warwick.

Gorner, Paul
Lecturer in Philosophy,
Department of Philosophy,
University of Aberdeen.

Jones, Barry
Formerly research student,
University of Manchester.

Kuehn, Manfred
Associate Professor of Philosophy,
Purdue University, Lafayette, Indiana.

Lacey, A. R.
Senior Lecturer in Philosophy (retired),
King's College, University of London.

Lamb, David
Reader in Philosophy, Department of
Biomedical Science and Bioethics,
University of Birmingham.

Lee, Keekok
Reader in Philosophy, University of
Manchester; Director of the Centre for
Philosophy and the Environment.

Leggatt, Stuart
Research student,
University of Reading.

Lewis, Peter
Lecturer in Philosophy,
University of Edinburgh.

Lyas, Colin
Senior Lecturer in Philosophy,
University of Manchester.

Martin, R. N. D.
Self-employed; part-time work for the Open
University.

Mason, Richard
Fellow of Wolfson, College, Cambridge
and Tutor in Philosophy, Madingley
Hall.

Mills, Stephen
Lecturer in Philosophy, University of
Ulster at Coleraine, Nothern Ireland.

Outhwaite, William
Professor of Sociology,
University of Sussex, Brighton.

Plant, Kathryn
Tutor in Philosophy,
Open University.

Pollard, Denis
Senior Lecturer in Philosophy,
University of Glamorgan.

Quinton, Lord Anthony
Formerly President of Trinity College,
Oxford and Fellow of the British
Academy.

Reck, Andrew
Professor of Philosophy, and Director of
Liberal Arts Program, Julane University,
New Orleans; Editor; *History of Philosophy
Quarterly.*

Reese, William
Former Professor of Philosophy,
State University of New York at Albany.

Rickamn, H. P.
Visiting Professor in Philosophy,
City University, London.

Sim, Stuart
Professor of English Studies,
University of Sunderland.

Singer, Marcus
Professor of Philosophy Emeritus,
University of Wisconsin, Madison.

Walford, David
Lecturer in Philosophy,
University of Wales, Lampeter.

Whitford, Margaret
Teacher, Queen Mary and Westfield College,
London.

Wilkinson, Robert
Staff Tutor and Senior Lecturer in
Philosophy, Open University.

Williams, James
Lecturer in Philosophy, University of
Dundee.

LIST OF ABBREVIATED SOURCES

These abbreviations appear in the **Sources** field at the end of an entry, where the author gives the sources used in compilation of the entry. Periodical abbreviations, including indexes, derive from the initial letters of each significant word in the title, and remain in italic. Books, including annuals, use the author's or editor's name(s), or a contraction of the title where this is not possible, and appear in roman.

AJP	*Australasian Journal of Philosophy*
Becker	*Encyclopedia of Ethics*, ed. Lawrence C. and Charlotte Becker, New York: Garland, 1992
Burkhardt	*Handbook of Metaphysics and Ontology*, ed. Hans Burkhardt, Munich: Philosophia Verlag, 2 vols, 1991
CA	*Contemporary Authors: A Bio-bibliographical Guide to Current Authors and their Works*, Detroit: Gale Research Inc., 1962–present
CBD	*Chambers Biographical Dictionary*, various editions; 1994 edition ed. Magnus Magnusson
Corsini	*The Concise Encyclopedia of Psychology*, ed. R. Corsini, New York: John Wiley, 1987
DAB	*Dictionary of American Biography*, Oxford: Oxford University Press and New York: Scribner's, various editions
Dancy & Sosa	*A Companion to Epistemology*, ed. J. Dancy and E. Sosa, Oxford: Blackwell, 1992
DAS	*Directory of American Scholars*, New York: R. R. Bowker, 1942–present
DFN	*Dizionario dei Filosofi dei Novecento*, Florence: Sansoni, 1976
DNB	*Dictionary of National Biography*, London: Oxford University Press, various editions
DSB	*Dictionary of Scientific Biography*, ed. G. C. Gillespie, New York: Scribner's, 1970–present
EAB	*Encyclopedia of American Biography*, second edition, ed. J. A. Garraty, HarperCollins (US), 1995
Edwards	*Encyclopedia of Philosophy*, ed. Paul Edwards, New York: Macmillan & Co., 1967
EF	*Enciclopedia Filosofica*, Florence: G. C. Sansoni, 6 vols, 1967
Flew	*A Dictionary of Philosophy*, ed. Antony Flew, New York: St Martin's Press, revised second edition, 1984
Goldenson	*Longman Dictionary of Psychology and Psychiatry*, ed. R. M. Goldenson, New York and London: Longman, 1984
Harré & Lamb	*The Encyclopedic Dictionary of Psychology*, ed. R. Harré and R. Lamb, Oxford: Basil Blackwell, 1983
IDPP	*International Directory of Philosophy and Philosophers*, Bowling Green, OH: Philosophy Documentation Center, Bowling Green State University, seventh edition, 1992
Kindler	*Kindlers Literatur Lexikon*, Zurich: Kindler Verlag, 1965 and 1970
Mittelstrass	*Enzyklopädie Philosophie und Wissenschaftstheorie*, ed. Jürgen Mittelstrass, Mannheim: Bibliographisches Institut AG, 1980–
MSSPNB	*Mémoires, Société des Sciences Physiques et Naturelles de Bourdeaux*
NÖB	*Neue Österreichische Biographie*, Vienna and Munich, Amalthea

Passmore 1957   *A Hundred Years of Philosophy*, John Passmore, London: Duckworth, 1957

Passmore 1985   *Recent Philosophers*, John Passmore, London: Duckworth, 1985

PBA   *Proceedings of the British Academy*

PI   *Philosopher's Index*, Bowling Green, OH: Philosophy Documentation Center, Bowling Green State University, various editions

RA   *Reader's Adviser*, Bowker (US), fourteenth edition, 1994

Reck 1968   *The New American Philosophers*, Andrew Reck, Baton Rouge: Louisiana State University Press, 1968

Reese   *Dictionary of Philosophy and Religion*, William L. Reese, New Jersey: Humanities Press, 1980

RPL   *Revue Philosophique de Louvain*

Turner   *Thinkers of the Twentieth Century*, ed. Roland Turner, Chicago: St James Press, second edition, 1987

Urmson & Rée   *The Concise Encyclopaedia of Western Philosophy*, ed. J. O. Urmson and J. Rée, London: Hutchinson, 1960

WD   *The Writer's Directory*, Chicago: St James Press, biennial

WW   *Who's Who*, London: A. & C. Black, 1843–present

WW(Am)   *Who's Who in America*, Chicago: Marquis Who's Who, 1899–present

WWW   *Who Was Who*, London: A. & C. Black, various editions

WWW(Am)   *Who Was Who in America*, Chicago: Marquis Who's Who, 1899–present

STRUCTURE OF AN ENTRY

There are three basic elements to each entry.

The opening section gives biographical details and summarizes the philosophical interests of the entrant. The first item of information after the name is nationality. Because of the difficulty of establishing entrants' preferences, English, Welsh and Scottish have been standardized as British. Cases of dual nationality or changes of citizenship have been noted. Following are dates and places of birth (*b:*), and death (*d:*) if appropriate, category (*Cat:*), interests (*Ints:*), higher education (*Educ:*), influences on the entrant (*Infls:*), and professional appointments (*Appts:*). The last are often posts held in higher education institutions, but where appropriate political and other activities are detailed.

A bibliographical section gives titles of major works by the entrant (**Main publications**), and critical or biographical works (**Secondary literature**), with dates, location and publisher where these are available. For books published before 1945, these details may not be so readily available; for political reasons also some works may be difficult to trace. The **Sources** field, at the end of the entry, lists works which were used in researching the entry, and not previously given in the **Secondary literature**. Many of these are reference works or journals, and are abbreviated. A list of the full titles can be found on page viii–ix.

Text paragraphs offer a description of the interests, ideas and work of the philosopher, expanding on the earlier summary. Influences (both on and by the entrant), central works, developments and changes in thought, alignments to schools or movements, may all be elements within this section. Names in bold type within the text are cross-references, indicating other entries that will be found in the book.

Adorno, Theodor Wiesengrund

German. *b:* 11 September 1903, Frankfurt am Main. *d:* 6 August 1969, Visp, Switzerland. *Cat:* Social philosopher; critical theorist; musicologist. *Ints:* Epistemology. *Educ:* University of Frankfurt, doctorate 1924; studied music with Alban Berg in Vienna, 1925–8. *Infls:* Walter Benjamin, Max Horkheimer, Hegel, Marx and Nietzsche. *Appts:* Editor, *Musikblätter des Anbruchs*, Vienna, 1928–1930; Privatdozent, University of Frankfurt, 1931–3; worked in Oxford, 1934–7; member of the Institute for Social Research, New York, from 1938; Beverly Hills from 1941; also worked with Paul Lazarsfeld on the Princeton Radio Research Project; Professor of Philosophy, University of Frankfurt, 1950–69; Assistant Director, 1950–5, Co-Director with Horkheimer, 1955–8, and Director, 1958–69, Institut für Sozialforschung, Frankfurt.

Main publications:

(1933) *Kierkegaard: Konstruktion des Ästhetischen*, Tünbingen: J. C. B. Mohr; second edition, Frankfurt: Suhrkamp, 1966 (English translation, *Kierkegaard: Construction of the Aesthetic*, trans. and ed. Robert Hullot-Kentor, Minneapolis: University of Minnesota Press, 1989).

(1947) (with Max Horkheimer) *Dialektik der Aufklärung*, Amsterdam: Querido (English translation, *Dialectic of Enlightenment*, trans. John Cumming, New York: Herder & Herder, 1972).

(1949) *Philosophie der neuen Musik*, Tübingen: J. C. B. Mohr (English translation, *Philosophy of Modern Music*, trans. Anne G. Mitchell and Wesley W. Bloomster, London: Sheed & Ward, 1949).

(1950) (with Elke Frenkel-Brunswick, Daniel J. Levinson and R. Nevitt Stanford) *The Authoritarian Personality*, New York: Harper & Brothers.

(1951) *Minima Moralia. Reflexionen aus dem beschädigten Leben*, Frankfurt: Suhrkamp (English translation, *Minima Moralia*, trans. E. F. N. Jephcott, London: New Left Books, 1974).

(1955) *Prismen. Kulturkritik und Gesellschaft*, Berlin and Frankfurt: Suhrkamp (English translation, *Prisms*, trans. Samuel and Shierry Weber, London: Neville Spearman, 1967).

(1956) *Zur Metakritik der Erkenntnistheorie. Studien über Husserl und die phänomenologischen Antinomien*, Stuttgart: W. Kohlhammer (English translation, *Against Epistemology: A Metacritique*, trans. Willis Domigno, Oxford: Blackwell, 1982).

(1956) (with Max Horkheimer) *Soziologische Exkurse*, Europäische Verlagsantalt (English translation, *Aspects of Sociology*, trans. John Viertel, London: Heinemann, 1973).

(1963) *Drei Studien zu Hegel*, Frankfurt: Suhrkamp.

(1963) *Eingriffe. Neun Kritische Modelle*, Frankfurt: Suhrkamp.

(1964) *Jargon der Eigentlichkeit. Zur deutschen Ideologie*, Frankfurt: Suhrkamp (English translation, *Jargon of Authenticity*, trans. Knut Tarnowski and Frederick Will, London: Routledge & Kegan Paul, 1964).

(1966) *Negative Dialektik*, Frankfurt: Suhrkamp (English translation, *Negative Dialectics*, trans. E. B. Ashton, New York: Seabury Press, 1973).

(1967) *Ohne Leitbild. Parva Aesthetika*, Frankfurt: Suhrkamp.

(1969) *Stichworte. Kritische Modelle 2*, Frankfurt: Suhrkamp.

(1969) (Introduction and contributions to) *Der Positivismusstreit in der deutschen Soziologie*, Neuwied and Berlin: Luchterhand (English translation, *The Positivist Dispute in German Sociology*, trans. Glyn Adey and David Frisby, London: Heinemann, 1976).

(1969) (ed.) *Spätkapitalismus oder Industriegesellschaft? Verhandlungen des 16 deutschen Soziologentages vom 8–11 April 1968 in Frankfurt am Main*, Frankfurt: Suhrkamp.

(1970) *Ästhetische Theorie*, ed. Gretel Adorno and Rolf Tiedemann, Frankfurt: Suhrkamp (English translation, *Aesthetic Theory*, trans. C. Lenhardt, London: Routledge & Kegan Paul, 1984).

(1970–86) *Gesammelte Schriften*, 20 vols, ed. Rolf Tiedemann, Frankfurt: Suhrkamp (the Theodor W. Adorno Archive plans to publish a further twenty volumes of posthumous papers).

(1973–4) *Philosophische Terminologie. Zur Einleitung*, 2 vols, ed. Rudolf Zur Lippe, Frankfurt: Suhrkamp.

Secondary literature:

Benjamin, Andrew (ed.) (1989) *The Problems of Modernity: Adorno and Benjamin*, London: Routledge.

Bernstein, J. M. (1992) *The Fate of Art: Aesthetic Alienation from Kant to Adorno*, Cambridge: Polity.
——(1994) *The Politics of Transfiguration*, London: Routledge.
Brunkhorst, Hauke (1990) *Theodor W. Adorno: Dialektik der Moderne*, Munich: Piper.
Buck-Morss, Susan (1977) *The Origin of 'Negative Dialectics': Theodor W. Adorno, Walter Benjamin and the Frankfurt Institute*, Hassocks: Harvester Press.
Friedeburg, Ludwig von and Habermas, Jürgen (eds) (1983) *Adorno-Konferenz 1983*, Frankfurt: Suhrkamp.
Jameson, Fredric (1990) *Late Capitalism: Adorno, or, the Persistence of the Dialectic*, London: Verso.
Jay, Martin (1973) *Adorno*, Glasgow: Collins Fontana.
——(1973) *The Dialectical Imagination: A History of the Frankfurt School and the Institute of Social Research, 1923–1950*, London: Heinemann (includes substantial bibliography).
——(1984) *Marxism and Totality*, Berkeley and Los Angeles: University of California Press.
Löbig, Michael and Schweppenhäuser, Gerhard (eds) (1984) *Hamburger Adorno-Symposium*, Lünneburg: Dietrich zu Klampen Verlag.
Rose, Gillian (1978) *The Melancholy Science: An Introduction to the Work of Theodor W. Adorno*, London: Macmillan (includes substantial bibliography).
Schweppenhauser, Hermann (ed.) (1971) *Theodor W. Adorno zum Gedächtnis*, Frankfurt: Suhrkamp (includes bibliography by Klaus Schultz).
Thyen, Anke (1989) *Negative Dialektik und Erfahrung: Zur Rationalität des nichtidentischen bei Adorno*, Frankfurt: Suhrkamp.
Wiggershaus, Rolf (1986) *Die Frankfurter Schule: Geschichte, theoretische Entwicklung, politische Bedeutung*, Munich: Hanser (English translation, *The Frankfurt School*, trans. Martin Robertson, Cambridge: Polity).
——(1987) *Theodor W. Adorno*, Munich: Beck.

Adorno is without question the most important thinker of the Frankfurt School, where he acted as a crucial mediating force between Marxism and the rest of philosophy, and between philosophy itself and sociology and cultural studies. His studies on Hegel, **Heidegger**, **Husserl**, Kierkegaard and other major philosophers are unequalled in their incisiveness, and are only now beginning to have the impact they deserve outside the German-language area. His critique of Husserl is also a critique of epistemology as traditionally conceived.

Adorno's own conception of 'negative' dialectic, a dialectic which rejects as utopian the possibility of total reconciliation, is central to neo-Marxist philosophy (see Jay 1984), as is the line of cultural criticism expressed throughout his work, notably in *Dialectic of Enlightenment* (1947), one of the central books of the twentieth century, and in his many works in the philosophy and sociology of music. Adorno's aesthetic theory has an importance far outside that field, and has been taken by many contemporary philosophers as a starting-point for reconceptualizing the role of philosophy as a whole. As Bernstein (1994) has shown, the tension between Adorno's speculative theorizing and **Habermas**'s more disciplined or, from this point of view, scientist approach, remains a fundamental legacy of the Frankfurt School.

In both philosophy and cultural theory Adorno combined a revolutionary modernism with a deep attachment to what he saw as the best elements of European thought and high culture, threatened by fascist and Stalinist totalitarianism and by commercial philistinism. *Jargon of Authenticity* (1964) is a powerful critique of the abuse of philosophical language. Adorno's own sensitivity to issues of language, including a Nietzschean hostility to terminological definition, comes out clearly in some of his more accessible works, such as his contributions to *Aspects of Sociology* (1956) and the Introductory Lectures published as *Philosophische Terminologie* (1973–4). Although his thought was sceptical, aphoristically formulated and often despairing, he was far from the nihilism and frivolity of later 'post-structuralist' thought, whose insights he may be seen to have anticipated and transcended.

WILLIAM OUTHWAITE

Althusser, Louis

Algerian-French. **b:** 1918, Birmendreis, Algeria. **d:** 1990, Yvelines, France. **Cat:** Marxist; political philosopher; epistemologist; metaphysician; philosopher of science. **Educ:** Studied at the École Normale Supérieure, Paris. **Infls:** Marx, Lenin, Gramsci, Lévi-Strauss, Gaston Bachelard and Mao Zedong. **Appts:** Professor of Philosophy, École Normale Supérieure.

Main publications:

(1959) *Montesquieu: la politique et l'histoire*, Paris: Presses Universitaires de France (English translation, *Politics and History: Montesquieu, Rousseau, Hegel and Marx*, trans. Ben Brewster, London: NLB, 1972).

(1965) *Pour Marx*, Paris: Maspero (English translation, *For Marx*, trans. Ben Brewster, London: NLB, 1969).

(1965) (with Étienne Balibar, Pierre Macherey, *et al.*), *Lire le Capitale*, Paris: Maspero; revised edition, 1968 (English translation, *Reading Capital*, trans. Ben Brewster, London: NLB,1970)

(1969) *Lénine et la philosophie*, Paris: Maspero (English translation, *Lenin and Philosophy and Other Essays*, trans. Ben Brewster, London: NLB, 1971).

(1974) *Éléments d'autocritique*, Paris: Hachette (English translation, *Essays in Self-Criticism*, trans. G. Lock, London: NLB, 1976).

(1974) *Philosophie et philosophie spontanée des savants*, Paris: Maspero (English translation, *Philosophy and the Spontaneous Philosophy of the Scientists*, trans. Ben Brewster *et al.*, London: NLB, 1990).

Secondary literature:

Assiter, Alison (1990) *Althusser and Feminism*, London: Pluto Press.

Benton, Ted (1984) *The Rise and Fall of Structural Marxism*, London and Basingstoke: Macmillan.

Callinicos, Alex (1976) *Althusser's Marxism*, London: Pluto Press.

Clarke, Simon (1980) *One Dimensional Marxism: Althusser and the Politics of Culture*, London: Allison & Busby.

Elliott, Gregory (1987) *Althusser: The Detour of Theory*, London: Verso.

Smith, Steven B. (1984) *Reading Althusser*, Ithaca, NY, and London: Macmillan.

Thompson, E. P. (1978) *The Poverty of Theory and Other Essays*, London: Cornell University Press.

Althusser is the leading figure in the movement known as structural Marxism, which sought to reinterpret Marx in the light of the work of structuralists like Lévi-Strauss. A member of the French Communist Party, Althusser's development as a philosopher is very much tied up with the fortunes of that organization, in particular with the intense policy debates that occurred within the party in the aftermath of the denunciation of Stalin at the 1956 Congress of the Soviet Communist Party, and in the context of the growing rift between Soviet and Chinese Communism. Most of Althusser's major contributions to Marxist theory, such as the theory of the symptomatic reading, the doctrine of the epistemological break, the Overdeterminism Thesis and the insistence on a sharp separation between science and ideology, stem from his interventions in these debates, as does his later interest in the work of **Mao Zedong**. Althusser's earliest intellectual influence was the philosopher of science Gaston **Bachelard**, from whose work he derived the basis for the doctrine of the epistemological break. Althusser also drew heavily on the work of **Lenin** and **Gramsci**, whose doctrine of hegemony and theories of the mutually interactive relationship between the economic base of a society and its cultural superstructure had a profound impact on Althusser's mature thought. The general drift of Althusser's project is to establish Marxism as a 'theoretical antihumanism'; that is, as a social theory whose concern is with historical process rather than with the actions of individual human beings: 'historical process without a subject' as it is known. Structuralism, with its commitment to independently operating deep structures of thought, and downgrading of the role of human agency within history, is an obvious point of reference here. Althusser's concern in his theoretical interventions was to press the claims for Marx's mature writings, *Capital* for example, over those of his youthful, so-called 'humanist' period of the early 1840s, such as the *Economic and Philosophical Manuscripts* of 1844. To counter the fashion of these largely Hegelian works amongst French humanist Marxists, Althusser posited the existence of a dramatic change in Marx's thought in the mid-1840s, a rupture or 'epistemological break', roughly from *The German Ideology* and *Theses on Feuerbach* onwards, which marked his coming of age as a 'scientific' theorist. Before 1845 Marx's thought is constrained by the ideological notions of its time; after 1845 he is conducting a scientific critique of his ideology and pointing out its deficiencies and internal contradictions. The key to identifying this break lies in Althusser's theory of the symptomatic reading, where the objective is to isolate the underlying structure of thought, or 'problematic' as Althusser terms it, which governs the production of the text and moulds its argument. It is in the nature of a problematic, whose family resemblance to **Kuhn**'s notion of 'paradigm' has been noted by several commentators, to set limits on what can be thought or called into question, and a symptomatic reading is concerned precisely to identify what those limits are. A sharp distinction is made in Althusser between ideology, a closed system of belief featuring internal contradictions which most of us are unaware of in everyday lived experience, and science, a system of enquiry open to change from within. Marxism, through its theory of dialectical materialism, is for Althusser a science, and sciences are seen to be beyond the reach of ideology. Theory is in fact an autonomous area of discourse, or 'practice', to Althusser, with Marxism being regarded as a self-validating science. In Althusser's social theory the superstructure of a culture consists of a series of such practices, variously political, ideological or theoretical, which are in a dialectical relationship with

the economic base. Taking his cue from Gramsci, Althusser treats the relationship as one of mutual interaction where base and superstructure can affect each other, whereas in a more traditional Marxist thought the base is held to be dominant. Althusser posits a 'relative autonomy' of the superstructure which is only in 'the last instance' (a thesis which remains fairly obscure) under the dominance of the base. Thus events in the superstructure are as capable of triggering a revolutionary situation as those in the base, since the former may well constitute the weak, or 'overdetermined', link in a given social formation: this is Althusser's 'Overdeterminism Thesis'. Such a relationship between base and superstructure actively precludes any possibility of meaningful human action, and historical process without a subject is primarily a matter of 'Repressive State Apparatuses' (instruments of state power such as the police or army) and 'Ideological State Apparatuses' (hegemonic institutions such as the church or universities) working through individuals. Those individuals simply act out the roles assigned to them by ideology, which provides little scope for human agency. Althusser was a major theoretical force in the French Communist Party, and his recasting of the fundamental elements of Marxist thought within a structuralist framework generated vigorous debate in Marxist circles, both inside and outside France. Arguably the most influential voice in Western Marxism during the 1960s and 1970s, Althusser's structural Marxism was much in vogue at the time and had a significant impact across a range of intellectual disciplines, such as political economy, sociology, anthropology, aesthetics and literary theory. Althusser's reputation has declined markedly since the 1970s, partly in the wake of the poststructuralist critique of the metaphysics underpinning structuralist methodology, as well as the postmodernist challenge to 'grand narrative' theories such as Marxism; and structural Marxism no longer commands much support on the left, where notions like the epistemological break are felt to be unhistorical and far too schematic. A common criticism of Althusser's work has been that it lacks a human dimension, and his theory of ideology is now considered to be overly determinist in character. E. P. Thompson, for example, has been particularly scathing of Althusser's denial of the role of human agency in history, and has also been one of a number of commentators to accuse Althusser of having Stalinist tendencies, although others, such as Steven B. Smith, have been just as keen to defend him from this highly emotive charge. Althusser's most committed disciples have been his ex-students Étienne Balibar and Pierre Macherey; the former being the co-author with Althusser of one of the central texts of structural Marxism, *Reading Capital* (revised edition); the latter having had notable success in the application of Althusserian ideas to literary theory in his widely admired study *A Theory of Literary Production* (1966).

STUART SIM

Anscombe, G(ertrude) E(lizabeth) M(argaret)

British. **b:** 1919. **Cat:** Analytic philosopher. **Ints:** Philosophy of mind; ethics; metaphysics; philosophy of religion; history of philosophy. **Educ:** Universities of Oxford and Cambridge. **Infls:** Aristotle, St Thomas Aquinas and Ludwig Wittgenstein. **Appts:** 1946–64, Research Fellowships, Somerville College, Oxford; 1964–70, Fellow of Somerville College, Oxford; 1970–86, Professor of Philosophy, University of Cambridge; 1970–86, Fellow of New Hall, Cambridge, Honorary Fellow since 1986. 1967, Fellow of the British Academy; 1979, Foreign Honorary Member, American Academy of Arts and Sciences.

Main publications:

(1939) (with Norman Daniel) *The Justice of the Present War Examined*, Oxford: published by the authors.
(1953) (trans.) Ludwig Wittgenstein, *Philosophical Investigations*, Oxford: Basil Blackwell.
(1956) 'Aristotle and the sea battle', *Mind* 65.
(1957) *Intention*, Oxford: Basil Blackwell.
(1957) *Mr Truman's Degree*, Oxford: published by the author.
(1958) 'Modern moral philosophy', *Philosophy* 33.
(1959) *An Introduction to Wittgenstein's 'Tractatus'*, London: Hutchinson.
(1961) (with Peter Geach) *Three Philosophers*, Ithaca: Cornell University Press.
(1971) *Causality and Determination*, Cambridge: Cambridge University Press.
(1975) 'The first person', in Samuel Guttenplan (ed.), *Mind and Language*, Oxford: Clarendon Press.
(1976) 'The question of linguistic idealism', in 'Essays on Wittgenstein in honour of G. H. von Wright', *Acta Philosophica Fennica* 28.
(1979) 'Under a description', *Noûs* 13.
(1981) *The Collected Philosophical Papers of G. E. M. Anscombe* (vol. 1, *From Parmenides to Wittgenstein*; vol. 2, *Metaphysics and the Philosophy of Mind*; vol. 3, *Ethics, Religion and Politics*), Oxford: Basil Blackwell.

Secondary literature:

Diamond, Cora and Teichman, Jenny (eds) (1979) *Intention and Intentionality: Essays in Honour of G. E. M. Anscombe*, Brighton: Harvester Press.
MacDonald, Scott (1991) 'Ultimate ends in practical reasoning: Aquinas's Aristotelian moral psychology and Anscombe's fallacy', *The Philosophical Review* vol. 100.

Anscombe converted to Roman Catholicism in her youth, and a substantial portion of her work on ethics and religion has been devoted to exploring and defending Catholic doctrines. As a research student in Cambridge she became a pupil of **Wittgenstein** and, although she was never a *disciple* of his views, much of her thought shows his influence. Like Wittgenstein's, much of Anscombe's work is devoted to the relation between thought and reality. Unlike Wittgenstein, however, she has a serious interest in the history of philosophy and much of her work has been done through the explicit discussion of such philosophers as Aristotle, Aquinas and Hume.

Her first published article was written in the early weeks of the Second World War. It argued, contrary to the usual assumption, that it was not a just war on the grounds that its aims were unlimited and that it would involve the unjustifiable killing of civilians. In its reliance on the theory of natural law this article foreshadowed much of her later work. It also embodied a conception of human action which she explored and developed in many later writings. According to this conception, actions have an intrinsic nature, which depends upon their direct intention, and this intrinsic nature is at least as relevant to their moral status as are their motives and any consequences they may have. For instance, it may be held that deliberately killing the innocent as a means to one's ends is murder—whatever one's motives and whatever the consequences— and is always wrong. (According to the Doctrine of Double Effect which Anscombe espoused, one may permissibly perform actions that have the deaths of innocents as a consequence only so long as this is not one's 'direct intention'.) So, in *Mr Truman's Degree* (1957) she opposed the University of Oxford granting an honorary degree to President Truman, on the ground that his ordering the use of atom bombs, with the intention of causing the deaths of innocent civilians as a means of wringing total surrender from the Japanese, was an act of mass murder. On this conception, the theory of moral evaluation depends upon the theory of action, and Anscombe argued in 'Modern moral philosophy' (1958)—an article that helped lay the groundwork for the reemergence in analytic ethics of Aristotelian virtue theory and natural law theory—that moral philosophy should be abandoned until we have an adequate philosophical psychology.

Her highly influential monograph *Intention* (1957) discussed at length a major element of this philosophical psychology, the notion of intention, although without overt reference to ethical issues. Most philosophers had thought of intentions as mental events which occurred prior to actions and caused them. Anscombe argued that we should not think of intentional action as behaviour brought about by a certain sort of *cause*, but behaviour for which it is appropriate to give a *reason* in response to the question why it occurred. She also held that one knows what one's intentions are *without observation* (in a way in which one cannot always know what, for instance, one's motives are); and this is possible only because there is a species of knowledge— *practical* knowledge—which has been much underplayed by philosophers, who have been obsessed with *theoretical* knowledge. Practical knowledge, however, could only be adequately understood through an understanding of practical reasoning, and this led Anscombe into an influential discussion of this topic and some of its ramifications.

She also drew attention to the importance of the fact that one and the same action may fall under many different descriptions, for instance 'ending a war', 'killing civilians' and 'displacing molecules of air'. Under some of these descriptions it would be intentional and under others not; and different intentional descriptions would evoke different moral evaluations. Is there, then, one *correct* description? This problem has been extensively discussed ever since.

Many of the positions that Anscombe proposed in *Intention* became, for a considerable time, extremely widely accepted. This cannot be said of much of her work. Her paper 'The first person' (1975), for instance, argues that the word 'I' is not a referring expression. Not understanding this, she held, forces us into postulating a Cartesian ego since, if 'I' were indeed a referring expression, it seems that a Cartesian ego is what it would have to refer to. Like much of Anscombe's work, this difficult paper has been much discussed, but without commanding widespread agreement.

To understand the idea of action one needs to understand causality, and some of Anscombe's most discussed work has been on this topic. In her Inaugural Lecture *Causality and Determination* (1971) (in *Collected Papers*, vol. 3) she attacked two views which, since the eighteenth century, have been widely accepted. First, she argued against what she called 'determinism', the view that every event is completely determined by a prior cause. Contrary to the view of Hume, she held that there are many sorts of cause, and some of them do not *necessitate*, or make inevitable, effects. Second, she attacked the view, deriving from Kant and which had been almost an orthodoxy for fifty years, that determinism would be consistent with freedom of the will.

After Wittgenstein's death Anscombe became one of his literary executors. In this capacity she has translated and edited many of his works. One of her own earliest works (1959) was a difficult, though highly influential, commentary on Wittgenstein's *Tractatus Logico-Philosophicus*, in which she combated the then prevalent interpretation according to which the work was a manifesto of logical empiricism. Anscombe is widely thought to be one of Britain's foremost postwar philosophers—'simply the most distinguished, intellectually formidable, original, and troublesome philosopher in sight' (J. M. Cameron, *The New Republic*, 19 May, 1982, p. 34). Her thought is almost always difficult, in large part because it raises questions at the most fundamental level. Consequently, many of her arguments have been more widely discussed than accepted. Her fierce intelligence has often found expression in a fierceness of style that not everyone has found likeable.

Sources: Passmore 1957; CA 129; WW 1992.

ANTHONY ELLIS

Arendt, Hannah

German-American (emigrated to USA in 1941). *b:* 14 October 1906, Hannover, Germany. *d:* 4 December 1975, New York. *Cat:* Social critic; political philosopher. *Educ:* Königsberg, Marburg, Freiburg and Heidelberg Universities. *Infls:* Husserl and Jaspers. *Appts:* 1946–8, Chief Editor, Schocken Books, New York; 1949–52, Executive Director, Jewish Cultural Reconstruction, New York; 1953–67, Professor, Committee on Social Thought, University of Chicago; 1967–75, Professor, Graduate Faculty, New School for Social Research, New York.

Main publications:

(1951) *The Origins of Totalitarianism*, New York: Harcourt, Brace.
(1958) *The Human Condition*, Chicago: University of Chicago Press.
(1961) *Between Past and Future: Six Exercises in Political Thought*, New York: Viking Press.
(1963) *Eichmann in Jerusalem: A Report on the Banality of Evil*, New York: Viking Press.
(1963) *On Revolution*, New York: Viking Press.
(1970) *On Violence*, New York: Harcourt, Brace.
(1978) *The Life of the Mind*, 2 vols, ed. Mary McCarthy, New York: Harcourt Brace.
(1982) *Lectures on Kant's Political Philosophy*, ed. R. Beiner, Chicago: University of Chicago Press.

Secondary literature:

Canovan, Margaret (1992) *Hannah Arendt: A Reinterpretation of Her Political Thought*, New York: Cambridge University Press.
Hill, Melvyn A. (ed.) (1979) *Hannah Arendt: The Recovery of the Public World*, New York: St Martin's Press.
O'Sullivan, Noel (1975) 'Hannah Arendt: Hellenic nostalgia and industrial society', in Anthony de Crespigny and Kenneth Minogue (eds), *Contemporary Political Philosophers*, New York: Dodd, Mead & Co.
Tolle, Gordon J. (1982) *Human Nature under Fire: The Political Philosophy of Hannah Arendt*, Washington: University Press of America.
Young-Bruehl, Elisabeth (1982) *Hannah Arendt: For Love of the World*, New Haven, Yale University Press (bibliography included).

Hannah Arendt was a complex and wide-ranging thinker whose work cannot easily be summarized. She was a critic of modern mass society which, with its tendency to atomization, alienation, anomie and diffusion of responsibility, was fertile ground for what she called 'totalitarianism', in which individual human life becomes meaningless and freedoms are eroded. To counteract this tendency she advocated the separation of public life from social and economic life. She looked back to the Greek polis and, to a lesser extent, the early United States of America as models for what public life should be. In these societies individual citizens sought to excel in service to the community, and authority was vested in institutions to which they were committed. Arendt's ideas have been extensively discussed and they have been widely influential. Her critics have, however, doubted their philosophical underpinning. One commentator (O'Sullivan 1975, p. 251) questions her identification of the broad notion of 'the public' with the comparatively narrow notion of 'the political'. Without that identification it is not so clear that political action is as central a part of a proper human life as Arendt maintained.

Sources: Derwent, May (1986) *Hannah Arendt* (biography), New York: Penguin; Turner.

STUART BROWN

Aurobindo, Ghose (popularly known as Sri Aurobindo)

Indian. **b:** 15 August 1872, Calcutta. **d:** 5 December 1950, Pondicherry. **Cat:** Metaphysician. **Educ:** St Pauls High School and King's College, Cambridge. **Infls:** Vedanta and evolutionists such as Henri Bergson and John Dewey. **Appts:** Founder of Aurobindo Ashram at Pondicherry, India.

Main publications:

(1947) *The Life Divine*, 2 vols, Calcutta: Arya Publishing House.
(1950) *The Ideal of Human Unity*, New York: Sri Aurobindo Library.
(1970–2) *Sri Aurobindo Birth Centenary Library*, Pondicherry: Sri Aurobindo Ashram (containing *Essays on the Gita*; *The Upanishad Texts, Translations and Commentaries*; *The Secret of the Veda*).

Secondary literature:

Chaudhuri, Haridas and Spiegelberg, Frederic (eds) (1961) *The Internal Philosophy of Sri Aurobindo: A Commemorative Symposium*, London: Allen & Unwin.
Chaudhuri, J. (1954) *The Philosophy of Integralism or the Metaphysical Synthesis Inherent in the Teaching of Sri Aurobindo*, Calcutta: Sri Aurobindo Pathamandir.
Pearson, Nathaniel (1952) *Sri Aurobindo and the Soul Quest of Man*, London: George Allen & Unwin.
Price, Joan (1977) *An Introduction to Sri Aurobindo's Philosophy*, Pondicherry: Sri Aurobindo Ashram.

Aurobindo, like the other twentieth-century Indian philosophers such as Radhakrishnan and Vivekananda, was deeply impressed by the idealism of Shankarite Vedanta. According to Shankara, the ultimate Reality, *Brahman*, is beyond space and time, non-dual, qualityless and indescribable. The world as we know it, that is, as consisting of objects in space and time, is *maya* or illusion. Aurobindo accepted *Brahman* as the ultimate reality:

[*Brahman*] cannot be summed up in any quantity or quantities, it cannot be composed of any quality or combination of qualities. It is not an aggregate of forms or a formal substratum of forms. If all forms, quantities or qualities were to disappear, this would remain. Existence without quantity, without quality, without form is not only conceivable, but it is the one thing we can conceive beyond these phenomena.

The Life Divine (1947, vol. I, p. 96).

However, he disagreed with Advaita Vedanta, who thought that the phenomenal world was unreal. Aurobindo believed that the truth did not lie either in idealism or in materialism since they both gave one-sided views about the nature of reality. The answer instead lay in integralism, according to which matter and consciousness are connected inseparably. In other words, matter and spirit are two aspects of a single whole; they are both real.

According to Aurobindo, Brahman is *sat* (being), *chit* (consciousness) and *ananda* (bliss, delight)—that is to say, *Braham* is, *Brahman* knows and *Brahman* is bliss. And all that is in space and time is real and is created by *Brahman* out of delight or *ananda*. *Brahman*, for Aurobindo, manifests itself through a process of transformation or involution as matter, and through a gradual process of evolution unfolds its many powers—life, mind and consciousness. Man is a synthesis of the universe and is comprised of physical matter, vital force, emotive qualities, elementary intellect and soul. His goal is one of realizing *Brahman* through knowledge of himself. In essence, Aurobindo's philosophy is largely influenced by the Advaita Vedanta of Shankara. He is, however, to be regarded as a modern interpreter who has tried to provide some justification for the objective existence of the phenomenal world despite accepting a non-dual *Brahman* as Reality.

INDIRA MAHALINGAM CARR

Austin, J(ohn) L(angshaw)

British. *b:* 1911, Lancaster, England. *d:* 1960, Oxford. *Cat:* Analytic philosopher. *Ints:* Epistemology; philosophy of language; philosophy of mind. *Educ:* Oxford University. *Infls:* Aristotle. *Appts:* Fellow, All Souls College, Oxford, 1933–35; Fellow, Magdalen College, Oxford, 1935–52; White's Professor of Moral Philosophy, Oxford; 1952–60; Visiting Professor, University of California at Berkeley, 1958–9.

Main publications:

(1961) *Philosophical Papers*, Oxford: Clarendon Press; second edition, 1970.
(1962) *How to Do Things with Words*, Oxford: Clarendon Press; second edition, 1975.
(1962) *Sense and Sensibilia*, Oxford: Clarendon Press.

Secondary literature:

Berlin, Isaiah *et al.* (1973) *Essays on J. L. Austin*, Oxford: Clarendon Press.
Fann, K. T. (ed.) (1969) *Symposium on J. L. Austin*, London: Routledge & Kegan Paul.
Warnock, G. J. (1991), *J. L. Austin*, London: Routledge.

After a distinguished undergraduate career as a classical scholar, Austin turned to philosophy. He was a Fellow of All Souls College from 1933 to 1935, and lectured in philosophy at Oxford from 1935 until the outbreak of war in 1939. After a notable career in intelligence, he returned to Oxford in 1945, and became Professor of Moral Philosophy in 1952. He had by then only edited a volume of H. W. B. Joseph's *Lectures on the Philosophy of Leibniz*, translated **Frege**'s *Grundlagen der Arithmetik* and published three papers. His influence rested very largely on his lecturing and seminars in Oxford. A considerable proportion of his work was reconstructed and published posthumously.

Austin thought that much philosophical work was characterized by haste and carelessness—about language, and about well-known facts of our experience—and this concern is clear in, for instance, 'The meaning of a word' (a lecture delivered in 1940 and published in *Philosophical Papers*). It can be seen most famously, however, in the series of lectures that he gave in various forms from 1947 to 1958, which were subsequently published as *Sense and Sensibilia* (1962). These lectures consist very largely of a minutely detailed examination of A. J. Ayer's exposition of the Argument from Illusion, an argument which had widely been taken to show that in perception we are only ever acquainted with sense data and never with material objects. Austin tried to show that the argument was vitiated from beginning to end by the failure to give any clear sense to the central terms.

Some have thought that Austin's best philosophical work is in his papers on the philosophy of action: 'A plea for excuses' (*Proceedings of the Aristotelian Society* 1956–7), 'Ifs and cans' (1956), 'Pretending' (1956–7) and 'Three ways of spilling ink' (1958). He thought that there was no way to understand philosophical puzzles about the nature of action, freedom and responsibility other than to examine in detail particular aspects of our talk about action, and the articles are characterized by an extraordinary sensitivity to the distinctions that we ordinarily make when we talk about action. Austin thought that 'our common stock of words embodies all the distinctions worth drawing, and the connexions worth marking, in the lifetimes of many generations: these surely are likely to be more numerous, more sound, since they have stood up to the long test of survival of the fittest, and more subtle, at least in all ordinary and reasonably practical matters, than any that you or I are likely to think up' ('A plea for excuses').

Probably Austin's most famous and influential contribution was the notion of 'speech acts'. The idea first makes its appearance (incipiently and unnamed) in 'Other minds' (1946), and was given fuller treatment in 'Performative utterances' and *How to Do Things with Words*. Austin seems initially to have been struck by such forms of speech as 'I promise to...', 'I name this ship ...', 'I hereby bequeath ...'—forms of speech

which *look* initially like ordinary indicative statements, but which in fact are not. When I say 'I promise to ...', I do not, according to Austin, thereby state *that* I promise; I *do*, by using that form of words, actually promise: my utterance is itself the *act* of promising. It seems initially tempting to contrast such speech forms, which Austin called 'performatives', with statements: doings as opposed to sayings. But Austin saw that this would be a mistake: after all, stating something is itself doing something, and Austin found no significant way to distinguish that sort of doing from other sorts of verbal doings.

The way forward, he thought, was to recognize that all speech consists of what he called 'speech acts'; and speech acts have different levels. When someone utters a sentence in a language, Austin called that a 'locutionary act'. But in performing a locutionary act one may thereby perform a further act: *in* saying, for instance, 'there is a bull in that field', I may, depending on the circumstances, either be merely *stating* that there is a bull or be *warning* you. Such further acts Austin called 'illocutionary acts'. I may also accomplish some effect by what I say: if I warn you that there is a bull in the field, and you are deterred from going into the field, *by* my warning I deter you. This Austin referred to as the 'perlocutionary effect' of my act.

Austin went on to distinguish five different types of illocutionary act, and he seems to have thought that attention to this variety would have significant philosophical implications. It would, for instance, wean us away from our obsession with the true–false distinction and the fact–value distinction.

There has been much discussion as to what Austin thought was the relevance to philosophy of the study of language. In part, it was no doubt that he thought that philosophers should use more care in the way that they treated an essential tool, and that this would lead to progress with old problems. In part, it was no doubt simply the sense that the phenomena of language raised problems which were interesting in themselves. Austin also toyed with the idea that, just as philosophy had given birth to such disciplines as psychology, it might one day give birth to a 'science of language', and this would no doubt be the home of much that he was interested in.

During the 1970s Austin's influence, which had been enormous in Britain during his lifetime and for some years thereafter, largely waned. However, detailed work was done on the notion of speech acts (by, for instance, J. R. **Searle**) and that notion itself has passed into common philosophical parlance. According to Geoffrey Warnock, Austin's contributions to philosophy 'were not predictable. They opened questions that had seemed closed, and brought in new questions. They followed no tramlines, deepened no dialectical ruts. They brought balloons down to earth—sometimes very visibly much the worse for wear when they got there' (1991, p. 153). Austin was a superb, and hilariously amusing, writer. *Sense and Sensibilia* is one of the funniest books of serious philosophy ever written.

Sources: Flew; Passmore 1957; Isaiah Berlin *et al.* (1973) Essays on J. L. Austin, Oxford: Clarendon Press; DNB; *The Times,* 10 Feb 1960, p. 13.

ANTHONY ELLIS

Main publications:

(1936) *Language, Truth and Logic*, London: Gollancz.
(1940) *Foundations of Empirical Knowledge*, London: Macmillan.
(1947) *Thinking and Meaning*, London: H. K. Lewis.
(1954) *Philosophical Essays*, London: Macmillan.
(1954) *The Problem of Knowledge*, London: Macmillan.
(1963) *The Concept of a Person and Other Essays*, London: Macmillan.
(1968) *The Origins of Pragmatism*, London: Macmillan.
(1969) *Metaphysics and Common Sense*, London: Macmillan.
(1971) *Russell and Moore: the Analytical Heritage*, London: Macmillan.
(1972) *Probability and Evidence*, London: Macmillan.
(1972) *Russell*, London: Fontana.
(1973) *The Central Questions of Philosophy*, London: Weidenfeld.
(1980) *Hume*, Oxford: Oxford University Press.
(1980) *Philosophy in the Twentieth Century*, London: Weidenfeld.
(1981) *Philosophy and Morality and Other Essays*, Oxford: Clarendon Press.

Secondary literature:

Foster, John (1985) *A. J. Ayer*, London: Routledge.
Hahn, L. E. (ed.) (1972) *The Philosophy of A. J. Ayer*, La Salle, Ill.: Open Court.
Joad, C. E. M. (1950) *Critique of Logical Positivism*, London: Gollancz.
Macdonald, G. F. (ed.) (1979) *Perception and Identity*, London: Macmillan.
Phillips Griffiths, A. (ed.) (1991) *A. J. Ayer: Memoral Essays*, Cambridge: Cambridge University Press.

Ayer, Alfred Jules

British. *b:* 29 October 1910, London. *d:* 27 June 1989, London. *Cat:* Logical positivist. *Ints:* Epistemology; philosophical logic; ethics. *Educ:* Christ Church, Oxford. *Infls:* Russell, Carnap and Ryle. *Appts:* Lecturer, Christ Church, Oxford 1933–40; Professor, University College, London 1946–59; Professor of Logic, Oxford 1959–78.

Ayer impressed himself emphatically on the philosophical consciousness of his age with the publication of *Language, Truth and Logic* in 1936. For the rest of his long career he was largely engaged in developing the ideas it contained, often by attenuating them. Its striking effect was due to a number of factors: the provocative nature and expression of its contents, its notable literary merits (clarity, force, elegance, firmness of outline and solidity of construction), perhaps, even, its refreshing brevity. The ideas it put

forward were not without British exponents—**Russell**, **Moore** and the marginally
British **Wittgenstein**—and, before them, W.
K. Clifford and Karl Pearson. But they had
been passed through the Vienna Circle,
which had endowed them with a particularly
uncompromising character.

The first, and crucial, thesis was that a
sentence is significant only if it is verifiable
by experience. From this it follows that
metaphysics, to the extent that it claims to
supply information about what lies beyond
or behind experience, is impossible. Metaphysical sentences are without meaning and
so neither true nor false. From this elimination of metaphysics it follows, in turn, that
the only proper business of philosophy is
analysis, the definition, in some sense, of
intellectually essential words and types of
sentence. The definitions in question will not
be explicit definitions of the sort to be found
in a dictionary. They will be definitions in
use, or 'contextual' definitions, giving rules
for translating sentences in which a problematic term occurs into sentences in which
only less problematic, epistemologically
more elementary, terms are to be found.

There is, however, one kind of non-
empirical, a priori, sentence which has an
acceptable method of verification. This is the
kind of sentence of which logic, mathematics
and, it turns out, philosophy proper are
composed. These sentences are analytic: true
(if true or, if false, false) in virtue of the
meaning of the terms they contain. In
elementary cases they cannot be understood
unless their truth (or falsity), is acknowledged. Others, whose truth is not intuitively
obvious, can be derived from them by proofs
which rely on rules which themselves correspond to evidently analytic truths. (This
account of the matter somewhat idealizes
Ayer's too headlong exposition.)

The most disconcerting consequence of
the verification principle was the insignif-
icance and emptiness, not of metaphysics,
but of moral utterances (indeed, of judgements of value of all kinds) and of the

doctrines of religion. Religious creeds are
transcendentally metaphysical. The basic
terms of morality and evaluation
generally—*good, right, ought*—are neither
natural, that is to say empirical (here Ayer
invokes Moore's argument that ethical naturalism is fallacious, improving its formulation in the process) nor can there be non-
empirical properties for them to apply to.
The function of value-judgements is to
express the emotions, favourable or unfavourable, of the speaker and to arouse, in a
way that is neither explained nor evidently
explainable, similar emotions in the hearer.

Attempts at the constructive task of
analysis are made on material objects, the
past, the self and the minds of others. What
is empirically given in perception is sense-
data, momentary and private to the percei-
ver (an ancient empiricist dogma Ayer could
never bring himself seriously to question),
so, Ayer concluded, material objects must be
logical constructions out of actual and
possible sense-data, Mill's phenomenalism
stated in more linguistic terms. The self,
equally, is not an underlying substratum of
experience, but the series, in each case, of the
experiences each of which contains as an
element an experience of a particular,
identifiable human body. Since experiences
can enter into the construction of both
bodies and minds they are neither mental
nor physical, but neutral, in the style of
neutral monism, as in Russell. Past events
are startlingly analysed in terms of the future
experiences which will verify their occurrence. Other people's minds are analysed in
terms of their empirical manifestations in
bodily behaviour.

Ayer's next book, *Foundations of Empirical Knowledge* (1940), develops in quite
persuasive detail the phenomenalist account
of material objects briefly sketched in its
predecessor. A wholly original idea—that
theories of perception are 'alternative languages', proposals, to be justified by their
convenience, for discussing the facts of
perception—was soon abandoned without

traces. There is further consideration of the problem of other minds, reinstating the argument from analogy by the supposition that it is only a contingent fact that another's experience is his and not mine. Ayer also gives up his earlier thesis that no empirical proposition can be known for certain to be true. He dilutes his phenomenalism by the admission that statements about material objects cannot strictly be translated into statements about sense-data; the two can be correlated only in an indefinite and schematic way.

Further concessions appear in the substantial introduction to the second edition of *Language, Truth and Logic*, ten years after its first publication. The chief of these concern the verification principle. It had originally been stated in a 'weak' form, as requiring, not conclusive verification, but only that observation be relevant to the determination of a statement's truth or falsehood. That, he saw, is weak in another way. The notion of relevance is too indefinite. Ayer proposed various, more precise versions of the principle, but admitted, in the face of criticism, that the aim of exact elucidation had eluded him. His earlier, weird, reductive accounts of statements about future events and the minds of others were rejected. But reductive enthusiasm is evident in his London inaugural lecture of the same year, *Thinking and Meaning*. Here the self that thinks, the process of supposed mental acts in which it does so and the substantive meanings on to which it is alleged to be directed are all analysed into the expression of thought in significant sentences.

In *Philosophical Essays* (1954) topics in philosophical logic receive serious attention. Discussing individuals, he defends the implication of Russell's theory of descriptions that a thing is no more than the sum of its qualities, something he was to reaffirm more forcefully later. Negation is ingeniously investigated. The rest of the collection covers familiar ground in epistemology and ethics, going fully for the first time into the problem of free will, opposing it, not to causation, but to constraint.

In *The Problem of Knowledge* (1954) three major issues with which he had been occupied throughout his career—perception, knowledge of the past and knowledge of other minds—are shown to have a common structure. In each case the only evidence that seems to be available—sense-impressions, current recollections, observed behaviour—falls short of the conclusions drawn about material things, past events and the minds of others. The possible reactions are appraised: scepticism, an a priori principle to bridge the gap, its closure by reducing the inferred items to the evidence for them, non-empirical direct access to the problematic items. Ayer offers a fifth option—roughly that of explaining the gap in detail and then doing nothing about it. The account of memory is excellent, dispelling an inheritance of confusion from Russell. In the opening chapter knowledge is distinguished from true belief by the 'right to be sure', an evaluative notion whose credentials to objectivity are not discussed.

Ayer's later writings do not contain many new ideas. There are two forceful and lucid historical studies: on **Peirce** and **James** and on Russell and Moore. Three more essay collections contain good things but no great surprises. There are small books on Hume, Russell and Wittgenstein and a history of twentieth-century philosophy written very definitely from his point of view. The best and most substantial of his later books is *The Central Questions of Philosophy* (1973) in which a very broad range of topics is treated with admirable liveliness and concision, but in which no new ideas are advanced.

Nearly all Ayer's doctrines were derived very recognizably from others, except for those he soon abandoned. The fact was not recognized at first because in 1936 they were exotic and unfamiliar. Most of his early thinking was fairly direct transcription of **Carnap**, modified, where particularly paradoxical, by infusions of **Schlick**. He was, nevertheless, an exemplary philosophical writer: presenting definite theses for discussion, backing them up with explicit and often ingenious argument and expressing his thoughts in superbly lucid, slightly chilly, prose. He deserved his fame. Ayer became immediately well-known on the publication of his first book and strongly influenced his young contemporaries, perhaps giving them the courage of their own developing convictions. After 1946, at University College, London, both staff and students philosophy of the department revealed the strong impress of his personality. But his self-regard did not take the form of requiring submissive disciples; philosophy to him was more a competitive game than a religious rite focussed on himself. His pupils have his intellectual style, but not usually his opinions. His department, in the early postwar years, was the main effective opposition to the uneasy coalition between Cambridge Wittgensteinianism and the Oxford philosophy of **Ryle** and **Austin**. He came back to Oxford just when the latter, on Austin's death, was disintegrating philosophically. In these years he was a dedicated and effective teacher and animator of philosophical discussion. In the view of the interested public he was gradually transformed from being the prophet of moral nihilism into the paradigm of a philosopher.

Sources: Passmore 1957; Edwards; Hill.

ANTHONY QUINTON

Bachelard, Gaston

French. *b:* June 1884, Bar-sur-Aube, France. *d:* October 1962, Paris. *Cat:* Scientist; critic. *Ints:* Philosophy of science and of criticism. *Educ:* Studied for a Mathematics degree, 1912; degree in Philosophy, 1920; agrégation, 1922. *Infls:* Nietzsche, Einstein and Jung. *Appts:* Began adult life as a clerk; served with gallantry during the First World War;

Professor of Philosophy, Dijon; Professor of the History and Philosophy of Science, the Sorbonne, retiring 1954; Légion d'Honneur, 1951.

Main publications:

On the philosophy of science:
(1928) *Essai sur la connaissance approchée.*
(1934) *Le Nouvel Esprit scientifique.*
(1940) *La Philosophie du non.*
(1949) *Le Rationalisme appliqué*, Paris: PUF.
(1953) *Le Matérialisme rationnel*, Paris: PUF.
Theory of criticism:
(1938) *La Psychanalyse du feu.*
(1940) *Lautréamont.*
(1942) *L'Eau et les rêves.*
(1943) *L'Air et les songes.*
(1948) *La Terre et les Rêveries de la volonté*, Paris: Corti.
(1948) *La Terre et les Rêveries du repos*, Paris: Corti.
(1957) *La Poétique de l'espace*, Paris: PUF.
(1961) *La Flamme d'une chandelle*, Paris: PUF.

Secondary literature:

Ginestier, P. (1968) *Pour connaître la pensée de Bachelard*, Paris: Bordas.
Lafrance, G. (ed.) (1987) *Gaston Bachelard*, Ottawa: University of Ottawa Press.
Quillet, P. (1964) *Bachelard*, Paris: Seghers.

The features of the world which most concerned Bachelard were change and discontinuity, especially in the working of the mind. Trained as a scientist and deeply impressed by relativity, he began his intellectual career with a sustained attack on the positivistic idea of scientific progress as a neat process of the accretion of truths. Discoveries, he argued, are more accurately regarded as discontinuities. Later in life, turning his attention to artistic creativity, he argued forcibly against the deterministic criticism of the school of Sainte-Beuve, in Bachelard's view false to the real workings of the imagination. Scientific discoveries and works of art are important discontinuities in the world.

The growth of scientific knowledge,

Bachelard argues, is not a neat, sequential piling up of new truths, as the positivists have presented it. Discoveries are made not by those who accept current science but by those who say no to it, those who correct errors (cf. 1940), and discoveries frequently involve revisions of concepts at all levels, down to the most fundamental. The assumption, for example, that the notion of reason as enshrined in traditional rationalism is fixed for all time is untenable: 'Reason must obey science ... which is evolving' (1940, p. 144; there is much in Bachelard which is Kuhnian *avant la lettre*). The outmoded assumptions of such rationalism Bachelard replaces by his preferred method, surrationalism: mutable, polymorphic and in principle revisable at all levels of conceptual generality. This method furthers rather than stifles the mental process at the heart of discovery, the sudden intuition which goes beyond currently received belief sets. Everything which presents itself as a final discovery or immutable principle is to be regarded with suspicion: stasis was not a property Bachelard saw around him either in the world or in our knowledge of it; what we call being at rest is merely 'a happy vibration' (*La Dialectique de la durée*, 1936, p. 6).

Partly for emotional reasons and partly as a result of his interest in the psychology of creativity, Bachelard was not content to remain solely a philosopher of science. From 1938 onwards he published a series of works which are centrally concerned with the processes of the artistic imagination, and his views have important consequences for the nature of criticism. The imagination is as valuable and as basic a mental faculty as reason. Its product is the image, irreducible to concepts, imprecise and suggestive. The process of the imagination cannot be predicted, and can be studied only a posteriori. The imagination works best in the state Bachelard calls reverie, by which he means neither a dream nor a dreamy condition but a contemplative state in which the surface ego is in abeyance, time consciousness is modified and the mind follows its own impulsions. Since the imagination is in principle unpredictable, criticism of the kind practised by Sainte-Beuve, further vitiated by its reliance on deterministic principles rejected by science, is a waste of effort. Nothing in the humdrum life of the artist allows us to predict the occurrence and nature of creative acts. It is more appropriate, in Bachelard's view, to classify artistic imaginations into types. His way of doing this was to associate them with one of the elements: hence the reference, in the titles of many of his literary works, to fire, earth, air and water.

ROBERT WILKINSON

Benjamin, Walter

German. **b:** 1892, Berlin. **d:** 1940, Port Bou, Franco-Spanish border. **Cat:** Marxist; cultural theorist; literary theorist. **Ints:** Art and society. **Educ:** Universities of Berlin, Freiburg, Munich and Bern. **Infls:** Goethe, Baudelaire, Marx, Lukács and Brecht. **Appts:** Benjamin held no formal academic position, working mainly as a freelance critic and translator, although he was associated with the Institute of Social Research at the University of Frankfurt (later relocated in New York).

Main publications:

(1928) *Der Ursprung des deutschen Trauerspiels*, (English translation, *The Origin of German Tragic Drama*, trans. John Osborne, London: NLB, 1977).
(1966) *Versuche über Brecht*, Frankfurt-am-Main: Suhrkamp Verlag (English translation, *Understanding Brecht*, trans. Anna Bostock, London: NLB, 1973).
(1968) *Illuminations*, ed. Hannah Arendt, trans. Harry Zohn, New York: Harcourt, Brace & World.
(1969) *Charles Baudelaire: Ein Lyriker in Zeitalter des Hochkapitalismus*, ed. Rolf Tiedemann, Frankfurt: Suhrkamp Verlag (English

translation, *Charles Baudelaire: A Lyric Poet in the Era of High Capitalism*, trans. Harry Zohn, London: NLB, 1973).
(1970) *Berliner Chronik*, Frankfurt: Suhrkamp Verlag.
(1979) *One-Way Street and Other Writings*, trans. Edmund Jephcott and Kingsley Shorter, London: NLB.

Secondary literature:

Benjamin, Andrew (ed.) (1989) *The Problems of Modernity: Adorno and Benjamin*, London: Routledge.
Bullock, Marcus Paul (1987) *Romanticism and Marxism: The Philosophical Development of Literary Theory and Literary History in Walter Benjamin and Friedrich Schlegel*, New York: Peter Lang.
Eagleton, Terry (1981) *Walter Benjamin*, London: Verso.
Jennings, Michael W. (1987) *Dialectical Images: Walter Benjamin's Theory of Literary Criticism*, Ithaca, NY, and London: Cornell University Press.
Nagele, Rainer (1988) *Benjamin's Ground: New Readings of Walter Benjamin*, Detroit: Wayne State University Press.
Smith, Gray (ed.) (1988) *On Walter Benjamin: Critical Essays and Recollections*, Cambridge, Mass.: MIT Press.

Although relatively little known during his lifetime, when only two of his books were published, Benjamin is now considered to be one of the leading Marxist aestheticians and cultural commentators of the twentieth century; in particular, he is credited with being one of the first to recognise the significance of art as a form of social production. A close associate of the playwright Bertolt Brecht, Benjamin was an enthusiastic proponent of 'epic theatre' and one of the few Marxist critics of his time to defend modernism as an aesthetic. Generally speaking, the Marxist critical establishment favoured realism and frowned on experiment in an era when the 'socialist realism' of Stalin's cultural commisar, A. A. Zhdanov, came to dominate the Marxist cultural agenda. Benjamin's championship of experiment - new cultural conditions required new

forms of art, in his opinion - has affinities with the work of the Frankfurt School, with which he was loosely associated in the 1920s and 30s; although the School's leading figures (Theodor **Adorno** and Max Horkheimer) often criticized Benjamin's cultural analyses as not being dialectical enough. Somewhat ironically, it is that very lack of dialectical orthodoxy and rigidity which has led to Benjamin's renewed popularity amongst the generally anti-Marxist postmodernist movement.

Benjamin's writings on epic theatre (the two versions of the essay 'What is Epic Theatre?', for example) help to theorise Brecht's artistic practice more fully. For Benjamin, epic theatre's role was to reveal the underlying socio-political conditions in such a way that the audience could not ignore them; if necessary to shock the audience into awareness of those conditions. By encouraging identification with the plight of the dramatic characters, traditional theatre ('culinary', as Brecht had dismissively referred to it) had helped to distract audiences from those socio-political realities. Epic theatre, therefore, for both Benjamin and Brecht, fulfilled a specifically Marxist function, although it would not be until after the Second World War, and Brecht's return to communist East Germany, that it would find acceptance in official Marxist political circles. During Benjamin's lifetime, however, epic theatre, and its attendant commitment to experimentation with form and rejection of the principles of realism, came under bitter attack from more orthodox Marxist critics such as Georg **Lukács** (although it is also worth noting that Benjamin was highly influenced by earlier theoretical works of Lukács, such as *History and Class Consciousness*).

Benjamin spent several years working on his so-called Arcades Project, a wide-ranging account of nineteenth-century Parisian city life going right down to the level of its incidental details, in an 'attempt to capture the portrait of history in the most insignificant representations of reality, its scraps, as it were'. He was fascinated by the notion (found in Baudelaire) of the flaneur, the figure strolling around the city taking in its sights and sounds, and in this fashion gaining an insight into the hidden meanings of both the city and its historical period. The Project was never completed, but its rather impressionistic approach could only appear undialectical and insufficiently analytical to Marxists of the Adorno stamp.

One of Benjamin's most important contributions to aesthetic theory can be found in the essay 'The Work of Art in the Age of Mechanical Reproduction', which introduces the concept of 'aura'. The latter refers to the sense of originality or authenticity of a work of art, derived from 'its presence in time and space, its unique existence at the place where it happens to be'. Benjamin argues that the advent of mechanically-reproducible art forms (film and photography being cases in point) led to a withering away of that aura, and thus of art's authority and cult status. This process, which for Benjamin shatters tradition, can have both negative and positive connotations, politically speaking. It can become implicated in mass movements such as fascism, which for Benjamin constitutes the politicization of aesthetics, or it can lead to the emancipation of artworks from 'dependence on ritual'. Either way, art is now unmistakably in the political domain as far as Benjamin is concerned.

Benjamin's commitment to artistic experimentation can be seen to particular effect in the essay 'The Author as Producer', where it is argued that the time has come radically to rethink our traditional notions of literary forms and genres. 'Novels did not always exist in the past', it is pointed out, 'nor must they always exist in the future'. What Benjamin saw happening in the modern world was a 'melting down' of literary forms, a process which called into question our traditional perceptions of literary value, and of the relationship between 'high' and 'low' art, author and reader. Once again, Brecht was taken as some kind of model of how we should proceed in this new cultural situation. This aspect of Benjamin's thought has been particularly influential on the development of cultural studies and postmodernist aesthetics, which have equally enthusiastically celebrated the breakdown in the distinction between high art and popular culture, and the assumed authority of the artistic producer.

Benjamin's call in 'The Author as Producer' for artists to make themselves aware of their position in the production process, is part of a general insistence in his writings that art should be treated as a form of social production. For him, the important issue is not where art stands with regard to the relations of production of its particular historical time, but where it stands within those relations. In this respect he lays the groundwork for much later theorizing in Marxist aesthetics, such as the work of the structuralist Marxist movement (Pierre Macherey and Terry Eagleton, for example), whose concern with the ideology of artistic production owes much to Benjamin's ideas. Indeed, the structuralist Marxist technique of reading texts 'against the grain' to make them reveal their ideological assumptions, is adapted from Benjamin's demand in his enigmatic, and somewhat mystically-inclined late work, 'Theses on the Philosophy of History', that in order to bring out the latent 'barbarism' in all documents of 'civilization' it is the critic's duty 'to brush history against the grain'.

STUART SIM

Bergson, Henri-Louis

French. **b:** 18 October 1859, Paris. **d:** 3 or 4 January 1941, Paris. **Cat:** Metaphysician; process philosopher. **Ints:** Evolution. **Educ:** Studied at École Normale, Paris, graduating in 1881, and taking his doctorate in 1889. **Infls:** Zeno of Elea, Plato, Aristotle, Plotinus, Oriental and Christian mystics, Descartes, Spinoza, Leibniz, Berkeley, Hume, Kant, Claude Bernard, Lachelier, Ravaisson, Spencer, Darwin and Einstein. (See also R. Berthelot, 1913.). **Appts:** Taught at Anger, 1881–3, Clermont-Ferrand, 1883–7, and Paris; Professor, Collège de France, in 1900; main works placed on Vatican's Index, 1914; Nobel Prize for Literature, 1927.

Main publications:

(1889) *Essai sur les données immédiates de la perception*, Paris: Alcan (English translation, *Time and Free Will*, trans. F. L. Pogson, London: Allen & Unwin, 1910).

(1896) *Matière et mémoire*, Paris: Alcan (English translation, *Matter and Memory*, trans. N. M. Paul and W. S. Palmer, London: Allen & Unwin, 1911).

(1900) *Le Rire*, Paris: Alcan (English translation, *Laughter*, trans. C. Brereton and F. Rothwell, London: Macmillan, 1911).

(1903) 'Introduction à la métaphysique', *Revue de Métaphysique et de Morale*, 29 January (see 1912, 1934 for translations).

(1907) *L'Evolution créatrice*, Paris: Alcan (English translation, *Creative Evolution*, A. Mitchell, London: Macmillan, 1911).

(1912) *Introduction to Metaphysics*, New York: Putnam's Sons (trans. by T. E. Hulme of 1903).

(1919) *L'Energie spirituelle: Essais et conférences*, Paris: Alcan (English translation, *Mind-Energy*, trans. H. W. Carr, London: Macmillan, 1920).

(1922) *Dureé et simultanéité: A propos de la théorie d'Einstein*, Paris: Alcan (English translation, *Duration and Simultaneity*, trans. with an introduction by H. Dingle, Indianapolis: Bobbs-Merrill, 1965).

(1932) *Les Deux Sources de la morale et de la réligion*, Paris: Alcan (English translation, *The Two Sources of Morality and Religion*, trans. R. A. Audra and C. Brereton with the assistance of W. H. Carter, London: Macmillan, 1935).

(1934) *La Pensée et le mouvant: Essais et conférences*, Paris: Alcan (English translation, *The Creative Mind*, trans. M. L. Andison, New York: Philosophy Library, 1946).

Collected editions:
(1959) *Oeuvres*, Paris: PUF.

(1972) *Mélanges*, Paris: PUF (includes 1922, which is not in 1959).

Secondary literature:

Barlow, M. (1966) *Henri Bergson*, Paris: Editions universitaires (brief biography linking life and works).

Berthelot, R. (1938) *Un Romantisme utilitaire*, troisième partie, Paris: Alcan (thorough but hostile).

Čapek, M. (1971) *Bergson and Modern Physics*, Dordrecht: Reidel (full, scholarly and largely sympathetic account, seeing Bergson against the intellectual background).

Gunter, P. A. Y. (ed. and trans.) (1969) *Bergson and the Evolution of Physics*, Knoxville, Tenn.: Tennessee University Press (reactions to Bergson by modern physicists and others; often technical).

——(1986) *Henri Bergson: A Bibliography*, Bowling Green, Ohio: Philosophy Documentation Centre (revised edition of 1984 original).

Hanna, T. (ed.) (1962) *The Bergsonian Heritage*, New York: Columbia Univeristy Press.

Husson, L. (1947) *L'Intellectualisme de Bergson*, Paris: PUF (claims Bergson is not anti-intellectualist).

Jankélévitch, V. (1959) *Henri Bergson*, Paris: PUF (much revised version of 1931 original).

Kolakowski, L. (1985) *Bergson*, Oxford: Oxford University Press (brief introduction).

Lacey, A. R. (1989) *Bergson*, London: Routledge (attempts down-to-earth assessment of Bergson's actual arguments, although it has been accused of not bringing out his importance).

Les Études bergsoniennes (1948–76) (periodical in eleven volumes).

Mossé-Bastide, R.-M. (1955) *Bergson éducateur*, Paris: PUF.

Papanicolaou, A. C. and Gunter, P. A. Y. (eds) (1987) *Bergson and Modern Thought*, Chur, Swit.: Harwood Academic Publishers (essays tending to stress anticipations of modern physics and pyschology, and also parapsychology).

Russell, B. (1914) *The Philosophy of Bergson*, Cambridge: Bowes & Bowes (includes H. W. Carr's reply and Russell's further reply).

One of the most striking things about Bergson is perhaps the extraordinary width of his cultural attainments. At 17 he won an open prize for an original solution to a mathematical problem, and in the same year solved a problem Pascal claimed to have solved but left unpublished (1972, pp.

247–55). His graduation thesis (in Latin) was on Aristotle's theory of place and he wrote a short commentary on Lucretius (both reprinted in *Mélanges*, 1972); and he lectured on Plato, Aristotle and Plotinus, among other things. He made a thorough study of the technical literature on the role of the brain in connection with aphasia (1972, p. 1209), quoted detailed scientific evidence when discussing evolution, and in later years took on Einstein in public debate on certain paradoxical implications of relativity theory—a debate he is generally regarded as having lost, but several of the leading physicists of the century have devoted articles to his work (see Gunter 1969; Papainicolaou and Gunter 1987).

Bergson is among the regrettably few great stylists in philosophy. His ideas are often intricate and difficult, but his exposition of them ranks with those of **Russell**, Berkeley, the early Plato and his cordial admirer William **James**, and this feature survives in the English translations (all the non-posthumous ones having his imprimatur, as he was bilingual because of his English mother). 'There is nothing in philosophy which could not be said in everyday language', he told an interviewer (1972, p. 939). Like Russell he tried to combine philosophy with action: 'one should act like a man of thought and think like a man of action', as he told a Danish congress in 1937 (1972, p. 1579). In 1917 he helped to bring America into the war, visiting for that purpose, and later helped to set up the educational side of the League of Nations, believing that education and mutual understanding would prevent war. For his last seventeen years he endured crippling arthritis. Fiercely patriotic, he died at the darkest moment of French history, of bronchitis possibly caused by several hours' standing in freezing conditions to register as a Jew, refusing, it is said, to desert his fellow Jews by accepting a presumably face-saving exemption offered by the authorities (he refused for the same reason to join the Catholic Church, to which he had by then became spiritually converted).

Bergson is often regarded as a rather unrigorous, if not hopelessly high-flown, thinker. His sympathy with mysticism, especially in his later writings (see 1932), such rather cloudy notions as the *élan vital* (1907), and his often rather lyrical and picturesque style, do give some countenance to this. The success of style meant that his prewar lectures became so crowded (a photograph shows people straining to listen through the open windows) that they were nearly moved to the Opera. But all this is only one feature of a complex whole, and is far removed from his actual intentions. Twenty years before his book on morality (1932) he explained his silence on that topic by saying he could not there reach results 'as demonstrable or as "presentable" [*montrables*]' as in his other works, adding that philosophy could 'claim an objectivity as great as that of the positive sciences, although of another nature' (1972, p. 964). Not only did he appeal to detailed scientific evidence when relevant, but he reached his main philosophical positions by starting not, as was commonly thought, from the intuitive data of lived experience but by reflecting on the treatment of time by science and mathematics. Like William James, with whose 'stream of consciousness' his own philosophy had so much in common, he insisted on the importance of introspective psychology; but whereas for James it was a starting-point, for himself it was a point of arrival: for all the similarities of their philosophies, he said, he and James had reached them quite independently (1972, pp. 656–61; 1959, pp. 1541–3): Bergson was rather suspicious of claims to see philosophical influences' (1972, p. 1480). His 1889 work, with its title and its opening chapter on the nature of experience, might seem to belie this; but the latter, at least, although it does of course represent his own view, was added for strategical reasons connected with getting a doctorate (1959, p. 1542).

In the same important autobiographical

fragment (ibid., pp. 1541–3), written in 1922, Bergson tells how in his youth he was confronted by two opposing currents of opinion, Kantian orthodoxy and Spencerian evolutionism. He preferred Spencer because of the 'concrete character of his mind' and his desire to keep always to the domain of facts. He has often been regarded as anti-intellectualist because of his emphasis on intuition, a faculty which evolved from instinct (and is first treated in 1903). (On the anti-intellectualism charge see Husson 1947.) Although he later abandoned Spencer (because his science was inadequate), and does indeed give pride of place to intuition as the highest human faculty, it is not at the expense of intellect in its own sphere, that of science and mathematics, which he never abandoned. The 'intuition of duration' is indeed the linchpin of Bergson's philosophy (1972, p. 1148), but intuition in general is 'instinct that has become disinterested, self-conscious, capable of reflecting upon its object and of enlarging it indefinitely' (1907, translation, p. 187). It is certainly not a substitute for hard work (1934, translation, p. 103. But Bergsons' treatment of intuition does seem to involve some confusions. Sometimes it seems to mean the getting of bright ideas, which both presupposes and involves intellectual hard work. But it is also a faculty which diverges from intellect, partly by apprehending duration as something essentially unified and continuous (and the qualitative aspects of our experiences in general) and partly as apprehending ineffable metaphysical reality, culminating in mysticism: here intuition is the method of philosophy as intellect is of science and mathematics—but does he distinguish philosophy as an intellectual study *about* intuition? Bergson's most lasting influence has certainly lain in his distinction between time as indivisible, qualitatively heterogeneous and known to experience (duration) and time as divisible, qualitatively homogeneous, and studied by science, which treats it as analogous to space; though from *Matière et*

mémoire (1896) on, both belong in the world itself. He solves Zeno's Achilles paradox by similarly distinguishing Achilles' indivisible motion from the divisible trajectory it covers, a solution which, along with his asymmetrical treatment of time and space, has been much criticized. Not only have these views on time been generally (though not undisputedly) taken to have influenced Proust and many other literary figures (see, for example, Delattre in *Les Études bergsoniennes*, 1948–76, vol. 1), but here and in his 'process philosophy' approach to substance (1896) and his views on determinism (1889) and on the influence of consciousness (1896) he is sometimes claimed to have anticipated features of relativity theory, microindeterminacy and modern scientific theories of the mind (see, for example, Papanicolaou and Gunter 1987).

Sources: Passmore 1957.

A. R. LACEY

Bradley, Francis Herbert

British. *b:* 1846, London. *d:* 1924, Oxford. *Cat:* Absolute idealist. *Ints:* Ethics; logic; metaphysics. *Educ:* MA, University College, Oxford. *Infls:* T. H. Green, E. Caird, Bosanquet and Hegel. *Appts:* Fellow of Merton College, Oxford, 1870–1924.

Main publications:

(1876) *Ethical Studies*, London; second edition, Oxford, 1927 (1962 edition cited here).
(1883) *Principles of Logic*, Oxford; second edition, Oxford, 1922.
(1893) *Appearance and Reality*, London: Allen & Unwin; second edition, 1897 (1969 edition cited here).
(1914) *Essays on Truth and Reality*, Oxford.
(1935) *Collected Essays*, Oxford.

Secondary literature:

Eliot, T. S. (1964) *Knowledge and Experience in the Philosophy of F. H. Bradley*, London: Faber & Faber.

Mander, W. J. (1994) *An Introduction to Bradley's Metaphysics*, Oxford: Clarendon Press.

Manser, A. (1983) *Bradley's Logic*, Oxford: Blackwell.

——and Stock, G. (eds) (1984) *The Philosophy of F. H. Bradley*, Oxford: Clarendon Press.

Taylor, A. E. (1924–5) Obituary, *Proceedings of the British Academy* 11.

Wollheim, R. (1959) *F. H. Bradley*, Harmondsworth: Penguin.

Bradley's central work in idealist metaphysics was expressed in *Appearance and Reality* (1893), although he did not regard this as a systematic exposition of his thinking. His earlier *Ethical Studies* (1876) and *Principles of Logic* (1883) were also important as critiques of utilitarianism and empiricism. *Ethical Studies* and the chapter on 'goodness' in *Appearance and Reality* stress the importance of *self-realization* as an end for morality, but Bradley was equally anxious to stress that this end could only be understood in a wide metaphysical context, rather than as an appeal to mere self-interest. The 'self to be realized' was not 'the self to be pleased' (1876, Essay V, p. 160). The 'real moral idea' was the community, which provided the only intelligible framework for realization (p. 210): Bradley's famous notion of 'My station and its duties'. 'There is nothing better than this', he wrote, 'nor anything higher or more truly beautiful' (ibid.). His scorn for utilitarian ethics was almost unlimited: happiness could have nothing at all to do with morality; the idea that any kind of pleasure principle could act as a moral motivation was incoherent. The general strategy of *Ethical Studies* was dialectical in a way that can mislead the unwary reader searching for clear conclusions. Essay VI, on 'Ideal morality', tries to explain how self-realization falls into his wider view: 'The general end is self-realization, the making real of the ideal self; and for morality, in particular, the ideal self is the good will, the identification of my will with the ideal as a universal will' (p. 230). However, none of the necessary superstructure for this was given in *Ethical Studies*. That had to wait for *Appearance and Reality*.

Principles of Logic, like *Appearance and Reality*, opens with a denial that it is a systematic treatise. Bradley also distances himself from Hegel, usually seen as his main source of influence: 'We want no system-making or systems home-grown or imported' (Preface). Although there are obvious differences, Bradley's logic can be appreciated best in contrast with that of **Frege**, his near contemporary (see Manser's paper in Manser and Stock 1984). Like Frege, he totally rejected psychologism in logic, sarcastically referring to Mill as our 'great modern logician' (1876, p. 113). But, also like Frege, he was preoccupied with whatever it was about or within a judgement that held it together, and with the connections between judgements that enabled logical relations to exist between them. Like Frege, but without any supporting symbolism, he repudiated subject—predicate logic and stressed the significance of logical as opposed to superficial forms (1883, pp. 618–19). (All of this may have influenced the early **Russell** far more than he claimed to remember). But extremely unlike Frege, Bradley drew idealist conclusions from his critiques of psychologistic logic: the unity within a statement, and the unity between logically related statements, could only be grasped truly as part of a wider metaphysical unity: 'All judgment is of Reality, and that means that it makes its idea the adjective of the real Universe' (Terminal Essay, 1922, II, p. 628). Again, as with his moral philosophy, the underlying metaphysics of this had to wait to be fully explained.

This explanation came in *Appearance and Reality*, where Bradley expounded his absolute idealism as fully as he ever did anywhere. The object of the book was 'to state merely a general view about Reality, and to defend this view against more obvious and prominent objections' (p. 403). His metaphysical thinking was not based on epistemology. Appearance and reality (as with **McTaggart**) were not aligned with phenomena and noumena (chapter XII). Although the ordinary, perceived world was not *Reality* for Bradley, he was at pains to stress that it was unreal in comparison with a higher ideal and, not in comparison with anything concealed behind the veil of perception inherited from egocentric epistemology: 'The assertion of a reality falling outside knowledge, is quite nonsensical' (p. 114). Experience, he held, was genuine enough in its own terms. Appearance was unreal mainly for logical reasons (see p. 334). The idea that anything could be only accidentally ('externally') related to anything else was a profound error. Deeper reflection would show that all relations were in some way essential or intrinsic ('internal'), and could not, in any event, be considered themselves, apart from the reality within which they existed. 'Reality is one. It must be single, because plurality, taken as real, contradicts itself (p. 460). So a full statement about anything—and hence a fully true statement about anything—could not be made without reference to everything else. Thus: 'There will be no truth which is entirely true, just as there will be no error which is totally false' (pp. 320–1). The repudiation of 'external relations' and the doctrine of degrees of truth and reality were seen by Bradley's pluralist critics, **Moore** and Russell, as well as by him, as logically fundamental.

The critical side of Bradley's metaphysics is often surprisingly trenchant. The positive characterization of the absolute is more elusive. 'There is but one Reality, and its being consists in experience' (p. 403). Any further categorical statement about it would be bound to be false since: 'any categorical judgment must be false. The subject and the predicate, in the end, cannot either be the other' (p. 319). Nevertheless, in a sense, it may be said that: 'the Absolute is actually good, and throughout the world of goodness it is truly realized in different degrees of satisfaction. Since in ultimate Reality all existence, and all thought and feeling, become one, we may even say that every feature in the universe is thus absolutely good' (p. 365). *Appearance and Reality* ends with what Bradley invokes as 'the essential message of Hegel': 'Outside of spirit there is not, and there cannot be, any reality, and the more that anything is spiritual, so much the more is it veritably real' (p. 489). Bradley, with McTaggart, is normally taken to be the principal figure in British idealism: a movement that now seems peculiar for the speed of its total downfall. Its culmination in Bradley's *Appearance and Reality* (1893) was succeeded, soon after 1898, by its alleged intellectual defeat by Moore and Russell. But its influence lasted longer than that, starting with the earlier work of Green, Bosanquet and Bradley himself, going on through McTaggart's *Nature of Existence* (1921–7) and lasting for the terms of many later university appointments of idealists in England and Scotland, half a century after their philosophy had been pronounced dead (Collingwood and Joachim were two notable examples in Oxford).

Russell tended to take Bradley as a main target of his 'revolt into pluralism', although it is striking that he engaged in direct published debate only with Joachim. Bradley scarcely mentioned his pluralist critics. His only sustained response was the posthumous 'Relations' (1923–4, in *Collected Essays*, 1935).

Bradley was a remarkable writer: powerful, allusive and scornful, and wholly undeserving of the charges of woolly unclarity brought against him by his later positivist critics. T. S. Eliot noted in his Preface (1964) to the reissue of his doctoral dissertation on Bradley how closely his own prose style was 'formed on that of Bradley and how little it has changed in all these years' (pp. 10–11). Bradley's colourful use of metaphor may be valued more highly as philosophical rhetoric becomes more appreciated. ('The Absolute has no seasons, but all at once bears its leaves, fruit, and blossoms. Like our globe it always, and it never, has summer and winter' (1893, p. 442).)

RICHARD MASON

Brentano, Franz

German-Austrian. *b:* 1838, Marienburg, Germany. *d:* 1917, Florence. *Cat:* Philosophical psychology. *Ints:* Intentionality; act psychology. *Educ:* Universtiy of Tübingen. *Infls:* Aristotle, Kant and the post-Kantians. *Appts:* Professor of Philosophy, first at the Catholic University of Würzburg, later at University of Vienna.

Main publications:

(1874) *Psychologie vom empirischen Standpunkt*, Leipzig: Duncker & Humblot, 1874; second edition in 2 volumes, 1911; third edition, ed. O. Kraus, Leipzig: F. Meiner, 1925 (English translation, *Psychology from an Empirical Standpoint*, ed. L. L. McAlister, London, 1973).

(1889) *Ursprung sittlicher Erkenntnis*, Leipzig: Duncker & Humblot; third edition, ed. Oskar Kraus, 1934 (English translation, *The Origins of Our Knowledge Right and Wrong*, trans. Cecil Hague, London: A. Constable, 1902).

(1893) *The Future of Philosophy*, Vienna: A. Holder

(1895) *Die vier Phasen der Philosophie* [The Four Phases of Philosophy], Stuttgart: J. C. Cott'schen Buchhandlung; ed. Oskar Kraus, Leipzig: F. Meiner, 1926.

(1907) *An Investigation of the Psychology of the Senses*, Leipzig: Duncker & Humblot.

(1925) *Versuch über die Erkenntnis* [Inquiry into the Nature of Knowledge] ed. Alfred Kastil, Leipzig: F. Meiner.

(1929) *Vom Dasein Gottes* [On the Existence of God], ed. Alfred Kastil, Leipzig: F. Meiner.

(1930) *Wahrheit und Evidenz* [Truth and Evidence], ed. Oskar Kraus, Leipzig: F. Meiner.

(1952) *Grundlegung und Aufbau der Ethik* [The Basis and Structure of Ethics], ed. F. Mayer-Hillebrand, Bern: A. Francke.

(1954) *Religion und Philosophie*, ed. F. Mayer-Hillebrand, Bern: Francke.

Secondary literature:

Chisholm, R. M. (ed.) (1960) *Realism and the Background of Phenomenology*, Glencoe, Ill.: Free Press (contains portions of *Psychologie vom empirischen Standpunkt*).

Kastil, A. (1951) *Die Philosophie Franz Brentano: Eine Einführung in seine Lehre*, Bern: A. Francke.

Moore, G. E. (1903) 'Review of Franz Brentano: The origins of the knowledge of right and wrong', *International Journal of Ethics* 14: 115–23.

Spiegelberg, H. (1960) *The Phenomenological Movement: A Historical Introduction*, 2 vols, The Hague: Nijhoff.

A philosopher and psychologist, Franz Brentano has a permanent place in the history of philosophy as the first to give a clear account of the intentionality, or object-relatedness, of mental phenomena. Born in the Rhineland, he became a Roman Catholic priest and Professor of Philosophy at the Catholic University of Würzburg. He resigned both priesthood and Chair after the Declaration of Papal Infallibility in 1871, and was appointed to a Chair of Philosophy at Vienna University. In a voluminous output, his most important work was *Psychology from the Empirical Standpoint*, first published in 1874, the same year as Wundt's *Foundations of Physiological Psychology*.

In the *Psychology* Brentano set out to provide an account of the structure of mind which would serve as a foundation for empirical psychology. He called this 'descriptive psychology' (and sometimes 'descriptive phenomenology'). He considered himself an empiricist: experience, he claimed, was his only teacher. Where Wundt was establishing psychology as an empirical science through the experimental investigation of the context of experience, Brentano's primary method was careful observation of the act of experience itself. Taking for granted a broadly dualistic view of the world (as divided into 'psychical' and 'physical' phenomena), he concentrated on two questions: What are the essential or defining characteristics of the mental?; Into what categories can mental phenomena be classified?

It was in attempting to answer the first of these questions that he developed his influential ideas on the intentionality of mind. Mental phenomena, he argued, are distinguished from physical by 'intentional inexistence', that is 'reference to a content' or 'direction upon an object'. Thus a thought is always a thought *about* something, a desire is always a desire *for* something, a perception is always a perception *of* something, and so on. This is more than a merely contingent matter. The 'something' may be some other mental content (an image, say). It may be something that does not exist (for example, a unicorn). Hence the intentionality of mind is not a relation between it and its object (which would entail that the object existed) it is 'relational' or 'relation-like'. But there must (logically must) always be something towards which a mental act is directed. In the absence of this, mental verbs are literally meaningless. Subjective experiences can only be understood as acts of consciousness directed towards objects.

As to the second question, Brentano allowed only three categories, or 'Grand Classes', of mental phenomena: representations, judgements and feelings (including both emotions and volitions). These reflect three ways in which mental phenomena may be directed upon their objects. Thus with a representation an idea is simply before the mind or 'present to consciousness'. But with a judgement we take up a stance towards an idea, an intellectual stance, which may be either of acceptance or rejection. A feeling also involves taking a stance. In this case the stance is emotional, a feeling being broadly either 'for' or 'against' the idea in question. (Brentano used 'love'/'hate' here to mean something along the lines of approach/avoidance.)

In this classification, representations are basic in the sense that we must have an idea before we can take up a stance towards it, intellectual or emotional. However, it is with the epistemological and ethical implications respectively of judgements and feelings that much of the remainder of Brentano's extensive philosophy is concerned. Thus representations, ideas directly present to consciousness, cannot be either correct or incorrect. They are as it were just there. But when we take up one or other of two opposed stances we open up the possibility of being right or wrong. In the case of judgements, then, one or other of the two opposed stances of affirmation or rejection must be correct in a given case: 'This is a pencil', or, 'This is not a pencil'. As to which is correct, we come to understand the difference by contrasting actual cases of judgements which are correct with those which are not. And judgements are objective in the sense that we cannot affirm correctly what anyone else denies correctly, or vice versa. This is a non-propositional theory of judgement. To affirm/deny that there is a pencil is not to affirm/deny the proposition 'my pencil exists'. It is to affirm/deny the existence of a pencil. The object of the affirmation/denial is not a proposition, nor even a state of affairs, but, like the object of the corresponding representation, the pencil. Indeed, terms like 'exist' do not refer: they are 'systematic', allowing us to express our acceptance or rejection of things.

Much the same, Brentano argued, is true of feelings and, hence, since this category includes the ethical stances of good and bad, morals. This is the basis of his moral philosophy. He considered morality, no less than epistemology, to be a branch of descriptive psychology. As with opposed intellectual stances, only one of two opposed emotional stances can be correct in a given case. Again, we grasp the difference between correct and incorrect emotional stances only by experience of contrasting cases, much as we learn what it is for something to be, say, red. Moreover feelings, like judgements, are objective in the sense that we cannot correctly have a pro-emotion towards an object towards which anyone can correctly have an anti-emotion, and vice versa. The correctness of feelings, then, including moral feelings, is, like the correctness of judgements, objective.

Brentano developed his ideas on truth and evidence in the posthumously published *Truth and Evidence* (1930). He distinguished *evident judgements* and *blind judgements*. The former we should perhaps call self-evident: they include judgements of inner awareness ('I seem to see a pencil') and judgements of necessary truth ('two pencils are more than one'). Blind judgements are all those that are not self-evident ('I see a pencil'). Most judgements of the outer world and all judgements of memory are blind; but, to the extent that they confirm each other, we can have confidence in them. The judgement, for instance, that there is a three-dimensional (spatial) world is, Brentano believed, so widely confirmed as to be infinitely more likely than any of its alternatives. Truth is then that which 'pertains to the judgement of one who asserts what the person who judges with evidence would assert' (p. 139).

Besides epistemology and moral philosophy, Brentano wrote on a wide range of other topics. First, on logic, developing a revised syllogism. Second, on the nature of categories, arguing that there are only concrete (as opposed to abstract) things, and that every judgement is an acceptance or rejection of a concrete thing (thus any true sentence which appears to refer to some abstract entity can be translated into a sentence which refers to a concrete thing— for example, 'he believes that there are horses' becomes 'he affirms horses'). Third, on God, whose existence, as a Necessary Being, he derived from the Principle of Sufficient Reason. Fourth, on the nature of chance, rejecting the notion of absolute chance as self-contradictory, and arguing that determinism is incompatible with the fact of freedom of the will. His ideas, though often speculative, were always sharp and challenging. In *Religion and Philosophy* (1954), for instance, he extended his dualistic view of the mind to incorporate a Christian picture of the soul as separate from the body and yet capable of acting through it. He argued that the soul was created *ex nihilo* at the time of conception, defending this idea by claiming that 'psychical' things are created *ex nihilo* every time we call an image to mind. He believed that philosophy went through cycles of flourishing and decline, the latter being marked by three phases: a shift of interest from theory to practice, scepticism, and mysticism. As well as being a prolific writer, Brentano was a charismatic and inspiring teacher. His pupils included Alexius **Meinong**, Karl Stumpf, Christian Ehrenfels and Edmund **Husserl**. Through the last, his ideas helped to establish the school of phenomenology, from which (though in a much modified form) modern descriptive psychopathology is derived. His picture of the mind as intentional rather than as a receptacle was an important formative idea for Freud in the development of psychoanalysis. Along with others who have sought a philosophical foundation for empirical science, his project failed: the positivist tendencies of scientific psychology owe more to Wundt. His account of the intentionality of subjective experience remains important in the philosophy of mind.

Sources: Goldenson; Reese; Corsini; Edwards; Urmson & Rée.

K. W. M. FULFORD

Camus, Albert

French. *b:* 1913, Mondovi, Algeria. *d:* 1960, near Paris (road accident). *Cat:* Philosopher of the absurd. *Ints:* Ethics. *Infls:* Greek thought, Augustine, Nietzsche and Sartre. *Appts:* Camus's student work on philosophy (on Plotinus and Augustine) was interrupted by illness, and up to the outbreak of the Second World War he had a number of theatrical and journalistic jobs in Algiers and Paris; active in the Resistance he became

Coeditor (with Sartre) of *Combat*; breaking with Sartre after the war, Camus devoted himself to writing. Nobel Prize for Literature, 1957.

Main publications:

(1942) *Le Mythe de Sisyphe*, Paris: Gallimard; second, expanded edition, 1945.
(1942) *L'Étranger*, Paris: Gallimard.
(1945) *Lettres à un ami allemand*, Paris: Gallimard.
(1947) *La Peste*, Paris: Gallimard.
(1950–3) *Actuelles: I and II*, Paris: Gallimard.
(1951) *L'Homme révolté*, Paris: Gallimard.
(1956) *La Chute*, Paris: Gallimard.

Secondary literature:

Ayer, A. J. (1946) 'Novelist-philosophers', *Horizon* 13: 155–68.
Braun, L. (1974) *Witness of Decline: Albert Camus, Moralist of the Absurd*, Cranbury, NJ: Farleigh Dickinson University Press.
Cruickshank, J. (1960) *Albert Camus and the Literature of Revolt*, London and New York: Oxford University Press.
Karpushin, V. A. (1967–9) 'The concept of the individual in the work of Albert Camus', *Soviet Studies in Philosophy*, 6, Winter, pp. 52–60.
Thody, P. (1957) *Albert Camus: A Study of His Work*, New York and London: Macmillan.
Trundle, R. C. and Puligandla, R. (1986) *Beyond Absurdity: The Philosophy of Albert Camus*, Lanham: University Press of America.

As with **Unamuno**, Camus is not an academic philosopher but rather a thinker concerned to work out a way of making sense of a life threatened with meaninglessness. Thanks to his literary skill, Camus's thought was widely diffused and influential and its embodiment in classics of fiction such as *L'Étranger* (1942) and *La Peste* (1947) continues to make it one of the most approachable of examples of recent French philosophy. His thought has two phases, epitomized in the two philosophical essays *Le Mythe de Sisyphe* (1942) and *L'Homme révolté* (1951). Common to each phase are the presuppositions of atheism, the mortality of the soul and the indifference of the

universe to human aspirations. The development lies in the value system for which these views form the basis.

The concept central to the early phase of Camus's thought is the absurd. Absurdity is a feeling which arises from the confrontation of the world, which is irrational, with the hopeless but profound human desire to make sense of our condition. The appropriate response to this situation, Camus argues, is to live in full consciousness of it. He rejects philosophies or courses of action which conjure the problem away, notably religious belief, suicide and existentialism, which in Camus's view deifies the irrational. From a lucid appreciation of the absurdity of our life three consequences flow, which Camus calls revolt, freedom and passion. By 'revolt' (in the early phase of his thought) Camus means defiance in the face of the bleak truth about the human condition, hopeless but not resigned, lending to life a certain grandeur. Again, recognition of absurdity frees us from habit and convention: we see all things anew, and are inwardly liberated. By 'passion' Camus means the resolve to live as intensely as possible, not so as to escape the sense of absurdity but so as to face it with absolute lucidity. The way to do this is to maximize not the quality but the quantity of one's experiences. Sisyphus is the hero who exemplifies these virtues. He is aware of the hopelessness of his task but rises above his destiny by facing it lucidly: we must imagine Sisyphus to be happy.

A further consequence difficult to avoid in such an outlook is that any course of action is permissible (*tout est permis*), provided we make no attempt to escape the consequences of our actions—witness the behaviour of Mersault in the fictional depiction of this philosophy, *L'Étranger*. The experience of war caused Camus to change his mind on this point, since it cannot be seriously advanced in the face of unquantifiable suffering. In *L'Homme révolté* and its fictional counterpart *La Peste* Camus seeks to ground values very close to those of liberal humanism on much the same bases as those of his earlier work. The major philosophical change, a marked break with Sartrean existentialism, is the view that there is such a thing as human nature, the conclusion Camus draws from his analysis of the concept of revolt in life and art. In the concept of human nature he finds a reason and a cause for union between human beings. The detachment of the absurdist is replaced by an ethic of sympathy, community and service to others.

ROBERT WILKINSON

Carnap, Rudolf

German. *b:* 18 May 1891, Ronsdorf (Wuppertal), Germany. *d:* 1970. *Cat:* Logician. *Ints:* Logic; semantics; philosophy of science; epistemology. *Educ:* University of Freiburg; University of Jena, PhD 1921; Harvard University, ScD(Hons) 1936. *Infls:* Kant, Frege, Russell and Wittgenstein. *Appts:* Professor of Natural Philosophy, German University, Prague, 1931–5; Professor of Philosophy, University of Chicago, 1936–52; subsequently Professor, University of California, Los Angeles from 1954–62; Visiting Professor, Harvard, 1941–2.

Main publications:

(1928) *Der Logische Aufbau der Welt*, Berlin: Weltkreis-Verlag (English translation, *The Logical Structure of the World and Pseudoproblems in Philosophy*, trans. R. George, Berkeley: University of California Press, 1969).
(1934) *Logische Syntax der Sprache*, Vienna: Springer (English translation, *The Logical Syntax of Language*, London: Routledge & Kegan Paul, 1937).
(1950) 'Empiricism, semantics and ontology', *Revue Internationale de Philosophie* 4; reprinted in Carnap (1956).
(1950) *The Logical Foundations of Probability*, University of Chicago Press.
(1956) *Meaning and Necessity*, second edition, University of Chicago Press.

(1959) 'The elimination of metaphysics through the logical analysis of language', in A. J. Ayer (ed.), *Logical Positivism*, Glencoe: Free Press.
(1987) 'On protocol sentences', *Nous* 21.

Secondary literature:

Sarkar, S. (ed.) (1992) 'Carnap: a centenary appraisal', *Synthese*, 93, 1–2.
Schilpp, P. A. (ed.) (1963) *The Philosophy of Rudolf Carnap*, La Salle: Open Court.

Carnap occupies an important position in the evolution of the analytic tradition in philosophy, not least in his appreciation of the significance for philosophy of the major developments in logic due to **Frege** and **Russell**. From the latter's influence he also conceived his own project of constructing material objects (or their concepts) from primitive elementary experiences. One important point of difference from the atomism of Russell, however, is that Carnap takes these basic experiences as states of consciousness, the experiences of an individual, and not sensations or simple impressions in the manner of earlier empiricism. He grew dissatisfied with this project, principally on the ground that scientific, and therefore public, knowledge could not plausibly be constructed on such a subjective base. This abandonment of the phenomenalist perspective was heavily influenced by his fellow positivist Neurath, whose commitment to physicalism he came to share. Along with this commitment he espoused the thesis, very characteristic of the positivists, of the unity of method in the sciences.

In the heyday of logical positivism Carnap led the assault on metaphysics. Like many empiricists he espoused a form of the analytic—synthetic distinction, according to which knowledge can be only of two basic kinds: 'necessary' truths or tautologies which hold independently of particular matters of fact and are true in all possible cases; and factual propositions about the world. Consequently there are just two permissible categories of proposition which exhaust what can be meaningfully said. By contrast, the assertions of traditional metaphysicians fail to qualify for either category, being neither tautological not empirically verifiable. Thus, while the sentences of metaphysics might, by virtue of their seductive syntactical appearance, suggest that great profundities were being communicated, they in fact lacked any literal sense at all, although they could have some emotional significance for those using them. Indeed Carnap stigmatized metaphysicians as frustrated poets or musicians, seduced by fundamental confusions about language. The principal source of this confusion is that philosophers have typically used what Carnap calls the 'material mode of speech' or 'thing'-language, and much metaphysics can arise from a failure to distinguish what are really sentences about language ('syntactical sentences') from sentences about objects ('object-sentences'). This produces sentences of a third category, ('pseudo-object sentences') which look as if they are about objects but, insofar as they are meaningful at all, could only be about language. The litmus test for items in this category is that there is no empirical test that could be made to determine their truth. For Carnap, therefore, metaphysical problems were totally spurious and did not admit of resolution. The implication of this for philosophy was far-reaching—philosophy had no business masquerading as a source of knowledge beyond science, and its proper role is to be concerned with the logical syntax of language, especially the language of science. Other disciplines with pretensions to scientific status, like psychology, would need to become thoroughly empirical, shedding discredited metaphysical preoccupations, and abandoning vacuous speculations about the mind.

On this approach syntax is a matter of conventions and the rules which license combinations of linguistic expressions. In his earlier work his concerns were largely of this formal complexion, and it was somewhat later that he took more serious account of substantial semantic issues, principally as a result of the influence of the Polish logician Alfred **Tarski**. The mature statement of his approach, which he called the method of extension and intension, was developed through a modification of more traditional concepts, such as those of class and property. He signalled a departure from a common assumption, that the role of an expression in language is that of naming some entity, whether abstract or concrete, preferring to talk of expressions as each possessing an intension and an extension. The intension is the meaning component which is grasped by anyone who understands the expression, while the extension is what is determined by observation or empirical investigation.

Carnap hoped to provide a basis for the analysis of modal logic, and while acknowledging the existence of the formal systems already available, he none the less felt that the fundamental notions themselves, for example necessity and possibility, had not been sufficiently clarified. He also endeavoured to extend the application of logical rigour to the topic of induction, seeking to provide a basis for measuring the degree of inductive support, and produced substantial work on probability.

In a later paper, 'Empiricism, semantics and ontology' (1950), Carnap delivered his most considered views on ontological questions. Maintaining his anti-metaphysical instinct, he distinguished between what he called 'external' and 'internal' questions. Acceptance of a kind of entity was ultimately a matter of adopting a linguistic framework, not one of belief, still less a commitment to some dubious metaphysical reality. So the question of which linguistic framework to adopt ultimately came down to a choice which was to be made on pragmatic grounds of expediency, fruitfulness or utility. Only once a framework was adopted, did it make sense to ask 'existential' questions. Thus the decision to adopt the mathematical framework of numbers was external, a practical question of whether to accept certain linguistic forms. An internal question say, about whether there exist prime numbers greater than a million was a matter of investigation and justification. This combination of pragmatism and empiricism was very much characteristic of Carnap's whole style of thought. Carnap's views attracted criticism from a number of quarters. Apart from those levelled against logical positivism as such, his stance on induction and probability brought him into conflict with Karl **Popper** who notoriously questioned whether any degree of inductive support or 'confirmation' increased either the probability of a theory being true or one's rational entitlement to believe in its truth. Carnap was also confronted by **Quine** with scepticism about modality and the very idea of analyticity as traditionally conceived. He and Quine additionally parted company on ontological commitment. Where Carnap saw a difference of kind between external and internal questions, Quine saw a difference of degree of generality. Others, on different grounds from Popper, have judged his forays into inductive logic to have been less than successful, albeit a substantial stimulus to subsequent work in the field. In other respects, his contributions to the study of syntax and semantics presaged much of the more recent work on truth-conditional semantics and possible worlds accounts of modality, and even logical pragmatics. Among those influenced by him in addition to Quine, were Hilary **Putnam** and the late R. M. Martin, the latter developing, in idiosyncratic style, a form of the logical pragmatics that Carnap had envisaged.

Sources: WW(Am) 1965.

DENIS POLLARD

Cassirer, Ernst

German. *b:* 28 July 1874, Breslau. *d:* 13 April 1945, New York. *Cat:* Neo-Kantian (Marburg School); historian of philosophy; epis-temologist. *Ints:* Culture. *Educ:* Berlin, Leipzig, Munich, Heidelberg and Marburg. *Infls:* Hermann Cohen, Edmund Husserl and Paul Natorp. *Appts:* Professor at Marburg and then at Hamburg University (Rector from 1930–3); Professor at Columbia University in New York; also taught at Oxford (1933–5), Göteborg, Sweden (1935–41) and Yale (1941–4).

Main publications:

Major editions of the works of Leibniz (1904–15) and Kant (1912).

(1899) 'Descartes, Kritik der Mathematischen und Naturwissenschaftlichen Erkenntnis', Marburg: Inaugural Dissertation.

(1906–20) *Das Erkenntnisproblem in der Philosophie und Wissenschaft der neueren Zeit*, 3 vols, Berlin: Bruno Cassirer (English translation of the third volume, *The Problem of Knowledge*, New Haven: Yale University Press, 1950).

(1910) *Der Substanzbegriff und der Funktionsbegriff*, Berlin: Bruno Cassirer (English translation, *Substance and Function, and Einstein's Theory of Relativity*, New Haven: Yale University Press, 1923).

(1918) *Immanuel Kants Leben und Lehre*, Berlin: Bruno Cassirer (English translation, *Kant's Life and Thought*, New Haven: Yale University Press, 1981).

(1923–9) *Philosophie der symbolischen Formen*, 3 vols, Berlin: Bruno Cassirer (English translation, *The Philosophy of Symbolic Forms*, New Haven: Yale University Press, 1953–7).

(1925) *Sprache und Mythos*, Leipzig: B. G. Teubner (English translation, *Language and Myth*, New York: Harper & Brothers, 1946).

(1927) *Individuum und Kosmos in der Philosophie der Renaissance*, Leipzig: B. G. Teubner (English translation, *The Individual and the Cosmos in Renaissance Philosophy*, Philadelphia: University of Pennsylvania Press, 1963).

(1932) *Die Platonische Renaissance in England und die Schule von Cambridge*, Leipzig: B. G. Teubner.

(1932) *Die Philosophie der Aufklärung*, Tübingen: J. C. B. Mohr (English translation, *The Philosophy of the Enlightenment*, Princeton: Princeton University Press, 1951).

(1936) *Determinismus und Indeterminismus in der modernen Physik*, Göteborg: Högskolas Årskrift.

(1939) *Descartes, Lehre, Persönlichkeit, Wirkung*, Stockholm: Berman Fischer Verlag.

(1942) *Zur Logik der Kulturwissenschaften*, Göteborg: Högskolas Arskrift (English translation: *The Logic of the Humanities*, New Haven: Yale University Press, 1974).
(1944) *An Essay on Man: Introduction to the Philosophy of Human Culture*, New Haven: Yale University Press.
(1946) *The Myth of the State*, New Haven: Yale University Press.
(1970) *Rousseau, Kant, Goethe*, Princeton: Princeton University Press.
(1971) *Idee und Gestalt, Goethe, Schiller, Hölderlin, Kleist*, Darmstadt: Wissenschaftliche Buchgesellschaft.
(1979) *Symbol, Myth, and Culture: Essays and Lectures of Ernst Cassirer, 1935–1945*, ed. Donald Philip Verene. New Haven: Yale University Press.
(1985) *Symbol, Technik, Sprache*, Hamburg: Meiner.

Secondary literature:

Braun, H.-J., Holzhey, H. and Orth, E. W. (1988) *Über Ernst Cassirers Philosophie der symbolischen Formen*, Frankfurt am Main: Suhrkamp.
Cassirer, Toni (1981) *Mein Leben mit Ernst Cassirer*, Hildesheim: Gerstenberg.
Hamburg, Carl H. (1956) *Symbol and Reality: Studies in the Philosophy of Ernst Cassirer*, The Hague: Martinus Nijhoff.
Itzkoff, Seymour W. (1971) *Ernst Cassirer: Scientific Knowledge and the Concept of Man*, Notre Dame: University of Notre Dame Press.
Lipton, David R. (1978) *Ernst Cassirer: The Dilemma of a Liberal Intellectual in Germany, 1914–1933*, Toronto, University of Toronto Press.
Schilpp, Paul (ed.) (1949) *The Philosophy of Ernst Cassirer*, La Salle: Open Court; reprinted 1973.

Cassirer was Hermann Cohen's most important student. His work is often considered to be the final testament of the Marburg school. Yet, there are important differences between him and the earlier Marburg neo-Kantians. Although he devoted himself to a critical and historical study of the problem of knowledge and the logic of the sciences, he was also interested in the problem of culture in general. Thinking of human beings as 'symbolic animals', he argued that all culture was based on our concept-ual ability that allows us to invent and use artificial signs and symbols. In many ways Cassirer takes up and develops also the ideas of the Baden (or Southwestern) School of neo-Kantianism as they were exemplified in the works of Wilhelm Windelband and Heinrich Rickert. Just as they did, he felt that it was necessary to move from a 'critique of reason' to a 'critique of culture'. However, his many historical studies were not only in the service of such a critique of culture. They were also meant to be contributions to the advancement of culture, for he believed that in order 'to possess the world of culture we must incessantly reconquer it by historical recollection'.

Like Kant and the neo-Kantians in general, he argued that our concepts determine the way we experience the world. Our experience does not mirror an objectively existing world or things in themselves. Rather, the world is actively constructed by us in accordance with our conceptual framework. In an important sense, we constitute it, using the materials given to us by the senses. For this reason Cassirer thought that philosophers should concentrate on the conceptual framework that enables us to experience the world in the way we do experience it. In more technical terms, we must employ a transcendental method in showing how these concepts make our experience possible. However, unlike Kant (but like some of his own neo-Kantian predecessors), he rejected the idea that the concepts and principles that make our experience possible are the static and forever fixed furniture of the human mind. He claimed that these concepts and principles constantly develop. Although one may speak of a 'natural symbolism' that characterizes all human consciousness, it can take many different forms. His philosophy started from the presupposition that, if there is a definition of the nature or 'essence' of human beings, it can only be functional. It cannot be substantial. Cassirer also thought that the original Kantian conception of critical philosophy was far too narrow. In particular, he argued that the transcendental investigation must be extended to the humanities and even to forms of representation that are often called primitive, namely mythologies. They also constitute conceptual systems worthy of analysis. Indeed, he argued that every manifestation of culture is an important subject of philosophical study in so far as our symbolizing nature is present in it. Cassirer felt that 'the artist is just as much a discoverer of the forms of nature as the scientist is a discoverer of facts or natural laws'.

This philosophy of culture had, for Cassirer, clear ethical consequences, for he believed that 'human culture taken as a whole may be described as the progress of man's progressive self-liberation. Language, art, religion, sciences, are various phases in this process. In all of them man discovers and proves a new power—the power to build up a world of his own, an 'ideal' world'. Being equally opposed to empiricism, naturalism, positivism and *Lebensphilosophie* (which he thought included the kind of existential thinking advocated by Martin **Heidegger**), he argued for a new kind of idealism and humanism. Indeed, he characterized his philosophy also as a 'humanistic philosophy of culture'. At the same time he was rather pessimistic about the influence of philosophy on politics: 'the role of the individual thinker is a very modest one. As an individual the philosopher has long ago given up all hopes to reform the political world'. And even though he also believed that 'philosophy as a whole' should not give up hope, he thought that all that could be done by philosophy was the debunking of political myths. As he said in one of his last lectures: 'To all of us it has become clear that we have greatly underestimated the strength of political myths. We should not repeat this error'. Cassirer had some followers in the USA during the early years after the Second World War, both among historians of philosophy and among philosophical critics. The best known among these was perhaps

Susanne **Langer**. However, his thought was then almost completely ignored in Germany. In the late twentieth century, a real interest in Cassirer's philosophy has developed in Germany. Some of his later essays, written in English, have recently been translated into German, and there is even talk of 'the beginning of a renaissance' of his thinking.

MANFRED KUEHN

Chisholm, Roderick Milton

American. *b:* 27 November 1916, North Attleborough, Massachusetts. *Cat:* Metaphysician; philosopher of mind. *Ints:* Phenomenology. *Educ:* Studied at Brown University, AB 1938; and Harvard, AM 1940, PhD 1942. *Infls:* Fichte, Reid, Brentano, Meinong, Husserl, Moore, C. I. Lewis, Cardinal Mercier and Ducasse. *Appts:* Taught at University of Pennsylvania, 1946–7; thereafter at Brown University; Andrew W. Mellon Professor of the Humanities, 1972; Visiting Professor at many universities, notably Graz in Austria; Editor of *Philosophy and Phenomenological Research*, 1980.

Main publications:

(1957) *Perceiving*, Ithaca: Cornell University Press.
(1960) (ed.) *Realism and the Background of Phenomenology*, Glencoe, Ill.: Free Press.
(1966) *Theory of Knowledge*, Englewood Cliffs: Prentice-Hall (substantially revised in second (1977) and third (1989) editions).
(1966) (ed., with others, and trans. Franz Brentano) *The True and the Evident*, (English edition (with others) translated by Chisholm).
(1973) (ed. with R. J. Swartz) *Empirical Knowledge: Readings from Contemporary Sources*, Englewood Cliffs, NJ: Prentice-Hall.
(1976) *Person and Object*, London: Allen & Unwin; La Salle: Open Court.
(1976) (ed. with S. Körner) *Philosophische Untersuchungen zu Raum, Zeit und Kontinuum*, Hamburg: F. Meiner.

(1978) (ed. with R. Haller) *Die Philosophie Franz Brentanos*, Amsterdam: Rodopi.

(1981) *The First Person*, Brighton: Harvester and Minneapolis: Minnesota University Press.

(1982) *Brentano and Meinong Studies*, Amsterdam: Rodopi.

(1982) *The Foundations of Knowing*, Brighton: Harvester and Minneapolis: Minnesota University Press.

(1985) (ed. with others) *Philosophie des Geistes, Philosphie der Psychologie: Akten des 9. Internationalen Wittgenstein Symposiums*, Vienna: Hölder-Pichler-Tempsky.

(1986) *Brentano and Intrinsic Value*, Cambridge: Cambridge University Press.

(1989) *On Metaphysics*, Minneapolis: Minnesota University Press.

Secondary literature:

Bogdan, R. J. (ed.) (1986) *Roderick M. Chisholm*, Dordrecht: Reidel (includes intellectual autobiography and full bibliography of his writings to date, partly annotated by himself).

David, M. and Stubenberg, L. (eds) (1986) *Philosophische Aufsätze zur Ehren von Roderick M. Chisholm*, Amsterdam: Rodopi.

Lehrer, K. (ed.) (1975) *Analysis and Metaphysics*, Dordrecht: Reidel.

Philosophia 1978 (special issue).

Sosa, E. (ed.) (1979) *Essays in the Philosophy of Roderick M. Chisholm*, (includes extended reply by Chisholm).

Chisholm stands firmly in the main Anglo-American tradition of analytic philosophy, in a broad sense, but he is unusual in the breadth of the influences that he has brought to bear upon it, ranging from the ancient Greeks (his first published paper, in *Philosophy of Science* for 1941, was on Sextus Empiricus) through Fichte, **Brentano** and **Meinong** to Cardinal Mercier and his own teacher C. J. Ducasse, as well as the standard sources. His earliest publications include many reviews, on topics covering, as well as central philosophy, symbolic logic, aesthetics, ethics and psychology—his war service was as a clinical psychologist. He has edited and contributed to the translation of works by Fichte, Brentano and Meinong.

Chisholm presents his own work in a direct no-nonsense style, using sets of definitions. These are built up gradually and form the skeleton for the main ideas. Despite this rather formal approach he eschews the technicalities of formal logic in his main works and writes in plain English. Apart from commentaries on writers like Brentano and Meinong his work mainly falls under epistemology, philosophy of mind, metaphysics and ethics.

A key motif throughout Chisholm's philosophy, and one heavily influenced by Brentano and the phenomenologists, is his emphasis on consciousness and on how things appear to one. Among his central concepts is one he develops from Brentano, that of evidence, and one of the central problems he sees for epistemology (one which links him with Sextus Empiricus) is that of the criterion for when we have adequate evidence for something. He distinguishes what is directly evident from what is indirectly evident (*Theory of Knowledge*, 1966), and the problem of the criterion concerns the passage from the indirectly evident to the directly evident. The directly evident is the 'self-presenting' (ibid., p. 28; later he prefers this term: *The Foundations of Knowing*, 1982, p. 26), or what we have when: 'What justifies me in counting it as evident that a is F is simply the fact that a is F' (*Theory of Knowledge*, 1966, p. 26). The indirectly evident can then hopefully be reached from this by applying certain epistemic rules or principles (ibid., p. 38). Chapter 3 of *The Foundations of Knowing* uses an elaboration of these ideas to defend a view of knowledge as justified true belief in the face of 'Gettier' counterexamples suggesting that such a belief may fail to be knowledge because its truth and the basis of its justification for the believer in question are irrelevant to each other (cf. chapter 10 of the third edition (1989) of *Theory of Knowledge*). All this forms part of the foundationalism, in the general tradition of Descartes, to which Chisholm adheres (*Foundations*, chapter 1; cf. Bogdan (ed.) 1986, p. 43). He is an 'internalist' rather than an 'externalist' (cf. *Foundations*, p. 29), claiming that justification must be 'epistemic' and rejecting various other kinds of justification (pp. 27–32). The third edition of *Theory of Knowledge* repeats or develops many of these points.

A further effect of Chisholm's foundationalism is his distinction between 'particularists' and 'methodists' (*Foundations*, p. 66). Particularists, of whom Chisholm is one, start from the question 'What do we know?' and only then go on to the question 'How can we decide whether we know?' Methodists do the reverse, while sceptics claim that neither question can be answered without first answering the other. Empiricism is one type of methodism, and can take two forms, a genetic doctrine about how we actually come by our knowledge, and a doctrine of justification. Chisholm rejects both of these in *Perceiving* (1957), but he shares something with them in that he accepts incorrigible states of mind, as a foundationalist perhaps must. These, however, are not sense-datum statements (he rejects substantial appearances, although he once accepted them: 1957, p. 117), but statements that one is in a certain state of mind, or is being appeared to in a certain way (he does not tell us how he would deal with unconscious beliefs and desires). Later, however, he rejected the view that there are first-person propositions, since this view cannot distinguish '*X* believes *X* is *F*' from '*X* believes he himself is *F*'. Instead he develops a theory of intentional states in terms of direct and indirect attribution, taking the 'he himself' locution as basic (*The First Person*, 1981, chapters 3 and 4; see also Boer's summary in Bogdan (ed.) 1986, p. 87).

Chisholm sees a strong analogy between epistemology and ethics. The first part of *Perceiving* borrows its title from W. K. Clifford: 'The ethics of belief' (cf. also *Theory of Knowledge*, (third edition) 1989, pp. 57–60). Belief, or its withholding, is 'required' of us in certain circumstances, and he is sympathetic to the view that requirements is the central concept of ethics (e.g.

1986, p. 53). *Brentano and Intrinsic Value* (1986) develops the ethics of Brentano along lines paralleling his own epistemology: we have incorrigible knowledge of our own valuings, and these are prima facie evidence for correct valuings—for emotions, like judgements, can be correct or incorrect. This is then applied to a detailed development of **Moore**'s notion of 'organic unities'. Throughout Chisholm assumes, in Moorean fashion, that 'whatever we are justified in assuming, when we are not doing philosophy, we are also justified in assuming when we *are* doing philosophy' (*Person and Object*, 1976, p. 16).

On the nature and existence of the self Chisholm rejects Hume's 'bundle of perceptions' view. Hume says that in seeking himself he always stumbles on some perception, but bundles don't stumble on their own contents; experiences need a subject just as qualities need a substance. But Kant too goes wrong in saying we can never know the self, since this is like saying we can never know the substance of an object as something distinct from the qualities which give us access to it. We know the self in knowing states of it, i.e. in having experiences (ibid.), although later he rejected the view that we have an individuating concept of ourselves, (1981, pp. 16–17, 86–90; but cf. Sosa (ed.) 1979, pp. 324–5). This same self is the cause of its own actions by 'immanent' as against 'transeunt' causation, a medieval distinction he revives between causation by agents and causation by events. He hopes thus to transcend the determinism–indeterminism impasse, each limb of which seems to make responsibility an illusion. The objection that attributing actions to an agent as cause is empty and tells us nothing beyond the mere sequence of events he dismisses as applying equally to transeunt causation: what does talk of 'causing' add there either? One might wonder, however, if this is fair: believers in transeunt causation need not be mere Humeans, and the question arises how agents manage to decide one way or the other.

(Chisholm takes his view further in Bogdan (ed.) 1986: see especially pp. 214–15, 223.)

An important contribution to the philosophy of mind is Chisholm's revival of Brentano's idea of intentionality as a mark of the mental, enabling him to maintain 'the primacy of the intentional' over the semantic (ibid., pp. 222, 231). Chisholm started a debate on the criteria for intentionality, offering three in the *Proceedings of the Aristotelian Society*, 1955–6. Later (in his entry on intentionality in P. Edwards (ed.), *Encyclopedia of Philosophy*, 1967), he added two more, but admitted that together they only provided sufficient conditions and not necessary ones (cf. also Bogdan (ed.) 1987, pp. 36–7, 232.

For all his adherence to Moorean common sense Chisholm is ready to distinguish, with Joseph Butler, 'strict and philosophical' from 'loose and popular' speech, especially when defending mereological essentialism, which he claims is really congenial to common sense (*Person and Object*, 1976, pp. 102–3, Appendix B). The self, however, is a continuant, and is immune to Lockean transfers from one substance to another, but none of this commits us to a doctrine of temporal parts (ibid., Appendix A). Perhaps Chisholm's most lasting influence lies in his revival of the ideas of the earlier Austrian philosophers, especially in the area of intentionality. His foundationalism is perhaps less in tune with modern views, although they would mostly (but not entirely) agree with his rejection of substantial appearances and sense data. His apparatus of direct and indirect evidence, and his epistemic principles, have been criticized as inadequate. The externalism–internalism debate is still in full swing. His views on agent causality have had some influence, and mereological essentialism is a currently debated topic, as are the ontological questions to which he has contributed.

Sources: DAS, 7th edn, 1978; Dancy & Sosa; personal communication.

A. R. LACEY

Chomsky, Avram Noam

American. *b:* 7 December 1928, Philadelphia. *Cat:* Linguist; cognitive scientist; libertarian socialist; philosopher of language; philosopher of mind. *Ints:* Philosophy of language; philosophy of mind. *Educ:* University of Pennsylvania. *Infls:* Zellig Harris, Nelson Goodman and W. V. O. Quine. *Appts:* 1951–5, Junior Fellow, Harvard University; from 1955, Assistant, Associate, then full Professor at the Massachusetts Institute of Technology; Institute Professor in the Department of Linguistics and Philosophy.

Main publications:

(1957) *Syntactic Structures*, The Hague: Mouton.
(1965) *Aspects of the Theory of Syntax*, Cambridge, Mass.: MIT.
(1972) *Language and Mind*, enlarged edition, New York: Harcourt Brace Jovanovich.
(1980) *Rules and Representations*, New York: Columbia University Press.
(1980) 'Rules and representations', with Open Peer Commentary and Author's Response, *Behavioral and Brain Sciences* 3: 1–61.
(1986) *Knowledge of Language: Its Nature, Origin and Use*, New York: Praeger.
(1988) *Language and Problems of Knowledge: The Managua Lectures*, Cambridge: Mass.: MIT Press.
(1993) *Language and Thought*, Wakefield, Rhode Island and London: Moyer Bell.
(1995) 'Language and nature', *Mind* 104: 1–61.

Secondary literature:

George, A. (ed.) (1989) *Reflections on Chomsky*, Oxford: Blackwell.
Harman, G. (ed.) (1974) *On Noam Chomsky: Critical Essays*, New York: Anchor.
Kasher, A. (ed.) (1991) *The Chomskyan Turn*, Oxford: Blackwell.

Koerner, K. and Tajima, M. (1986) *Noam Chomsky: A Personal Bibliography, 1951–1986*, Amsterdam: J. Benjamins.

Salkie, R. (1990) *The Chomsky Update: Linguistics and Politics*, London: Unwin Hyman.

Sgroi, S. C. (1983) *Noam Chomsky: Bibliografia 1949–81*, Padua: CLESP.

Noam Chomsky is both an eminent linguist and a prominent political activist. His creation and constant elaboration of generative grammar has been profoundly influential within linguistics and has contributed significantly to the development of cognitive science. As a libertarian socialist he has trenchantly and tirelessly criticized US foreign policy and sought to correct deception and narrowness of debate within the mainstream media. While Chomsky's politics has philosophical underpinnings and is related very generally to his linguistics, his important philosophical views are located predominantly in the latter.

Chomsky holds that scientific linguistics, his fundamental concern, should focus its attention on questions which can be given clearly formulated and empirically testable answers; further, that there are three basic questions of this type: *What constitutes knowledge of language? How is such knowledge acquired?* and *How is such knowledge put to use?* Since the introduction of generative grammar in *Syntactic Structures* (1957) he has concentrated upon the first two questions.

For Chomsky a rigorous scientific description of the knowledge of language possessed by a mature speaker-listener is possible in the form of a particular generative grammar. In this context such a grammar is a fully explicit formal theory which purports to describe precisely the principles and rules in the mind/brain of a speaker-listener which characterize the grammatical sentences of the speaker-listener's particular language. These principles and rules comprise a grammar. Hence, in a second sense, a grammar is a complex mental structure. To possess such a structure is to be in a mental state of unconscious knowledge of the principles and rules involved and it is this state which constitutes knowledge of language.

Scientific linguistics, then, is conceived as a part of psychology since its proper object of study is language understood as a psychological structure. This runs wholly counter to the widespread view that the proper object of study is language understood as a public phenomenon and, in fact, Chomsky denies that a clear concept of this alleged object is possible. His account entails a rejection of theories which analyse knowledge of language in terms of use and, more generally, it requires a sharp theoretical distinction between knowledge of language and performance. The latter is made prominently in his distinction between *competence* and *performance*. Reference must be made to performance for certain purposes but it is a theory of competence, that is to say, of tacit knowledge of grammar, which is a viable scientific goal. Major questions can be asked about performance: for example, how are people able to consistently produce utterances appropriate to their changing circumstances? In Chomsky's view, however, these are far beyond the reach of foreseeable scientific investigation.

Granted his account of a speaker-listener's knowledge of his or her language, the second, and for Chomsky the most fundamental, question for scientific linguistics can be asked: how is such knowledge acquired? Chomsky is adamant that all answers which in effect say that knowledge of grammar is learned from experience are mistaken. Crucial to his arguments for this and for his alternative answer is a strong claim, for which he holds there is detailed support, *viz.*, that children acquire principles of language for which there was no evidence in their experience. This phenomenon, often called the poverty of the stimulus, can be explained in only one general way in Chomsky's view: the principles are innate features of the child's mind.

Chomsky offers a more detailed nativist theory. Common to all humans is a genetic language-programme which encodes linguistic principles. It is not the mind/brain as a whole which is thus programmed, rather a distinct subsystem, the language faculty. Prior to a child experiencing language the language faculty is in its *initial state*, which comprise the genetically encoded principles and is called by Chomsky *Universal Grammar*. The language faculty develops until it reaches its *steady state*, the mature speaker-listener's state of knowledge of his or her particular language. In order for this development to take place it is certainly necessary for the child to experience its native language, the experience having such roles as 'triggering' the innate mechanisms and 'shaping' acquisition to the particular language. Nevertheless the contribution of experience is relatively superficial, being severely constrained by the genetically determined principles of Universal Grammar, and the whole process of development is characterized as one of biological growth or maturation rather than learning. Thus, for Chomsky, a proper answer to the second question involves a precise specification of the principles of Universal Grammar and a rigorous account of how these interact with experience so as to yield knowledge of a particular language.

A recent revision in his views is pertinent to such an answer. Chomsky has always been concerned to reduce the number of principles and rules postulated by generative grammar. Transformational rules have this effect and were prominent in his earlier work, but his revised theory suggests that only one highly abstract transformational principle is required. Indeed he now proposes that a very small number of highly abstract simple principles which interact can explain language acquisition. Crucial to this is relaxing the notion of a principle of Universal Grammar so that rather than being a rigid rule it permits a narrow range of options, called parameters, with different languages

taking different options. As a child acquires a language it effectively fixes a particular parameter on the basis of a small amount of positive evidence in its linguistic experience. Since each principle applies to every sentence as a licenser and since the principles interact, each instance of fixing a parameter can have widespread grammatical effects. It is therefore possible that rules in the traditional sense do not exist. Since Chomsky's views are both influential and controversial they have been subject to a large number of criticisms, many by philosophers. These include arguments that the theory of an innate grammar is biologically implausible (**Piaget**), that the notion of an internal grammar is threatened by indeterminacy of translation (**Quine**), that the idea that general learning procedures are not involved in language acquisition is implausible (**Putnam**), that language is properly conceived as a social phenomenon (**Dummett**) and that innate knowledge is conceptually impossible. Chomsky has responded to these and other criticisms, often at length—a practice which has enabled him to elaborate his position. For Chomsky philosophy is continuous with science, a view that he holds to be exemplified in the work of such writers as Descartes and Leibniz in whose rationalist tradition he locates himself.

STEPHEN MILLS

Collingwood, Robin George

British. *b:* 22 February 1889, Cartmel Fell, Lancashire. *d:* 9 January 1943, Coniston, Cumbria. *Cat:* Neo-idealist; archaeologist; historian. *Ints:* Metaphysics; epistemology; philosophy of history; aesthetics; ethics; political philosophy; philosophy of mind. *Educ:* Rugby Public School and University College, Oxford. *Infls:* Hegel, Vico, Croce, De Ruggiero, Hobbes and Hume. Personal: J. A. Smith, H. H. Joachim, E. F. Carritt and F. J. Haverfield. **Appts:** Fellow of Pembroke College, Oxford, 1912–34; University Lecturer in Philosophy and Roman History, Oxford, 1912–35: Waynflete Professor of Metaphysical Philosophy, University of Oxford, 1934–41; Fellow of the British Academy, 1934.

Main publications:

(1913) (trans.) B. Croce, *The Philosophy of Giambattista Vico*, London: H. Latimer.

(1916) *Religion and Philosophy*, London: Macmillan; reprinted, Bristol: Thoemmes Press, 1994.

(1923) *Roman Britain*, London: Oxford University Press; revised editions, Oxford: Clarendon Press, 1932, 1934.

(1924) *Speculum Mentis: or, the Map of Knowledge*, Oxford: Clarendon Press.

(1925) *Outlines of a Philosophy of Art*, London: Oxford University Press; reprinted in *Essays in the Philosophy of Art*, 1964; also reprinted, Bristol Thoemmes Press, 1994.

(1927) (trans.) B. Croce, *An Autiobiography*, Oxford: Clarendon Press.

(1933) *An Essay on Philosophical Method*, Oxford: Clarendon Press.

(1936) (with J. N. L. Myres) *Roman Britain and the English Settlements*, Oxford: Clarendon Press; second edition, 1937.

√(1938) *The Principles of Art*, Oxford: Clarendon Press.

√ (1939) *An Autobiography*, London: Oxford University Press.

(1940) *An Essay on Metaphysics*, Oxford: Clarendon Press.

(1942) *The New Leviathan: or, Man, Society, Civilization and Barbarism*, Oxford: Clarendon Press; revised edition, ed. David Boucher, Oxford: Clarendon Press, 1992.

(1945) *The Idea of Nature*, ed. T. M. Knox, Oxford: Clarendon Press.

√(1946) *The Idea of History*, ed. T. M. Knox, Oxford: Clarendon Press; revised edition, ed. Jan van der Dussen, Oxford: Clarendon, 1993.

(1964) *Essays in the Philosophy of Art*, ed. Alan B. Donagan, Bloomington: Indiana University Press.

(1965) *Essays in the Philosophy of History*, ed. William Debbins, Austin, Texas: University of Texas Press.

(1968) *Faith and Reason: Essays in the Philosophy of Religion*, ed. Lionel Rubinoff, Chicago: Quadrangle.

(1989) *Essays in Political Philosophy*, ed. David Boucher, Oxford: Clarendon Press.

Secondary literature:

Boucher, David (1989) *The Social and Political Thought of R. G. Collingwood*, Cambridge: Cambridge University Press.

——(ed.) (1992) *Collingwood Studies* (the journal of the Collingwood Society) 1.

Donagan, Alan (1962) *The Later Philosophy of R. G. Collingwood*, Oxford: Clarendon Press; second edition, Chicago and London: University of Chicago Press, 1985.

Krausz, Michael (1972) *Critical Essays on the Philosophy of R. G. Collingwood*, Oxford: Clarendon Press.

Mink, Louis O. (1969) *Mind, History and Dialectic: The Philosophy of R. G. Collingwood*, Bloomington, Indiana: Indiana University Press.

Rubinoff, Lionel (1970) *Collingwood and the Reform of Metaphysics: A Study in the Philosophy of Mind*, Toronto: University of Toronto Press.

Taylor, Donald S. (1988) *R. G. Collingwood: A Bibliography*, New York and London: Garland Publishing Co.

Van der Dussen, W. J. (1981) *History As Science: The Philosophy of R. G. Collingwood*, The Hague: Nijhoff.

Collingwood is distinguished by his outstanding achievements in history as well as philosophy. One of the few students of F. J. Haverfield to survive the First World War, Collingwood was internationally recognized at his death as the leading authority on Roman Britain. In the last decade of his life, despite severe illness, he produced a series of philosophical works which in their scope, depth and scholarship are without parallel in twentieth-century British philosophy. But his work has failed to influence the mainstream of modern philosophy.

In his autobiography Collingwood explains how his involvement in archaeological fieldwork became the inspiration for his reevaluation of the nature of philosophy. His interests in history linked him with philosophers such as **Croce** in the Italian idealist tradition deriving from Vico and Hegel, but brought him into conflict with

Oxford realists such as Joseph and Prichard. Collingwood justly describes his life's work as 'in the main an attempt to bring about a *rapprochement* between philosophy and history' (1939, p. 77), although scholars dispute his account of the development of his ideas.

Many of the themes of Collingwood's mature work make their appearance in his first two books: in *Religion and Philosophy* (1916) he maintains that philosophy and history are 'the same thing'; in *Speculum Mentis* (1924) he articulates a theory of mental life which systematically relates 'forms of experience' from pure feeling to rational self-consciousness. In later works such doctrines are reinterpreted in the light of Collingwood's changing conception of history, philosophy and the mind.

In the later philosophy of art he continues to think that art, as an imaginative or non-assertive form of experience, both makes possible and affects the character of rational thought. But, whereas in *Speculum Mentis* imagination is in contradiction with expression, in *The Principles of Art* (1938) art is identified with imaginative expression of feeling. Such expression involves bodily gesture, which is language in its primitive stage, verbal language being a refinement facilitating the expression of intellectual ideas. Through a synthesis of Crocean idealism with Humean phenomenalism Collingwood maintains that artistic activity, by raising feelings to consciousness, is at once the beginning of self-knowledge and the making of the world known in language. Since denial of feeling is corruption of consciousness or bad art, the artist proper bears the responsibility of speaking on behalf of his community. The theory of mind and language is further elaborated in *The New Leviathan* (1942) as the basis of Collingwood's liberal view of freedom as mental maturity attainable within a society of people conscious of one another's freedom.

At the centre of Collingwood's philosophy is his denial of what he saw as the principle of propositional logic, that the proposition is the 'unit of thought' (1939, p. 36). Parallel to **Wittgenstein**'s concern with the role of words in language-games, Collingwood emphasizes the place of a proposition in a complex structure of questions and answers. Every proposition is an answer to a question: the significance and the truth or falsity of a proposition depend on what question it is meant to answer. Every question involves presuppositions, some of which are themselves answers to yet further questions, while those that are not count as absolute presuppositions. In *An Essay on Metaphysics* (1940) Collingwood maintains that the aim of metaphysics is to identify the constellations of absolute presuppositions taken for granted by systematic thinkers in different eras. (*The Idea of Nature*, 1945, is Collingwood's account of the presuppositions of European cosmology). However, since absolute presuppositions cannot be either true or false, metaphysics must forgo assessment of them and is thereby revealed to be—contrary to the conclusion of *An Essay on Philosophical Method* (1933)—a historical discipline.

'The logic of question and answer' emerged from Collingwood's reflection on historical methodology and informs the philosophy of historical understanding presented in *The Idea of History* (1946). Historians study, not sheer events, but past actions, traces of which survive into the present. But actions are performed for particular reasons in specific circumstances. So the historian is obliged to discern the thoughts which determined the actions in question. Thus all history is the history of thought. Furthermore, the historian can understand past thoughts only by rethinking them in his own mind, just as the spectator appreciates a work of art by reconstructing in his own imagination the emotions expressed by the artist. On this account understanding the thoughts of others requires understanding one's own thoughts. Thus historical knowledge is a form of self-knowledge. As such it is the science of history, rather than the pseudoscience of psychology, which can provide the insight needed for control of human affairs. Collingwood's opposition to the divorce between theory and practice culminates in *The New Leviathan*, his analysis of the psychological and ethical foundations of European civilization and of the forces threatening to undermine it.

Sources: ENP; Turner; obituary, R. B. McCallum, T. M. Knox and I. A. Richmond, *PBA* 29 (1943): 463–80.

PETER LEWIS

Croce, Benedetto

Italian. *b:* 25 February 1866, Pescasseroli, Italy. *d:* 20 November 1952, Naples. *Cat:* Philosopher of spirit. *Appts:* Croce held no university appointment; he was a man of independent means.

Main publications:

The collected works number over 70 volumes; the philosophical core, however, are the works which constitute the philosophy of the spirit:
(1902) *Estetica.*
(1909) *La logica.*
(1909) *La Filosofia della practica.*
(1917) *Teoria e storia della storiografia.*
Also notable are:
(1900) *Materialismo storico ed economia marxista.*
(1910) *Problemi di estetica.*
(1911) *La filosofia di G. B. Vico* (English translation), *Poetry and Literature*, trans. G. Gullace, Southern Illinois University Press, 1981).
(1913) *Saggio sul Hegel.*
(1920) *Brevario di estetica.*
(1925) *Elementi di politica.*
(1928) *Estetica in nuce* (English translation, 'Aesthetics', in *Encyclopaedia Britannica*, fourteenth edition).
(1939) *La poesia.*
English editions of most of these exist; there is also a collection by Cecil Sprigge (1966) *Philosophy, Poetry and History*, Oxford: Oxford University Press.

Secondary literature:

Carr, H. W. (1917) *The Philosophy of Benedetto Croce*, New York: Russell & Russell.
Gullace, G. (1981) *Poetry and Literature*, Southern Illinois University Press (translation of *La Poesia* with a full introduction to Croce's work).
Moss, M. (1987) *Benedetto Croce Reconsidered*, University of New England Press.
Niccolini, Fausto (1960) *L'editio ne varietur' delle opere di B. Croce* (full bibliography).
Orsini, G. (1961) *Benedetto Croce*, Southern Illinois University Press.
Piccoli, R. (1922) *Benedetto Croce*, New York: Harcourt, Brace & Co.

Croce is one of the central figures in the cultural and political life of Italy in the first half of the twentieth century. As founder and editor of *La critica* he exercised an extraordinary influence on Italian letters. He was a practising politician, a government Minister, a Senator, during the long years of fascism a focus of sustained opposition, and a member of the postwar Provisional Government. His enormously erudite writings range over the whole of European and world literature, philosophy, and political and economic theory. He never held a university position, having the means to live an independent life amid his magnificent collection of books in Naples. Most Italian philosophers addressed his work, **Gramsci**, indeed, asserting that a close reading of Croce was a prerequisite for contemporary philosophy. Together with **Gentile**, with whom, before an intellectual and political estrangement, he was friend and cothinker, Croce set the agenda (both for his supporters and opponents) of much Italian philosophizing, and, through R. G. **Collingwood**'s acceptance of many of his doctrines his influence extended into the English-speaking world, most noticeably in aesthetics and the philosophy of history. Croce spent much time on Hegel and was one of the earliest debaters of Marxism (Croce, Labriola, who introduced the study of Marx to Italy, and Sorel were known as the Holy Trinity of Latin Marxist studies, although Labriola was to condemn the revisionism of the other two). Croce found Marx's views, which he took to be deterministic, at odds with his own categorical commitment to freedom.

Following the tragic death of his family in an earthquake, and after brief periods of study in Rome, Croce returned to Naples and spent the early years of his intellectual life exploring the history and culture of that city. The *Scienza Nuova* of Vico awoke his mind to philosophy and he became interested in the much debated question whether history be an art or a science. This led him in turn to think about the nature of art, a thinking that was to issue in his first major work, and the work by which he is best known in the English-speaking world, *Estetica* (1902). In the course of writing this work what had started as an interest in the particular questions of art and history widened itself into a systematic philosophy, what he was to call the philosophy of spirit. Although that philosophy is elaborated in the four works mentioned above, the best short introduction to it is *Estetica*, for that work came to be not merely an account of art but an account that placed art in an overarching account of all the faculties of the human mind.

The drift of the philosophy of spirit may be grapsed by considering a stone warmed by the sun. Here the stone passively receives stimuli. Compare this to the receipt of stimuli by a human being. Here the recipient of the stimuli is active in processing them. The first thing the recipient does is to impose a form on the welter of experience. This is the aesthetic stage, which therefore lies at the root of all that we can subsequently do. In that stage we impose order on chaos by finding a way of expressing (intuiting, representing—the terms are interchangeable) the stimuli. That expression issues in language and art and is something that every human and not merely every artist does. In this activity we find expressed our categorical freedom: nothing can in advance determine the direction our expression will take, for until expression has taken place

there is nothing formed to do the determining. Croce's commitment to freedom in the active struggle against fascism has, therefore, a foundation in the core of his philosophy. Having given form to our sensations we can now grasp particulars, this stone, this man, this water. At the next stage, which presupposes and is therefore secondary to the aesthetic, comes the stage at which we extract the general from the particular and talk in general terms of stones, water, men by forming concepts. This is the stage of logic, which is investigated more fully in the second of the volumes of the philosophy of spirit. The aesthetic and the logical stages exhaust the theoretical activities of the mind. But there is also the practical. This, too, has two stages: the economic, in which we try to get what we have conceptualized (so that the economic depends on the logical, which depends on the aesthetic; for, Croce asks, how could we seek something if we did not have a concept of what we seek?); the final stage is the moral, not merely wanting, but being able to distinguish between what ought and what ought not to be wanted. This is further investigated in the third of the works of the philosophy of spirit, *La filosofia della practica* (1909). In these four stages the whole life of the mind is laid before us.

Two aspects of this philosophy deserve brief further comment: first, the account of aesthetics. Initially Croce had said that art simply is expression or intuition so that any intuition or expression is art. Later he was to further characterize art as a certain kind of intuition, first as lyrical intuition and later as cosmic intuition. These notions are continually applied in the actual study of works of art and literature (although it has been argued that examples that would demonstrate their applicability to the plastic arts and to music are distinctly lacking). Some, including Gentile, found the assertion of the existence of such distinctions somewhat at odds with the unifying impulse of idealism, to which Croce felt an affinity. Second, Croce thought history to be allied with art rather than science, being concerned with the particular rather than the general. That influential view of history is set out in the fourth volume of the philosophy of spirit, *Teoria e storia della storiografia* (1917). An implication is that to attempt to find in history scientific laws of progress is to misconstrue that subject, a conclusion which has obvious implications for Marxism.

COLIN LYAS

Davidson, Donald Herbert

American. *b:* March 1917, Springfield, Massachusetts. *Cat:* Philosopher of mind; philosopher of language. *Ints:* Casuation; meaning. *Educ:* Harvard University, BA 1939, MA 1941, PhD 1949. *Infls:* Carl Hempel, Hans Reichenbach, Rudolf Carnap, Willard Van Orman Quine and Alfred Tarski. *Appts:* Instructor, Queen's University (NY) College, 1947–56; Stanford University, California, 1951–67; Professor, Princeton University, 1967–70; Professor, Rockefeller University, 1970–6; Professor, University of Chicago, 1976–81; Professor, University of California, Berkeley, from 1981; John Locke Lecturer, University of Oxford, 1970.

Main publications:

(1972) (ed. with Gilbert Harman) *Semantics of Natural Language*, Dordrecht: Reidel.
(1980) *Essays on Actions and Events*, Oxford: Clarendon Press.
(1984) *Inquiries into Meaning and Truth*, Oxford.

Secondary literature:

Evnine, S. (1991) *Donald Davidson*, Polity Press.
Lepore, E. (ed.) (1986) *Truth and Interpretation: Perspectives on the Philosophy of Donald Davidson*, Oxford: Blackwell.
——and McLaughlin, B. (eds) (1985) *Actions and Events: Perspectives on the Philosophy of Donald Davidson*, Oxford: Blackwell.

Donald Davidson is one of the major contributors to contemporary analytic philosophy. Over a period of three decades he has outlined and developed two distinctive and intimately related theoretical perspectives in the philosophy of mind and the philosophy of language. Some of his earliest work was devoted to uncovering the logical form of causal and action statements, already demonstrating the close relation between semantic and other substantive issues. Dissatisfied with standard analyses of such statements, he argued that legitimate inferences, for example from 'Caesar stabbed Brutus with a knife' to 'Caesar stabbed Brutus' were not recoverable unless such statements were analysed in terms of relations between events, where these latter were taken as belonging to an ontological category distinct from things and their properties. Espousing a materialist position, Davidson had to accommodate prima facie conflicting theses: that as human beings we were part of the natural order, but that our mental life and voluntary action failed to fit the requirements of deterministic law. Davidson disputes that there are strict laws connecting the mental and the physical, or connecting mental events with one another, despite being committed to the view that each mental event is a physical event. This controversial view, which he calls 'anomalous monism', itself supplies an interesting twist to the debates between proponents of soft and hard determinism, the point being that it is only under a physical description that mental events instantiate deterministic laws. Yet for Davidson causation is essential to understanding the idea of acting with a reason, and we can make singular causal claims without reference to any laws that they might instantiate. Reasons are not only causes, but also explanatory of what people do. Thus Davidson's strategy is appropriately described as rationalizing one, in that normative principles embody all that we know about mental life and human action. So while we might defer to experts about the nature of copper or quarks, our everyday or 'folk-psychology' requires no such deference.

In his treatment of the mental Davidson concentrates on 'propositional attitudes', states with propositional content as expressed in statements like 'Joan believes that snow is white'. He sees beliefs as explanatory, but also as showing how other beliefs and actions can be reasonable, given those initial beliefs. Being a believer-agent, therefore, amounts to being more or less rational. Not only is this strategy normative, it is holistic in that we cannot ascribe beliefs and other attitudes in isolation, but only as elements in a web of attitudes. This holistic dimension owes much to the influence of **Quine**, and this influence is visible elsewhere in Davidson's work.

Undoubtedly Davidson's most significant and influential work has been in the field of what is known as 'truth-conditional semantics', the theoretical position according to which the meaning of a sentence in a language is given by stating the conditions under which it is true. Furthermore, this type of theory purports to show how the truth-conditions of sentences are determined by the semantic properties of the component expressions such as nouns and verbs. Such a theory might be expected to yield for any sentence S, a sentence of the form 'S means p', in which the meaning of S is given by whatever sentence replaces p. However, again under Quinean influence, Davidson regards any appeal to 'meanings' as opaque and, drawing on the work of Alfred **Tarski**, substitutes locutions of the form 'S is true if, and only if, p', claiming that a theory based on the notion of truth is both more perspicuous and can do all that a theory of meaning is supposed to do. Davidson does, however, depart from Tarski in certain respects: the latter's work was exclusively with formalized technical languages, and was combined with a scepticism about the applicability of formal techniques to natural languages, everyday languages being too messy, changeable and inconsistent. It is precisely these features which pose the most acute problems for Davidson himself, especially indexicality (involving terms like 'I', 'this' and 'now'), attributive adjectives like 'good' and 'large', and indirect speech contexts as instanced by 'Galileo said that the earth moves'. Attempts by Davidson and his followers to deal with these problems, while exhibiting considerable ingenuity and innovation, have met with a mixed reception from critics.

The two main strands of Davidson's work have a wider purport which goes beyond their narrower technical interest. It has to be shown how the theory of meaning can be put to work in interpreting the utterances of speakers of an alien tongue, using the strategy of 'radical interpretation'. Davidson imposes a constraint on this, called the 'principle of charity', by which we seek to maximize agreement between ourselves and the speakers of the other language. We are to assume that most of what those natives say is true by our lights. Davidson sets himself against scepticism and relativism, arguing that there is no sense to be attached to the notion of radically divergent or alternative conceptual schemes. Local untranslatability is unremarkable; wholesale untranslatability between languages is unintelligible. Davidson has influenced many younger philosophers including John McDowell, Colin McGinn and Mark Platts. He has also attracted spirited criticisms from thinkers as diverse as Michael **Dummett** (on the question of the form a theory of meaning should take) and Jerry Fodor (on the status of the mental within the natural order). More generally, his anomalous monism has been condemned as an unstable compromise, and theorists otherwise sympathetic to his semantical project have none the less suggested that appeal to truth-conditions is at best necessary but not sufficient to account for how and why people behave and speak as they do. Overall his work has had a conspicuous impact on some major philosophical issues such as relativism, objectivity

and rationality, and as such has a relevance to debates in discipline areas outside the traditional boundaries of philosophy.
Sources: WWW(Am).

DENIS POLLARD

Derrida, Jacques

Algerian-French. **b:** 1930, Algiers. **Cat:** Poststructuralist; phenomenologist; philosopher of language; metaphysician; aesthetician. **Ints:** Deconstruction. **Educ:** École Normale Supérieure and Harvard University. **Infls:** Sartre, Husserl, Heidegger and others in the phenomenological tradition, as well as Saussure and structuralist theorists. **Appts:** Philosophy at the Sorbonne and École Normale Supérieure; Visiting Professor, Johns Hopkins, Yale and the University of California at Irvine; key figure in the development of the International College of Philosophy, Paris.

Main publications:

(1962) (trans. and intro.) *L'Origine de la géométrie*, Paris: Presses Universitaires de France (English translation, *Edmund Husserl's 'Origin of Geometry': An Introduction*, trans. John P. Leavey, Pittsburgh: Duquesne University Press, 1978).
(1967) *La Voix et la phénomène: introduction au problème du signe dans la phénoménologie de Husserl*, Paris: Presses Universitaires de France (English translation, *'Speech and Phenomena' and Other Essays on Husserl's Theory of Signs*, trans. David B. Allinson, Evanston, Ill.: Northwestern University Press, 1973).
(1967) *De la grammatologie*, Paris: Minuit (English translation, *Of Grammatology*, trans. Gayatri Chakravorty Spivak, Baltimore: Johns Hopkins University Press, 1976).
(1967) *L'Écriture et la différance*, Paris: Seuil (English translation, *Writing and Difference*, trans. Alan Bass, London: RKP, 1978).
(1972) *La dissémination*, Paris: Seuil (English translation, *Dissemination*, trans. Barbara Johnson, London: Althone Press, 1981).
(1972) *Positions*, Paris: Minuit (English translation, *Positions*, trans. Alan Bass, London: Althone Press, 1981).

(1972) *Marges de la philosophie*, Paris: Minuit (English translation, *Margins of Philosophy*, trans. Alan Bass, Chicago: Chicago University Press, 1982).
(1974) *Glas*, Paris: Galilée.
(1978) *Éperons: Les styles de Nietzsche*, Paris: Flammarion (English translation, *Spurs: Nietzsche's Styles*, trans. Barbara Harlow, Chicago: Chicago University Press, 1979).
(1978) *La Vérité en peinture*, Paris: Flammarion (English translation, *The Truth in Painting*, trans. Geoffrey Bennington and Ian McLeod, Chicago: Chicago University Press, 1987).
(1980) *La Carte postale de Socrate à Freud et au-delà*, Paris: Aubier-Flammarion (English translation, *The Post Card: From Socrates to Freud and Beyond*, trans. Alan Bass, Chicago: Chicago University Press, 1987).
(1993) *Spectres de Marx*, Paris: Galilée (English translation, *Spectres of Marx*, trans. Peggy Kamuf, London: Routledge, 1994).

Secondary literature:

Gasché, Rodolphe (1986) *The Tain of the Mirror: Derrida and the Philosophy of Reflection*, Cambridge, Mass.: Harvard University Press.
Llewelyn, John (1986) *Derrida on the Threshhold of Sense*, London, Macmillan
Norris, Christopher (1987) *Derrida*, London: Collins.
Ryan, Michael (1982) *Marxism and Deconstruction: A Critical Articulation*, Baltimore: Johns Hopkins University Press.
Sallis, John (ed.) (1987) *Deconstruction and Philosophy: The Texts of Jacques Derrida*, Chicago and London: University of Chicago Press.
Staten, Henry (1984) *Wittgenstein and Derrida* Lincoln, Neb.: University of Nebraska Press.
Wood, David and Bernasconi, Robert (1988) *Derrida and Différance*, Evanston, Ill.: Northwestern University Press.

Derrida is the founder and prime exponent of deconstruction, a method of textual analysis applicable to all writing, philosophy no less than creative literature, which by means of a series of highly controversial strategies seeks to reveal the inherent instability and indeterminacy of meaning. One of his primary objectives is to draw attention to the inescapably *textual* character of all philosophical writing, which he feels that most philosophers try to deny, regarding it as pure argument instead. Deconstruction is best approached as a form of radical scepticism and antifoundationalism (Derrida's philosophical project has been variously compared to those of Hume, **Nietzsche** and **Wittgenstein**), and Derrida adopts an oppositional stance towards Western philosophy from Plato onwards for its unacknowledged commitment to a 'metaphysics of presence', the belief that meaning *is* essentially stable and determinate and can be grasped in its entirety. Western philosophy is in this sense logocentrist, committed to the idea that words are capable of communicating unambiguously meanings that are present in the individual's mind. It is further to be regarded, Derrida argues, as phonocentrist, believing that speech more authentically communicates meaning than writing, being closer to the original thought than writing is. For Derrida, on the other hand, meaning is marked by the continual play of difference, and his entire oeuvre is designed to show how this calls into question the logocentrist and phonocentrist assumptions underlying philosophical discourse. Derrida's is essentially a linguistic enquiry—he takes his lead from **Saussure**'s identification of the sign as arbitrary—although it has involved excursions into metaphysics, aesthetics, ethics, literary criticism and art criticism over the course of what has been a highly prolific writing career. His roots lie in phenomenology, with his earliest important publications being commentaries on **Husserl**, whose concepts of bracketing, *epoché* and phenomenological reduction all play a crucial part in Derrida's development. He argues that, for all the radicalism of the concepts above, Husserl is still caught up in the metaphysics of presence and that it is not until the work of **Heidegger**, a critical influence on Derrida's thinking and the source of the idea of deconstruction, that presence is subjected to close scrutiny. A major target of Derrida's critique of Western philosophical method has been structuralism, which he feels largely ignores the implications of the arbitrariness of the sign, and he has delivered some devastating attacks on the notion of there being underlying structures to discourse. Derrida is particularly critical of Lévi-Strauss's belief that myths can be reduced to a common structure, since it requires the existence of an originary myth—an indefensibly essentialist line of argument in Derrida's view. Derrida is notorious for deploying a range of concepts in his writing—*différance*, supplement, force, for example—while denying that they have the status of concepts. The practice of erasure, derived in the first instance from Heidegger, is taken to sanction the use of a word minus its metaphysical commitments. *Différance* is probably Derrida's best-known 'concept', and it is designed to illustrate the shifting and indeterminate nature of meaning since it can be heard as either *différence* (difference) or *différance* (deferral), with both meanings being kept in play at any one time. Such cases bear out Derrida's point about the indeterminacy of meaning and the arbitrariness of the sign, as well as enabling him to call into question the law of identity and thus strike a blow at the very foundations of philosophy. Derrida is also notorious for the obscurity and eccentricity of his style, in which punning and word-play, applied examples of Saussure's associative relation, are important parts of a strategy to locate gaps (aporias) in our discourse. The end-result is a form of philosophy which looks closer to game-playing than to traditional philosophical argument; but since it is part of Derrida's concern to problematize the division between philosophy and literature, as well as to insist that philosophy is above all a form of writing as dependent as any other on the operation of figures of speech, such practices have become an integral part of the project to deconstruct Western metaphysics. The general thrust of Derrida's work is antifoundationalist, and he is in fact one of the most uncompromising antifoundationalists in modern philosophy, part of a general trend in this respect which encompasses figures such as fellow French poststructuralists Michel **Foucault** and Jean-François **Lyotard** and the American pragmatist philosopher Richard **Rorty**. Derrida has had an enormous impact on modern thought, with deconstruction proving itself to be one of the most controversial as well as most stimulating developments in late twentieth-century intellectual life. There is now what amounts to a Derrida industry—Christopher Norris has spoken of a 'deconstructive turn' to academic discourse in recent years—and few works in the general field of cultural studies fail to acknowledge Derrida's influence or engage with his ideas. Response to Derrida's theories tends to be highly polarized and he arouses extreme hostility and passionate advocacy in almost equal measure. Perhaps his greatest area of success has been in American academic life, where he has inspired the work of the Yale School of literary critics, Harold Bloom, Paul de Man, J. Hillis Miller and Geoffrey Hartman, and through their writings a whole generation of literary academics. Derrida himself has expressed misgivings about the use made of his ideas in 'American deconstruction', 'disagreeably surprised' being his comment, but there is no denying the extent of his impact. In Britain Derrida's ideas have met with a greater degree of resistance, both from the left, which has persistently criticized the deconstructive enterprise as essentially apolitical in character, and from the British philosophical establishment, which, with a few notable exceptions, hardly considers what Derrida does to count as philosophy at all. Charges of intellectual charlatanism are not uncommon, with Derrida's obsession with such philosophically marginal details as the status of signatures being cited as evidence. The literary theorist Christopher Norris has proved to be Derrida's most able apologist from within British academic life, with the philosophers John Llewelyn and David Wood providing sympathetic defences of Derrida's philosophical credibility. On the whole, however, Derrida has exerted far greater influence among culture theorists and literary critics than amongst the philosophical community.

STUART SIM

Dewey, John

American. **b:** 20 October 1859, Burlington, Vermont. **d:** 1 June 1952, New York City. **Cat:** Philosopher of education; pragmatist. **Ints:** Social philosophy. **Educ:** University of Vermont, BA 1879; Johns Hopkins University, PhD 1884. **Infls:** Hegel and James. **Appts:** 1884–8, 1889–94, Professor, University of Michigan, Ann Arbor; 1888–9, Professor, University of Minnesota; 1894–1904, Professor and Head, Department of Philosophy, Psychology and Pedagogy, University of Chicago; 1904–30, Professor, Columbia University.

Main publications:

(1969–90) *The Works of John Dewey*, general editor, J. A. Boydston, Carbondale and Edwardsville: Southern Illinois University Press (divided into three parts: (1967–72) *John Dewey: The Early Works, 1882–1898*, 5 vols, referred to below as *EW*; (1976–83) *John Dewey: The Middle Works, 1899–1924*, 15 vols, referred to below as *MW*; (1981–90) *The Later Works, 1925–53*, 17 vols, referred to below as *LW*).

(1887) *Psychology*, New York: Harper & Brothers; reprinted in *EW* 2.

(1899) *The School and Society*, Chicago: University of Chicago Press; reprinted in *MW* 1.

(1902) *The Child and the Curriculum*, Chicago: University of Chicago Press; reprinted in *MW* 2.

(1903) *Studies in Logical Theory*, Chicago: University of Chicago Press; reprinted in *MW* 2.

(1910) *The Influence of Darwin on Philosophy and Other Essays in Contemporary Thought*, New York: Henry Holt & Company; reprinted in *MW* 4.

(1916) *Democracy and Education: An Introduction to the Philosophy of Education*, New York: Macmillan; reprinted in *MW* 9.

(1916) *Essays in Experimental Logic*, Chicago: University of Chicago Press; reprinted in *MW* 10.

(1920) *Reconstruction in Philosophy*, New York: Henry Holt & Co.; reprinted in an enlarged edition with new introduction by John Dewey, Boston: Beacon Press, 1924; reprinted in *MW* 12.

(1922) *Human Nature and Conduct. An Introduction to Social Psychology*, New York: Henry Holt: reprinted in *MW* 14.

(1925) *Experience and Nature*, Chicago: Open Court; reprinted in a revised edition, New York: W. W. Norton, 1929; reprinted in *LW* 1.

(1927) *The Public and its Problems*, New York: Henry Holt; reprinted in *LW* 2.

(1929) *The Quest for Certainty*, New York: Minton, Balch; reprinted in *LW* 4.

(1932) *Individualism, Old and New*, New York: Minton, Balch; reprinted in *LW* 5.

(1932) (with James Hayden Tufts) *Ethics*, revised edition, New York: Henry Holt; reprinted in *LW* 7.

(1934) *A Common Faith*, New Haven: Yale University Press; reprinted in *LW* 9.

(1934) *Art as Experience*, New York: Minton, Balch; reprinted in *LW* 10.

(1935) *Liberalism and Social Action*, New York: G. P. Putnam; reprinted in *LW* 11.

(1938) *Experience and Education*, New York: Macmillan; reprinted in *LW* 13.

(1938) *Logic: The Theory of Inquiry*, New York: Henry Holt & Company; reprinted in *LW* 12.

(1939) *Freedom and Culture*, New York: G. P. Putnam, reprinted in *LW* 13.

(1939) *Theory of Valuation. International Encyclopedia of Unified Science*, vol. 2, ed. Otto Neurath, Rudolf Carnap and Charles Morris, Chicago: University of Chicago Press; reprinted in *LW* 13.

(1949) (with Arthur F. Bentley) *Knowing and the Known*, Boston: Beacon Press; reprinted in *LW* 16.

Secondary literature:

Boydston, J. A. and Poulos, K. (eds) (1978) *Checklist of Writings about John Dewey, 1877–1977*, second edition, Carbondale: Southern Illinois University Press.

Coughlan, N. (1975) *Young John Dewey: An Essay in American Intellectual History*, Chicago: University of Chicago Press.

Dykhuizen, G. (1973) *The Life and Mind of John Dewey*, ed. J. A. Boydston, Carbondale: Southern Illinois University Press.

Rockefeller, Steven C. (1991) *John Dewey, Religious Faith and Democratic Humanism*, New York: Columbia University Press.

Schilpp, P. A. (ed.) (1939) *The Philosophy of John Dewey*, Evanston, Ill.: Northwestern University Press, The Library of Living Philosophers; second edition, New York: Tudor Publishing Company, 1951.

Thomas, M. H. (1962) *John Dewey: A Centennial Bibliography*, Chicago: University of Chicago Press.

W'estbrook, R. B. (1991) *John Dewey and American Democracy*, Ithaca and London: Cornell University Press.

Dewey began his career as a Hegelian idealist. His 1887 textbook on psychology sought to synthesize a Hegelianized faculty psychology with the newly emerging experimental psychology.

At the University of Chicago Dewey had assembled an imposing group of thinkers including G. H. Mead, Tufts, Ames and A. W. Moore. He founded the famous laboratory school for education. Further, he participated in numerous social reform organizations, most notably Jane Addams' Hull House. Appearing as a decentennial publication of the university, *Studies in Logical Theory* (1903) contained essays by Dewey and his colleagues William **James** at Harvard hailed it as a sign of the birth of a new school of philosophy, the Chicago School. Dewey's philosophy had evolved from Hegelian absolute idealism to experimental pragmatism, James's *Principles of Psychology* (New York: Henry Holt, 1890) having exerted the decisive influence on his thinking. Evolutionary biology also profoundly shaped Dewey's philosophy. Experimental pragmatism, which Dewey preferred to call 'instrumentalism', grounded cognition in action and noncognitive experiences. Although Dewey abandoned the Hegelian ideal of an absolute whole of experience, and stressed the biological basis of experience and the need to experiment, he retained the Hegelian strategy of overcoming dualism by the dialectical discovery of organic unities.

Because of conflict with the administration over the laboratory school Dewey left the University of Chicago and joined the faculty of Columbia University. Affiliated with Columbia Teachers College, Dewey continued his work in education, rising to the forefront of the educational reform movement. He rejected both the formalistic approach and the romantic approach to the education of children since these approaches reflected false psychological theories. He proposed overhauling the system of education. The interests of children, portrayed as naturally curious and active, had to be captivated and cultivated by means of educational experiences which would foster creativity and independence.

Dewey's conception of human nature, basic to his educational theories, stressed the malleability of human nature. He esteemed growth to be the aim of education and of life, growth that should never end. Dewey's zeal for educational reform was at one with his zeal for social reform.

Dewey's conception of experience is crucial to the understanding of his philosophy. It is active as well as passive, social as well as individual, objective as well as subjective, dynamic and continuous. Dewey's metaphysics is focused on the description of the generic traits of existence. In primary experience he found the polarity of stability and uncertainty and the polarity of the actual and the ideal; he also detected qualities, events, histories. These traits discovered in experience are traits of existence and so of nature. Human beings create the meanings that serve to stabilize the uncertain flux of events. Their political economies, their art, their religion, their science, their philosophy are the human enterprises on behalf of meaningful stability. Dewey distinguished philosophy from metaphysics. Philosophy is wisdom; its task is the criticism of cultural values. Metaphysics, by contrast, is a general empirical science; its task is to present the generic traits of existence to serve as the ground-map for philosophy as cultural criticism.

Dewey's penchant for reform extended to philosophy itself. He held that traditional philosophers, while reacting to the problems in the civilizations in which they arose, flew from practical solutions into imagined domains of certainty. Hence Dewey called for the reconstruction of philosophy to confront what he deemed to be the major crisis of his time—the discrepancy between inherited values and ideals and the new forces of control over nature unleashed by science and technology—and to resolve this crisis by applying the method of enquiry that had succeeded in natural science to social and moral problems.

Committed to democracy and its values, Dewey participated in significant public events: he headed the commission that exonerated Leon **Trotsky** of the Stalinist charges in 1937, and he joined in the defence of Bertrand **Russell** against the denial of his teaching post in New York in 1941. Dewey called for the reform of traditional liberalism. Centred on the self-reliant individual and his rights to *laissez faire*, liberalism had to be reconstructed, since the industrialization and urbanization of society by means of new technologies produced a new social environment which called for a type of individual different from the old type of pioneer in the wilderness.

Dewey condemned fascism and communism because they abandoned democracy and resorted to violence. He advocated the method of enquiry and democratic processes.

Dewey's philosophical labours extended to all the fields of human experience. His philosophy of art reinstates the ideal of organic unity which he had derived from Hegelian thought. It also stresses the primacy of immediately felt quality. Such quality may occur in my experience; it is consummatory. Aesthetic values are consummatory qualities, experienced not merely in the presence of art objects stored in a museum, but encountered every day in ordinary life. In philosophy of religion

Dewey's position is that of humanistic naturalism. He interpreted religion, not as a personal experience in the manner of William James, but as a non-sectarian social effort on the march to realize the ideal.

In his closing years Dewey associated with logical empiricism, although he maintained his intellectual autonomy. He never yielded in his naturalistic theory of values and his cognitivist theory of value judgements.

For the professional philosopher and scientist, Dewey's method of enquiry is his most important work. This instrumentalist or pragmatist methodology has won him his distinctive niche in the history of philosophy. Enquiry is defined as the process of moving from an indeterminate situation that blocks action towards a determinate situation in which action may proceed. Four stages are described: (i) defining the problem by observation and analysis; (ii) imaginative construction of hypotheses to explain and resolve the problem; (iii) explication of the meanings of the concepts in the hypotheses, in regard to mathematical formulations, experimental design and further deductions; and (iv) actual testing. The method is instrumentalist, not simply because ideas are construed metaphorically as tools for action, but also because, as any experimental laboratory illustrates, instrumentation is employed in nearly every phase of the process.

Dewey's belief that the method of enquiry, the scientific method, should be applied to practical problems lent philosophical support to the rise and the vogue of the social sciences.

Sources: Edwards; DAB, supplt 5, 1951–5; EAB.

ANDREW RECK

Dilthey, Wilhelm

German. **b:** 19 November 1833, Biebrich, Germany. **d:** 1 October 1911, Siez (Bozen).

Cat: Philosopher of culture (close to the neo-Kantians of the Baden school); epistemologist. **Educ:** Theology, Philosophy and History in Heidelberg and Berlin. **Infls:** Kuno Fischer, Edmund Husserl and Friedrich Adolf Trendelenburg. **Appts:** Professor at Basel, Kiel, Breslau and Berlin.

Main publications:

Dilthey's works are available in his *Gesammelte Schriften*, 20 vols. Stuttgart: B. G. Teubner; Göttingen: Vandenhoek & Ruprecht, 1914–90). Many of the essays and reviews found in this edition were scattered in various places, and were difficult to obtain before. Apart from the works published by Dilthey himself, this edition also includes a number of manuscripts that were not available before.

(1870) *Das Leben Schleiermachers* vol. I, vol. II 1922, *Gesammelte Schriften* XIII and XIV.

(1883) *Einleitung in die Geisteswissenschaften*, vol. I, Leipzig, *Gesammelte Schriften* I (English translation, *Introduction to the Human Sciences*, trans. R. J. Bretanzos, Detroit: Wayne State University Press, 1989).

(1894) *Ideen über eine beschreibende und zergliedernde Psychologie, Gesammelte Schriften* V, 139–237 (English translation in *Descriptive Psychology and Historical Understanding*, trans. R. H. Zaner and K. L. Heiges, The Hague: Nijhoff, 1977).

(1905) *Erlebnis und Dichtung*, Stuttgart: B. G. Teubner.

(1907) *Das Wesen der Philosophie, Gesammelte Schriften* V, pp. 339–428 (English translation, *The Essence of Philosophy*, trans. S. A. and W. T. Emery, New York: AMS Press, 1969).

(1910) *Der Aufbau der geschichtlichen Welt in den Geisteswissenschaften, Gesammelte Schriften* VII, 79–190.

(1961) *Pattern and Meaning in History. Thoughts on History and Society*, trans. H. P. Rickman, London: Allen & Unwin (represents a collection of translated passages from volume VII of the *Gesammelte Schriften*).

(1989–) *Dilthey's Selected Works*, ed. Rudolf A. Makkreel and Frithjof Rodi, Princeton: Princeton University Press. This edition is projected to have six volumes. Two of these have appeared, including vol. I, *Introduction to the Human Sciences* (1989) which includes a translation of *Einleitung in die Geisteswissenschaften*, vol. I and the drafts for vol. II and vol. V, *Poetry and Experience* 1985).

Secondary literature:

Biemel, Walter (ed.) (1968) 'Der Briefwechsel Dilthey–Husserl', *Man and World* 1: 428–46.

Bollnow, O. F. (1955) *Dilthey: Eine Einführung in seine Philosophie*, second edition, Stuttgart: Kohlhammer; originally Leipzig and Berlin 1936.

Hodges, H. A. (1944) *Wilhelm Dilthey: An Introduction*, London: Kegan Paul, Trubner & Co.

——(1952) *The Philosophy of Wilhelm Dilthey*, London: Routledge & Kegan Paul.

Makkreel, Rudolf A. (1969) 'Wilhelm Dilthey and the Neo-Kantians: the distinction of the Geisteswissenschaften and the Kulturwissenschaften', *Journal of the History of Philosophy* 4: 423–40.

——(1992) *Dilthey: Philosopher of Human Studies*, second edition, Princeton: Princeton University Press.

Misch, Clara (ed.) (1960) *Der junge Dilthey: Ein Lebensbild in Briefen und Tagebüchern, 1852–1870*, Göttingen: Vandenhoek & Ruprecht (first published in 1933).

Misch, Georg (1967) *Lebensphilosophie und Phänomenologie. Eine Auseinandersetzung der Diltheyschen Richtung mit Heidegger und Husserl*, Darmstadt: Wissenschaftliche Buchgesellschaft, originally Berlin 1930).

——(1985) Orth, E. W. (1985) *Dilthey und die Gegenwart der Philosophie*, Freiburg/Munich: K. Alber.

Of interest for Dilthey's life are:

Briefe Wilhelm Dilthey's an Rudolf Haym, 1861–1873, ed. Erich Weiniger, Berlin, 1936.

Dilthey's thinking starts from the philosophy of Kant and Schleiermacher. Although he is often described as an idealist and romantic, this characterization of him is rather misleading. In many ways he might be better described as an empiricist. Yet he rejected that label as well. His stance was thoroughly antimetaphysical, and he was more interested in analysing particular problems than in providing a theory of the nature of reality. Starting from what he thought was 'the standpoint of experience and unprejudiced empirical inquiry', his works constituted a series of attempts at establishing the foundation of the experiential sciences of the mind, called by Dilthey *Geisteswissenschaften*. While the term 'Geisteswissenschaften' is usually translated as 'human sciences' or 'human studies', it was originally closer to what John Stuart Mill designated the 'moral sciences'.

Today Dilthey is mainly known for his epistemological analysis of historiography as involving a special kind of mental operation called 'Verstehen' (understanding). Yet, while history and the problems concerned with the writing of history were extremely important to him, his philosophy was much more broadly conceived than this view suggests. His projected 'Critique of historical reason' was to cover all of the human sciences. Arguing that historical reality was 'truncated' and 'mutilated' by those who were trying to force the human sciences into the same mould as the natural sciences, he attempted to establish a new methodology and foundation for these sciences. He rejected positivism not because he felt that the kind of certainty they were seeking could not be had, but because he thought that they were sacrificing the 'legitimate independence of the particular sciences'. Dilthey's new foundation of the human sciences involved a critique of consciousness in a Kantian sense. Yet, unlike Kant, who believed that his critique could uncover universal conditions of the possibility of experience, i. e. categories, principles, and ideas of the human mind that would hold anywhere and at any time, Dilthey thought of these conditions as being embedded in a consciousness of a particular time and place. He found that no 'real blood flows in the veins of the knowing subject constructed by Locke, Hume, and Kant, but rather the diluted extract of reason as a mere activity of thought'. He wished to explain even knowledge and its concepts in terms of the manifold powers of a being that wills, feels, and thinks, and thus rejected, as 'fixed and dead' the rigid a priori epistemology of Kant in favour of a developmental history that started 'from the totality of our being'.

This does not mean that Dilthey believed historians can look merely at the motives and the actions of individuals. For him the individual is always part of a certain culture, and to understand the individual is also to understand that culture. Dilthey's 'philosophy of life' (*Philosophie des Lebens*) is an expression of his belief that we must see and understand ourselves as part of the larger whole that has been created by human beings and that forms our social and historical reality. Furthermore 'every expression of life has meaning insofar as it is a sign which expresses something that is part of life. Life does not mean anything other than itself. There is nothing in it which points to a meaning beyond it.' The expressions of life form the subject matter of the human sciences. It is the realm of the method of understanding in the sense of *Verstehen*.

Although different times and different individuals may belong to cultures quite foreign to ours, we can, according to Dilthey, understand the historical and social processes in them because we are living individuals who know 'the process by which life tends to objectify itself in expressions'. Understanding is a process *sui generis*. We cannot explain it by reducing it to other, more basic processes. Nor should it be confused with 'understanding' in the ordinary sense, which signifies any kind of comprehension. Dilthey describes it as the 'rediscovery of the I in the Thou', or as a form of knowing that is concerned with intellectual processes. It is the comprehension of intentions, motives, feelings or thoughts as they are expressed in gestures, words, works of literature, legal codes, etc.

Dilthey is also famous for his analysis of *Weltanschauungen* or world views. Differentiating between three different types: materialism or positivism, objective idealism, and idealism of freedom, he himself could not identify with any one of them. All three of them appeared to him as honest but one-sided views of reality. Dilthey's greatest influence began only after his death. Thus he has had some influence on the contemporary discussion of the philosophy of

history. Although his concept of *Verstehen* is often misunderstood, it has generated a great deal of controversy. Dilthey also had an indirect influence on early sociological theories through the works of Max Weber and Talcott Parsons. Most importantly, perhaps, early existentialist thought, such as that of Karl **Jaspers** and Martin **Heidegger**, is unthinkable without Dilthey. Thus Heidegger claimed that his own analysis of temporality and historicity in *Being and Time* was 'solely concerned with preparing the way for the assimilation of the investigations of W. Dilthey'. And Bollnow's introduction to Dilthey was perhaps more an introduction to existential thinking than to Dilthey's theory.

MANFRED KUEHN

Duhem, Pierre Maurice Marie

French. *b:* 9 June 1861, Paris. *d:* 14 September 1916, Cabréspine Ande. *Cat:* Physicist. *Ints:* Philosophy and history of science; intellectual history; science and religion. *Educ:* Paris, École Normale Supérieure, 1882–7, PhD 1888. *Infls:* B. Pascal, J. W. Gibbs, H von. Helmholtz, H. St Clair Deville, J. Moutier, J. Tannery and L. Blondel. *Appts:* Lille 1887–93, Rennes 1893–4, Bordeaux 1894–1916; Member of Académie des Sciences (non-resident).

Main publications:

(1886) *Le Potentiel thermodynamique*, Paris: Hermann.

(1892) 'Quelques réflexions au sujet des théories physiques', *Revue des Questions Scientifiques* 31: 139–77.

(1892) 'Notation atomique et hypothèse atomistiques', *Revue des Questions Scientifiques* 31: 391–454.

(1893) 'Physique et métaphysique', *Revue des Questions Scientifiques* 34: 55–83.

(1893) L'École anglaise et les théories physiques, *Revue des Questions Scientifiques* 34: 345–78.

(1894) 'Quelques réflexions au sujet de la physique expérimentale', *Revue des Questions Scientifiques* 36: 179–229.

(1900) *Les Théories électriques de J. Clerk Maxwell*, Paris: Hermann.

(1902) *Le Mixte et la combinaison chimique*, Paris: C. Naud.

(1902) *Thermodynamique et chimie*, Paris: Gauthier-Villars (English translation, *Thermodynamics and Chemistry*, New York: Wiley, 1903).

(1903) 'Analyse de l'ouvrage de Ernst Mach', *Bull. Sci. Math.* 2/27: 261–83.

(1903) 'Étude sur l'oeuvre de George Green', *Bull. Sci. Math.* 2/27: 237–56.

(1903) *L'Évolution de la mécanique*, Paris: A. Joanin (German translation, *Die Wandlunger der Mechanik*, Leipzig: J. A. Barth, 1921).

(1905–6) *Les Origines de la statique*, Paris: Hermann (English translation, *The Origin of Statics*, trans. Leneaux *et al.*, Dordrecht: Kluwer, 1991).

(1906) *La Théorie physique, son objet et sa structure*, Paris: Chevalier et Rivière; second edition, 1913 (English translation, *The Aim and Structure of Physical Theory*, trans. Wiener, Princeton: Princeton University Press, 1954; German translation, *Ziel und Struktur physikalischer Theorien*, trans. Adler, Leipzig: J. A. Barth, 1908, reprinted with introduction and bibliography of secondary literature by L. Schäfer, 1978).

(1906–13) *Études sur Léonard de Vinci*, Paris: Hermann.

(1908) ΣΟΖΕΙΝ ΤΑ ΨΑΙΝΟΜΕΝΑ *Essai sur la notion de théorie physique de Platon à Galilée*, Paris: Hermann (English translation, *To Save the Phenomena*, trans. Dolland and Maschler, Chicago: University of Chicago Press, 1969).

(1913–58) *Le Système du monde, histoire des doctrines cosmologiques de Platon à Copernic*, 10 vols, Paris: Hermann.

(1915) *La Science allemande*, Paris: Hermann (English translation, *German Science*, La Salle: Open Court, 1991).

(1916) *La Chimie est-elle une science française?*, Paris: Hermann.

(1917) 'Notice sur les travaux scientifiques de Duhem', *Mémoires de la Société des Sciences Physiques et Naturelles de Bordeaux* 7/I: 71–169.

(1985) *Medieval Cosmology*, trans. Ariew, Chicago: University of Chicago Press (partial translation of later volumes of *Le Système du Monde*, 1913–58).

(1987) *Prémices philosophiques*, ed. S. L. Jaki, Leiden: Brill.

Secondary literature:

Ariew, A. and Barker, P. (eds) (1990) 'Pierre Duhem, historian and philosopher of science', *Synthese* 83: 177–453.

Brenner, A. (1990) *Duhem, science, réalité et apparence*, Paris: Vrin.

Harding, S. G. (1976) *Can Theories be Refuted? Essays on the Duhem–Quine Thesis*, Dordrecht: Reidel.

Jaki, S. L. (1984) *Uneasy Genius: The Life and Work of Pierre Duhem*, The Hague, Martinus Nijhoff (fullest bibliography in print to date of Duhem's writings).

Lowinger, A. (1941) *The Methodology of Pierre Duhem*, New York: Columbia.

Maiocchi, R. (1985) *Chimica e filosofia, scienza, epistemologia, storia e religione nell'Opera di Pierre Duhem*, Florence: La Nuova Italia (a good critical account with a full bibliography).

Martin, R. N. D. (1982) 'Darwin and Duhem', *History of Science* 20: 64–74.

——(1987) 'Saving Duhem and Galileo', *History of Science* 25: 302–19.

——(1991) *Pierre Duhem: Philosophy and History in the Work of a Believing Physicist*, La Salle. Ill.: Open Court.

——(1991) 'The trouble with authority: the Galileo affair and one of its historians', *Modern Theology* 7: 269–80.

Paul, H. W. (1979) *The Edge of Contingency: French Catholic Reaction to Scientific Change from Darwin to Duhem*, Gainesville: University Presses of Florida.

Popper, K. R. (1959) *The Logic of Scientific Discovery*, London: Hutchinson.

——(1963) *Conjectures and Refutations*, London: Routledge.

Schäfer, L. (1974) *Erfahrung und Kovention*, Stuttgart-Bad Cannstatt: F. Fromman.

Pierre Duhem was a major physicist at the turn of the nineteenth and twentieth centuries, a prolific contributor to the development of the theories of heat, physical chemistry, hydrodynamics and electrodynamics, but opposed to the atomism that ultimately triumphed. He was also a seminal writer on the philosophy of science and on the history of science—particularly the medieval period. The general character and themes of his work as it evolved have to be understood against the broad background of late nineteenth-century physics and philosophy, as well as his avowed Catholicism.

Interpretation of his work is complicated by his habit of reusing earlier work in a new context in ways liable to blind the unwary reader to his changes of point of view. At the outset his views were obvious variations on late nineteenth-century positivist themes. Physical theory was to offer a purely symbolic representation of the facts and to assist the memory by providing a classification of them. It was quite distinct from metaphysics and from common-sense knowledge. How this could have been achieved can perhaps be seen from the much more detailed discussion offered by Moritz **Schlick** in his *Allgemeine Erkenntnislehre*, where the relationships established between different concepts are thought of as a kind of net giving each concept, and therefore the reality it represents, its place in the scheme of things. Duhem supported his approach with an instrumentalist account of atomistic symbolism in chemistry, and by some rationally reconstructed history of a kind already familiar in the work of Eugen Dühring and Ernst Mach. At this point he showed no sign of any interest in or knowledge of medieval science. The first criticisms were Catholic in origin. Duhem was attacked for allegedly disdaining metaphysics, and for conceding too much to scepticism, an important point for Catholics because of their official commitment to a semi-rationalist apologetic. Duhem's initial response, a quasi-Thomist account of the mutual independence of physics and metaphysics, was never afterwards repeated or referred to. His long-term response was twofold: to draw out of his initial doctrine that physical theories were symbolic systems a fully fledged doctrine of the theoreticity of facts, and to flesh out what he meant by classification into his still controversial doctrine of natural classification. Experimental laws depended on other theoretical commitments to state them, so that the very notion of experimental refutation became logically ambiguous; so that, necessary as logic was to physical theory, it was not all-sufficient and not the

ultimate arbiter. Experimental refutation and the response of physicists to it were matters of intuitive judgement. Physicists had to judge whether an experimental result refuted the theory or whether it was merely the effect of some other theory involved in the experimental situation. They also had to judge how to amend their theories in the light of accepted experimental refutations. Duhem also claimed that the goal of physics was the intuitively judged improving classification which increasingly reflected the ontological order. This doctrine of a fallible natural classification plays in Duhem's mature system of the *Théorie physique* a role like **Popper**'s notion of fallible truth in his. As Duhem matured, he came increasingly to cite Pascal's *Pensées* at crucial points in his argument. Prone as he was to suggest in the first part of his career that the natural classification looked for by physicists would have a scholastic form, these suggestions do not reflect his deeply Pascalian temper, made very explicit at the end of his life in his *Science allemande*. His later historical work lends itself to a like conclusion. After a decade of work that denied the existence or relevance of medieval science he was genuinely surprised to discover evidence of it while working on the *Origines de la statique* in the early winter of 1903. Thereafter his historical work changed its character. He did not, though, align himself with the Catholic neoscholasticism of the period, but emphasizes those aspects of the Middle Ages with which it was least compatible, claiming indeed that Thomism was incoherent.

Sources: Edwards; Mittelstrass; E. Jordan (1917) 'Duhem, Pierre', *MSSPNB 7/I:* 3–40; H. Pierre-Duhem (1936) *Un Savant français*, Paris: Plon; DSB 4: 225a–233b (bibliography); P. Brouzeng (1987) Duhem 1861–1916: *Science et Providence*, Paris: Belin; S. L. Jaki (1988) *The Physicist as Artist*, Edinburgh: Scottish Academic Press; S. L. Jaki (1992) *Reluctant Heroine: the Life and Work of Hélène Duhem*, Edinburgh: Scottish Academic Press.

R. N. D. MARTIN

Dummett, M(ichael) A(nthony) E(ardley)

British. **b:** 1925, London. **Cat:** Analytic philosopher. **Educ:** University of Oxford. **Infls:** Frege and Wittgenstein. **Appts:** Assistant Lecturer, University of Birmingham, 1950–1; Commonwealth Func Fellow, University of California at Berkeley, 1955–6; Reader in the Philosophy of Mathematics, University of Oxford, 1962–74; Fellow of All Souls College, Oxford, 1950–79; from 1979, Wykeham Professor of Logic, and Fellow of New College, Oxford; other visiting positions in Europe, the USA and Africa.

Main publications:

(1973) *Frege: Philosophy of Language*, London: Duckworth.
(1977) (with the assistance of Roberto Minio) *Elements of Intuitionism*, Oxford: Clarendon Press.
(1978) *Truth and Other Enigmas*, London: Duckworth.
(1991) *Frege and Other Philosophers*, Oxford: Clarendon Press.
(1991) *Frege: Philosophy of Mathematics*, London: Duckworth.
(1991) *The Logical Basis of Metaphysics*, London: Duckworth.
(1993) *Origins of Analytic Philosophy*.
(1993) *The Seas of Language*, Oxford: Clarendon Press.

Secondary literature:

McGuinness, Brian and Oliveri, Gianluigi (eds) (1993) *The Philosophy of Michael Dummett*, Dordrecht: Reidel.
Wright, Crispin (1986) *Realism, Meaning and Truth*, Oxford: Basil Blackwell.

In his 1959 article 'Truth' (*Proceedings of the Aristotelian Society* 59, 1958–9) Dummett proposed the idea that for a proposition to be true is for it to be correctly assertible, and that no statement can be correctly assertible if it is such as to transcend all possibility of our verifying or falsifying it. If this is correct then the correct analysis of some types of statement might reveal that they do not have what Dummett called a 'realist' meaning; that is to say, they will not be true or false in virtue of a reality independent of our cognitive powers. Indeed, some perfectly clear and precise statements of the given class may turn out to be neither true nor false, and a central thrust of Dummett's philosophy has been to question the Principle of Bivalence.

The issue of anti-realism, as Dummett called it, has been the main focus of Dummett's work. It concerns, in his view, a cluster of problems which, though having different subject matters, none the less have a structural similarity. Are statements about the external world, for instance, statements about a reality that exists independently of our knowledge of it? Or are they merely statements about our actual and possible sense experiences? Are statements about the mind statements about a reality for which observable behaviour is merely evidence? Or are they, for instance, really just statements about that observable behaviour? Again, to take an example that has been central in Dummett's discussion, are mathematical statements to be understood as being about a mathematical realm that exists independently of us? Or are they simply statements about a mental realm constructed by what we regard as mathematical proofs?

Although highly sympathetic to intuitionism in mathematics, a form of anti-realism, and although he holds that the argument for anti-realism in many other areas presents a major challenge, Dummett has never been committed to anti-realism generally; in large part, this has been a response to the difficulty in articulating an acceptable anti-realist view of the past. Much of Dummett's work has been pursued through the study of other major philosophers, and one of his significant achievements has been to make the work of **Frege** central to contemporary philosophy.

Dummett has been particularly influential in Great Britain, especially at Oxford. Some, however, have thought that his anti-realism is, in substance, no more than a reversion to the verificationism of the 1930s. It has also been objected that it is an over-hasty extrapolation from a view that is plausible (though controversial) when applied to the realm of mathematics.

Dummett resigned his Fellowship with the British Academy in protest at its failure, as he saw it, to protest sufficiently effectively against the cuts in university funding instituted by the Thatcher government of the 1980s.

Sources: WW 1992.

ANTHONY ELLIS

Feng Youlan (Fung Yu-lan)

Chinese. *b*: 1895, Tangho, Honan Province, China. *d*: 1990, Beijing. *Cat*: Neo-Confucian. *Ints*: History of Chinese philosophy; neo-Confucian rationalism. *Educ*: University of Beijing and Columbia University, USA. *Infls*: John Dewey and Frederick J. E. Woodbridge, Neo-Confucianism, daoism, Buddhism, and Western logic and metaphysics. *Appts*: 1923–5, Professor of Philosophy, Zhongzhou University, Kaifeng; 1926–8, Professor of Philosophy, Yenching University, Beijing; 1933–52, Professor of Philosophy, Qinghua University, Beijing: 1933–52, Dean, College of Arts, and Head of Philosophy Department, Qinghua University; 1939–46, Dean, College of Arts, Southwest Associated University, Kunming; 1952–90, Professor, Peking University; 1954–66, Chief, Division of Chinese Philosophy, Research Institute of Philosophy, Academia Sinica; 1946–7, Visiting Professor, University of Pennsylvania, USA; 1947–8, Visiting Professor, University of Hawaii.

Main publications:

(1924) *A Comparative Study of Life's Ideals: the Way of Decrease and Increase with Interpretations and Illustrations from the Philosophies of the East and West*, Shanghai.

(1924) *A Philosophy of Life*, Shanghai.

(1924) *A View of Life*, Shanghai.

(1930–6) *A History of Chinese Philosophy*, 2 vols, Shanghai: Commercial Press (English translation, Derk Bodde, Princeton: Princeton University Press).

(1931) *Zhuangzi: A New Selected Translation with an Exposition of the Philosophy of Guo Xiang*, Shanghai.

(1934) *A Brief History of Chinese Philosophy*, Shanghai.

(1936) *A Supplement to the History of Chinese Philosophy*, Shanghai.

(1938) *A New Treatise on Neo-Confucianism*, Changsha: Commercial Press.

(1939) *China's Road to Freedom*, Kunming: Commercial Press.

(1939) *A New Treatise on the Way of Living*, Kunming.

(1940) *New Culture and Society*, Kunming: Commercial Press.

(1940) *New Self*, Kunming: Kaiming.

(1942) *New Morality*, Chongqing: Commercial Press.

(1943) *A New Treatise on the Nature of Man*, Shanghai: Commercial Press.

(1944) *The Spirit of Chinese Philosophy*, Chongqing (English translation, E. R. Hughes, London: Kegan Paul).

(1944) *New Philosophy*, Chongqing, Commercial Press.

(1946) *New Scholarship*, Shanghai: Commercial Press.

(1946) *A New Treatise on the Methodology of Metaphysics*, Shanghai.

(1948) *Collected Essays in Wartime*.

(1948) *Short History of Chinese Philosophy*, in English, ed. Derk Bodde, Macmillan: New York.

(1958) *Essays on the History of Chinese Philosophy*, Shanghai: Shanghai Renmin Publishing House.

(1983–90) *A New History of Chinese Philosophy*, 7 vols, Beijing: Renmin Publishing House.

(1984) *My Memoirs*.

(1985–) *The Collected Works of Feng Youlan*, 14 vols.

(1991) *Selected Philosophical Writings of Fung Yu-Lan*, in English, Beijing: Foreign Languages Press.

Secondary literature:

Boorman, H. (ed.) (1970) *Biographical Dictionary of Republican China*, New York and London: Columbia University Press.

Briere, O. (1956) *Fifty Years of Chinese Philosophy 1898–1950*, London: George Allen & Unwin Ltd.

Chan, W. T. (1963) *A Source Book in Chinese Philosophy*, Princeton: Princeton University Press.

Complete Chinese Encyclopedia (1987) Philosophy Volumes, Beijing: Chinese Encyclopedia Publications.

Louie, K. *Inheriting Tradition: Interpretations of the Classical Philosophers in Communist China 1949–1966*, Hong Kong: Oxford University Press.

Masson, M. C. (1985) *Philosophy and Tradition: The Interpretation of China's Philosophical Past Fung Yu-Lan 1929–1949*, Taipei: Institut Ricci.

Feng was a creative philosopher of outstanding ability as well as the century's most important historian of Chinese philosophy. His concern for metaphysics, logical analysis, tradition, culture and morality and his masterly appreciation of Western and Chinese philosophy produced a philosophical system marked by intellectual depth and elegance. Feng was a materialist throughout his career, but after 1949 political pressure and his own desire to place his work in a Marxist context led to repeated self-criticism and to fierce attack by others, not exclusively in the Cultural Revolution. Even during this latter phase his work often displayed subtlety and balance.

Feng's doctoral training at Columbia University under the pragmatist John **Dewey** and the neo-realist Frederick Woodbridge led him to demand clear argument and analytical rigour in the statement and defence of philosophical positions. Feng reinterpreted allusive and aphoristic Chinese texts to meet his own high standards of cogency. He sought to determine a great tradition of Chinese philosophy, saving what could contribute to a modern flowering of Chinese thought and rejecting the rest. His rejection of Han and Qing learning and his method of determining what belonged to tradition were the focus of exciting controversies. Some critics complained that his perspective altered from one major historical study to another, while others thought that tradition should be a matter of passive discovery rather than active construction. Many contested his assessment of particular figures or schools or rejected his division between the Period of Philosophers (up to about 100 BC and the Period of Classical Learning (after 100 BC). China's most serious philosophers, especially those associated with the periodical *Philosophical Review*, admired Feng's deep ingenuity in using sophisticated Western techniques to adapt traditional philosophy to the needs of contemporary China. These philosophers also admired his attempt to resolve crucial controversies over the relative value of Western and Chinese thought which preoccupied Chinese intellectual life in the early part of the century.

The focus of the philosophical system Feng developed in the 1930s and 1940s was *A New Treatise on Neo-Confucianism* (1938), more literally rendered 'A new study of principle'. For this work, Feng drew on the Cheng-Zhu school of rationalist neo-Confucianism, especially the work of Zhu Xi (1130–1200), daoism, Chan Buddhism, and Western logical analysis from Plato and Aristotle to the modern day. He identified four fundamental notions in his metaphysics: *li* (principle), *qi* (matter); *dao di* (the evolution of the *dao* or way); and *da quan* (the Great Whole). All are Chinese philosophical concepts, but they are related to the Western concepts of being, non-being, becoming and the absolute. They differ from their Chinese predecessors and Western counterparts, according to Feng, because of his methodological insistence that his analysis provide 'empty' or formal concepts and that associated principles yield no knowledge of actuality. Philosophy was also useless in shaping practice, yet 'sageness within and kingliness without' from a standpoint of transcendence remained the highest pursuit of man as man.

Much of Feng's thought can be related to his realist understanding of the status of universals and his view that metaphysics derived ultimately from logic. All things or events are what they are in virtue of being things or events of certain kinds. Each thing is actual, but its *li* or principle, which makes it be of its kind, is real and exists abstractly outside space and time. Without the distinction between real and actual Feng thought that formality would be lost and that the criticisms of traditional metaphysics would overwhelm his formal system. In Feng's view the Great Whole, as everything there is, cannot be thought or said. If it could the thinking or saying would stand outside it, and it would lack at least one constituent of everything there is. It is therefore unsayable, like Laozi's *dao* and like that which can be shown but not said in Wittgenstein's *Tractatus*. The metaphysics of the unsayable, for Feng, made room for philosophical appreciation of the sublime.

Feng used his metaphysics as a framework for discussions of morality, culture and art. He considered the moral to be that which is in accord with the *li* of society and the immoral to be that which conflicts with the *li*. By introducing the amoral he placed large areas of life outside the scope of traditional Confucian ethical assessment. He argued that cultures should be understood in terms of types rather than in terms of particular historical instantiations and that types of culture could be explained by underlying material causes. He applied this view to Chinese intellectual history and the problem of inheriting the Chinese past. After the establishment of the People's Republic in 1949 Feng set out a doctrine of abstract inheritance, according to which concepts like the Confucian virtue *ren* (humanity or benevolence) could be abstracted from their concrete class circumstances and used without the taint of past oppression in contemporary society. Some of the most important and bitter philosophical debates of the 1950s and 1960s surrounded this claim. Like most

eminent intellectuals Feng was badly treated in the Cultural Revolution. His final major history of Chinese philosophy, although displaying great intellectual power, also showed the effects of his maltreatment.

NICHOLAS BUNNIN

Feyerabend, Paul Karl

Austrian. *b:* 13 January 1924, Vienna. *d:* 11 February 1994. *Cat:* Anti-empiricist; anti-rationalist. *Ints:* Philosophy of science. *Educ:* Institute for the Methodological Renewal of the German Theatre, Weimar; PhD, University of Vienna. *Infls:* Lakatos, Felix Ehrenhaft, David Bohm, Wittgenstein and (though sometimes denied) Popper. *Appts:* Professor, Yale University; Free University, Berlin; University College, London; University of Auckland; University of California at Berkeley; Federal Institute of Technology, Zurich; many visiting appointments.

Main publications:

(1975) *Against Method*, London: NLB.
(1978) *Science in a Free Society*, London: NLB (contains short intellectual autobiography, section 2.11).
(1981) *Philosophical Papers*, 2 vols, Cambridge.
(1987) *Farewell to Reason*, London: Verso.
(1991) *Three Dialogues on Knowledge*, Oxford: Blackwell.
(1995) *Killing Time*, Chicago: University of Chicago Press (posthumous autobiography).

Secondary literature:

Munévar, Gonzalo (ed.) (1991) *Beyond Reason: Essays in the Philosophy of Paul Feyerabend*, Dordretch: Kluwer.

Feyerabend's work in the 1950s and 1960s, much of it collected in his *Philosophical Papers* (1981), contained detailed studies in the development of the sciences. Along with **Kuhn**, Lakatos and Hesse, he was associated with the view that a historical perspective on scientific change can be at least as fruitful as any logical analysis of scientific methods. Independently of Kuhn, he was an originator of a historical thesis that there are frameworks of thought which are incommensurable (in the sense that logical relations cannot hold between the contents of different frameworks). He believed that so-called scientific observation terms 'are not merely theory-*laden* ... but *fully theoretical* (observation statements have no "observational core" ... Or, to express it differently: there are only theoretical terms' (1981, Introduction, p. x). This provided one basis for his critique of empiricism, both in the philosophy of science and more widely.

Feyerabend's later work, from *Against Method* (1975), argued that changes in science cannot proceed according to any specific method (and hence any 'rational' method: this step is indistinct). That led him to increasingly strong attacks on what he saw as rationality and rationalism. He shares with **MacIntyre** a belief in 'traditions' which can be defended or criticized appropriately only in their own terms. He wrote in *Science in a Free Society* (1978): 'There is ... hardly any difference between the members of a "primitive" tribe who defend their laws because they are the laws of the gods ... and a rationalist who appeals to "objective" standards, except that the former know what they are doing and the latter does not' (p. 82). He has argued for the democratic control of science against its control by scientists, and took this case as far as its practical consequences in his interest in non-conventional medical treatment.

In his last work he acknowledged that he had relied on concepts such as 'democracy', 'tradition' and 'relative truth' which he had come to see to be as rigid as 'truth', 'reality' and 'objectivity', 'which narrow people's vision and ways of being in the world' (*Killing Time*, 1995, p. 179). Feyerabend had no wish to be accepted as a respectable, academic, professional philosopher. His arguments against rationality, expressed in a violently polemical style (but with a lively sense of humour), provoked the most extreme reactions. The fact that many of his detractors believe that his later writings cannot be taken seriously did not strike him as altogether negative.

RICHARD MASON

Foucault, Michel

French. *b:* 1926, Poitiers, France. *d:* 1984, Paris. *Cat:* Post-structuralist; historian of ideas. *Educ:* École Normale Supérieure, Paris. *Infls:* Marx, Nietzsche, Heidegger, Merleau-Ponty, Jean Hyppolite and Georges Canguilhem. *Appts:* Professor of Philosophy, University of Clermont-Ferrand; Professor of History and Systems of Thought, Collège de France.

Main publications:

(1954) *Maladie mentale et psychologie*, Paris: Presses Universitaires de Frances (English translation, *Mental Illness and Psychology*, trans. Alan Sheridan, New York: Harper Colophon, 1976).
(1961) *Folie et déraison: histoire de la folie à l'âge classique*, Paris: Plon (English translation, *Madness and Civilization: A History of Insanity in the Age of Reason*, trans. Richard Howard, New York: Mentor Books, 1965).
(1963) *Naissance de la clinique: une archéologie du regard medical*, Paris: Presses Universitaires de France (English translation, *The Birth of the Clinic: An Archaeology of Medical Perception*, trans. Alan Sheridan, New York: Vintage Books, 1973).
(1966) *Les Mots et les choses: une archéologie des sciences humaines*, Paris: Gallimard (English translation, *The Order of Things: An Archaeology of the Human Sciences*, trans. Alan Sheridan, New York: Random House, 1970).
(1969) *L'Archéologie du savoir*, Paris: Gallimard (English translation, *The Archaeology of Knowledge*, trans. Alan Sheridan, New York: Harper & Row, 1972).
(1977) *Surveiller et punir: naissance de la prison*, Paris: Gallimard (English translation, *Discipline*

and Punish: The Birth of the Prison, trans. Alan Sheridan, New York: Pantheon, 1977).

(1976–84) *Histoire de la sexualité*, I–III, Paris: Gallimard (English translation, *The History of Sexuality*, I–III, trans. Robert Hurley, New York: Pantheon, 1978–85).

(1980) *Power/Knowledge: Selected Interviews and Other Writings 1972–1977*, ed. Colin Gordon, Leo Marshall, John Mepham and Kate Soper.

Secondary literature:

Arac, Jonathan (ed.) (1988) *After Foucault: Humanistic Knowledge, Postmodern Challenges*, New Brunswick, NJ: Rutgers University Press.

Cousins, Mark and Hussain, Athar (1984) *Michel Foucault*, London and Basingstoke: Macmillan.

Diamond, Irene and Quinby, Lee (1988) *Feminism and Foucault: Reflections on Resistance*, Boston: Northeastern University Press.

Dreyfus, Hubert L. and Rabinow, Paul (1982) *Michel Foucault: Beyond Structuralism and Hermeneutics*, New York and London: Harvester.

During, Simon (1992) *Foucault and Literature: Towards a Genealogy of Writing*, London: Routledge.

Sheridan, Alan (1986) *Michel Foucault: The Will to Truth*, London and New York: Tavistock Publications.

Originally trained as a philosopher, Foucault subsequently worked in the fields of psychology and psychopathology, the subject of his first book, *Mental Illness and Psychology* (1954), before returning to philosophy and, more specifically, to the history of ideas. He drew inspiration from Marxist, structuralist and Freudian theory at various points in his career, although he tended to disclaim any lasting influence on his thought from these traditions. The main thrust of Foucault's work is to merge philosophy with history such that large-scale analyses, or 'archaeologies' as he has termed them, can be undertaken of those historical 'discourses' (Foucault's name for thought when it is realized as a social practice) that have led to the present rationality-biased discourse of Western culture. Foucault sets himself the objective of constructing 'a history of the

present' by means of these archaeologies, which have encompassed such diverse topics as changing attitudes to insanity in post-Renaissance European society, the development of the prison system within the same society, and the codes governing sexual practice in classical times. In each case Foucault's concern is to trace the mechanisms involved in the development of the various discourses of social control in modern culture. There is a consciously anti-Enlightenment strain in Foucault's enquiries, and somewhat notoriously he proclaims 'the death of man' in *The Order of Things* (1966), arguing, as do so many structuralist and poststructuralist thinkers, that the concept of 'man', in particular 'rational' man, is a very recent, and in many ways very regrettable, cultural invention. Foucault's archaeologies tend to identify discontinuities in history, and he insists that his cultural analyses are specifically directed against all notions of teleology or assumptions of transcendental vantage points. Thus in *Madness and Civilization* (1961) he traces a radical change in social attitudes towards the phenomenon of madness over a relatively short historical period, whereby behaviour tolerated at one point within civil society was very soon designated as a social 'problem' requiring an institutional response. Foucault describes this cultural phenomenon of the seventeenth and early eighteenth centuries as 'The Great Confinement', and emphasizes the discontinuity involved in such a significant shift in perception. The underlying ideological reason for this change, Foucault claims, is to be located in the growing cult of reason, which led to insanity, or 'unreason', taking on negative connotations that were unthinkable before. A whole new structure of power evolved, as it did also in the rise of the modern prison system with its systematized methods of repression and punishment, and Foucault is a particularly acute analyst of power in its institutionalized forms. The analysis of power is a continuing concern throughout his career, surfacing in all his major works. Foucault's approach to cultural history is fairly broad-brush in style and can involve some questionable generalizations. He adopts a rather cavalier attitude to historical research, much influenced by **Nietzsche**'s iconoclasm about such matters, denying the possibility of historical objectivity and dismissing academic history as being merely 'the history of the historians'. The latter requires a vantage-point outside history in order to make it work, Foucault argues, and he is harshly critical of all such examples of 'transcendental narcissism'. Foucault pursues his archaeological enquiries throughout his oeuvre, culminating in his monumental three-volume history of sexuality in classical times, where the concern is to establish the process whereby the relatively guilt-free view of male sexuality in Greek times, including what is by modern standards a very relaxed attitude towards homosexual practices such as pederasty, evolved into the more repressive, as well as recognizably more modern, codes of behaviour of later Roman society. What Foucault identifies yet again is the development and institutionalization of methods of social control that are unacceptable to his quasi-anarchistic outlook. Like so many other French intellectuals in the post-1968 *événements* period, Foucault comes to display a deep distrust of all institutional power and its tendency towards overt control of individual behaviour. Foucault has been a highly controversial figure and his broadly based interdisciplinary-minded analyses of culture and the nature of institutional power have made him a difficult thinker to categorize. Purists are only too apt to see his projected merger of philosophy and history as lacking the intellectual rigour required of either discipline. There is no doubt, however, that he qualifies as one of the most influential contributors to the field of history of ideas in the modern era. Discourse theory, one of the liveliest areas of debate in recent cultural theory, largely derives from the work of Foucault, and his project to map out a 'history of the present' through archaeological analyses of past discourses has been enthusiastically followed up by a host of scholars across the humanities and social sciences. Foucault has attracted criticism from various quarters. The left, for example, has denounced his anarchistic tendencies and quasi-Nietzschean outlook as inimical to socialist ideas (Foucault's political and intellectual position might best be summed up as post-Marxist). A more general criticism has been, that his archaeologies, with their sweeping historical generalizations and often highly selective use of sources, have been wildly over-schematic. Rather in the manner of the structuralist and Marxist thinkers he affects to disdain, Foucault has been accused of imposing a model on the past which cannot always be substantiated by the available evidence: 'tall orders largely unsupported by the facts' being one not untypical verdict on his archaeological enquiries (J. G. Merquior). Foucault's self-consciously anti-Enlightenment stance has also been the subject of much unfavourable comment, with Jürgen **Habermas**, for example, arguing that the abandonment of any commitment to universal reason on the part of poststructuralist thinkers like Foucault ultimately leads to the end of philosophy, and to any possibility of being able to discriminate between the claims of competing theories or discourses. In common with most poststructuralist theories Foucault espouses antifoundationalism— he claims that the theories in *The Archaeology of Knowledge* are 'groundless', for example—and this aspect of his thought has come under considerable attack as well, on the fairly predictable grounds that it undermines the validity of his own theories and cultural analyses.

STUART SIM

Frege, Friedrich Ludwig Gottlob

German. **b:** 1848, Weimar, Germany. **d:** 1925, Bad Kleinen, Germany. **Cat:** Logicist; Platonist philosopher of mathematics; analytic philosopher. **Ints:** The epistemological foundations and ontology of number theory. **Educ:** Universities of Jena (1869–70) and Göttingen (1871–3); doctorate in Mathematics. **Appts:** 1874–1918, Lecturer, Assistant Professor, then Honorary Ordinary Professor of Mathematics at the University of Jena.

Main publications:

(1879) *Begriffsschrift, eine der arithmetischen nachgebildete Formelsprache des reinen Denkens*, Halle (English translation in J. van Heijenoort (ed.), *Source Book in Mathematical Logic*, Harvard University Press, 1967; and in *Gottlob Frege: Conceptual Notation and Related Articles*, Terrell Ward Bynum, Oxford: Oxford University Press, 1972).

(1884) *Die Grundlagen der Arithmetik, ein logisch-mathematische Untersuchung über den Begriff der Zahl*, Breslau (reprinted with English translation in *The Foundations of Arithmetic: A Logico-mathematical Enquiry into the Concept of Number*, J. L. Austin, Oxford: Oxford University Press, 1953).

(1891) 'Funktion und Begriff', an Address given to the Jenaische Gesellschaft für Medicin und Naturwissenschaft, 9 January 1891 (English translation in *Translations from the Philosophical Writings of Gottlob Frege*, ed. and trans. P. Geach and M. Black, Oxford: Oxford University Press, 1980).

(1892) 'Über Sinn und Bedeutung', *Zeitschrift für Philosophie und philosophische Kritik* 100 (English translation in *Translations from the Philosophical Writings of Gottlob Frege*, ed. and trans. P. Geach and M. Black, Oxford: Oxford University Press, 1980).

(1893) *Grundgesetze der Arithmetik, Begriffsschriftlich abgeleitet Bd. I*, Jena (English translation of Preface, Introduction and Part 1 in *The Basic Laws of Arithmetic*, trans. and ed. with an introduction by Montgomery Furth, Berkeley and Los Angeles: University of California, 1964).

(1903) *Grundgesetze der Arithmetik, Begriffsschriftlich abgeleitet Bd. II*, Jena (English translation of extracts in *Translations from the*

Philosophical Writings of Gottlob Frege, ed. and trans. P. Geach and M. Black, Oxford: Oxford University Press, 1980).

(1918) 'Der Gedanke: eine logische Untersuchung', *Beiträge zur Philosophie des deutschen Idealismus* 1 (English translation in P. F. Strawson (ed.), *Philosophical Logic*, Oxford: Oxford University Press, 1967).

(1979) *Posthumous Writings*, ed. H. Hermes, F. Kambartel and F. Kaulbach, trans. P. Long and R. White, Oxford: Blackwell 1979).

Secondary literature:

Baker, G. P. and Hacker, P. M. S. (1984) *Frege: Logical Investigations*, Oxford: Basil Blackwell.

Bell, D. (1979) *Frege's Theory of Judgement*, Oxford: Clarendon Press.

Benacerraf, P. (1981) 'Frege: the last logicist', in P. French *et al.* (eds), *Midwest Studies in Philosophy VI*, Minneapolis: Minneapolis University Press.

Currie, G. (1982) *Frege: An Introduction to his Philosophy*, Brighton: Harvester.

Dummett, M. A. E. (1981) *Frege: The Philosophy of Language*, London: Duckworth.

——(1982) *The Interpretation of Frege's Philosophy*, London: Duckworth.

——(1991) *Frege: Philosophy of Mathematics*, London: Duckworth.

Mind (1992) 101, 404, October (issue to honour the publication in 1892 of Gottlob Frege's 'Über Sinn und Bedeutung').

Resnik, M. (1980) *Frege and the Philosophy of Mathematics*, Ithaca, NY: McGraw-Hill.

Schirn, Mathias (ed.) (1976) *Studien zu Frege*, 3 vols, Stuttgart-Bad Canstatt.

Sluga, H. (1980) *Gottlob Frege*, London: Routledge & Kegan Paul.

Wright, C. J. G. (1983) *Frege's Conception of Numbers as Objects*, Aberdeen: Aberdeen University Press.

Wright, Crispin (ed.) (1984) *Frege: Tradition and Influence*, Oxford: Basil Blackwell.

Frege was influenced by the technical development of number theory in the nineteenth century combined with, as it seemed to him, the 'scandalous' state of its foundations. He set himself the task of giving epistemologically secure foundations for number theory and a proper delineation of its subject matter. Frege rejected, in particular, attempts to ground mathematics in human psychology. He also rejected attempts, like that of

John Stuart Mill, to construe number theory as an empirical science. Further, he rejected attempts to portray mathematics as a subject without a subject matter: that is, as the formal manipulation of empty signs with no intrinsic meaning. He took number theory to be the study of the necessary relations between numbers, and he took numbers to be mind-independent abstract objects. This view is known as Platonism after Plato's own similar view. Frege conceived his task as one of setting out precise and self-evident truths of pure logic in terms of which numerical concepts could be defined, and from which the accepted theorems of number theory could be rigorously deduced. This programme is known as logicism, the grounding of number theory in pure logic. In the course of this enterprise Frege made three momentous contributions to philosophy.

First, he developed a radically new way of treating quantifiers in logic. Quantifiers are expressions like 'something', 'all' and 'everything' which can fill the gap in predicates like '—is red' to form sentences which are true or false—for example, 'Something is red', 'Everything is red'. Frege's technique enables us to see a complex expression like '—is red and—is round' as a unitary predicate, from a logical point of view if not from a grammatical point of view. There is no limit to the complexity of predicates which quantifiers can turn into sentences, for example, 'if — is red then all bulls hate —' is a predicate in Frege's logic, and one which itself embeds the quantifier 'all'. Frege deployed his quantifiers in a novel formal language of his own, the first semantically precise language in which logic and set theory could be rigorously formulated.

Frege's discovery was the most important breakthrough in logic since Aristotle had founded the subject some two millennia before. It provided the first successful treatment of relations, and made possible the explosive development of logic in this century. The development of the theory of proofs, in particular the work of Alfred

Tarski and Kurt **Gödel**, stems directly from Frege's pioneering work. The logic which Frege invented is now so widely accepted that it is taught as a standard toolkit without attribution to its inventor, like elementary mathematics itself. However some, notably Brouwer, Heyting and perhaps **Dummett**, accept Frege's formal language but not all of the logic he used it to express.

Second, Frege used his formal language to present, in his *Grundgesetze der Arithmetik Band I*, the first system of axioms and definitions of what we would now call logic and set theory, and he commenced the rigorous deduction of the accepted truths of number theory from those axioms and definitions. This was a programme he intended to continue in volume II. But it was a spectacular failure, since, while the second volume was in press, Bertrand Russell showed that Frege's axioms allowed the rigorous deduction of a contradiction, known to subsequent generations as Russell's Paradox. Frege did not find a way of recasting his axioms which satisfied him, and his private papers show he eventually abandoned logicism, coming round to the view that number theory cannot after all be deduced from the necessary truths of pure logic. The trouble lay not in Frege's logical axioms but in his axioms of set theory. Those axioms combine the view that every predicate can be used to define a set, *viz.* the set of objects of which that predicate is true, and the view that every predicate must be true or false of every object there is. So Russell took the predicate '— is not a member of itself' and defined the set of things which are not members of themselves, and he then asked whether the predicate is true or false of that very set. It's easy to see that if it is then it isn't, and if it isn't then it is, which is paradoxical.

Frege had formulated what we would now call Naive Set Theory. However, it is 'naive' only in the sense that to hold such a set theory is naive given Frege's rigorous formulation of it and Russell's exploitation of that rigorous formulation to develop his paradox. Prior to these developments Naive Set Theory had been the intuitively appealing set theory. Frege's contribution here was to produce a rigorous formulation of Naive Set Theory whose rigour Russell could exploit to develop his paradox, thus, between them, ending an age of innocence and prompting the modern development of set theories.

Frege's Platonism has fared better. His basic idea is generally accepted—*viz*. that once a theory is adequately formulated in Frege's formal language, and supposing the theory is true, then its ontological commitment, whether Platonic or not, can be read off from its syntax. This approach is common to, for example, Crispin Wright who has defended Platonism, and to W. V. O. **Quine** and Nelson **Goodman**, who oppose Platonism by seeking to reformulate number theory in a way which eliminates or minimizes its commitment to abstract objects. It is shared also by Hartry Field, but leads him to conclude that number theory is not true but a useful fiction.

Frege's third great contribution was his theory of meaning. Frege needed a theory of meaning to show that his novel formal language, unlike our natural languages, is ontologically perspicuous. The key notions he used were sense and reference (*Sinn* and *Bedeutung*). Roughly, the sense of an expression is what a mind grasps, and sense mediates the connection between mind and the worldly entity (the referent) which the expression is about. More precisely, the sense of an expression (i) is grasped by a mind, but (ii) is not a psychological entity, since two minds may grasp the very same sense. Further, (iii) sense connects an expression with its referent in the world—Frege calls sense 'the mode of presentation of the referent'. Finally, (iv) the sense of an expression contributes to the truth-conditions of sentences in which that expression occurs. To grasp the sense of a sentence involves knowing its truth-conditions.

On the other hand, the referent of an expression is (i) its semantic role: that is, what that expression contributes to determining the truth-values of sentences in which it occurs. It follows that *all* categories of expression have referents—predicates, logical constants, whole clauses, as well as noun phrases. But (ii) Frege also thinks of reference as analogous to the relation between a name and its bearer. So the world contains, he thinks, entities corresponding to predicates, logical constants and whole clauses, as it contains objects corresponding to noun phrases. These additional entities are concepts, truth-functions and truth-values, respectively.

This theory of Frege's has been immensely influential. Wittgenstein radically reworked it in his *Tractatus*, and rejected it root and branch in his *Philosophical Investigations*. **Davidson** claims a Fregean pedigree for his influential blueprint for a theory of meaning, and Dummett criticizes Davidson from a Fregean point of view.

Frege's entire career was passed quietly at the University of Jena, where he was well thought of. But, to his disappointment, his work did not attract much interest in his own lifetime. However, there were illustrious exceptions: Peano, **Husserl**, **Russell**, **Wittgenstein** and **Carnap** all studied Frege. His posthumous recognition and his influence upon analytic philosophy have been enormous.

Sources: M. A. E. Dummett (1982) *The Interpretation of Frege's Philosophy*, London: Duckworth (with bibliography); Terrell Ward Bynum (1993) *Gottlob Frege: Conceptual Notation and Related Articles*, Oxford: OUP (with bibliography).

JIM EDWARDS

Gadamer, Hans-Georg

German. *b:* 11 February 1900, Marburg, Germany. *Cat:* Hermeneutic philosopher. *Ints:* Hermeneutic theory; classical thought; technology (especially medicine). *Educ:*

University of Marburg. **Infls:** Heidegger. **Appts:** Professor of Philosophy, University of Marburg, 1937–9; Professor of Philosophy, 1939–47, and Rector, 1946–7, University of Leipzig; Professor of Philosophy, University of Frankfurt, 1947–9; Professor of Philosophy, University of Heidelberg, 1949–68.

Main publications:

(1942) *Volk und Geschichte im Denken Herders,* Frankfurt: Klostermann.
(1960) *Wahrheit und Methode. Grundzüge einer philosophischen Hermeneutik;* fourth edition, Tübingen: J. C. B. Mohr, 1975 (English translation, *Truth and Method,* trans. William Glyn-Doepel, New York: Seabury Press).
(1964) (ed.) *Hegel-Tage, Royaumont,* Bonn: Bouvier.
(1967) *Kleine Schriften,* 3 vols, Tübingen: J. C. B. Mohr.
(1968) *Platos Dialektische Ethik;* second edition, Hamburg: Meiner, 1983 (English translation, *Plato's Dialectical Ethic,* trans. Robert M. Wallace, 1983).
(1968) *Um die Begriffswelt der Vorsokratiker.*
(1976) *Hegel's Dialectic: Five Hermeneutical Studies,* trans. P. Christopher Smith, New Haven: Yale University Press.
(1976) *Philosophical Hermeneutics,* trans. David Linge, Berkeley: University of California Press (contains essays from *Kleine Schriften*).
(1976) *Vernunft im Zeitalter der Wissenschaft,* Frankfurt: Suhrkamp (English translation, *Reason in the Age of Science,* trans. Frederick Lawrence, Cambridge, Mass.: MIT Press, 1981).
(1977) *Kleine Schriften,* vol 4, Tübingen: J. C. B. Mohr.
(1977) *Philosophische Lehrjahre,* Frankfurt: Klostermann (English translation, *Philosophical Apprenticeships,* trans. Robert R. Sullivan, Cambridge, Mass: MIT Press, 1985).
(1979) *Das Erbe Hegels: 2 Reden aus Anlass der Verleihung des Hegel-Preises der Stadt Stuttgart an Hans-Georg Gadamer am 13 Juni 1979,* Frankfurt: Suhrkamp.
(1979) (ed. with G. Boehm) *Seminar: Philosophische Hermeneutik,* second edition, Frankfurt: Suhrkamp.
(1980) *Dialogue and Dialectic: Eight Hermeneutical Studies on Plato,* trans. P. Christopher Smith, New Haven: Yale University Press.
(1982) *Heidegger Memorial Lectures,* ed. Werner Marx, trans. Steven W. Davis, Pittsburgh, PA: Duquesne University Press.

(1983) *Heideggers Wege. Studien zum Spätwerk,* Tübingen: J. C. B. Mohr.
(1984) 'Text und Interpretation', in Philippe Forget (ed.), *Text und Interpretation: Deutsch-Französische Debatte,* Munich: Fink.
(1986) *The Idea of the Good.*
(1986) *The Relevance of the Beautiful.*
(1986–) *Gesammelte Werke,* 7 vols, Tübingen: J. C. B. Mohr.
(1989) *Das Erbe Europas. Beiträge,* Frankfurt: Suhrkamp.
(1990) *Gedicht und Gespräch,* Frankfurt: Insel-Verlag.
(1993) *Über die Verborgenheit der Gesundheit. Aufsätze und Vorträge,* Frankfurt: Suhrkamp (English translation, *The Enigma of Health,* Cambridge: Polity, 1995).

Secondary literature:

Bernstein, Richard J. (1983) *Beyond Objectivism and Relativism,* Philadelphia: University of Pennsylvania Press; Oxford: Blackwell.
Bleicher, Josef (ed.) (1980) *Contemporary Hermeneutics,* London: Routledge & Kegan Paul.
——(1982) *The Hermeneutic Imagination,* London: Routledge & Kegan Paul.
Böhler, Dietrich (1977) 'Philosophische Hermeneutik und hermeneutische Methode', in Fuhrmann *et al., Text und Applikation: Theologie, Jurisprudenz und Literaturwissenschaft im hermeneutischen Gespräch,* Poetik und Hermeneutik 9, Munich: Fink.
Buber, R. *et al.* (eds) (1970) *Hermeneutik und Dialektik I. Festschrift für Hans-Georg Gadamer,* Tübingen: J. C. B. Mohr.
Dallmayr, Fred (1987) *Critical Encounters,* Notre Dame: Notre Dame University Press.
——and McCarthy, Thomas (eds) (1977) *Understanding and Social Inquiry,* Notre Dame: Notre Dame University Press.
Grondin, Jean (1982) *Hermeneutische Wahrheit? Zum Wahrheitsbegriff Hans-Georg Gadamers,* Königstein: Forum Academicum.
Habermas, Jürgen (1967) *On the Logic of the Social Sciences;* trans. Shierry Weber Nicholsen and Jerry A. Stark, London: Heinemann, 1989.
——(1979) 'Urbanisierung der heideggerschen Provinz' (English translation, 'Urbanizing the Heideggerian province in Habermas', *Philosophical-Political Profiles,* trans. Frederick G. Lawrence, London: Heinemann, 1983, pp. 189–97).
Henrich, Dieter (ed.) (1960) *Die Gegenwart der Griechen im neueren Denken. Festschrift für Hans-Georg Gadamer zum 60 Geburtstag.*

Hermeneutik und Dialektik I. Festschrift für Hans-Georg Gadamer, (1970) Tübingen: J. C. B. Mohr.

Hermeneutik und Ideologiekritik (1971) (various authors) Frankfurt: Suhrkamp.

Howard, Roy (1981) *Three Faces of Hermeneutics: An Introduction to Current Theories of Understanding*, Berkeley: University of California Press.

Hoy, David (1978) *The Critical Circle*, Berkeley: University of California Press.

Jauss, Hans Robert (1982) *Toward an Aesthetic of Reception*, trans. Timothy Bahti, Minneapolis: University of Minnesota Press.

Lang, Peter Christian (1982) *Hermeneutik, Ideologiekritik, Ästhetik*, Königstein: Forum Academicum.

Linge, D. (ed.) (1976) *Philosophical Hermeneutics*, Berkeley: University of California Press.

MacIntyre, Alasdair (1976) 'Contexts of interpretation: reflections on Hans-Georg Gadamer's *Truth and Method*', *Boston University Journal* 27, 1.

Michaelfelder, Diane P. and Palmer, Richard E. (eds) *Dialogue and Deconstruction: The Gadamer-Derrida Encounter*, Albany: SUNY Press.

Misgeld, Dieter (1977) 'Discourse and conversation: the theory of communicative competence and hermeneutics in light of the debate between Habermas and Gadamer', *Cultural Hermeneutics* 4.

Outhwaite, William (1985) 'Hans-Georg Gadamer', in Quentin Skinner (ed.), *The Return of Grand Theory in the Human Sciences*, Cambridge: Cambridge University Press.

——(1987) *New Philosophies of Social Science: Realism, Hermeneutics and Critical Theory*, London: Macmillan.

Ricoeur, Paul (1973) 'Ethics and culture: Habermas and Gadamer in dialogue', *Philosophy Today*, 17.

Schmidt, Lawrence Kennedy (1985) *The Epistemology of Hans-Georg Gadamer: An Analysis of the Legitimation of the Vorurteile*, Frankfurt: Peter Lang.

Silverman, Hugh J. (ed.) (1991) *Gadamer and Hermeneutics*, New York: Routledge, Chapman & Hall.

Sullivan, Robert R. *Political Hermeneutics: The Earlier Thinking of Hans-Georg Gadamer*, Pennsylvania State University Press.

Thompson, John (1981) *Critical Hermeneutics: A Study in the Thought of Paul Ricoeur and Jürgen Habermas*, Cambridge: Cambridge University Press.

Wachterhauser, Brice (ed.) (1986) *Hermeneutics and Modern Philosophy*, Albany: SUNY Press.

Warnke, Georgia (1987) *Gadamer: Hermeneutics, Tradition and Reason*, Cambridge: Polity.

Weinsheimer, Joel (1985) *Gadamer's Hermeneutics: A Reading of Truth and Method*, New Haven: Yale University Press.

——(1991) *Philosophical Hermeneutics and Literary Theory*, New Haven: Yale University Press.

Wright, Kathleen (ed.) *Festivals of Interpretation: Essays on Hans-Georg Gadamer's Work*, Albany: SUNY Press.

Gadamer's philosophical hermeneutics is conceived in opposition to the methodological emphasis of traditional hermeneutic theories and their concern with the accuracy of interpretation. Gadamer's aim is to describe the underlying process, an existential encounter between two perspectives or horizons of expectation, which makes interpretation possible in the first place. Understanding is not just a matter of immersing oneself imaginatively in the world of the historical actor or text, but a more reflective and practical process which operates with an awareness of the temporal and conceptual distance between text and interpreter and of the ways in which the text has been and continues to be reinterpreted and to exercise an influence over us. This effective history (*Wirkungsgeschichte*), which traditional historicist hermeneutics tends to see as an obstacle, is for Gadamer an essential element which links us to the text. Our prejudgements or prejudices are what make understanding possible.

Although Gadamer has often stressed the distinction between his philosophical hermeneutics, with its origin in **Heidegger**'s hermeneutic ontology, and hermeneutics as a *technique* of interpretation, his approach clearly poses a challenge to more traditional interpretations. These differences are brought out in particular in Gadamer's exchanges in the 1960s with Emilio Betti, whose *General Theory of Interpretation* was published in 1955. The alternative conception of the human sciences or *Geisteswissenschaften* put forward in Gadamer's work also made it central to Jürgen **Habermas**'s reformulation of the *Logic of the Social Sciences*. Habermas welcomed Gadamer's critique of hermeneutic objectivism, which he saw as the equivalent of positivism in the philosophy of the natural sciences, and also his stress on the totalizing character of understanding. For Habermas, however, Gadamer's stress on the fundamental nature of language, expressed in his claim that 'Being that can be understood is language', amounted to a form of linguistic idealism. Together with Gadamer's stress on the importance of tradition and his rehabilitation of the category of prejudice, this suggested an ultimately conservative approach which was unable to deal with the systematic distortion of communicative processes by relations of power and domination. Habermas and Gadamer debated these issues in the late 1960s and early 1970s; more recent theorists have tended to stress the compatibility of hermeneutics and critical theory (notably the Frankfurt School) in a conception of critical hermeneutics (cf. Thompson 1981, Outhwaite 1983). More recently, Gadamer also engaged briefly with the French deconstructionist philosopher Jacques **Derrida** (see Gadamer 1984), whose conception of interpretation is more sceptical.

Gadamer has also published an enormous amount of work on the history of philosophy, notably on Greek thought, scientific rationality and other topics, including, most recently, essays on the history and philosophy of medicine.

WILLIAM OUTHWAITE

Geach, P(eter) T(homas)

British. **b:** 1916, London. **Cat:** Analytic philosopher. **Ints:** Logic; metaphysics; philosophy of mind; philosophy of religion; ethics. **Educ:** Balliol College, Oxford and St Deiniol's Library, Hawarden. **Infls:** Aristotle, Aquinas, Gottlob Frege, J. M. E. McTaggart and Ludwig Wittgenstein. **Appts:** 1951–61, Assistant Lecturer, Lecturer, Senior Lecturer, University of Birmingham; 1961–6, Reader in Logic, University of Birmingham; 1966–81, Professor of Logic, University of Leeds; 1985, Visiting Professor, University of Warsaw; 1965, Fellow of the British Academy.

Main publications:

(1956) 'Good and evil', *Analysis*, 17.
(1956) *Mental Acts*, London: Routledge & Kegan Paul.
(1960) (trans. with Max Black) *Translations from the Philosophical Writings of Gottlob Frege*, Oxford: Blackwell.
(1962) *Reference and Generality*, Ithaca: Cornell University Press; amended edition, 1968.
(1969) *God and the Soul*, London: Routledge & Kegan Paul.
(1972) *Logic Matters*, Berkeley: University of California Press.
(1973) (with Elizabeth Anscombe) *Three Philosophers*, Oxford: Basil Blackwell.
(1977) *Providence and Evil*, Cambridge: Cambridge University Press.
(1977) *The Virtues*, Cambridge: Cambridge University Press.
(1977) (trans. with R. H. Stoothoff) Gottlob Frege, *Logical Investigations*, Oxford: Basil Blackwell.
(1979) *Truth, Love, and Immortality: An Introduction to McTaggart's Philosophy*, Berkeley: University of California Press.

Secondary literature:

Evans, Gareth, (1977) 'Pronouns, quantifiers, and relative clauses', *Canadian Journal of Philosophy* 7.
Griffin, Nicholas (1977) *Relative Identity*, Oxford: Clarendon Press.

Geach has written influentially in many of the central areas of philosophy, but his most important contribution has been the application of logical techniques to problems of language and metaphysics. His first book gives a logical analysis of the notion of mental acts. Its greatest influence, however, came from its opposition to the empiricist doctrine of abstractionism, the view that concepts are formed by abstracting them from recurrent features of experience. In general, Geach's view of the mind owes much to both **Wittgenstein** and Aristotle.

Geach was never sympathetic to the 'linguistic philosophy' of the 1950s and 1960s, and *Reference and Generality* (1962) used the techniques of formal logic to understand how referring expressions, and expressions of generality, are used in everyday language and thought. Its most influential view was perhaps the claim that identity claims are meaningless except as relative to some general term: 'x = y' can only ever mean 'x is the same something or other as y'.

Geach's work in ethics has promoted the 'doctrine of the virtues', and part of the groundwork for this was laid in his influential article 'Good and evil' (1956). Here Geach attacked the prescriptivism that was fashionable at the time, arguing that the primary sense of 'good' is in fact descriptive. Goodness is not, however, a *sui generis* property, as the intuitionists had thought: rather, to be good is to be a good *something*, and the nature of the something supplies the standards of goodness.

His work in the philosophy of religion has used the techniques and results of modern logic to defend traditional Roman Catholic doctrines. Geach's work continues to be discussed, although the notion of relative identity, highly influential during the 1960s and 1970s, has now largely been rejected. In ethics, however, the theory of the virtues remains central.

Sources: WW 1992; 'A philosophical autobiography', in Harry A. Lewis (ed.) (1991) *Peter Geach: Philosophical Encounters*, Dordrecht: Kluwer.

ANTHONY ELLIS

Gentile, Giovanni

Italian. *b:* 30 May 1875, Castelvetrano, Sicily. *d:* 14 April 1944, Florence. *Cat:* Idealist metaphysician. *Ints:* History of philosophy; moral philosophy; philosophy of education. *Educ:* Pisa 1893–97, PhD 1897. *Infls:* Hegel, D. Jaja and B. Spaventa. *Appts:* Campobasso, 1897–1902; Naples, 1902–6; Palermo, 1906–13; Pisa, 1914–16; Rome, from 1917; Minister of Education, 1922–4; associated with the Fascist regime until its fall and his death at the hands of Italian partisans in 1944.

Main publications:

(1898) *Rosmini e Gioberti*, Pisa: Fratelli Nistri (PhD thesis).
(1899) *La Filosofia di Marx Studi Critici*, Pisa: Spoerri.
(1903) *Dal Genovesi al Galuppi*, Milan: Treves.
(1908) *Scuola e Filosofia*, Palermo: Sandron.
(1913) *I Problemi della Scolastica e il Pensiero Italiano*, Bari: Laterza.
(1913) *La Riforma della Dialettica Hegeliana*, Messina: Principato.
(1916) *Teoria generale dello Spirito come Atto Puro*, Pisa: Vallecchi (English translation, London, Macmillan, 1922).
(1917) *Sistema di Logica come Teoria del Conoscere*, 2 vols, Pisa: Spoerri.
(1920) *Discorsi di Religione*, Florence: Vallecchi.
(1920) *Giordano Bruno e il Pensiero del Renascimento*, Florence: Vallecchi.
(1920) *La Riforma dell'Educazione* Bari: Laterza (English translation, London: Benn, 1923).
(1920) *La Riforma dell'Educazione*, Bari: Laterza.
(1923) *Dante e Manzone*, Florence: Vallecchi.
(1929) *Origine e dottrina del Fascismo*, Rome: Libreria del Littorio.
(1931) *Filosofia dell'Arte*, Milan: Treves (English translation, Ithaca: Cornell University Press, 1972).
(1933) *Introduzione alla Filosofia*, Milan: Treves.
(1936) *Memorie, Italiane e Problemi*, Florence: Sansoni.
(1945) *Genesi e Struttura della Società*, Florence: Sansoni (English translation, Urbana: University of Illinois Press, 1960).
(1964) *Storia della Filosofia, dalle Origine a Platone*, ed. V. Bellezza, Florence: Sansoni.
(1969) *Storia della Filosofia Italiana*, 2 vols, ed. E. Garin, Florence: Sansoni.
(1973) *Italian Fascism from Pareto to Gentile*, ed. Lyttleton, London: Cape.

Secondary literature:

Agosti, V. (1977) *Filosofia e Religione nell'Attualismo Geniliano*, Brescia: Paideia.

Baraldi, G. (1976) 'Divenire e Trascendenza' (PhD thesis), Fribourg.

Calendra, G. (1987) *Gentile e il Fascismo*, Rome: Laterza.

Crespi, A. (1926) *Contemporary Thought in Italy*, London: Williams & Norgate.

Croce, B. (1981) *Lettere a Giovanni Gentile*, Milan: Mondadori.

Harris, H. S. (1960) *The Social Philosophy of Giovanni Gentile*, Urbana: University of Illinois Press.

Holmes, R. W. (1937) *The Idealism of Giovanni Gentile*, New York: Macmillan.

Janowski, F. (1889) 'Gentile, Giovanni', *Metzler Philosophenlexikon*, Stuttgart: Metzlersche Verlagsbuchhandlung, pp. 284–7.

Lion, A. (1932) *The Idealistic Conception of Religion: Vico, Hegel, Gentile*, Oxford: Clarendon.

Minio-Paluello, L. (1946) *Education in Fascist Italy*, London and New York: Oxford University Press.

Natoli, S. (1989) *Giovanni Gentile Filosofo Europea*, Turin: Bollati Boringheri.

Negri, A. (1975) *Giovanni Gentile*, 2 vols, Florence: La Nuova Italia.

Pardo, F. (1972) *La Filosofia di Giovanni Gentile*, Florence: Sansoni.

Romanell, P. (1938) *The Philosophy of Giovanni Gentile*, New York: S. F. Vianni.

——(1947) *Croce versus Gentile*, New York: S. F. Vianni.

Romano, S. (1984) *Giovanni Gentile la Filosofia al Potere Sergio Romano*, Milan: Bompiani.

Signore, M. (1972) *Impegno Etico e formzione del'uomo nel Pensiero Gentiliano*, Galatina: Editrice Salentina.

Spirito, U. (1969) *Giovanni Gentile*, Florence: Sansoni.

——(1976) *Dal Attualismo al Problematicismo*, Florence: Sansoni.

Gentile propounded a system known as actual idealism, in which thought was held to be pure activity and united with action. For Gentile there was no sense in seeking the cause of experience within the content of experience, and belief in an external world was the product of our attempt to organize our experience in thought, a so-called concrete logic. Sensation was the spontaneous activity of self-affirmation and because thought had to be embodied in language, our individual self-consciousness or moral personality was united into the collective consciousness of what he called the transcendental ego or state, although perhaps it could be interpreted as culture. In the interpretation of Harris the state here was not—though some of his wrritings might imply otherwise—necessarily the concrete state to be joyfully obeyed but more the future world of the individual's unrealized ideals but it was at this point that Gentile became, with many of his followers (but in contrast to **Croce**, his one-time collaborator on the *Giornale Critica della Filosofia Italiana*), a supporter of Italian fascism and able to serve it as a Minister of Education while carrying through educational reforms in line with his ideals. Gentile was a dominating influence on Italian intellectual life even after the fall of fascism in the postwar era. He founded and edited the journal *Saggi Critici* and was a principal editor of the *Enciclopedia Italiana* (1925ff, 37 vols).

Sources: Edwards; V. A. Bellezza (1950) *Bibliografia degli Scritti di Giovanni Gentile*, Florence: Sansoni; Höllhuber, I. (1969) *Geschichte der Italienischen Philosophie*, Munich and Basel: Reinhardt; Mittelstrass; G. M. Pozzo (1986) 'Gentile, Giovanni', in *Dizionario Critica della Letteratura Italiana*, Turin: Unione Tipografica-editrice.

R. N. D. MARTIN

Gilson, Étienne Henri

French. *b:* 13 June 1884, Paris. *d:* 19 September 1978, Auxerre, France. *Cat:* Neoscholastic. *Ints:* History of philosophy; metaphysics; epistemology; aesthetics. *Educ:* University of Paris. *Infls:* Lucien Lévy-Bruhl, Descartes, Aquinas and Bonaventure. *Appts:* 1921–32, University of Sorbonne; 1932–51, Collège de France; 1929–78, Institute of Medieval Studies, University of Toronto.

Main publications:

(1919) *Le Thomisme*, Strasbourg: Vix, sixth edition, Paris: Vrin, 1986 (English translation of fifth edition, *The Christian Philosophy of St. Thomas Aquinas*, London: Gollancz, 1957).

(1937) *The Unity of Philosophical Experience*, New York: Charles Scribner's Sons.

(1948) *L'Etre et l'essence*, Paris: Vrin, second edition, 1962 (English translation, *Being and Some Philosophers*, Toronto: Pontifical Institute of Medieval Studies, 1949; second edition, 1952).

(1960) *Le philosophe et la théologie*, Paris: Fayard (English translation *The Philosopher and Theology*, New York: Random House, 1962).

(1963) *Introduction aux arts de beau*, Paris: Vrin (English version, *The Arts of the Beautiful*, New York: Charles Scribner's Sons, 1965).

Secondary literature:

McCool, Gerald A. (1989) *From Unity to Pluralism*, New York: Fordham University Press, pp. 161–99.

McGrath, Margaret (1982) *Étienne Gilson: A Bibliography. Une Bibliographie*, Toronto: Pontifical Institute of Medieval Studies (complete bibliography of Gilson's works).

Quinn, John M. (1971) *The Thomism of Étienne Gilson*, Villanova, Pa.: Villanova University Press.

Shook, Laurence K. (1984) *Étienne Gilson*, Toronto: Pontifical Institute of Medieval Studies.

Van Riet, Georges (1965) *Thomistic Epistemology*, 2 vols, St Louis & London: Herder, vol. II, pp. 153–74.

Van Steenberghen, Fernand (1979) 'Étienne Gilson: historien de la pensée médiévale', *Revue Philosophique de Louvain* 77: 487–508.

Gilson was the most influential historian of medieval philosophy in the twentieth century. His historical studies led him to adopt the philosophy of Thomas Aquinas as his own, and to expound a metaphysics and a theory of knowledge which, despite his claim that they were simply the views of Aquinas himself, disturbed, or at least irritated, many advocates of orthodox Thomism.

His studies of the medieval period began by a kind of accident, when it was suggested to him that he should examine the medieval provenance of Descartes's thought. He quickly came to the conclusion not only that

Descartes had deep roots in medieval philosophy, but also that Cartesian philosophy was in some ways inferior to it. Thenceforward he immersed himself in medieval philosophy, and argued constantly that the great medieval thinkers attained a level of sophistication and insight superior to any philosophy before or after.

One of the first shocks that Gilson administered to conventional Thomists was to show that medieval philosophy was not a simple homogeneous body of thought, still less a mere reworking of Aristotle. In a number of brilliant studies of Aquinas (1919), Bonaventure (1924), Augustine (1929), St Bernard (1934) and Duns Scotus (1952), as well as shorter pieces on Abelard and Albertus Magnus, and other works on medieval philosophy as a whole, he demonstrated that there were radical differences amongst its greatest figures. He thus permanently changed the map of medieval philosophy, and also indirectly challenged the very conception of a homogeneous 'Scholastic Philosophy', whether conceived of as a medieval phenomenon or as a single tradition surviving intact to the present day.

The only incontestable constant in medieval philosophy, according to Gilson, was that it was practised within the context of a belief in God and an acceptance of Christian revelation. (In the same way, contemporary philosophy is practised in a context of quantum mechanics, evolutionism, biogenetic theory, and the like.) This is why he described it as 'Christian' philosophy. By this he meant, not that philosophy and theology, or reason and faith, were confused with one another, but that faith provided insights and data for philosophy to examine and exploit. Christian revelation was, as he put it, 'an indispensable auxiliary to reason'. Gilson's view that medieval philosophy was Christian philosophy was vigorously contested by several of his scholastic contemporaries, most notably by Fernand Van Steenberghen.

One of the most decisive insights borrowed by philosophy from Christian faith, according to Gilson, was found in Exodus 3:14, in the Vulgate *ego sum qui sum*, 'I am who am'. In neo-Platonic thought, the creative source of the universe was regarded as something beyond being, therefore something unknowable and unnameable except as non-being. Augustine was inspired by Exodus, Gilson argued, to transform this creative source from non-being into being, and to identify it with the Christian God. Thus, from Augustine onwards the concept of being came to occupy a central role in metaphysics. For Augustine, however, heavily influenced as he still was by Platonic thought, God's being was an immutable essence, from which created being flowed and in which it participated. Knowledge, for instance, was an illumination by the divine intellect, since there could be no other source of its being than the divine being himself.

Aquinas, whose classical mentor was Aristotle, transformed the concept of being again, according to Gilson, this time into the idea of an activity: being as analogous to kicking or throwing. Being in this sense, Gilson argues, refers primarily to existence, not to essence. For Augustine, God had been an immutable essence; for Aquinas, God was the pure act of existence, He whose entire nature it is to exist. His essence is existence. Furthermore, God is not so much the source as the cause of finite existents. He communicates existence to them; and in them, too, existence is an act-of-being, although one which is limited and determined by the essence whose existence it is.

Gilson's theory of knowledge flows from his metaphysics of existence, although, as Georges Van Riet has shown, it underwent various changes and perhaps was never wholly satisfactory. The problem of knowledge, for Gilson, was the problem of explaining our knowledge of an external reality, which is in large part a world of objects. Finite objects possess both essence and existence. The intellect enables us to know the essence of things, but their existence is not conceptualizable. Neither is

their existence a sensible quality. How, then, can really existing objects be known? Gilson's answer is that they can be known in a judgement of existence. This kind of judgement differs from the judgement of attribution, which is the judgement studied in logic. In the judgement of existence, the verb 'to be' is not a copula: it is used, not to affirm a predicate of a subject, but rather to affirm its reality.

In his later years Gilson turned his hand to aesthetics; or rather, to the philosophy of art. The roots of art, he argued, lie in the fecundity and dynamism of being, in being-as-act. In humankind, this dynamism generates the order of factivity, of making as opposed to knowing. There is an infinite variety in human making, much of it for utilitarian ends or else for the sake of knowledge or desire. The fine arts, however, have as their end the production of beautiful objects, that is, objects of which the sensuous apprehension is pleasing. Objects of this kind possess the properties of wholeness, proportion and clarity.

The production of beautiful objects is the only purpose of art. Art is not knowledge, nor intuition, nor expression; nor is it symbolical. Works of art may, of course, contain other elements: dramatic, expressive, cognitive, conative; but in so far as they are works of art, they are simply objects of beauty. Similarly, our experiences of art may have a cognitive element, and in the case of a poet such as Dante this may be powerful and significant. But in so far as we experience Dante's poetry as a work of art, we sensuously perceive it just as a beautiful object made out of language. For Gilson, the order of knowing and the order of making might be mingled in artistic realities, but they were conceptually distinct, and were the product and the object of different mental activities.

Sources: DFN; EF; WWW.

HUGH BREDIN

Gödel, Kurt

Austrian-American (American citizen from 1948). **b:** 28 April 1906, Brunn, Austria (now Brno, Czech Republic). **d:** 14 January 1978, Princeton, New Jersey. **Cat:** Mathematical logician and philosopher of mathematics. **Ints:** Platonism in mathematics. **Educ:** 1924, University of Vienna, PhD 1930; associated with Vienna Circle. **Infls:** Plato, Leibniz, and David Hilbert. **Appts:** 1933–40, University of Vienna; 1933–8, Privatdocent; 1953–76, Professor, Institute for Advanced Studies, Princeton; 1951, Einstein Award; 1975, National Medal for Science. Honorary doctorates from Universities of Yale, Harvard, Rockefeller, and from Amherst College, Mass. Member of the National Academy of Sciences, the American Academy of Arts and Sciences, and the Royal Society of London, corresponding member of the Academie de Science Morale et Politique, Paris, and the British Academy.

Main publications:

(1986–) *Collected Works*, ed. S. Feferman, Oxford: Clarendon Press. Includes:
(1930) (thesis) 'Über die Vollständigkeit des Logikalkulas' [On the completeness of the logical calculus].
(1930) 'Die Vollständigkeit der Axiome des logischen Funktionenkalkuls' [The completeness of the axioms of the logical calculus of functions].
(1930) 'Einige metamathematische Resultate über Entscheidungsdefinitheit und Widersprufsfreiheit' [Some metamathematical results concerning completeness and consistency].
(1931) 'Über formal unentscheidbare Sätze der *Principia Mathematica* und verwandter systeme' [On formally undecidable propositions of *Principia Mathematica* and related systems] (published in English, New York: Dover Books, 1992).
(1936) 'Über die Länge von Beweisen' [On the length of proofs].
(1938) 'The consistency of the axioms of choice and of the generalized continuum hypothesis with the axioms of set theory' (reprinted Princeton, NJ: Princeton University Press, 1970).
(1939) 'Consistency-proof for the generalized continuum-hypothesis'.

(1940) 'The consistency of the continuum-hypotheisism' (third edition, corrected, 1953).
(1944) 'Russell's mathematical logic', in P. A. Schilpp, ed., *The Philosophy of Bertrand Russell* (Library of Living Philosophers series).
(1947) 'What is Cantor's continuum problem?'
(1949) 'A remark about the relationship between relativity theory and idealistic philosophy' in P. A. Schilpp (ed.) *A. Einstein: A Philosopher Scientist.*
(1958) 'Über eines bisher noch nicht benutzte Erweiterung des finitem Standpunktes' [On a hitherto unused amplification of the finite point of view].

Secondary literature:

Dawson, J. W. (1969) *The Foundations of Mathematics: Symposium Papers Commemorating the Sixtieth Birthday of Kurt Gödel*, Berlin/Heidelberg/NY: Springer Verlag.
——(1984) *The Papers of Kurt Gödel: An Inventory*, Princeton, NJ: The Institute for Advanced Studies.
Kurt Gödel Colloquium (1989) *Proceedings of the First Kurt Gödel Colloquium Sept 1989*, Vienna: Kurt-Gödel-Gesellschaft.
Lolli, Gabrielle (1992) *Incompletezza: saggio su Kurt Gödel*, Bologna: Il Mulino.
Nagel, E. and Newman, J. R. (1958) *Gödel's Proof*, New York: New York University Press.
Shanker, S. G. (ed.) (1988) *Gödel's Theorem in Focus*, Croom Helm.

Between 1930 and 1940 Gödel was responsible for three significant developments in mathematical logic. These were, first, the completeness proof relating to the first-order functional calculus; second, the theorem known as Gödel's Theorem, (the first incompleteness theorem); and third, a demonstration that the system of **Russell**'s and **Whitehead**'s *Principia Mathematica*, which the incompleteness theorem showed to be apparently inconsistent, could be rendered consistent.

Gödel's Theorem constituted a major challenge not only to the generally-held assumption that basic systems in mathematics are complete in that they contain no statements that can be either proved or disproved, but also to Hilbert's view that proofs of the consistency of such a system can be formulated within the system itself. Briefly, the theorem states that in a formal system S of arithmetic, there will be a sentence P of the language of S such that if S is consistent neither P nor its negation can be proved within S. The impact of this on *Principa Mathematica* was to undermine the latter's project of providing a set of logical axioms from which the whole of pure mathematics, as well as the non-axiomatic residue of logic, were deducible, since the theorem showed that mathematics contains propositions that are neither provable nor disprovable from the axioms. Gödel's ingenious argument revealed that in proving the consistency of the system one would also secure a proof that a particular statement, T, could not be proved, and also a proof of statement T. This shows that a consistency proof of ordinary arithmetic is not possible using finite procedures. In connection with this it has been claimed that Gödel's theorem demonstrates that human beings are superior to machines since they can know to be true propositions that no machine programmed with axioms and rules can prove.

After 1940 Gödel extended his interests in the philosophy of mathematics, working in greater detail on the relationship of the continuum hypothesis and the axiom of choice to set theory. His 1949 paper includes a curious argument for the unreality of time. But it is the famous first incompleteness proof that has generated, and continues to generate, lively debate among philosophers.

Sources: Turner.

DIANÉ COLLINSON

Goodman, Nelson

American. **b:** 7 August 1906, Somerville, Massachusetts. **Cat:** Analytic philosopher. **Ints:** Philosophy of science; philosophy of language; aesthetics. **Educ:** Harvard University. **Infls:** Carnap and C. I. Lewis. **Appts:** Instructor and Professor, University of Pennsylvania, 1946–64; Professor, Brandeis University, 1964–7; Professor, Harvard, 1967–77.

Main publications:

(1951) *The Structure of Appearance*, Cambridge, Mass.: Harvard University Press.
(1954) *Fact, Fiction and Forecast*, London: Athlone Press.
(1968) *The Languages of Art*, London: Oxford University Press.
(1972) *Problems and Projects*, Indianapolis: Bobbs-Meuil.
(1978) *Ways of World-Making*, Inianapolis: Hachett.
(1984) *Of Mind and other Matters*, Cambridge: Mass.: Harvard University Press.
(1988) *Reconceptions in Philosophy* (with Catherine Z. Elgin), London: Routledge.

Secondary literature:

Ayer, A. J. *Philosophy in the Twentieth Century*, c. ix, 4.

Goodman, after undergraduate study of philosophy, worked for some years as an art dealer and then returned to the subject. After writing a distinguished thesis, which was the core of his first major publication, *The Structure of Appearance* (1951), he entered the academic philosophical profession. Even more than **Quine**, his early collaborator and for many years his colleague at Harvard, Goodman is remarkable for his combination of extreme conceptual austerity with speculative intrepidity. He also has a stylistic likeness to Quine: both combine exquisite concision with a measure of playfulness. In an early article which he wrote with Quine they declared their predilection for nominalism. But it emerged that they understood it in different ways. Quine wanted to countenance only concrete individuals: Goodman had no objection to the abstract, but reserved his hostility for classes, which Quine thought had to be admitted to make sense of mathematics. In that first book he took as his starting-point **Carnap**'s *The Logical Construction of the World*. There Carnap had sought to display the entirety of the linguistic apparatus with which matters of fact are described as reducible by definitions and the instruments of formal logic to the smallest possible undefined basis: the single empirical concept of recollection of similarity. Goodman endorsed Carnap's procedure, contrasting his book as a unique example of serious philosophy with everything else, described as 'amorphous philosophical discourses'. But he was highly critical of its detail, replacing its account of definition, providing it with a formal theory of simplicity and rejecting one of its main purposes, that of basing the whole construction on what is epistemologically primary or fundamental. In constructing a phenomenalistic system, he said, he was not claiming that it was in any way 'closer to the facts' than a physicalistic one. The elements he selects are individuals, but they are abstract ones, sense-qualia such colours and, more disputably, places and times. A concrete phenomenal item is the sum of a colour, a place and a time. Another object of Goodman's distaste, along with classes, is similarity. In an early article on likeness of meaning he argued against the notion of synonymy in a way that to some extent prefigured Quine's 'Two dogmas of empiricism' and the protracted campaign against meaning, intensions, properties and so forth that he developed from that article. Later Goodman generalized his critique of similarity, denying its explanatory power in any application. For him denotation or extension is intelligible and that is all there is to general terms applying to a multiplicity of things. Nothing is added by saying that things to which such a word applies are connected by similarity to each other. Congruous with Goodman's preference for individuals is his actualism, his unwillingness to countenance possibilities over and above what there actually is. These have been invoked by philosophers to explain the difference between laws of nature and merely accidental generalities and also to interpret counterfactual conditionals. Laws of nature, it has been suggested, are those from which we are prepared to infer counterfactuals. A most effectively argued paper on this (now the first chapter of *Fact, Fiction and Forecast* (1955)) concludes that counterfactuals, such as 'if this had been put in water it would have dissolved' (also expressible with the use of 'dispositional predicate this is soluble') amount to ascribing some property, presumably microstructural, which is possessed by all those things that do dissolve in water, to the thing of which the disposition is being predicated. He went on, in *Fact, Fiction and Forecast*, to propound what he called a 'new riddle of induction'. Why do we take 'all emeralds up to now have been green' to confirm 'all emeralds whatever are green' and not 'all emeralds are grue', where 'grue' means 'green up to now and blue from now'? Neatly parrying objections, obvious and subtle, Goodman concludes that we project those predicates into unrestricted generalizations and singular predictions ('the next emerald I come on will be blue') that are *entrenched*, that we have got into the habit of projecting. An early paper with the economical title 'About' foreshadowed the elaborate account of the nature of representation in art in his *Languages of Art* (1968). In it the view that art represents the world mimetically by resembling it is emphatically rejected. Works of art are symbols, like sentences, and, like sentences, they have cognitive value and enlarge our knowledge or understanding of the world. In *Ways of World-Making* (1978) a multitude of world-versions, over and above those of art and science, are countenanced, such as the world (or world-version) of common sense, which is not too disturbing, but also those of particular artists or even musical composers. Analogies of denotation or representation are here stretched, many would feel, to breaking point, while the incompatibility, as contrasted with the different selectivenesses, of the apparently competing versions is overdramatized. Much of Goodman's work has been very widely and actively discussed. His early Carnapian idea of formally systematic philosophy has not been carried on by him or others but his philosophical conscience ('I do not want there to be more things in my philosophy than there are in heaven and earth') has been a valuable example.

Sources: Edwards; Passmore 1985.

ANTHONY QUINTON

Gramsci, Antonio

Italian. *b:* 1891, Ales, Sardinia. *d:* 1937, Rome. *Cat:* Marxist; political philosopher; culture theorist. *Educ:* 1911, University of Turin, but did not complete his degree. *Infls:* Marx, Hegel, Lenin, Croce and Sorel. *Appts:* Gramsci held no formal academic appointments, working as a journalist and politician.

Main publications:

(1948–51) *Quaderni del carcere*, Turin: Einaudi (*Prison Notebooks*, trans. Quintin Hoare and Geoffrey Nowell Smith, London: Lawrence & Wishart, 1971).
(1957) *The Modern Prince* (selection from papers given at Institutio Gramsci, Rome), trans. Louis Marks, New York: International Publishers.
(1965) *Lettere del carcere*, Turin: Einaudi (*Letters from Prison*, trans. Lynne Lawner, New York: Harper & Row, 1973).

Secondary literature:

Adamson, Walter L. (1977) *Hegemony and Revolution: A Study of Antonio Gramsci's Political and Cultural Theory*, Berkeley, Los Angeles and London: University of California Press.
Buci-Glucksmann, Christine (1980) *Gramsci and the State*, London: Lawrence & Wishart.
Cammett, John M. (1967) *Antonio Gramsci and the Origins of Italian Communism*, Stanford, CA: Stanford University Press.
Dombroski, Robert S. (1989) *Antonio Gramsci*, Boston: Twayne.
Joll, James (1977) *Gramsci*, London: Collins.
Pozzolini, A. (1970) *Antonio Gramsci: An Introduction to his Thought*, London: Pluto Press.
Williams, Gwyn A. (1975) *Proletarian Order: Antonio Gramsci, Factory Councils and the Origins of Communism in Italy*, London: Pluto Press.

Generally regarded as one of the most creative and original thinkers within the Marxist philosophical tradition, Gramsci spent most of his career in journalism and politics. He was active in the Turin Factory Council movement (a soviet-style workers' organization) in 1919–20, and after its suppression he edited *L'Ordine Nuovo*, later to become a Communist Party journal, and sat as a Deputy in the Italian Parliament. Gramsci was one of the founders of the Italian Communist Party, and although he was a political prisoner for the last ten years of his life, he went on to become one of the Party's major theorists through his prison writings. The earliest intellectual influence on Gramsci was the Italian idealist philosopher and aesthetician Benedetto **Croce**, whose work formed a lifelong source of inspiration despite the fact that its author ultimately turned fascist sympathizer. From Croce, Gramsci derives his deeply held belief in the importance of history as an intellectual activity. Another important source of influence for Gramsci's intellectual development was the French syndicalist theorist Georges Sorel, whose faith in the working class and admiration for the organizational powers of the Catholic Church throughout history, Gramsci shared. Despite the strong pull of Marx and **Lenin**, Gramsci also retained a distinctly Hegelian bias to his thought, conceiving of the dialectic in primarily Hegelian terms. Gramsci's early concern as a Marxist theorist was to find ways of countering the fairly crude and mechanical forms of dialectical materialism being propounded by such Bolshevik theorists as Nikolai Bukharin. Marxism was for

Gramsci not so much a sociological as a historical theory, and he differed considerably from Soviet orthodoxy on this issue, with his interest invariably being concentrated on cultural and historical factors rather than on purely economic considerations.

Gramsci can be credited with expounding a more human version of Marxist doctrine than most of his contemporaries, one less driven by the dictates of economic determinism and more committed to keeping the political leadership of a Marxist revolutionary movement in touch with the rank and file of its working-class members. Throughout his life Gramsci remained a firm believer in the use of persuasion to achieve political aims, as opposed to the more widespread Marxist–Lenin method of the imposition of party discipline and policy from above. The vision of the Communist Party put forward by Gramsci was a markedly less authoritarian one than usual, closer perhaps to the model of organization presented by the Catholic Church. Gramsci's major contributions to Marxist theory, including the enormously influential doctrine of hegemony, come mainly from his prison writings, not published until after the Second World War. 'Civil hegemony', to give it its full title, represents Gramsci's attempt to provide an explanation for history's periodic failure to conform to the determinist model of Marxism: if the conditions were ripe for the total collapse of the capitalist system, why did it not occur? A ruling class, Gramsci maintained, could keep control over the masses by means other than brute force or economic power. If it could encourage the masses to share its social, cultural and moral values then its dominant position, or 'hegemony', was assured. Thus the working class could often prove to be a reactionary rather than a revolutionary force, even though it could never be in its long-term interests to be so and despite the presence of the correct economic conditions for revolution, because it had internalized the values of its rulers.

The continuing strength of capitalism could be attributed to the prevailing influence of hegemonic factors, hence the need for Marxist theorists to turn their attention to the cultural realm, where the ruling class's values were constructed. Intellectuals were allotted a key role in this process, and Gramsci set great store by education as a political weapon. The emphasis on ideas as a means of bringing about effective change is typical of Gramsci, who did not believe that change would be lasting unless individuals truly desired it and political leadership was based on cultural and moral ascendancy rather than just economic power. In *The Modern Prince* Gramsci reformulated Machiavelli's ideas about leadership so that the Communist Party was seen to be just such an instrument of cultural and moral ascendancy. Throughout the prison writings Gramsci evinces a greater interest in analysing the past and identifying historical laws than in laying down specific rules for future political action. He represents a humanist strain of thought within Marxism which owes much to a long-running tradition of humanism in Italian culture stretching back to the Renaissance period, and he remains one of the least 'economist', as well as least dogmatic, of Marxist theorists. Gramsci's humanistic interpretation of Marxist theory has exerted a considerable appeal amongst those Marxists unhappy with the excesses of Stalinism or the cruder forms of dialectical materialism favoured in Russian Communist circles. His reputation has grown steadily since his death and he is generally considered to be the most approachable of Marxist theorists to non-believers, given his lack of dogmatism. Within Italian political and cultural life since the collapse of fascism Gramsci has been a major force. The Italian Communist Party of the post-war period took much of its lead from Gramsci's example as both theorist and political activist, and showed itself more disposed to compromise than most such organizations. In Marxist circles outside Italy, Gramsci's influence is most clearly seen in the work of the French structural Marxist philosopher Louis Althusser, a great admirer of the Italian's ideas, particularly his analyses of the relationship between economic base and cultural superstructure (Althusser's notion of the relative autonomy of the superstructure echoes Gramsci's insistence on the latter's importance vis-à-vis the base) and his doctrine of hegemony. The latter doctrine has won wide acceptance among theorists and has been used to considerable effect in fields such as political science, sociology and aesthetics. Theorists of popular culture, as a case in point, rely heavily on the notion of hegemony in their analyses, and most Western Marxist aesthetic theorists have adopted the doctrine in order to draw attention to the crucial ideological role played by the arts within culture.

STUART SIM

Habermas, Jürgen

German. *b:* 18 June 1929, Dusseldorf. *Cat:* Post-Marxist critical theorist. *Ints:* Social philosophy; hermeneutics; modernist (emancipatory) thought; communication (speechact) theory; historical and socio-political criticism. *Educ:* 1954, doctorate, University of Bonn; 1961, second doctorate (*Habilitation*), University of Mainz. *Infls:* Hegel, Kant, Marxist philosophy, Schelling, Fichte, Dilthey, Weber, Adorno, Horkheimer, Lukács, Searle and Anglo-American linguistic philosophy. *Appts:* 1954, Adorno's assistant, University of Frankfurt's Institute for Social Research; 1961, professorship, University of Heidelberg; 1964, taught philosophy and sociology at Frankfurt; 1971–84, Director of the Max Planck Institute, Starnburg; 1984, Professor of History of Philosophy, University of Frankfurt.

Main publications:

(1962) *Strukturwandel der Öffentlichkeit*, Berlin: Leuchterhand.
(1970) *Zur Logik der Sozialwissenschaften*, Frankfurt am Main: Suhrkamp.
(1971) (with Niklaus Luhmann) *Theorie der Gesellschaft oder Sozialtechnologie: Was leistet die Systemforschung?*, Frankfurt am Main: Suhrkamp.
(1973) *Kultur und Kritik*, Frankfurt am Main: Suhrkamp.
(1975) *Legitimation Crisis*, trans. T. McCarthy, Boston: Beacon Press 1975.
(1977) 'The analytical theory of science and dialectics' and 'A positivistically bisected rationalism', in *The Positivist Dispute in German Sociology*, ed. Adey and Frisby, London: Heinemann.
(1984) *The Theory of Communicative Action and the Rationalisation of Science*, 2 vols, trans. T. McCarthy, London: Heinemann.
(1987) *The Philosophical Discourse of Modernity*, trans. F. Lawrence, London: Blackwell.

Secondary literature:

Adey and Frisby (eds) (1977) *The Positivist Dispute in German Sociology*, London: Heinemann.
Bernstein, R. (1985) *Habermas and Modernity*, Oxford: Polity Press.
Held, D. (1980) *Introduction to Critical Theory*, London: Hutchinson.
White (1990) *Recent Works of Jürgen Habermas*, London: Cambridge University Press.

Jürgen Habermas is the most notable and independent-minded successor to the Frankfurt School of Philosophy, which attempted to retrieve Marxism from Stalinist orthodoxy and remould it into an incisive form of ideological and cultural criticism. Habermas has extended that concern into a broad preoccupation with those cultural and political factors which distort and disrupt the assumed openness of human communication. His distinctive contribution to contemporary European thought is his thesis that perfectible structures of reasoning and cumulatively liberating insights into truth are tangibly accessible as they are embedded within our ordinary communicative practices: they are neither grounded in nor reflections of an alleged external reality, but are to be found within the socially constructed discourses which constitute our 'life-world'.

Habermas's thought ranges through an incisive attack upon positivism and Popperian notions of rationality, an attempt to revitalize Marxism as a culturally critical tool, a critique of the conservative foundations of Gadamerian hermeneutics and a stalwart defence of the enlightening capacities of modernist thought against the critical onslaught of French deconstruction. His thinking is not so much marked by distinct transitions as by a continuous bringing forward of one or other of a cluster of themes that bind his overall position together. These include an intense resistance to scientific, political and philosophical attempts to monopolize knowledge and truth, a passionate commitment to open and undistorted communication as a means to truth and the conviction that vigilant criticism of untruth offers the only route to an intellectually open and politically unrepressive society.

Habermas acquired the basis of his conception of emancipatory truth from his initial deep involvement with the Frankfurt School. Marx's teleological framework commences with an abstract notion of mankind as a *potentia* containing the as yet unrealized creative potential. Although the Frankfurt School abandoned the conviction that only the alienating process of historical labour could actualize this truth, Habermas retained through its influence the Marxist notion of truth as a yet to be realized historical situation in which that which was potentially true could be realized as actually true. The importance of this notion for Habermas is that it offers an ideal facilitating a critique of events as a deviation from the envisaged norm, as well as the basis of an ideological critique the task of which is to unmask the social and political factors which hide the anticipated truth. As the realization of individual creative potential depends upon the extent of social emancipation, cultural critique cannot be dissociated from political critique. In its critical and emancipatory capacities, Habermas's ideal of undistorted communication is a true child of this Marxist motif.

In his antipositivist critique of **Popper**'s and Albert's 'critical rationalism' (see Adley and Frisby, 1977), Habermas refuses to allow the motif of an emancipatory truth to be marginalized by a methodology that refuses sense to all except that which can be explicated through scientific analysis. Decisions and values relevant to moral and political life cannot be replaced or rationalized by scientific calculation (*Zweckrationalität*). Curiously, **Gadamer**, Habermas's next chosen opponent, would concur; but just as Habermas resists the ideologically acquired authority of scientific reasoning to legislate upon questions of social and political value, so he disputes the authority of historical and cultural tradition to be the sole opponent of technological thinking. To resist the one-sidedness of scientific reasoning with the evident partisanship of inherited tradition is merely to replace one distorted truth with another. Habermas supports his claim by arguing for an analogy between the problems posed by tradition and those confronted by psychoanalysis. Just as neurotic behaviour entails the suppression of its causes, so tradition can be unknowingly blind to values not its own and to the ideological presuppositions which underwrite is own truth claims.

In his debate with Gadamer, Habermas's commitment to emancipatory truth was not the sole basis of his opposition. He responded profoundly to Gadamer's dialogical model of understanding, fusing it with aspects of **Searle**'s speech-act theory. His famous essay 'The hermeneutic claim to universality' (1980) argues that 'truth ... measures itself as an idealised consensus achieved in unlimited (and unforced) communications'. That which validates the procedures of a discourse as truthful is not metaphysically or ontologically distinct from the discourse but emerges historically from within it. Thus once questions concerning the truth claims of tradition are raised, the participants of that tradition need not remain passively subject to their received authority but are rationally invited to critically reappropriate them and by means of critical involvement extend their claims. A variation of the argument appears in *Knowledge and Human Interests* (1968), where Habermas argues that all knowledge has a sociological origin, suggesting the possibility of a rational discourse permitting the participants the opportunity to revise or make more adequate the norms underwriting its operating consensus. If discourse about the assumptions underwriting knowledge is possible, it is also possible to anticipate more comprehensive (i.e. emancipatory) assumptions for that discourse. Habermas's central contention is that built into the very notion of rational discourse is the anticipation of acheiving for it more adequate and more open foundations. This intrinsic discursive logic impels all rational discourses towards an ever more open and enlightened stance.

In *The Theory of Communicative Action* (1984), Habermas explores the pretheoretical understandings legitimating speech acts. He argues that in the understanding of something said, understanding occurs not because the interlocutors share the same experiences but because one can grasp the point of what the other is saying despite any expressive idiosyncrasy. This effectively reformulates Habermas's ideal speech situation, for if it is in the nature of discourse to generate intersubjective meanings which can transcend a particular interlocutor, it is possible by means of sound argument to arrive at the emancipatory potential within such meanings and expand them beyond the originating discourse. Whosoever speaks a language both belongs to and aspires to the widening of a universal community grounded upon the openness and free consensus of communica-

tion. The argument that such a consensus is neither forced on us nor the result of happenstance but springs from actual everyday lingustic practice—is something that we actually talk ourselves into—is Habermas's profoundest contribution to European philosophy.

Habermas's defence of such ideality has drawn the fire of post-structuralist and deconstructivist criticism on the grounds that both his ideal speech act and his espousal of an as yet to be arrived at historical truth are merely fictive vehicles for the peddling of his particular political commitments. Not only, it is said, do his arguments perpetrate the fiction of an end truth of discourse—the realization of a truly free communicative society—but they exhibit an authoritarian attempt to straightjacket the direction of history. In *The Philosophical Discourse of Modernity* (1987), Habermas responds by arguing that any empirically rooted ideal as that of the undistorted speech situation cannot be falsified by genealogical reductivism. The claim to truth, just as the claim to meaning, always reaches beyond the empirical circumstances which initially generate it. Exploding the universality of a political truth claim by exposing the particularist interests which might hypocritically nurture it, does nothing, he maintains, to undermine the critical potential that truth might have. Furthermore, if there is difference over an issue there is at least agreement over what the issue is; and if there is that, the logical possibility exists of rationally arriving at a consensus as to how such differences might be resolved. In this respect the notion of emancipatory critique is pehaps one of the last defences against the murderous threat ever present within religious and political bigotry.

Habermas's defence of modernity carries with it a political import of some weight. Post-structuralist criticism may expose the particular wills to power sustaining progressivist notions of philosophical and cultural modernism, but what are the consequences of allowing the idealistic aspirations of modernism to fall completely to such cynicism? Post-structuralist criticism may delight in exposing the alleged elitist authoritarianism of modernism, but is not the dream of every political tyranny to convince those under its subjection that there is no other actuality than the immediate? If any claim to meaning or truth which seeks to transcend the horizons of its socio-political origin is disallowed, the claim of the ideal, so necessary for any aspiration to reformulate positions in a more embracing manner, will wither. With that withering comes what Habermas is afraid of. Without an awareness of a responsiveness to the wider claims of rational criticism, capable of reminding us of how a situation or argument might be structured differently from previous or present exemplars, humanity's consciousness will be imprisoned within the horizon of the immediate and its freedom to imagine and act beyond that horizon irredeemably impaired.

NICHOLAS DAVEY

Hare, R(ichard) M(ervyn)

British. *b:* 1919, Backwell, near Bristol. *Cat:* Analytic philosopher. *Ints:* Ethics; political philosophy; philosophy of language. *Educ:* University of Oxford, 1945–7. *Infls:* G. E. Moore, J. L. Austin and Ludwig Wittgenstein. *Appts:* Fellow of Balliol College, Oxford, 1947–66; White's Professor of Moral Philosophy, Oxford, and Fellow of Corpus Christi College, 1966–83; Graduate Research Professor, University of Florida at Gainesville, from 1983; Fellow of the British Academy, 1964.

Main publications:

(1952) *The Language of Morals*, Oxford: Clarendon Press.

(1963) *Freedom and Reason*, Oxford: Clarendon Press.

(1971) *Practical Inferences*, London: Macmillan.

(1971) *Essays on Philosophical Method*, London: Macmillan.

(1972) *Essays on the Moral Concepts*, London: Macmillan.

(1972) *Applications of Moral Philosophy*, London: Macmillan.

(1981) *Moral Thinking: Its Levels, Method and Point*, Oxford: Clarendon Press.

(1982) *Plato*, Oxford: Oxford University Press.

(1989) *Essays in Ethical Theory*, Oxford: Clarendon Press.

(1989) *Essays on Political Morality*, Oxford: Clarendon Press.

(1992) *Essays on Religion and Education*, Oxford: Clarendon Press.

(1993) *Essays on Bioethics*, Oxford: Clarendon Press.

Secondary literature:

Hudson, W. D. (1983) *Modern Moral Philosophy*, London: Macmillan.

Seanor, Douglas and Fotion, N. (eds) (1988) *Hare and Critics*, with comments by R. M. Hare, Oxford: Clarendon Press.

Hare's first published work, *The Language of Morals* (1952), has been one of the most influential works of moral philosophy in the English-speaking world since the Second World War. He argued that moral judgements, though fundamentally imperative in form, could none the less be rational. His later works elaborated these themes and, especially in *Moral Thinking* (1981), developed the claim that a certain sort of utilitarianism must be the correct ethical theory. He has also published a considerable amount of work in practical ethics, increasingly so in the latter half of his career.

When Hare started working on ethics, the emotivism of philosophers such as A. J. **Ayer** and C. L. Stevenson was in the ascendant. Hare's view was that emotivism was right to deny that moral judgements were factual, or descriptive, statements of any kind, but wrong to hold that they were merely expressions of emotion or attempts to influence the emotions of others. In particular, it went wrong in not distinguishing clearly the claim that moral utterances are attempts *to influence* the actions of others (a claim Hare held to be false) from the view that moral utterances are an attempt *to tell people what to do* (which he held to be true). And this rendered emotivism unable to give a satisfactory account of how ethics could be a *rational* endeavour. So Hare wished to propound a theory which would be 'a rationalist kind of non-descriptivism' (Seanor and Fotion 1988: 210).

According to Hare, moral judgements were fundamentally imperative in their logical form, which is why any form of naturalism must be incorrect: it would involve the attempt to derive imperative conclusions from factual, and therefore non-imperative, premises. And this was the fault which G. E. **Moore**, although not properly diagnosing it, had labelled the Naturalistic Fallacy. Moral judgements are not usually, of course, imperative in their *grammatical* form. The nub of Hare's claim that they were logically imperative was this: it is a conceptual truth that sincerely accepting a moral judgement commits the speaker to *acting* upon it on appropriate occasions if it is within his power. Thus, if someone does not act upon a moral judgement on the appropriate occasions, then we may logically conclude that either that he *could not* do so or that he did not accept the moral judgement. This view of ethical judgements came to be known as prescriptivism.

Hare was at pains, however, to show that imperatives are subject to logical constraints, just as factual assertions are, and this is part of what brings morality within the domain of reason.

Hare's second major claim is that a genuine moral judgement, such as that I ought not, for instance, to have my pregnancy aborted, must be based upon some *principles*. Hare's claim is that it is a conceptual truth that moral principles are

universal in form. This does not mean that they need be wide generalizations; indeed they may be very specific. But they must not contain references to particular individuals. And this in turn generates the thesis of the Universalizability of Moral Judgements. To accept a particular moral judgement, *as* a moral judgement, involves accepting it also as a universal principle. If I really think that it would be morally wrong for me to have an abortion then I must think that it would be morally wrong for anyone relevantly like me, in relevantly similar circumstances, to have an abortion. Hare's theory thus came to be known as Universal Prescriptivism.

The practical force of the marriage of prescriptivism and universalizability became clearer in *Freedom and Reason* (1963) and, in particular, *Moral Thinking* (1981). In these works, Hare developed a form of utilitarianism. Like most modern utilitarians, he thought of the individual good as consisting in one's desires being fulfilled, rather than in happiness, a conception known as preference utilitarianism. Desires, which he claimed were the *subject matter* of morality, could be ordered according to their strength, and independently of whose desires they were or what they were desires for. He then argued that a sympathetic identification with the desires of others would make us come to identify with those desires as we identify with our own. We should thus come to want the satisfaction of desires generally, ranked according to their strength, and with no concern for *whose* desires they were nor what they were desires for; and, Hare argued, this would lead us to desire the maximum satisfaction of desires generally.

In *Moral Thinking* Hare worked more concentratedly towards a theory that combined the advantages of both act utilitarianism and rule utilitarianism. Although, at the level of what he called critical thinking—the level of the utterly impartial, rational and knowledgeable agent—an individual act is right if and only if it maximizes the satisfaction of desire, he argued that in making moral decisions we should not usually consider the consequences of each individual act. Doing so would not in fact produce the desired result, since our judgements would often go wrong. Rather, we should generally follow those rules that have been tried and tested—for example, rules against lying, cheating, stealing and so forth. We should rest content with what Hare calls our intuitive judgements. Indeed we should try to mould our sentiments, and those of our children, to make it psychologically difficult for us to act against them save in exceptional circumstances. So Hare does not suggest that utilitarian thinking should replace an adherence to many of our ordinary, intuitive moral principles. Indeed the fact that a general adherence to these principles maximizes utility explains, in his view, why they have grown up. Hare's work has been the subject of continuous discussion, and virtually every aspect of it has been criticized. It has been argued, for instance, that the diversity of moral utterances cannot be reduced satisfactorily to the imperative model. Many have argued that there is no fact–value distinction of the sort that is central to his work. Others, again, have held that moral judgements are not essentially universalizable. And many philosophers have thought that his recent work commits Hare to a sort of naturalism which his theory was supposed to reject. Allan Gibbard remarks: 'Perhaps no philosopher since Kant has developed a theory of moral judgement and moral reasoning so ingenious and so carefully worked through as R. M. Hare' (in Seanor and Fotion 1988, p. 57).

Sources: Flew; Becker; WW 1992; personal communication.

ANTHONY ELLIS

Hartmann, Nicolai

German. **b:** 20 February 1882, Riga, Lativa. **d:** 9 October 1950, Göttingen, Germany. **Cat:** Metaphysician; ethicist. **Ints:** Ontology; ethics. **Educ:** St Petersburg (gymnasium; Philology), Dorpat, Estonia (Medicine) and University of Marburg (Philosophy PhD). **Infls:** Plato, Kant, Hegel, Aristotle, Hermann Cohen, Husserl and Max Scheler. **Appts:** 1920–5, Professor of Philosophy, University of Marburg; 1925–31, Professor of Philosophy, University of Cologne; 1931–45, Professor of Philosophy, University of Berlin; 1945–50, Professor of Philosophy, University of Göttingen.

Main publications:

(1909) *Platos Logik des Seins* [Plato's Logic of Being], Geissen: A. Thopelmann.

(1921) *Grundzüge einer Metaphysik der Erkenntnis* [Outlines of a Metaphysics of Knowledge], Berlin: W. de Gruyter.

(1923–9) *Die Philosophie des deutschen Idealismus* [The Philosophy of German Idealism], 2 vols: vol. I, *Fichte, Schelling und die Romantik* vol. II, *Hegel*, Berlin: W. de Gruyter.

(1926) *Ethik*, Berlin: W. de Gruyter (English translation, *Ethics*, trans. Stanton Coit, 3 vols, London: Macmillan, 1932).

(1933) *Das Problem des geistigen Seins* [The Problem of Ideal Being], Berlin: W. de Gruyter.

(1935) *Zur Grundlegung der Ontologie* [Foundations of Ontology], Berlin: W. de Gruyter.

(1938) *Möglichkeit und Wirklichkeit* [Possibility and Reality], Berlin: W. de Gruyter.

(1940) *Der Aufbau der realen Welt* [The Structure of the Real World], Berlin: G. A. Hain.

(1940) 'Neue Wege der Ontologie', in *Systematische Philosophie*, Stuttgart: N. W. Kohlhammer. (English translation, *New Ways of Ontology*, trans. Reinhard C. Kuhn, Chicago: Henry Regnery, 1953).

(1953) *Asthetik* [Aesthetics], Berlin: W. de Gruyter.

(1955–8) *Kleinere Schriften* [Shorter Writings], 3 vols, Berlin: W. de Gruyter (includes reprints of journal articles).

Secondary literature:

Cadwallader, Eva H. (1984) 'The continuing relevance of Nicolai Hartmann's theory of value', *Journal of Value Inquiry* 18: 113–21.

——(1984) *Searchlight on Values: Nicolai Hart-mann's Twentieth Century Value Platonism*, Lanham, Md.: University Press of America.

Hook, Sidney (1930) 'A critique of ethical realism', *International Journal of Ethics* 40 (Jan.): 179–210.

Kuhn, Helmut (1951) 'Nicolai Hartmann's ontology', *Philosophical Quarterly* 1 (July): 289–318.

Mohanty, Jitendra N. (1957) *Nicolai Hartmann and Alfred North Whitehead: A Study in Recent Platonism*, Calcutta.

Werkmeister, W. H. (1990) *Nicolai Hartmann's New Ontology*, Tallahassee: University of Florida Press, 1990.

Nicolai Hartmann, a major German philosopher of the first half of the twentieth century, was primarily a metaphysician, but is best known in the English-speaking world for his monumental *Ethics*. The most characteristic features of his work are his 'aporetic method', and his insistence on the priority of ontology over epistemology. He saw his aporetic method as continuous with the best in Plato and Aristotle, as consistent with the scientific spirit and as central to productive philosophizing. The aporetic method consists of two phases: first, a careful phenomenology of relevant facts (whether ontological, epistemological, ethical or aesthetic); second, a dialectical clarification of the problems they present. Wherever possible, Hartmann formulated problems as antinomies (paradoxes), assessing each side carefully. Hartmann thus eschewed the German tradition of system-building in favour of his unique aporetic approach.

Hartmann fully ontologized the relation (regarding both being and value) between knower and known. Setting the two 'modes of Being' (particulars and universals) on an equal footing in so far as they are both objective and independent of the knower, he proceeded to articulate them by a method partly phenomenological, partly logical and partly metaphysical. This resulted in 'ontological stratifications', Hartmann's unique metaphysical approach. *New Ways of Ontol-ogy* and *Ethics* contain its most important examples.

Hartmann's most enduring contribution to philosophy will undoubtedly be his *Ethics*, the aretaic aspect of which has probably already exerted invisible influences. The *Ethics* comprises both a general theory of value (the Platonism of which is universally rejected today) and a revival of the long-neglected aretaic method of doing ethics, originated by Aristotle. Aretaic ethics is virtue-centred ethics, an alternative to utilitarianism and formalism. Hartmann's phenomenology of virtues is in volume II, written in lucid, sometimes austerely poetic prose, illuminating and inspiring. It is governed, Hartmann says, by a 'logic of the heart', and the influence of **Nietzsche** is as powerful as that of Aristotle. Volume I is an aporetic phenomenology of morality and a history of normative ethics and ethical theory. Fortunately, volume III's unconvincing attempt to solve the problem of freedom does not impair the majesty of the second volume.

Certain aspects of Hartmann's philosophy have been compared with Anglo-American work. His value Platonism has been compared with A. N. **Whitehead**'s (Mohanty 1957) and contrasted with G. E. **Moore**'s (Cadwallader 1984). Several factors in Hartmann's epistemology are reminiscent of C. S. **Peirce**, 'Father of American Pragmatism', namely Peirce's subtle balancing of anti-dogmatic objectivism with non-nihilistic fallibilism. On the other hand, Hartmann's value intuitionism, seemingly incorrigible although radically pluralistic, stands in a paradoxical relation to fallibilism (the view that one can always be mistaken). Hartmann claims to resolve this antinomy with a searchlight metaphor according to which values themselves do not change but rather our perceptions of them.

Although this Kantianized value Platonism runs against the current of the times, Hartmann shares the existentialist conviction that human beings must heroically endow reality with meaning. For, despite the partial intelligibility and orderliness of reality and ideality, neither God nor cosmic purpose exists. Despite his objectivism, Hartmann's interests are not religious. Nevertheless, his 'emotional apriorism' ('logic of the heart') imparts a spiritual tone to the *Ethics* which will always appeal to some. In a century starved of sober inspirational thoughts on the virtues, *Ethics II* towers alone.

Sources: Abdulla K. Badsha 'Nicolai Hartmann', in *Great Lives from History: Twentieth Century Series*, vol. 2, ed. F. Magill, Englewood Cliffs, NJ: Salem Press; Edwards.

EVA CADWALLADER

Hartshorne, Charles

American. **b:** 5 June 1897, Kittaning, Pennsylvania. **Cat:** Process metaphysician; panentheist; panpsychist. **Ints:** Philosophy of religion. **Educ:** Haverford College, Harvard University, BA 1921, MA 1922, PhD 1923; the Universities of Freiburg and Marburg, 1923–5. **Infls:** Emerson, Peirce and Whitehead. **Appts:** 1925–8, Instructor and Research Fellow, Harvard University; 1928–55, Instructor to Professor, University of Chicago; 1955–62, Professor, Emory University; from 1962, Ashbel Smith Professor of Philosophy (1962–76) and Emeritus Professor (from 1976), University of Texas at Austin.

Main publications:

(1931–5) (ed. with P. Weiss) *Collected Papers of Charles Sanders Peirce*, 6 vols, Cambridge, Mass.: Harvard University Press.

(1934) *The Philosophy and Psychology of Sensation*, Chicago: University of Chicago Press.

(1937) *Beyond Humanism: Essays in the New Philosophy of Nature*, Chicago: Willet, Clark & Company; reprinted with new Preface, Lincoln: University of Nebraska Press, 1968.

(1941) *Man's Vision of God and the Logic of Theism*, Chicago: Willet, Clark & Company;

reprinted, New York: Harper & Brothers, 1948, and Hamden, CT: Archon Books, 1964.

(1947) *The Divine Relativity: A Social Conception of God*, New Have, CT: Yale University Press.

(1953) *Reality as Social Process: Studies in Metaphysics and Religion*, Glencoe and Boston: Free Press; reprinted, New York: Hafner, 1971.

(1953) (with W. L. Reese) *Philosophers Speak of God*, Chicago: University of Chicago Press.

(1962) *The Logic of Perfection and Other Essays in Neoclassical Metaphysics*, La Salle, Ill.: Open Court.

(1965) *Anselm's Discovery*, La Salle, Ill.: Open Court.

(1967) *A Natural Theology of Our Time*, La Salle: Open Court.

(1970) *Creative Synthesis and Philosophic Method*, London: SCM Press Ltd and La Salle, Ill.: Open Court.

(1972) *Whitehead's Philosophy: Selected Essays, 1935–1970*, Lincoln: University of Nebraska Press.

(1976) *Aquinas to Whitehead: Seven Centuries of Metaphysics of Religion. The Aquinas Lecture, 1976*, Milwaukee: Marquette University Publications.

(1983) *Insights and Oversights of Great Thinkers: An Evaluation of Western Philosophy*, Albany: SUNY Press.

(1984) *Omnipotence and Other Theological Mistakes*, Albany: SUNY Press.

(1984) *Creativity in American Philosophy*, Albany: SUNY Press.

(1987) *Wisdom as Moderation: A Philosophy of the Middleway*, Albany: SUNY Press.

(1990) *The Darkness and the Light: A Philosopher Reflects upon his Fortunate Career and Those who Made it Possible*, Albany: SUNY Press.

Secondary literature:

Cobb, Jr, J. B. and Gramwell, F. I. (eds) (1985) *Existence and Actuality: Conversations with Charles Hartshorne*, Chicago: Chicago University Press.

Hahn, L. E. (ed.) (1991) *The Philosophy of Charles Hartshorne*, La Salle: Open Court, The Library of Living Philosophers.

Peters, E. H. (1970) *Hartshorne and Neoclassical Metaphysics: An Interpretation*, Lincoln: University of Nebraska Press.

Reese, W. L. and Freeman, E. (eds) (1964) *Process and Divinity: The Hartshorne Festschrift*, La Salle: Open Court.

Viney, D. W. (1984) *Charles Hartshorne and the Existence of God*, Albany: SUNY Press.

Wood, Jr, F. and De Armey, M. (eds) (1986) *Hartshorne's Neo-Classical Theology*, New Orleans: Tulane Studies in Philosophy.

Second only to **Whitehead** in the leadership of process philosophy, Hartshorne has redirected its course from science to religion and theology. He professedly reached his basic philosophical position before becoming Whitehead's assistant at Harvard and working on the *Collected Papers of Charles Sanders Peirce* (1931–5). In *The Philosophy and Psychology of Sensation* (1934) he drew upon scientific psychology and philosophy to demonstrate that sensation is an evaluative feeling exhibiting continuity, a thesis he subsequently elaborated into a panpsychist or psychalist philosophy according to which life or feeling permeates the cosmos, concentrated in individualized centres, identical to Whitehead's 'actual entities' or 'occasions of experience'. Hartshorne held, like Whitehead before him, that recent developments in natural science require a radical reconception of nature. Since nature is reconceived as an affective continuum of valuational feelings, furthermore, a new theology replaces the classical conception of God. Hartshorne's speculations came to fruition in his 1946 Terry Lectures at Yale University, published in *The Divine Relativity* (1947). Hartshorne's process deity has a dipolar nature—an abstract, eternal nature and a concrete, temporal nature. It mirrors Whitehead's distinction between the primordial and consequent natures of God. The unity of these two aspects of God embraces the World, God being supreme as the eternal–temporal consciousness, knowing and including the world. Hence Hartshorne has advocated panentheism, the doctrine that God includes the world yet transcends it. Hartshorne has sought to employ the instruments of modal logic to prove the existence of God. Thus he has contributed to the revival of interest in the ontological argument in recent decades. His endeavours to rehabilitate the reputation of Anselm and to resuscitate the ontological

argument illustrate the 'neo-classical' turn of his thought. Hartshorne's hobby in birdwatching and listening to birdsong has resulted in his international reputation as an ornithologist. He published a prize-winning work, *Born to Sing: An Interpretation and World Survey of Bird Song* (Bloomington: Indiana University Press, 1973).

Sources: Reck 1968; RA, 4; WW(Am).

ANDREW RECK

Heidegger, Martin

German. *b:* 26 September 1889, Messkirch, Germany. *d:* 26 May 1976. *Cat:* Phenomenologist; ontologist. *Ints:* The question of being. *Educ:* Theology and Philosophy, University of Freiburg. *Infls:* The pre-Socratics, Plato, Aristotle, St Paul, Augustine, Aquinas, Duns Scotus, Meister Eckhart, Angelus Silesius, Luther, Leibniz, Kant, Hegel, Hölderlin, Schelling, Kierkegaard, Nietzsche, Brentano, Carl Braig, Dilthey, Husserl and Max Scheler. *Appts:* 1919–23, Privatdozent and Assistant of Husserl, University of Freiburg; 1923–8, Professor, University of Marburg; 1928–46, Professor, University of Freiburg; 1946–51, forbidden to teach; 1952–76, Emeritus Professor, University of Freiburg.

Main publications:

(1927) *Sein und Zeit*, Tübingen (English translation, *Being and Time*, trans. J. Macquarrie and E. Robinson, Oxford: Basil Blackwell, 1962).
(1975) *Grundprobleme der Phänomenologie*, Frankfurt (English translation, *Basic Problems of Phenomenology*, trans. A. Hofstadter, Bloomington: Indiana University Press, 1982).
(1978) *Metaphysische Anfangsgründe der Logik*, Frankfurt (English translation, *Metaphysical Foundations of Logic*, trans. M. Hein, Bloomington: Indiana University Press, 1984).
(1929) *Kant und das Problem der Metaphysik*, Bonn (English translation, *Kant and the Problem of Metaphysics*, trans. R. Taft, Bloomington: Indiana University Press, 1990).

(1929) *Grundbegriffe der Metaphysik*, Frankfurt.

(1929) *Was ist Metaphysik?*, Bonn (English translation, 'What is metaphysics?', D. F. Krell, in *Martin Heidegger: Basic Writings*, ed. D. F. Krell, London: Routledge, 1993).

(1929) *Vom Wesen des Grundes*, Halle (English translation, *The Essence of Reasons*, trans. T. Malick, Evanston: Northwestern University Press, 1969).

(1940) *Über den Humanismus*, Frankfurt (English translation, 'Letter on humanism', trans. F. Capuzzi, in *Basic Writings*, ed. D. F. Krell, London: Routledge, 1993).

(1943) *Vom Wesen der Wahrhreit*, Frankfurt (English translation, 'On the essence of truth', trans. John Sallis, in *Basic Writings*, ed. D. F. Krell, London: Routledge, 1993).

(1950) 'Der Urpsprung des Kuntswerks', in *Holzwege*, Frankfurt, (English translation, 'The origin of the work of art', trans. A. Hofstadter, in *Basic Writings*, ed. D. F. Krell, London: Routledge, 1993).

(1953) *Einführung in die Metaphysik*, Tübingen (English translation, *An Introduction to Metaphysics*, trans. R. Manheim, Garden City, NY: Doubleday-Anchor Books, 1961).

(1954) *Was heisst Denken?*, Tübingen (English translation, *What is Called Thinking?*, trans. F. D. Wieck and J. Glenn Gray, New York: Harper & Row, 1968).

(1957) *Der Satz vom Grund*, Pfullingen (English translation, *The Principle of Reason*, trans. R. Lilly, Bloomington: Indiana University Press, 1991).

(1957) *Identität und Differenz*, Pfullingen (English translation, *Identity and Difference*, trans. J. Stambaugh, New York: Harper & Row, 1969).

(1959) *Unterwegs zur Sprache*, Pfullingen (English translation, *On the Way to Language*, trans. P. D. Hertz and J. Stambaugh, New York: Harper & Row, 1971).

(1961) *Nietzsche*, 2 vols, Pfullingen (English translation, *Nietzsche* 4 vols, trans. D. F. Krell, New York: Harper & Row, 1979–87).

(1986) *Beiträge zur Philosophie: vom Ereignis*, Frankfurt.

Secondary literature:

Biemel, Walter (1973) *Martin Heidegger*, Hamburg (English translation, *Martin Heidegger: An Illustrated Study*, London: Routledge, 1977).

Caputo, John D. (1978) *The Mystical Element in Heidegger's Thought*, Athens, Ohio: Ohio University Press.

Dreyfus, H. (1991) *Being-in-the-World: A Commentary on Heidegger's 'Being and Time', Division I*, Cambridge, Mass.: MIT Press.

Dreyfus, H. and Hall, H. (eds) (1992) *Heidegger: A Critical Reader*, Oxford: Blackwell.

Franzen, Winfried (1976) *Martin Heidegger*, Stuttgart.

Gadamer, H.-G. (1983) *Heideggers Wege*, Tübingen.

Guignon, Charles (1993) (ed.) *The Cambridge Companion to Heidegger*, Cambridge: Cambridge University Press.

Macann, Christopher (ed.) (1992) *Martin Heidegger: Critical Assessments*, 4 vols, London: Routledge.

Olafson, F. A. (1987) *Heidegger's Philosophy of Mind*, New Haven: Yale University Press.

Ott, Hugo (1988) *Martin Heidegger: Unterwegs zu einer Biographie*, Frankfurt and New York.

Pöggeler, O. (1990) *Der Denkweg Martin Heideggers*, Pfullingen (English translation, *Martin Heidegger's Path of Thinking*, trans. D. Magurshak and S. Barber, Atlantic Highlands, NJ: Humanities Press International, 1987).

Safranski, Rüdiger (1994) *Ein Meister aus Deutschland: Heidegger und seine Zeit*, Munich.

Stern, P. (trans.) (1986), *Self-consciousness and Self-determination*, Cambridge, Mass.: MIT Press (originally published as *Selbstbewusstsein und Selbstbestimmung*).

Tugendhat, E. (1970) *Der Wahrheitsbegriff bei Husserl und Heidegger*, Berlin, 1979.

Herrmann, F.-W. von (1985) *Subjekt und Dasein*, Frankfurt.

——(1987) *Hermeneutische Phänomenologie des Daseins*, Frankfurt.

For Heidegger there was only one question, *die Seinsfrage* (the question of being). While still at school he read **Brentano**'s *On the Manifold Meaning of Being according to Aristotle* and as a theology student he studied *On Being: An Outline of Ontology* by Carl Braig. At the same time he became acquainted with something called 'phenomenology' through the study of **Husserl**'s *Logical Investigations*, a work which exercised a fascination on him which was to remain for the rest of his life. He never accepted Husserl's phenomenology in its transcendental and idealistic form but in Husserl's early phenomenology he saw a way of *seeing* which could provide the method for ontology. Husserl's devastating critique of psychologistic accounts of logic was put to effective use in Heidegger's doctoral thesis on the theory of judgement. The influence of the early Husserl is still strong in Heidegger's habiltation thesis on Duns Scotus. In 1919 Heidegger became Husserl's assistant. Under the influence of Husserl, but also drawing on such figures as Kierkegaard and **Dilthey**, Heidegger began to develop his own brand of phenomenology which focuses on the facticity of lived existence rather than transcendental consciousness and its pure ego. This culminated in *Sein und Zeit* (in English, *Being and Time*), which appeared in 1927 and confirmed a reputation which Heidegger had already established through his teaching.

In the early 1930s, having previously been unpolitical, Heidegger began to be attracted by the National Socialist movement and its charismatic leader, Adolf Hitler. Like many German intellectuals of the time he saw in the movement a force for renewal and regeneration. This led him to accept the rectorship of his university, Freiburg, in April 1933 and shortly afterwards to join the Nazi Party. He was active in the Nazi cause for ten months, resigning the rectorship in February 1934 after it had become clear that he did not have the support needed to implement his romanticized and rather idiosyncratic version of Nazism. Although Heidegger certainly did some shameful things in the early days of the Third Reich it must also be acknowledged that he was deeply critical of what passed in Nazi circles for 'philosophy' (racism and biologism). In 1942 he resigned from the committee charged with editing the works of **Nietzsche** after the committee had been ordered to remove those passages in which Nietzsche speaks contemptuously of antisemitism. After the war Heidegger paid for what he called his *Dummheit* (stupidity or silliness) by being forbidden to teach. His fate was sealed by a damning report written on him by his former friend Karl **Jaspers** (although in 1933 Jaspers had been enthusiastic about

the content of Heidegger's rectoral speech). The rest of his life was like that of Kant: uneventful.

Heidegger's major work, (*Being and Time*) explicitly raises the question which had begun to exercise him even as a student: the question of the meaning or sense (*Sinn*) of being. The method of such ontology he calls phenomenology. In the formal sense this is simply adherence to the maxim made famous by Husserl and his followers: 'To the things themselves!' It is the letting be seen of that which shows itself. But as philosophy phenomenology is the letting be seen of what primarily and for the most part does not show itself, but which is the ground of what does show itself. The phenomenon of philosophical phenomenology is not this or that being or entity but the being of beings or entities (*das Sein des Seienden*). Being is that which determines entities as entities, that on the basis of which entities are always already understood. Understanding of being makes all comportment to entities—both those which I am not and that which I myself am—possible. Being (*Sein*) is not something laid up in some realm to which the phenomenologist has some mysterious access. It is what is understood in the always understanding of being which already belongs to the being of *Dasein* (Heidegger's term for the being which we ourselves are).

Consider the kind of being of the things with which we have-to-do, things which Heidegger calls *Zeug* (equipment). One gets clear about the mode of being of *Zeug* by making explicit, and conceptualizing, the understanding of being which is already implicit in our circumspective having-to-do-with things. We do not have to put ourselves into this mode of comportment; we are always already in it. Phenomenology, as the letting be seen of being, is the laying bare of the conditions of the possibility of entities showing themselves or of our comportment to entities.

Phenomenology, as understood by Heidegger, is phenomenology of *Dasein*. The absolute prerequisite for doing philosophy, in Heidegger's view, is recognition of what he calls the ontological difference (being is not a being). But *Dasein* is a being, so how can phenomenology which makes being thematic be phenomenology of *Dasein*? *Dasein* is a being, but not just *a* being, occurring among other beings. The being of *Dasein*, what Heidegger calls *existence*, is such that *Dasein* understands its own being, but in understanding its own being it at the same time understands the being of entities other than itself. Heidegger calls the understanding of being disclosedness (*Erschlossenheit*). The *Da* in *Da-sein* is disclosedness. *Dasein* is the clearing (*Lichtung*) which makes possible the openness of what is.

It is because *Dasein* is the ontological being that the posing and answering of the question of the meaning of being as such (*überhaupt*) requires an analysis of the fundamental structures of the being of *Dasein*. And this is largely what *Being and Time* provides.

Although *Being and Time* is a very large book it is only part of a much larger projected work. *Being and Time*, one might say, answers the question: how is comportment to entities possible? What makes comportment to entities possible is the understanding of being. But how is the understanding of being possible? The complete work was to have shown how *time* is the 'horizon' by reference to which being is understood. Heidegger's lectures of 1927, *Basic Problems of Phenomenology*, go some way to carrying out this task.

There are two ways of interpreting *Being and Time* which make it seem that there is a complete break between the phenomenological Heidegger and the later Heidegger who describes his philosophy as *Denken* (thought or thinking). According to the first interpretation Heidegger's phenomenology of *Dasein* is just a modification of Husserl's phenomenology of *consciousness*. Heidegger's *Dasein* is Husserl's consciousness or subject but with a practical twist (practical

engagement with things is given greater emphasis than mere perception). But as Heidegger sees it the move from consciousness to *Dasein* is much more radical than this. *Dasein* as the understanding, or disclosedness, of being makes possible *both* theoretical *and* practical modes of comportment to what is. According to the second interpretation Heidegger is an existentialist. It is true that *Being and Time* contains some brilliant analyses of such typically existentialist themes as *Angst*, guilt and death. But these are not examined for their own sake but rather for their specially disclosive function in relation to the being of *Dasein*. Their treatment is subservient to the question of the meaning of being as such.

But even when such misinterpretations have been put aside it can still be difficult to see the continuity between early and late Heidegger. The late Heidegger is still talking about being but in ways which make it more tempting for the English-speaker to write 'Being'. 'There is being only so long as *Dasein* is' ('Nur solange Dasein ist, gibt es Sein') he says in *Being and Time*. Being only 'is' in *Dasein*'s understanding of being. But understanding, it would seem, is something we do, so being is the product of human beings. In his later thought it is made clear that we stand in the truth of being. The truth (or unconcealedness) of being as the clearing (*Lichtung*) in which what is shows itself as what is is not in any sense something which we make or which is at our disposal. But although the truth of being is not at our disposal it is not an *eternal* truth. Heidegger speaks of *Seinsgeschichte*, the history of being. There is a necessity about the elements of this history but, unlike Hegel, Heidegger does not think in terms of an inevitable progression towards *the* truth of being. He does, however, talk as though there had been a falling away from a primordial experience of being had by the pre-Socratics. The truth of being which animates our own technology-dominated age is such that entities are experienced as material for use. Underlying such experience is the metaphysics of subjectivity according to which the being of what is is being an object (*Gegenstand*).

Presenting Heidegger in such abbreviated form inevitably makes him seem more abstract than he is. Although he thinks the question of being is *the* philosophical question this does not mean he talks about nothing else and that those who have difficulty with such talk will find nothing valuable in him. His essay on the work of art, for example, in which he overcomes the subjectivist view that the work of art is the object of 'aesthetic experience', but also the Hegelian view that it merely points to a truth which only philosophy can adequately express, has an immediacy and concreteness and wealth of insight which should impress anyone who approaches it in an unprejudiced way. And similar claims can be made for his essay on technology and some of his writings on language.

The same people who dismiss Heidegger as unintelligible sometimes, in contradictory fashion, deplore the extent of his influence. That he has been influential is undeniable. In philosophy **Sartre** would be unimaginable without Heidegger, and **Merleau-Ponty** clearly owes much to him (although perhaps more to Husserl). Philosophical hemeneutics (**Gadamer**) would not have been possible without Heidegger. But his influence has not been confined to philosophy. For example, a distinctive form of psychotherapy was developed under the influence of Heidegger's analysis of *Dasein* (Ludwig Binswanger). And in theology, both Protestant and Catholic, Heidegger's influence is unmistakable (e.g. Rudolf Bultmann, Paul **Tillich**, Karl Rahner). But these are just examples of direct influence. In more subtle ways his thought has had a profound impact in fields as diverse as literary theory, envionmental studies, social science and aesthetics.

PAUL GORNER

Hempel, Carl Gustav

German-American. *b:* 8 January 1905, Oranienburg, Germany. *Cat:* Philosopher of science. *Educ:* Göttingen, Heidelberg, Berlin and Vienna, originally Physics and Mathematics, then Philosophy (PhD, Berlin, 1934, with dissertation on 'Beiträge zur logischen Analyse des Wahrheitsbegriff', published in part at Jena, 1934); member of Berlin Gesellschaft für empirische (later: wissenschaftliche) Philosophie (allied to Vienna Circle); research with P. Oppenheim in Brussels and Carnap in Chicago, 1934–9. *Infls:* H. Behmann, Hilbert, P. Oppenheim, Shlick, Carnap, Reichenbach, R. A. Fisher, O. Helmer, Nicod, Goodman, Tarski, Grelling and Dray. *Appts:* Taught at City College, New York, 1939–40; Queen's College, Flushing, New York, 1940–8; Yale, 1948–55; Stuart Professor of Philosophy, Princeton, 1955–73; University Professor of Philosophy, Pittsburgh, 1977; Visiting Professor at Columbia, 1950, at Harvard, 1953–4, at Hebrew University in Jerusalem, 1974, at Berkeley, 1975 and 1977, and at Pittsburgh, 1976; President of APA (Eastern Division), 1961; Member of American Academy of Arts and Sciences; sometime Editor of *Erkenntnis*.

Main publications:

(1936) (with P. Oppenheim) *Der Typusbegriff im Lichte der neuen Logik*, Leiden: A. W. Sijthoff.
(1945) 'Studies in the logic of confirmation', *Mind* (reprinted with some changes and postscript in (1965).
(1952) *Fundamentals of Concept Formation in Empirical Science, Internat. Encyc. of Unified Science*, II, 7, Chicago: Chicago University Press (expanded in German translation, *Grundzüge der Begriffsbildung in der empirischen Wissenschaft*, Düsseldorf, 1934).
(1958) 'The theoretician's dilemma', in H. Feigl, M. Scriven and G. Maxwell (eds), *Minnesota Studies in the Philosophy of Science* II, Minneapolis: Minnesota University Press.
(1962) 'Deductive–nomological *vs.* statistical explanation', in H. Feigl and G. Maxwell

(eds), *Minnesota Studies in the Philosophy of Science III*, Minneapolis: Minnesota University Press.

(1963) (ed. with R. G. Colodny) *Frontiers of Science and Philosophy*, Pittsburgh, PA: Pittsburgh University Press.

(1965) *Aspects of Scientific Explanation and Other Essays in the Philosophy of Science*, New York: The Free Press and London: Collier-Macmillan (includes new title essay and eleven reprinted items, many revised and three with Postscripts; expanded and revised in German translation, *Aspekte der wissenschaftliche Erklärung*, Berlin and New York, 1972).

(1966) *Philosophy of Natural Science*, Englewood Cliffs, NJ: Prentice-Hall.

(1983) (ed. with H. Putnam and W. K. Essler) *Methodology, Epistemology, and Philosophy of Science: Essays in Honour of Wolfgang Stegmüller on the Occasion of his Sixtieth Birthday*, Dordrecht: Reidel (reprinted from *Erkenntnis* 19, 1–3, 1983).

Secondary literature:

Carnap, R. (1950) *Logical Foundations of Probability*, §87-8, Chicago: Chicago University Press.

Dray, W. H. (1957) *Laws and Explanation in History*, London: Oxford University Press.

Essler, W. K., Putnam, H. and Stegmüller, W. (eds) (1985) *Epistemology, Methodology, and Philosophy of Science: Essays in Honour of Carl G. Hempel on the Occasion of His Eightieth Birthday*, Dordrecht: Reidel (includes bibliography; reprinted from *Erkenntnis* 22, 1–3, 1985).

Gunnell, J. G. (1975) *Philosophy, Science, and Political Inquiry*, Morristown, NJ: General Learning Press.

Kyburg, H. E. and Nagel, E. (eds) (1963) *Induction: Some Current Issues*, Middletown, CT: Wesleyan University Press (discussions of Hempel and Carnap with replies).

Mandelbaum, M. (1984) *Philosophy, History, and the Sciences*, Baltimore, MD: Johns Hopkins University Press (especially chapter 7).

Rescher, N. (ed.) (1969) *Essays in Honour of Carl G. Hempel: A Tribute on the Occasion of his Sixty-Fifth Birthday*, Dordrecht: Reidel (includes biographical note, and bibliography).

Scheffler, I. (1963) *The Anatomy of Inquiry*, New York: Knopf; London: Routledge & Kegan Paul, 1964.

Hempel's early work primarily aims at analysing confirmation, considered purely as a 'classificatory' concept and postponing questions of degrees or numerical values. Assuming a universal hypothesis is confirmed by positive instances of it, he insists that whatever confirms a hypothesis must confirm all its logically equivalent formulations. A white shoe therefore (or, better (1965, p. 22), a sentence reporting an observation of one) confirms 'All ravens are black' because (being a non-black non-raven) it confirms 'All non-black things are non-ravens'. Hempel simply accepts this, adding that it sounds odd because we normally come to *know* things about the evidence in one order and not another. Not everyone is so sanguine, and this 'paradox of confirmation' has been extensively discussed (see, for example, Scheffler 1963). After adding some further requirements Hempel claims that, roughly, an observation statement confirms a hypothesis if it entails what the hypothesis would say if only the objects mentioned in the observation statement existed (1965, pp. 36–7); it shows that part of what the hypothesis says is indeed true (1966, p. 64). Confirmation so defined is purely syntactical, holding between sentences; but later, answering **Goodman**'s 'grue' paradox, he admits that confirmation must be partly pragmatic, involving restrictions on the kinds of predicates allowed (1965, pp. 50–1).

Hempel also discusses meaning, rejecting both verifiability and falsifiability as adequate criteria (and also **Popper**'s use of falsifiability to demarcate empirical science), and claims that cognitive significance is a matter of degree and no simple criterion can be given (ibid., p. 117). He also agreed with **Quine** in rejecting the analytic/synthetic distinction (1985, p. 1).

But Hempel's other main contribution that has proved controversial is his account of scientific explanation. He develops a 'covering-law model', where to explain something is basically to infer it from a law plus initial conditions. The law may be universal in form or merely statistical, the inference being deductive in the former case and usually (but not always) inductive in the latter. The laws must not be mere accidental generalizations, and explanation is not mere reduction to a familiar, though the inductive kind, unlike the deductive, is relative to the background of knowledge (1965, pp. 397–403). As with Braithwaite, the emphasis is on subsumption into a system. Hempel is concerned with an idealized sort of explanation (ibid., pp. 425–8), but controversy has mainly arisen over his claims to extend it over subjects like history and psychology (pp. 231–43, 463–87).

Sources: *PI;* Edwards; Mittelstrass; IDPP.

A. R. LACEY

Husserl, Edmund

German. *b:* 8 April 1859, Prossnitz, Moravia. *d:* 27 April 1938, Freiburg, Germany. *Cat:* Phenomenologist. *Ints:* Epistemology; ontology. *Educ:* Universities of Leipzig, Berlin, Vienna and Halle. *Infls:* Literary influences include Descartes, the British empricists and Kant; personal influences include Franz Brentano and Thomas Masaryk. *Appts:* 1891–1901, Privatdozent, University of Halle; 1906–16, Ordinarius, University of Göttingen; 1916–28, Professor, University of Freiburg.

Main publications:

(1900–1) *Logische Untersuchungen*, Halle (English translation, *Logical Investigations*, trans. J. N. Findlay, London: Routledge, 1970).
(1913) *Ideen zu einer reinen Phänomenologie und phänomenologischen Philosophie*, Tübingen (English translation, *Ideas Pertaining to a Pure Phenomenology and to a Phenomenological Philosophy, First Book*, trans. F. Kersten, Dordrecht: Kluwer, 1982).
(1928) *Phänomenologie des inneren Zeitbewusstseins*, Tübingen (English translation, *The Phenomenology of Internal Time-Consciousness*, trans. J. Churchill, Bloomington: Indiana University Press, 1964).

(1929) *Formale und transzendentale Logik*, Tübingen (English translation, *Formal and Transcendental Logic*, trans. D. Cairns, The Hague: Nijhoff, 1969).
(1950) *Cartesianische Meditationen*, The Hague (English translation, *Cartesian Mediations*, trans. D. Cairns, The Hague: Nijhoff, 1960).
(1954) *Die Krisis der europäischer Wissenschaften und die transzendentale Phänomenologie*, The Hague (English translation, *The Crisis of the European Sciences and Transcendental Phenomenology*, trans. D. Carr, Evanston: Northwestern University Press, 1970).

Secondary literature:

Dreyfus, H. (ed.) (1982) *Husserl, Intentionality and Cognitive Science*, Cambridge: Mass.: MIT Press.
Elliston, F. and McCormack, P. (1977) *Husserl: Expositions and Appraisals*, Notre Dame University Press.
Hammond, M., Howarth, J. and Keat, R. (1991) *Understanding Phenomenology*, Oxford: Blackwell, chapters 1–3.
Heidegger, M. (1985) *History of the Concept of Time*, trans. T. Kisiel, Bloomington: Indiana University Press, pp. 27–126.
Kern, I. (1964) *Husserl und Kant*, The Hague: Nijhoff.
Lauer, Q. (1958) *The Triumph of Subjectivity*, New York: Fordham University Press.
Mohanty, J. N. (1990) *Transcendental Phenomenology*, Oxford: Blackwell.
Smith, D. W. and McIntyre, R. (1982) *Husserl and Intentionality*, Dordrecht: Reidel.

Edmund Husserl, the founder of phenomenology, first came to prominence through the publication of his *Logical Investigations* (1900–1). It was on the basis of this book that the phenomenological movement was formed. The early phenomenologists were most impressed by the call to a return to the things themselves ('Zu den Sachen selbst!') in the sense of giving precedence to how things (material objects but also numbers, institutions, works of art, persons, etc.) present themselves in actual experience over the dictates of some theory or system as to how they must be. Such philosophers were strongly influenced by Husserl's arguments against psychologism, were profoundly realist in outlook and generally exhibited a marked anti-Kantian tendency. It therefore came as something of a shock when Husserl published his next main work, *Ideas Pertaining to a Pure Phenomenology and to a Phenomenological Philosophy* (1913). For this seemed to represent a reversal of all that phenomenology had come to stand for. It was not the idea of arriving at pure consciousness by a process of reduction which was found objectionable. Nor was it the idea of intuiting and describing the essential structures of such consciousness (for according to the phenomenologists everything has its essence). Rather what was found objectionable was the idea that everything else is *constituted* in pure consciousness. This seemed like a capitulation to the neo-Kantians. Thereafter it was no longer possible to speak of a Husserlian school. Husserl himself would continue to insist that the reluctance to follow him in the transcendental direction laid down in his *Ideas* was based on a failure properly to understand the nature of his trancendentalism. In 1916 he moved to Freiburg, where three years later Martin **Heidegger** became his assistant. Husserl had great hopes for Heidegger, seeing in him someone of matchless ability who would continue to develop phenomenology along the lines he, Husserl, had laid down. Although not mistaken about Heidegger's ability, he was mistaken about his identification which his conception of phenomenology. The publication in 1927 of *Being and Time*, and Heidegger's succession to Husserl's Chair a year later, served only to accelerate a process which had been underway for some years: the emergence of Heideggerian phenomenology as the dominant force in German philosophy. As Husserl was Jewish the advent of National Socialism resulted in even greater isolation. But then Husserl always thought of genuine philosophy as an essentially lonely task. He continued to be creative, producing in the last years of his life his monumental *Crisis of the European Sciences* (1954).

In attempting to convey the essential character of Husserl's phenomenology it is perhaps best to begin with the notion of the intentionality of consciousness. Consciousness in its various modes has the property of being 'of' something or being directed towards something. For example, in thinking something is thought about, in perception something is perceived, in imagining something is imagined, in fear something is feared. Husserl calls these various modes of consciousness intentional experiences or acts. Unlike his teacher **Brentano** he does not regard the object of consciousness as being in all cases an inner mental entity. When I think about a mental image my consciousness is directed towards a mental entity. But when, for example, I see this book on my desk this intentional experience, the seeing, is directed towards a material object. What I am concious of is not an inner mental picture of a book but, precisely, a book. Even when I merely imagine a book it is not the case that my consciousness is directed towards a mental image. Each intentional experience, and not just those which essentially involve the use of language, contains something Husserl calls a sense or meaning (*Sinn*), and it is this which is responsible for the experience's directedness towards its object.

Intentionality is not a property which consciousness just happens to have. Without it consciousness would not be consciousness. It belongs to the *essence* of consciousness. The various modes of consciousness, as well as having the fundamental essential feature of intentionality, also have more specific essential features: for example, perception essentially involves sensation. The sense or meaning of the experience 'animates' sensation in such a way that it becomes an appearance of an object. In perception the object perspectivally adumbrates itself (*schattet sich ab*). The perceptually presented front-side of the object refers beyond itself to the unseen rear-side.

Normally consciousness is directed towards some item in the world and normally this item is regarded as really existing and as really possessing such and such properties. But whether or not the object of consciousness in fact exists, and whether or not it possesses the properties it is intended as having, this mode of consciousness, with this object, exists and can be described by the subject whose consciousness it is. It is possible to describe intentional experiences independently of the question of the real existence and real being-thus of their object. Moreover it is possible to describe the essence of such experiences, the features and structures without which they would not be the experiences they are.

However, even if we disregard the question of the reality of the object of an experience we still regard the experience itself as an event in the world, as belonging to a psycho-physical reality, the human being, which is one item among others in the world. And even when we disregard the question of the reality of a particular object we still take for granted the existence of the world as a whole. This taking-for-granted, which Husserl calls the general thesis of the natural attitude, can be suspended or 'put out of action' in an operation which he calls the transcendental reduction. Consciousness on which this operation has been carried out is not itself an item *in* the world but rather that *for which* there is a world. Phenomenology as the mature Husserl understands it is the description of the essential structures of this transcendental consciousness or subjectivity. These structures are not inferred by any kind of Kantian transcendental argument but are 'seen' by the phenomenological 'observer' in the phenomenological, as opposed to the natural, attitude.

Anything, of whatever ontological type, can be an object of consciousness. In the case of each type of entity phenomenology describes the structures of consciousness *of* such an entity. This includes a description of the entity itself but as object of consciousness, i.e. as phenomenon. In abstraction

from questions of real existence and real nature one considers the entity simply as it shows itself to consciousness. Phenomenology also describes the world, as the universal horizon of all that shows itself. The world is not just the totality of objects of consciousness, not just one great big object, but that from within which entities show themselves.

What is the purpose of such description? It is supposed by Husserl to yield ultimate understanding of things. To describe the structures of transcendental consciousness in which something becomes an object of consciousness is to describe the 'constitution' of that thing. The world and everything in it, including human beings, is constituted in transcendental subjectivity. As Husserl uses the term, 'constitution' suggests a kind of making, a bringing into being. It was in this 'creationist' sense that Husserl's transcendental idealism was generally understood—and generally rejected. However, it has recently been argued that such an interpretation is mistaken. What is constituted in consciousness is not things but senses, not the things that consciousness intends but the senses 'through' which it intends them.

In the final phase of his phenomenology Husserl introduces the notion of the lifeworld (*Lebenswelt*), the world of lived experience. What he calls objectivism seeks to eliminate everything subjective from our representation of the world by allowing as real only those aspects of experience which can be represented by means of the concepts of the mathematical natural sciences. Such objectivism dismisses the lifeworld as mere appearance. But this is to call in question the lifeworld from ths standpoint of what is itself a construction formed on the basis of the lifeworld. The properties and structures attributed by the objectifying sciences to the 'objective' world are themselves the product of a process of idealization and mathematization of 'lifeworldly' structures. The task of philosophy is not to downgrade the lifeworld but to remove from it the 'garment of ideas' which science has thrown over it. However, Husserl's emphasis on the lifeworld in his later philosophy does not represent a fundamental change in his conception of phenomenology as transcendental phenomenology. The lifeworld does not represent the ultimate foundation, for it is itself constituted in transcendental subjectivity.

PAUL GORNER

Ingarden, Roman

Polish. *b:* 5 February 1893, Cracow, Poland. *d:* 14 June 1970, Poronin, near Cracow. *Cat:* Phenomenological philosopher; realist. *Ints:* Ontology, epistemology and philosophy of aesthetics; major contributor to the realism/idealism debate. *Educ:* 1912–17, studied in Germany under Edmund Husserl, first at the University of Göttingen (from 1912) and then at the University of Freiburg im Breisgau (from 1916). *Infls:* Bergson and Husserl. *Appts:* 1924, Privatdozent (unsalaried lecturer), John Casimir University of Lvov (Lemberg) in Poland; 1933, Associate Professor; 1935, Full Professor; 1945–63, Professor, Jagiellonian University, Cracow (from 1949–56, during the Stalinist period, he was forbidden to teach and instead was attached to the Academy of Sciences and Letters where his duties left him considerable free time for his own researches); from 1963, Emeritus Professor at the University of Cracow, and Honorary Professor of the University of Lvov.

Main publications:

(1921) 'Über die Gefahr einer Petitio Principii in der Erkenntnistheorie' [On the danger of a petitio principii in the theory of knowledge], *Jahrbuch für Philosophie und Phänomelogische Forschung* 4: 545–68.
(1922) 'Intuition und Intellekt bei Henri Bergson' [Intuition and intellect by Henri Bergson], *Jahrbuch für Philosophie und Phänomelogische Forschung* 5: 286–461.
(1925) 'Essentiale Fragen. Ein Beitrag zum Problem des Wesens' [Essential questions. A contribution to the problem of essence], Halle an der Saale: Max Niemeyer.
(1925) *Über die Stellung der Erkenntnistheorie im System der Philosophie* [On the Position of Theory of Knowledge in the System of Philosophy], *Jahrbuch für Philosophie und Phänomelogische Forschung* 7.
(1929) 'Bemerkungen zum Problem "Idealismus–Realismus"' [Remarks on the problem 'idealism-realism'], *Jahrbuch für Philosophie und Phänomelogische Forschung* 10.
(1931) *Das literarische Kunstwerk* (original in German), Halle an der Saale: Max Niemeyer (English translation, *The Literary Work of Art*, trans. George G. Grabowicz, Evanston Ill.: Northwest University Press, 1973).
(1937) *The Cognition of the Literary Work of Art* (original in Polish; German translation 1968, English translation, Evanston, Ill.: Northwestern University Press, 1973).
(1946) *O budowie obrazu* [On the Structure of Painting], Cracow: Polish Academy of Sciences.
(1947) *Szkize z filozofii literatury* [Essays on the Philosophical Literature], Lodz.
(1947–8) *Spór o istnienia świata* 2 vols [The Controversy about the Existence of the World] (German translation, 1964/65/74), Cracow: Polish Academy of Sciences.
(1958) *Studia z estetyki* [Studies on Aesthetics] 2 vols, vol. 3, Warsaw: PWN, 1970; reviewed in *Journal of Aesthetics and Art Criticism* (1959) 17 by A.-T. Tymieniecka.
(1962) *Untersuchungen zur Ontologie der Kunst, Musikwerk, Bild, Architektur, Film* [Investigations on the Ontology of Art, Music Work, Pictures, Architecture and Film], Tübingen: Niemeyer.
(1963) *On the Motives which Led Husserl to Transcendental Idealism* (English translation, Dordrecht: Kluwer, 1973–5).
(1966) *Przezycie-dzielo-wartosc* [Experience of Artwork and Value], Cracow: Polish Academy of Sciences. (German translation, 1969).
(1971) *U podstaw teorii poznania* [At the Foundation of the Theory of Knowledge], Cracow: Polish Academy of Sciences.
(1974) *Wstep do fenomenologii Husserla* [Introduction to the Phenomenology of Husserl], Warsaw: PWN.
(1984) *Man and Value*, Washington: Catholic University Press.
(1985) *Roman Ingarden: Selected Papers in Aesthetics*, ed. P. J. McCorkick, Munich: Philoso-

phia, and Washington: Catholic University Press.

(1986) *The Work of Music and the Problem of its Identity*, trans. A. Czerniawski, ed. Jean G. Harrell, Berkeley: University of California Press.

(1986) *Ontology of the Work of Art*, Ohio University Press.

Secondary literature:

'Bibliografia Praz Filosoficznych Romana Ingarden, 1915–1965, Odbitka z Ksiazki R. Ingarden', *Studi z estetyki* T. II, 495–527.

Dzmiemidok, B. and McCormick, P. (eds) (1989) *The Aesthetics of Roman Ingarden: Interpretations and Assessments*, Dordrecht: Kluwer.

Mays, W. *et al.* (eds) *Journal of the British Society for Phenomenology* 6, 2, May (Ingarden issue).

Tymieniecka, A.-T. (1955) 'Le Dessein de la philosophie de Roman Ingarden', in *Revue de Métaphysique et de Morale*: 32–57.

——(1957) *Essence et existence. Étude à propos de la philosophie de Roman Ingarden et Nicolai Hartmann*, Paris.

——(ed.) (1976) *Analecta Husserliana*, vol. 4; 'Ingardeniana', Dordrecht: D. Reidel.

Van Breda, H. L. (1970) 'Professor Roman Ingarden', Obituary, *The Journal of the British Society for Phenomenology* I, 3, October: 100.

Although Ingarden is perhaps best known to English speakers for his philosophy of aesthetics, this needs to be seen within the perspective of his lifelong concern with the problems of epistemology and ontology. In his dissertation on **Bergson**, for example, he interprets such Bergsonian themes as the flux of consciousness and its immediate givens in the light of the phenomenologically based epistemological framework of consciousness, content of consciousness and object of consciousness. His 'Essentiale Fragen' (1925) is likewise a work in which he is concerned to delimit the field of phenomenology by a systematic demonstration of the existence of such objective essences as are implied by 'essential questions' of the type '*What* is x?'. Gilbert **Ryle** reviewed this work sympathetically in *Mind* 36 (1927), although he pointed out that Ingarden admits to being unable to solve the old problem of how an *infima species* (individual essence) can realise itself in concrete individuals.

The alien, neo-Kantian climate of Freiburg brought Ingarden and **Husserl** very close together and, although Ingarden returned to Poland at the end of the First World War and did not see Husserl again until 1927, the two philosophers remained lifelong friends and correspondents. Ingarden perhaps kept in closer touch with Husserl's developing thought than any other of the latter's Göttingen students, but it was always the *objects* of consciousness which preoccupied him and not, as it came to be with Husserl, the intentional analysis of consciousness itself. In his 'Bemerkungen zum Problem "Idealismus–Realismus"' (1929) Ingarden's argument is that it is necessary first to investigate the mode of being of objects before drawing conclusions about their relationship to, and possible dependency upon, consciousness .

Perhaps Ingarden's most original phenomenological work has been in the analysis of various works of art, beginning with his book *The Literary Work of Art* (1931) where, utilizing a theory developed by Alexander Pfänder on the basis of suggestions by Husserl, he first discloses the various strata of intentional constituents which interact to form the 'harmonious polyphony' of each art work. However, Ingarden's interest in the philosophy of art arose out of his concern with the ontological problem of idealism–realism, and *The Literary Work of Art* is actually subtitled *An Investigation on the Borderlines of Ontology, Logic and Theory of Literature*. Ingarden's ontological position in this work is that, since works of art are created by human subjects, they are—and may be perceived to be—ontically *heteronomous* (or dependent) objects. In contradistinction, real objects and the objects of mathematics do not depend upon consciousness. They are self-sufficient or ontically *autonomous*.

Ingarden's *chef-d'oeuvre* is almost certainly his massive, three-volume *Spór o istnienia świata* [The Controversy About the Existence of the World]. Volume I, 'Existential ontology', concerns the modal analysis of real, ideal and possible being. Volume II, 'Formal ontology', has two parts. Part II/1 is called 'Form and Essence' and Part II/2 'World and Consciousness'. These first two volumes are reviewed by Anna-Teresa Tymieniecka in *Mind* 56 (1957). He did not live to complete the culminating Volume III, 'Material ontology', but in 1974 a contribution to it was published posthumously in German called 'On the causal structure of the real world'. The full import of these remarkable volumes has yet to be assessed, but it is clear that Ingarden has done much work towards an ontology based on what is given to consciousness which avoids any recourse to transcendental idealism.

BARRY JONES

Irigaray, Luce

Belgian with French nationality. *b:* Either 1930 or 1932, Blaton, Belgium. *Cat:* Feminist philosopher; psychoanalyst. *Educ:* University of Louvain, the University of Paris and the Paris Institute of Psychology; trained as a psychoanalyst with the École Freudienne de Paris. *Infls:* Freud, Lacan, Derrida, Hegel, Nietzsche and Heidegger. *Appts:* Taught sixth-formers in Belgium, 1956–9; attached to the Centre National de Recherches Scientifiques in Paris since 1964; Lecturer, University of Paris VIII (Vincennes) 1969–74; Lecturer, École des Hautes Études en Sciences Sociales, since 1985; attached to the International College of Philosophy in Paris since 1987.

Main publications:

(1973) *Le Langage des déments*, Paris: Mouton.

(1974) *Speculum of the Other Woman*; Ithaca, NY: Cornell University Press, 1985.
(1977) *This Sex Which Is Not One*; Ithaca, NY: Cornell University Press, 1985.
(1980) *Marine Lover of Friedrich Nietzsche*; Columbia University Press, 1991.
(1981) *Le Corps-à-corps avec la mère*, Éditions de la pleine lune.
(1982) *Elemental Passions*, Athlone.
(1983) *L'Oubli de l'air. Chez Martin Heidegger*, Minuit.
(1984) *An Ethics of Sexual Difference*; Ithaca, NY: Cornell University Press, 1993.
(1985) *Parler n'est jamais neutre*, Minuit.
(1987) *Sexes and Genealogies*; Columbia University Press, 1993.
(1989) *Thinming the Difference: For a Peaceful Revolution*; Athlone, 1994.
(1990) *Je, Tu, Nous: Towards a Culture of Difference*; Routledge, 1993.
(1991) *The Irigaray Reader*, ed. Margaret Whitford, Oxford: Blackwell (provides a selection of extracts).
(1992) *J'aime à toi*, Grasset.
(1994) *Essere due*, Editore Bollati Boringhieri.
(1994) *La Democrazia comincia a due*, Editore Bollati Boringhieri.

Secondary literature:

Burke, Carolyn, Schor, Naomi and Whitford, Margaret (eds) (1994) *Engaging with Irigaray*, Columbia University Press (includes a wide range of critical accounts).
Grosz, Elizabeth (1989) *Sexual Subversions*, Sydney: Allen & Unwin, chapters 4 and 5.
Whitford, Margaret (1991) *Luce Irigaray: Philosophy in the Feminine*, Routledge (includes an ample bibliography of primary and secondary texts).

Irigaray was initially attracted to literature, writing her master's thesis on the poet Paul Valéry, whose work privileges consciousness and reflexivity. It was not until she left Belgium for Paris, where she undertook a diploma in psychopathology and began training as a psychoanalyst, that she turned her attention to the unconscious, and in particular to the notion of a cultural unconscious (or cultural 'imaginary' as it has come to be called). She was analysed by Serge Leclaire, one of the original members of **Lacan**'s École Freudienne, and until the publication of *Speculum* in 1974 seems to have been uncontroversially Lacanian.

Speculum fused a psychoanalytic attention to what is repressed by culture with a Derridean-inspired account of the repressions required by metaphysics. In both cases, Irigaray argues, the feminine is excluded. She concludes that 'woman' does not yet exist in the cultural imaginary of the West; that Western culture is founded on an originary matricide more ancient than the parricide of **Freud**'s *Totem and Taboo*. The feminist critique contained in *Speculum* led to Irigaray's expulsion from the Lacanian School of Psychoanalysis at Vincennes and launched her on her public career as feminist and philosopher of sexual difference.

Her subsequent work has explored the question of sexual difference in three areas in particular. First, she has looked for the forgotten woman in the history of philosophy; second, she has examined the sexual bias in language; third, she has considered the issues of women's civil status and rights. Along with Hélène Cixous and Julia **Kristeva**, Irigaray is probably one of the best-known representatives of French feminism in Europe, the USA and Australasia. Her international reputation, however, is often based on a misapprehension of her thought. She has been well understood and influential in countries like Holland and Italy which have a strong tradition in continental philosophy, but has so far had no significant effect on philosophy in Britain, where her work has been appreciated predominantly by literary critics.

Sources: CV supplied by Luce Irigaray.

MARGARET WHITFORD

James, William

American. *b:* 1 January 1842, New York City. *d:* 26 August 1910, Chocorua, New Hampshire. *Cat:* Psychologist; pragmatist. *Ints:* Philosophy of religion. *Educ:* University of Geneva, 1859–60; Harvard University, 1861–7; University of Berlin, 1867–8; Harvard University, 1868–9, MD 1869. *Infls:* Renouvier and Peirce. *Appts:* 1872–80, Instructor, 1880–5, Assistant Professor, 1885–1907, Professor of Psychology and Philosophy, Harvard University.

Main publications:

(1975–90) *The Works of William James*, ed. F. H. Burkhardt, F. Bowers and I. K. Skrupselis, 21 vols, Cambridge, Mass.: Harvard University Press (cited below as *WWJ*).

(1890) *The Principles of Psychology*, 2 vols, New York: Henry Holt; reprinted in 3 vols in *WWJ*, 1981.

(1892) *Psychology, Briefer Course*, New York: Henry Holt; reprinted in *WWJ*, 1984.

(1897) *The Will to Believe and Other Essays*, New York: Longmans, Green & Co.; reprinted in *WWJ*, 1979.

(1898) *Human Immortality: Two Supposed Objections*; second edition, Boston: Houghton Mifflin, 1899; reprinted in *WWJ*, 1986.

(1899) *Talks to Teachers on Psychology: and to Students on Some of Life's Ideals*, New York: Henry Holt & Company; reprinted in *WWJ*, 1983.

(1903) *The Varieties of Religious Experience: A Study of Human Behaviour*, New York: Longmans, Green & Co.; reprinted in *WWJ*, 1985.

(1907) *Pragmatism*, New York: Longmans, Green & Co.; reprinted in *WWJ*, 1975.

(1909) *The Meaning of Truth: A Sequel to 'Pragmatism'*, New York: Longmans, Green & Co.; reprinted in *WWJ*, 1975.

(1909) *A Pluralistic Universe*, New York: Longmans, Green & Co.; reprinted in *WWJ*, 1975.

(1911) *Some Problems of Philosophy: A Beginning of an Introduction to Philosophy*, prepared for press by H. M. Kallen and edited by H. James, Jr, New York: Longmans, Green & Co.; reprinted in *WWJ*, 1979.

(1912) *Essays in Radical Empiricism*, ed. R. B. Perry, New York: Longmans, Green & Co.; reprinted in *WWJ*, 1979.

Secondary literature:

Allen, G. W. (1967) *William James: A Biography*, New York: Viking.

Myers, G. E. (1987) *William James: His Life and Thought*, New Haven: Yale University Press.

Perry, R. B. (1935) *The Thought and Character of William James*, 2 vols, Boston: Little, Brown.

Reck, A. J. (1967) *Introduction to William James*, Bloomington: Indiana University Press.

Seigfried, C. H. (1990) *William James's Radical Reconstruction of Philosophy*, Albany: SUNY Press.

William James was the son of Henry, an eminent transcendentalist writer and lecturer, and the younger brother of Henry, the famous novelist. Educated informally in Europe as a child, and after a brief period in Newport, Rhode Island, preparing to become a portrait artist, James enrolled in Harvard. He interrupted his formal education to participate in the scientific expedition to the Amazon led by Louis Agassiz and also to study in Europe. Hobbled by poor health and psychological depression in his youth, James credited the writings of the French philosopher Charles Renouvier for releasing him from depression by providing the formula of choosing or willing to be free. In 1876 he established one of the first psychology laboratories in the United States at Harvard. His comprehensive work *The Principles of Psychology* (1890) won him international fame. In the Preface James announced the intention of establishing psychology as a natural science. Incorporating the findings and theories of the experimental psychologists, primarily German, the *Principles* also drew upon the entire history of introspective psychology, primarily British. Thus James's psychology contains two strands. One is based in biology, revolutionized by Darwinian evolution; it is amenable to experimental investigations of physiology and behaviour. Consciousness is conceived to be a function of the biological organism dependent on the brain, instrumental to the organism's coping with its environment and struggling to realize its purposes. The other strand, based on the introspective method, renovated associationist psychology by describing consciousness as a stream of feelings and ideas. The 'stream of consciousness' concept spread to literature, manifest in the writings, for example, of Gertrude Stein, who had been James's student. In psychology James's influence was profound; it promoted the establishment of experimental methods. In philosophy it influenced **Dewey**'s shift from Hegelianism to instrumentalism and contributed to **Husserl** some of the terminology and insights for phenomenology. James's interest in philosophy preceded and paralleled his interest in psychology. His earliest papers discussed the sentiment of rationality, the dilemma of determinism, the moral philosopher and the moral life. In 'The will to believe' (in 1897) James argued for the right to hold religious and moral beliefs even when logical or factual evidence is unavailable. If the option for belief in an hypothesis is live, forced and momentous—that is, if believing it will make a major difference in life—then, assuming it is compatible with logic and the facts, our passional, volitional nature should seize belief despite the absence of evidence. Religious belief, James contended, contains two propositions: (i) that God guarantees the everlastingness of ideals and values cherished by humans; and (ii) that the belief in (i) encourages humans to make a better world, enhancing the survival and triumph of these ideals and values. James's interest in religion was long-standing. In filial devotion to his father's memory James had edited, with a long introductory essay, *The Literary Remains of the Late Henry James* (Boston: James R. Osgood & Company, 1885). But where the father philosophized, drawing upon transcendentalism and Swedenborg's mystical theology, the son psychologized, relying on empirical reports and case studies. On the one hand James lent his name to psychical research and the investigation of occult phenomena, falling into the embrace of the spiritualists while reaping the scorn of the professional psychologists. On the other hand he produced one of the greatest works on the psychology of religion, *The Varieties of Religious Experience* (1903). Based on his Gifford Lectures at Edinburgh, James's

Varieties examines religion as it occurs in individual cases of experience. Religion is treated as distinctively individual, not social or institutional. James's typology of religious experience—for example, 'the healthy-minded', 'the sick soul'—has persisted, but his theory of the common structure of all religious experience remains sketchy. The structural dynamics characteristic of religious experience involves initially a psychological state in which a need is felt; second, a step into a deeper level of consciousness, itself connected to a cosmic consciousness; and, finally, reparation of the initial state by re-energizing the individual.

In 1898, in his address, 'Philosophical conceptions and practical results', delivered before the Philosophical Union at the University of California in Berkeley, James used the term 'pragmatism', which he attributed to Charles **Peirce**, to designate his philosophy. It stressed action as the goal of thought and clarified concepts in terms of their practical effects. Thus James unleashed pragmatism to the world. Affiliated with a host of thinkers in America and Europe—Ostwald in Berlin, Papini in Rome, F. C. S. Schiller at Oxford, **Bergson** in Paris and Dewey in Chicago—James's pragmatism, to Peirce's consternation, was also allied with such currents of thought as positivism, utilitarianism, nominalism and anti-intellectualism. James dedicated his book *Pragmatism* to J. S. Mill, claiming that it applied to the concept of truth the principle of utility that Mill had used in the analysis of the good. Pragmatism for James was both a method for settling metaphysical disputes and a theory of truth. As a method pragmatism prescribed that rival metaphysical theories be evaluated by reference to the differences they make in the lives of those who hold them. If there are no differences then the controversies over the theories are fruitless. The pragmatist conception of truth is dynamic: it maintains that the truth of a proposition consists in the successful consequences of holding it. James's theory of truth immediately aroused criticisms, and his replies to his critics, along with other essays on the topic, were collected in *The Meaning of Truth* (1909). James also espoused radical empiricism. In contrast to traditional empiricism, radical empiricism found that relations are as immediately given in experience as qualities; this James considered to be a matter of fact. In addition, it postulates methodologically that nothing be admitted as a fact except what some experient can experience at some time. Further, it is the generalized conclusion that the parts of experience hang together by means of experienced relations without resort to any trans-empirical principle. Just as James's pragmatism has had a profound impact on American philosophy, especially in the instrumentalism of John Dewey, his radical empiricism contributed to the rise of new realism and subsequently to logical empiricism. James's endeavour to articulate the metaphysics suggested by the generalization of radical empiricism finds expression in the last book he published during this lifetime, *A Pluralistic Universe* (1909). Based on his Hibbert Lectures at Oxford, this work offers a sustained criticism of absolute idealism and intellectualism, and finds in the works of Bergson and Peirce the hope of a temporalist metaphysics of change, chance and pluralism. James had intended to formulate this metaphysics in a comprehensive work comparable to his *Principles of Psychology*. Although James discernibly anticipated the rise of process philosophy, death cut his efforts short. His unfinished manuscript was published posthumously under the title *Some Problems of Philosophy* (1911).

Sources: EAB: Edwards; H. James (ed.) (1920) *Letters of William James*, 2 vols, Boston: Atlantic Monthly Press; DAB.

ANDREW RECK

Jaspers, Karl

German. *b:* 23 February 1883, Oldenburg,

Germany. *d:* 26 February 1969, Basle, Switzerland. *Cat:* Existentialist; psychologist; philosopher; historian of philosophy. *Ints:* History of philosophy. *Educ:* Studied medicine, Universities of Berlin, Göttingen and Heidelberg (1902–8). *Infls:* Literary influences: Kant, Hegel, Kierkegaard, Nietzsche, Plotinus, Bruno, Spinoza and Schelling. Personal influences: Max Weber and Heidegger. *Appts:* Independent Assistant, Heidelberg Psychiatric Clinic, 1908–15; (1909–20); University of Heidelberg, Psychology (1915–19), then in Philosophy, initially as *Extraordinarius* (1919–21) and then as *Ordinarius* (1921–37 and 1945–8).

Main publications:

(1913) *Allgemeine Psychopathologie*, Berlin: J. Springer (English translation, *General Psychopathology*, trans. J. Hoenig and M. W. Hamilton, Manchester: Manchester University Press, 1962).

(1914) *Psychologie der Weltanschauungen*, Berlin: J. Springer.

(1932) *Philosophie*, 3 vols, Berlin: J. Springer (English translation, *Philosophy*, trans. E. B. Ashton, 3 vols, Chicago: Chicago University Press, 1969–71).

(1935) *Vernunft und Existenz*, Groningen: J. W. Wolters (English translation, *Reason and Existenz*, trans. W. Earle, London: Routledge & Kegan Paul, 1956).

(1947) *Von der Wahrheit*, Munich: R. Piper.

(1949) *Vom Ursprung und Ziel der Geschichte*, Zurich: Artemis and Munich: R. Piper (English translation, *The Origin and Goal of History*, trans. M. Bullock, New Haven: Yale University Press, 1953).

(1957) *Philosophical Autobiography*, in Schilpp (revised and enlarged, 1981); also in Piper (ed.) 1967.

(1962) *Der philosophische Glaube angesichts der Offenbarung*, Munich: R. Piper (English translation, *Philosophical Faith and Revelation*, trans. E. B. Ashton, New York: Harper & Row, 1967).

(1967) *Karl Jaspers: Schicksal und Wille. Autobiographische Schriften*, ed. H. Saner, Munich: R. Piper.

Secondary literature:

Ehrlich, L. H. (1975) *Karl Jaspers: Philosophy as Faith*, Amherst, Mass.: University of Massachusetts Press.

——and Wisser, R. (eds) (1988) *Karl Jaspers Today: Philosophy at the Threshold of the Future*, Washington: University Press of America.

Gefken, G. and Kunert, K. (1978) *Karl Jaspers. Eine Bibliographie*, Oldenburg.

Olson, A. M. (1979) *Transcendence and Hermeneutics: An Interpretation of the Philosophy of Karl Jaspers*, Amsterdam: Kluwer Academic.

Piper, K. (ed.) (1967) *Karl Jaspers. Werk und Wirkung*, Munich: R. Piper.

Samay, S. (1971) *Reason Revisited: The Philosophy of Karl Jaspers*, Notre Dame, Ind.: Gill & Macmillan.

Saner, H. (1970) *Karl Jaspers in Selbstzeugnissen und Bilddokumenten*, Hamburg: Rowohlt.

Schilpp, P. A. (ed.) (1957) *The Philosophy of Karl Jaspers*, New York: Tudor Publishing; second edition, 1981.

Schragg, O. O. (1971) *Existence, Existenz, and Transcendence: An Introduction to the Philosophy of Karl Jaspers*, Pittsburg, PA: Duquesne University Press and Louvain: Editions E. Nauwelaerts.

Wallraff, C. F. (1970) *Karl Jaspers. An Introduction to his Philosophy*, Princeton, NJ: Princeton University Press.

The prewar years were for Jaspers dominated by his friendship with **Heidegger** during 1920–33 and the publication of his chief philosophical work, *Philosophie* (1932). The war years were spent, stripped of his Chair and silenced by the authorities, in Heidelberg with his Jewish wife, working on his second most important philosophical work, *Von der Wahrheit* (1947). At the end of the war Japsers was restored to his Chair but he declined the Rectorship of the University, although he was actively involved in its reform. In 1948 he left Germany to take up the Chair of Philosophy at the University of Basle, where he spent the rest of his life, continuing to publish prolifically, both on philosophy and, controversially, on sensitive issues of postwar German politics.

Jaspers's earliest major work, his *Allgemeine Psychopathologie* (1913), while containing a classification of psychological abnormalities and diagnostic techniques, foreshadows his later philosophical preoccupations in its concern to formulate a methodology for psychiatric medicine suitable for its 'object', a suffering human being. Fundamental to Jaspers's approach is the adoption of a phenomenological method and the deployment of a distinction, deriving from Dilthey and Max Weber, between causal-explanatory methods (*erklären*) and a method involving an intuitive-sympathetic understanding of the 'patient' as a living whole (*verstehen*). Hence Jaspers's emphasis on biography or 'pathography'. His classic study established the methodology of a phenomenological and existential psychiatric medicine.

His two chief philosophical works are *Philosophie* (1931) and *Von der Wahrheit* (1947). The central theme of his thought may be described as the finitude of human existence and the limits of human experience. Jaspers contrasts the truths of philosophy with those of science and religion. The truths of philosophy are forms of *faith*; the truths of natural science are alone objectively true, and are characterized by their 'compelling certainty' and their 'universal validity'; the truths of religion are symbolic, forms of *chiffre*. Philosophy has many possible starting-points; the starting-point of Jaspers's own philosophy is the ultimate experience of knowing (*erkennen*), and the fundamental question arising therefrom: How does Being manifest itself?

All knowing is referential and intentional. As such it involves the fissuring of subject and object (*die Subjekt–Objekt-Spaltung*). This fissure is the *locus* of all beings, all objects, all knowing. It both marks the limits of objectivity and points beyond itself to the transcendent, to the Unfissured (*das Ungespaltene*), the Encompassing (*das Umgreifende*). Jaspers distinguishes two senses of this last term: (i) the Encompassing as such (*das Umgreifende schlechthin*) or Being in itself (*das Sein an sich*); (ii) the Encompassing which we ourselves are (*das Umgreifende,*

das wir selbst sind), this latter splintering into a diversity of the ways in which we are (as existence (*Dasein*), existenz (*Existenz*), understanding, reason, consciousness).

The Encompassing as such transcends the subject–object fissure, and is thus not a possible object of knowledge. Being in itself is absolutely inaccessible to thought; ontology is, accordingly, impossible. Only the modes of Being (*die Weisen des Seins*), which mark the limits and the horizon of our experience, can be illuminated (*erhellt*) and clarified (*geklärt*) but not explained (*erklärt*). Such 'illumination' (*Erhellung*) is contrasted with ontology—a project doomed to failure (*scheitern*) and called 'periechontology' (*Periechontologie*).

Although Being as such is inaccessible to thought, we, as conscious beings, enjoy a kind of immediate access to our own lived and experienced Being, the Being of possibilities. Although not capable of conceptual (categorial) articulation or expression, our Being (*Existenz*) can be illuminated by means of tokens (*signa*). Jaspers, in his 'illumination' of our Being or Existenz (*Existenzerhellung*) distinguishes three such *signa*: (i) *Freedom*, the Being of possibilities of Being, is neither conceptually determinable nor knowable as an object; it can only be lived and experienced in choice and action; (ii) *Communication* (*Kommunikation*) with others springs from the existential ground of our Being, involves recognition of the freedom of the other, manifests itself in loving conflict (*liebender Kampf*), and may save us from the isolation and loneliness, to which our singularity and individuality may seem to condemn us; (iii) *Fundamental situations* (*Grundsituationen*) mark the limits of our finitude, include origin, mortality, guilt, conflict, accident and historicality, and become, when recognized and accepted (lived and experienced), *limiting situations* (*Grenzsituationen*); they then mark the transition from mere existence (*Dasein*) to authentic existenz (*Existenz*).

Jaspers emphasizes the antinomial character of our Being, which is rooted in our striving to transcend the limits of our Being and in attempting to penetrate the inaccessible realm of the Encompassing. This self-transcending tendency of our finite Being towards the infinite manifests itself in universal symbolic forms (*chiffres*), man's attempt to express the inexpressible and the unknowable, finite 'expressions' of the infinite. Such *chiffres* find their expression in art, poetry, myth, religion and metaphysics, but nowhere more vividly and dramatically than in the failure (*Scheitern*) of ontology itself. Although regarded as one of the three leading exponents of existentialism, Jaspers has been overshadowed by the genius of Heidegger and the celebrity of **Sartre**. The neglect from which Jaspers has suffered, particularly in Anglo-Saxony, has been, in part, due to the fact that, until recently, none of his greatest philosophical works has been available in English (*Von der Wahrheit* remains untranslated). On the other hand, most of his popular and semi-popular writings have been translated. Unfortunately, these works often slide into the vacuous, the vague and the platitudinous, and they have won for Jaspers an unfortunate and undeserved reputation for superficiality and banality. This situation is gradually being remedied as Jaspers's importance is slowly coming to be recognized.

Sources: Edwards; EF; Kindler 1964; Kindler 1988; Saner 1970; Wallraff 1970.

DAVID WALFORD

Kripke, Saul Aaron

American. *b:* 1940, New York. *Cat:* Logician; philosopher of language. *Ints:* Logic; philosophy of language; philosophy of mind. *Educ:* Harvard University and University of Oxford. *Infls:* S. Kleene, Bertrand Russell, Alfred Tarski and Ludwig Wittgenstein. *Appts:* Rockefeller University, New York; McCosh Professor of Philosophy, Princeton University.

Main publications:

(1959) 'A completeness theorem in modal logic', *Journal of Symbolic Logic* 24: 1–14.
(1963) 'Semantical analysis of modal logic 1', *Zeitschrift für Mathematische Logik und Grundlagen der Mathematik*, 9: 67–96.
(1965) 'Semantical considerations on modal logic', *Acta Philosophica Fennica* 16: 83–94.
(1965) 'Semantic analysis of modal logic 2', in J. Addison, L. Henkin and A. Tarski (eds) *The Theory of Models*, Amsterdam: North Holland, pp. 206–20.
(1975) 'Outline of a theory of truth', *Journal of Philosophy* 72.
(1976) 'Is there a problem about substitutional quantification?' in G. Evans and J. McDowell (eds) *Truth and Meaning: Essays in Semantics*, Oxford: Clarendon Press.
(1980) *Naming and Necessity*, Oxford: Blackwell.
(1982) *Wittgenstein on Rules and Private Language*, Oxford: Blackwell.

Secondary literature:

Forbes, Graeme (1985) *The Metaphysics of Modality*, Oxford: Clarendon Press.
Katz, J. (1990) *The Metaphysics of Meaning*, MIT Press.
Linksy, Leonard (ed.) (1971) *Reference and Modality*, Oxford: Oxford University Press.
Martin, R. M. (ed.) (1984) *Recent Essays on Truth and the Liar Paradox*, Oxford: Clarendon Press.
Salmon, Nathan, U. (1982) *Reference and Essence*, Oxford: Blackwell.

Kripke's remarkable career commenced with the publication of his first paper when he was nineteen years of age. Thereafter his work in logic provided a major impetus to the development of 'possible world' semantics, an approach which has had a wide application in philosophy. Having its origins in the Leibnizian idea of necessary truth as truth in all possible worlds, it provided a systematic framework for clarifying problems arising in relation to the plethora of already existing systems of modal logic. These systems, while formally well developed, had yet to be provided with a satisfactory semantics. Among the other applications in which Kripke has played a leading part are those to do with intuitionistic logic, which is of particular interest and concern for philosophers of mathematics. Such was the potential of this framework, that it took in studies of all manner of notions over and above the basic modalities of necessity and possibility.

This very diversity of modal logics posed problems, for the question immediately arose of whether there was any overall unifying perspective under which modal inferences could be systematically treated. Unfortunately some of the best known of these logical systems delivered different accounts of what qualified as correct inferences. It was all very well to have elegantly presented axiomatic systems, but without proper interpretation it was impossible to supply any definition of validity, and hence any satisfactory proofs of completeness for such systems. At best, logicians managed to give rather informal readings of their logical operators of necessity or possibility. The distinctiveness of Kripke's approach was in his definition of what he described as a 'model-structure', comprising a set of possible worlds with relations of accessibility or 'relative possibility' between those worlds. So, with respect to any given modal logic, the model assigns a truth-value to each atomic formula or proposition. So any given formula is either true or false in, or at, a world in the set. Kripke then defined the notion of validity for the given logic, a formula being valid in this sense if it came out true in all models. He went on to develop quantified modal logic, i.e. that which deals with modalized formulae involving the apparatus of quantification (informally expressed by 'all' and 'some'). In this logic an interpretation is provided for predicate expressions, specifying the sets of objects to be assigned to those expressions. In this way Kripke supplied the desired overall framework for accommodating the different logics—the

same fundamental ideas were in play, the individual systems embodying specific restrictions or conditions imposed on the relations between worlds. Subsequently Kripke has gone on to make pioneering contributions to the theory of truth and the analysis of the more recalcitrant of the logical and semantic paradoxes, as well as further developments in the field of quantification theory.

He made his greatest impact in a series of lectures (1970) which appeared in revised form in 1980. At the centre of his analysis was an assault on the long-cherished distinction between necessary and a posteriori truths. It was here that Kripke introduced his famous idea of the 'rigid designator' in his discussion of proper names, a topic which had already received extensive treatment since **Russell**'s analysis of 1905. Kripke's thesis was that proper names pick out their bearers or referents quite independently of any descriptions that might be associated with them. Additionally, he espoused what is known as the causal theory of meaning, i.e. that speakers' use of names is grounded ultimately in an original 'dubbing' of the object with the name, and subsequent use is sustained by a causal chain reaching back to that original episode in which the name was first assigned to the object. This had the immediate implication that names were not to be construed as in any way equivalent in meaning to any associated description or set of descriptions, and this in turn entailed dispensing with any Fregean-type distinction between the sense and reference of terms. Kripke's view also had the consequence that identity statements featuring only proper names were, if true, necessarily true. There were immediate implications here for the philosophy of mind: some of the proponents of the view known as 'central state' materialism had stressed the contingency of the identity of thoughts and brain processes; now the idea of contingent identity was in question.

Another interesting outcome of Kripke's

work was a renewed interest in the issue of essentialism, i.e. in whether a distinction between an entity's essential and its merely contingent properties was sustainable. At an intuitive level it seems quite natural to say that some properties are essential to an object or a person, as Kripke would say that having a specific biological parentage was essential to an individual, whereas their becoming a famous philosopher was not. The distinction, and Kripke's account, continues to be hotly debated. Kripke has not ceased to be controversial. In his 1982 monograph he ventured a provocative, and to some minds totally wrong-headed, interpretation of parts of **Wittgenstein**'s *Philosophical Investigations* according to which he attributes to Wittgenstein a comprehensively sceptical position on meaning and rule-following. His influence on both seniors and contemporaries has been considerable, sharpening up the debates with other and more extravagant possible-worlds theorists like David **Lewis**, and attracting a lengthy chapter of critical appraisal from the pro-Fregean Michael **Dummett**. Others, like Hilary **Putnam**, have applied the notion of rigid designation to kind terms as well as individual terms. Inevitably, the notion of possible worlds has itself come into question despite its utility, and few have been convinced by Kripke's arguments for propositions which can be both necessary and a posteriori.

Sources: See secondary literature.

DENIS POLLARD

Kristeva, Julia

Bulgarian. *b:* 1941, Bulgaria. *Cat:* Psychoanalyst; aesthetician; linguist; semiologist; feminist theorist. *Ints:* Cultural history. *Educ:* 1966, University of Paris; École Pratique des Hautes Études. *Infls:* Marx, Freud, Lacan, Barthes, Jakobson, Lévi-Strauss, Hegel, Bakhtin and Georges Bataille. *Appts:* Professor of Linguistics, University of Paris VII.

Main publications:

(1969) *Séméiotiké: Recherches pour une sémanalyse*, Paris: Seuil.

(1974) *La Révolution du langage poétique*, Paris: Seuil (English translation, *Revolution in Poetic Language*, trans. Margaret Waller, New York: Columbia University Press, 1984).

(1974) *Des Chinoises*, Paris: Editions des Femmes (English translation, *About Chinese Women*, trans. Anita Burrows, New York and London: Marion Boyars, 1986).

(1977) *Polylogue*, Paris: Seuil.

(1980) *Pouvoirs de l'horreur: essai sur l'abjection*, Paris: Seuil (English translation, *Powers of Horror: An Essay on Abjection*, trans. Leon S. Roudiez, New York: Columbia University Press, 1982).

(1980) *Desire in Language: A Semiotic Approach to Literature and Art*, ed. Leon S. Roudiez, trans. Thomas S. Gora, Alice Jardine and Leon S. Roudiez, New York: Columbia University Press.

(1981) *Le langage, cet inconnu*, Paris: Seuil (English translation, *Language the Unknown: An Initiation into Linguistics*, trans. Anna M. Menke, Hemel Hempstead: Harvester, 1989).

(1983) *Histoires d'amour*, Paris: Deneol (English translation, *Tales of Love*, trans. Leon S. Roudiez, New York: Columbia University Press, 1987).

(1986) *Au commencement était l'amour: psychanalyse et foi*, Paris: Hachette (English translation, *In the Beginning was Love: Psychoanalysis and Faith*, trans. Arthur Goldhammer, New York: Columbia University Press, 1987).

(1988) *Étrangers à nous-mêmes*, Paris: Fayard (English translation, *Strangers to Ourselves*, trans. Leon S. Roudiez, New York: Columbia University Press, 1989).

Secondary literature:

Allen, Jeffner and Young, Marion (eds) (1989) *The Thinking Muse: Feminism and Modern French Philosophy*, Bloomington, Ind.: Indiana University Press.

Benjamin, Andrew (ed.) (1990) *Abjection, Melancholia and Love: The Work of Julia Kristeva*, London and New York: Routledge.

Lechte, John (1990) *Julia Kristeva*, London and New York: Routledge.

Miller, Nancy K. (ed.) (1986) *The Politics of Gender*, New York: Columbia University Press.

Kristeva's original subject was linguistics but she has since branched out to become a major theorist in semiotics, psychoanalysis and feminism. She first came to prominence in the late 1960s through her association with the radical Parisian journal *Tel Quel*. Barthes was a key influence on her semiotic enquiries, where her early concern was to develop a semiotic theory capable of describing poetic language, with particular reference to modernism. One of her most important contributions to semiotic theory has been the concept of intertexuality, the idea, derived from her study of Bakhtin, that any text is a 'mosaic of quotations' from other textual sources. Another key Kristevian semiotic concept is *chora*, a kind of disruptive energy operating within the semiotic enterprise. A basically untheorizable entity, *chora*, is identified as a feminine element, a receptacle or womb in its original Greek sense, which for Kristeva corresponds to the poetic in language. From the 1970s onwards, after qualifying as a psychoanalyst (with **Lacan** as a major influence), Kristeva's work becomes increasingly preoccupied with psychoanalysis and its application to problems of feminism. Kristeva is a feminist theorist of less radical disposition than such 'second-generation' feminists as Luce **Irigaray** and Hélène Cixous, with their commitment to a 'feminism of difference' and specifically feminine discourse (*écriture féminine*). Reconciling this second-generation feminism with the first-generation feminism of theorists like de Beauvoir has been a particular project of Kristeva in her feminist writings, and she has claimed, in opposition to the second generation's sectarian impulses, that 'the dichotomy man/woman' belongs to metaphysics rather than to biology. Kristeva has been a leading voice in French intellectual life since the 1960s and has had a significant impact in her various chosen fields of enquiry. The concept of intertextuality, for example, has passed into general usage in literary and cultural studies. The most contentious part of Kristeva's work remains her feminist theories, which are almost provocatively reactionary by the standards of recent French feminism and have aroused considerable controversy in feminist circles worldwide.

STUART SIM

Kuhn, Thomas S(amuel)

American. **b:** 18 July 1922, Cincinnati, Ohio. **Cat:** Historian of science; philosopher of science. **Educ:** 1943, graduated in Physics, Harvard University. **Infls:** Alexandre Koyré, Emile Meyerson, Hélène Metzer, Anneliese Maier, Jean Piaget, B. L. Whorf, W. v. O. Quine and Ludwig Fleck. **Appts:** 1948–56, Junior Fellow, then Assistant Professor, General Education and History of Science, Harvard University; 1961–4, Professor, History of Science, University of California, Berkeley; 1968–79, M. Taylor Pine Professor of the History of Science, Princeton University; 1979–83, Professor, Philosophy and History of Science, Massachusetts Institute of Technology; 1983–91, Laurance S. Rockefeller Professor of Philosophy, MIT; 1991–, Professor Emeritus, MIT.

Main publications:

(1957) *The Copernican Revolution: Planetary Astronomy in the Development of Western Thought*, Cambridge, Mass.: Harvard University Press.

(1962) *The Structure of Scientific Revolutions*, Chicago: Chicago University Press; second enlarged edition, 1970.

(1966) (with John L. Heilbron, Paul L. Forman and Lini Allen) *Sources for History of Quantum Physics: An Inventory and Report*, Philadelphia: Memoires of the American Philosophical Society.

(1977) *The Essential Tension: Selected Studies in Scientific Tradition and Change*, Chicago: University of Chicago Press.

(1978) *Black-Body Theory and the Quantum Discontinuity, 1894–1912*, Oxford: Oxford University Press.

(1983) 'Rationality and theory choice', in *Journal of Philosophy* 80, pp. 563–71.

(1992) 'The natural and the human sciences', in D. Hiley et al. (eds) *The Interpretive Turn: Philosophy, Science and Culture*, Ithaca, NY: Cornell University Press.

(1994) 'Afterwords', in P. Horwich (ed.) *World Changes: Thomas Kuhn and the Nature of Science.*

Secondary literature:

Barnes, Barry (1982) *T. S. Kuhn and Social Science*, New York: Columbia University Press.

Buchdahl, Gerd (1965) Review of *The Structure of Scientific Revolutions, British Journal of the History of Science* 4: 55–69.

Gutting, Gary (ed.) (1980) *Paradigms and Revolutions*, Notre Dame: University of Notre Dame Press.

Horwich, Paul (ed.) (1994) *World Changes: Thomas Kuhn and the Nature of Science*, Cambridge, Mass.: MIT Press.

Hoyningen-Huene, Paul (1993) *Reconstructing Scientific Revolutions: Thomas S. Kuhn's Philosophy of Science*, Chicago: University of Chicago Press (published in an earlier version in 1989 as *Die Wissenschaftsphilosophie Thomas S. Kuhns: Rekonstruktion und Grundlagenprobleme*).

Lakatos, Imré and Musgrave, Alan (eds) (1970) *Criticism and the Growth of Knowledge*, Cambridge: Cambridge University Press.

Laudan, Larry (1977) *Progress and Its Problems*, Berkeley: University of California Press.

Putnam, Hilary (1981) 'The corroboration of theories', in I. Hacking (ed.), *Scientific Revolutions*, Oxford: Oxford University Press.

Shapere, Dudley (1964) Review of *The Structure of Scientific Revolutions, Philosophical Review* 73: 383–94.

Siegel, Harvey (1987) *Relativism Refuted: A Critique of Contemporary Epistemological Relativism*, Dordrecht: D. Reidel.

Kuhn's work falls into two main categories—his writings as a historian of science and his more controversial contribution to the philosophy and sociology of science. His former preoccupation appears to have influenced the latter domain but not vice versa. His reputation as a historian of science is indisputably solid, but his fame, transcending subject boundaries, rests primarily on *The Structure of Scientific Revolutions*, which admirers and critics tend to concentrate on, often excluding much else which might serve to modify the dominant theme which appears to them to emerge from its initial publication in 1962.

That thesis is perceived to consist of: (i) a paradigm establishing itself constitutes the maturity of a science; (ii) paradigms (embodying exemplars) are scientific achievements universally recognized and accepted by the community of practitioners to provide model problems and solutions, permitting normal science to occur; (iii) paradigm changes involve revolutionary science; (iv) competing paradigms are incommensurable because each selects different problems as significant to solve, using in turn different standards to count as success of solution; furthermore, no common observational data exist that could function as a neutral standard for comparing them, as each involves perceiving different 'facts'; (v) neutral rules and facts cannot, therefore, determine paradigm change; (vi) paradigm change is accounted for by the decisions of the scientific community, namely, justification by authority of persons, not by impersonal criteria like logical or methodological rules.

Philosophers of science tend to conclude irrationalism or relativism from the above. If so, there can be no philosophy but only sociology (and history) of science. On the other hand, historians and sociologists of science, while welcoming the treatment of cognitive beliefs and interests by the ordinary methods of empirical sociology, nevertheless, think that Kuhn has underplayed the influence of external factors, such as political and social ones, on scientific research. Kuhn himself, however, moans that he has been much misunderstood. But he is satisfied that Hoyningen-Huene (1993) has done justice to the complexities of his own position and the controversies surrounding it since the publication of *The Structure of Scientific Revolutions*.

Kuhn shares with **Popper** the honour of

laying the agenda, in the main, of (Anglo-American) philosophy of science in the last thirty years. Popper and positivists adhere to **Reichenbach**'s distinction between the context of justification and the context of discovery, thereby defending the thesis of scientific rationality and of progress which is linear and continuous. *The Structure of Scientific Revolutions* is perceived as a thought-provoking seminal work posing a powerful challenge to this 'traditional' view. By decentring the formal logical dimension, the Kuhnian account bears some affinity to the writing of French historians and philosophers of science like Gaston **Bachelard**, as well as that of **Feyerabend**, not to mention Michael **Polanyi**. Kuhn himself explicity acknowledges the influence of **Koyré**, another historian of science on his thoughts.

Sources: CBD; DAS; Turner; WD; *PI*; personal communication.

KEEKOK LEE

Lacan, Jacques

French. *b:* 1901, Paris. *d:* 1981, Paris. *Cat:* Psychoanalyst. *Ints:* Philosophy of mind; philosophy of language. *Educ:* Trained in Medicine and Psychiatry at the Paris Medical Faculty. *Infls:* Sigmund Freud and Ferdinand de Saussure. *Appts:* 1932, Chef de Clinique, Paris Medical Faulty; 1964, founded the École Freudienne, Paris, and became President of the Champ Freudien at the University of Vincennes.

Main publications:

(1966) *Écrits I and II*, Paris: Éditions du Seuil.
(1974) *Télévision*, Paris: Éditions du Seuil.
(1975) *Encore, 1972–3*, Paris: Éditions du Seuil.
(1978) *Le Séminaire, Livre II: Le Moi dans la théorie de Freud*, Paris: Éditions du Seuil (English translation, *The Ego in Freud's Theory*, ed. J.-A. Miller, Cambridge: Cambridge University Press.

(1981) *Le Séminaire, Livre VII: L'Ethique de la psychanalyse*, Paris: Éditions du Seuil.
(1986) *Le Séminaire, Livre VIII: Le Transfert*, Paris: Éditions du Seuil.
(1991) *Le Séminaire, Livre XVII: L'Envers de la psychanalyse*, Paris: Éditions du Seuil.

Secondary literature:

MacCannell, J. (1986) *Figuring Lacan: Criticism and the Cultural Unconscious*, London: Croom Helm.
Schneiderman, S. (1983) *Jacques Lacan: Death of an Intellectual Hero*, Cambridge, Mass.: Harvard University Press.
Sturrock, J. (ed.) (1979) *Structuralism and Since*, Oxford and New York: Oxford University Press (contains a short bibliography).

It is not easy to encapsulate Lacan's work because of his persistent refusal to state and develop any systematic theories, but one approach to his ideas is, first, to consider his views on language, and then to take in other concepts with which these views are closely interrelated.

According to Lacan, language has two aspects. There is the public, rule-governed and syntactical structure, but this is counterbalanced by the alternative level of free association in pun, word-play and dreams. Lacan's views on language owe much to **Saussure**, but he stresses to a much greater extent this second, free-association aspect.

The unconscious is both created by and reflects language. The rule-governed aspect of the latter constricts and suppresses the unconscious, which in its turn asserts its freedom and psychical energy through its persistent attempt to undermine and destabilize syntax and fixed meaning by the use of free association.

The unconscious is also in tension with the ideal ego, or persisting and integrated self. It is at the 'mirror phase' that a child makes the first of lifelong attempts to create a self, or to gain a sense of identity. Such attempts always fail, because the self is merely a constantly shifting, fluidly organized matrix or nexus which projects and objectifies itself into a deceptive and ficti-tious wholeness. Syntactical language is the ground and agent of this deception: the order found within this level of language both allows and directs such objectification.

What we view as reality is also con-structed by and reflected in language and changes with linguistic developments. Rea-lity is given its structure by, and is parasitic on, language. There is no metalanguage to describe any ultimate reality 'behind' what is given to us by the language we use. Lacan thus reverses the traditional order between the symbolic (in this case, language) and what it symbolizes: the former creates the latter.

Lacan was concerned to break down the barriers between different intellectual disci-plines, and his work ranges freely over the concepts of such traditionally diverse areas as psychoanalysis, linguistics, the theories of knowledge and mind, and literary and critical theory. His interest in, and applic-ation of his work to, the latter two areas can be illustrated by his treatment, in *Écrits* (1966), of Edgar Allan Poe's story 'The purloined letter'. According to Lacan's analysis, the letter of the story's title is a symbol of language: as it passes through the hands of the various characters it takes on a different meaning by playing a different role in each life.

There is a strong feminist interest in Lacan's works. According to one feminist interpretation the public aspect of language is male-oriented and paternalistic, whereas conversely the subversive struggle of the free-association aspect of language is a reflection of the attempts of the feminist principle to assert itself.

Lacan's writings are self-critical: his later works examine and destabilize the concep-tual structure of the earlier, thus leading to difficulties in giving an exposition of his views. He deliberately incorporates ambigu-ity, pun, word-play and multiple meaning into his publications, to highlight his posi-tion on the continuous slippage of language.

However, there must be some statements, or a metalanguage used about language, which are not subject to such a factor: the meaning of the assertion that there is continuous slippage in language must be fixed, so that we can know this alleged fact about lan-guage.

KATHRYN PLANT

Langer (née Knauth), Susanne Katerina

American. *b:* 20 December 1895, Manhattan, New York. *d:* 17 July 1985, Old Lyme, Connecticut. *Cat:* Neo-Kantian symbolist. *Ints:* Aesthetics; philosophy of mind; philo-sophy of language. *Educ:* Radcliffe College, Cambridge, Mass., and the University of Vienna (1921–2). *Infls:* C. S. Peirce, L. Wittgenstein, A. N. Whitehead, Ernst Cas-sirer and Charles Morris. *Appts:* Tutor in Philosophy, Radcliffe College, Harvard, 1927–42; Lecturer in Philosophy, Columbia University, 1945–50; Professor of Philosophy and Professor Emerita, Connecticut College, New London, 1954–85.

Main publications:

(1930) *The Practice of Philosophy*, New York: Holt.
(1937) *An Introduction to the Study of Symbolic Logic*, Boston: Houghton Mifflin and London: Allen & Unwin.
(1942) *Philosophy in a New Key: A Study in the Symbolism of Reason, Rite and Art*, Cambridge, Mass.: Harvard University Press; third edition, 1957.
(1953) *Feeling and Form: A Theory of Art*, New York: Scribner and London: Routledge.
(1957) *Problems of Art: Ten Philosophical Lec-tures*, New York: Scribner and London: Routle-dge.
(1958) (ed.) *Reflections on Art*, Baltimore: Johns Hopkins University Press.
(1962) *Philosophical Sketches*, Baltimore: Johns Hopkins University Press and London: Oxford University Press.

(1967–82) *Mind: An Essay on Human Feeling*, 3 vols, Baltimore: Johns Hopkins University Press.

Secondary literature:

Danto, Arthur, de Sousa, Ronald B. and Morawski, Stefan (1984), essays in *Journal of Philosophy* 81: 641–63.
Gosh, Ranjan K. (1979) *Aesthetic Theory and Art: A Study in Susanne Langer*, Delhi: Ajanta.

Although Susanne Langer is famous as an aesthetician, her work in aesthetics is interwoven with her contributions to the philosophy of mind and the philosophy of language. Like her mentors, A. N. **Whitehead** and Ernst **Cassirer**, she is a systematic thinker. But Langer worked in a period when philosophical systems were unfashionable: in the 1940s and 1950s she set about constructing a theory of art when her contemporaries questioned the very possibility of such a theory. However, Langer's theory of art itself originated in her semantic theory and was in its turn the basis of her theory of mind, the crowning achievement of her long career.

The major themes of Langer's philosophy are sounded in *Philosophy in a New Key* (1942), where she identified the 'keynote' of twentieth-century philosophy as a concern with the nature of symbolism. Langer's interest in art led her to a conception of the symbol stemming from the Kantian analysis of experience as developed by Cassirer rather than to that current in logic and positivist epistemology. She argues that the symbolic ordering of experience occurs at all levels of sensitive life through the making of abstractions, understood as the perception of form. Consequently, Langer distinguishes two kinds of symbol. Discursive symbols, the paradigm of which is verbal language, are characterized by fixed units of meaning and syntactic relations. Non-discursive symbols, found in sensory experience, ritual, myth and art, are characterized as articulated wholes whose function is the presentation of forms of experience incapable of linguistic expression. It is this expanded notion of symbol which has been the target of criticism from contemporary philosophers (see, for example, the review of *Philosophy in a New Key* by Ernst Nagel, *Journal of Philosophy* 40 (1943): 323–9).

Having originally taken music to exemplify her view of art as presentational symbol, Langer proceeds in her next book, *Feeling and Form* (1953), to provide a detailed account of the principles of creation and expression in the great orders of art. Art, for Langer, is significant form, and the arts are unified through the notion of expression. The forms of art are abstracted from their everyday employment to create, in Schiller's terms, a semblance or illusion which presents or symbolizes ideas of feeling, the artist's knowledge of feeling, as opposed to signalling his currently felt emotions. Thus the significance of art is that it enables the beholder to recognize directly the forms of human feeling, 'growth, movement, emotion, and everything that characterizes vital existence' (1953, p. 82). The artistic illusion (not delusion), which is not a mere arrangement of given materials in an aesthetically pleasing pattern but what results from the arrangement, Langer calls 'living form'; and "living form" is the most indubitable product of all good art' (ibid.).

However, 'why must artistic form, to be expressive of feeling, always be so-called "living form"?' Moreover, why need art 'only seem, not actually be, life-like'? That is to say: 'Why is semblance necessary?' These questions, prompted by her theory of art, were the origins of the final phase of Langer's philosophy, culminating in the three volumes of *Mind: An Essay on Human Feeling* (1967–82). Here she investigates 'actual living form as biologists find it ... and the actual phenomena of feeling' in order to show that the fundamental division between human and animal mentality is 'a vast and special evolution of feeling in the hominid stock' (see the Introduction to *Mind*, vol. 1). Langer's theory of mind is resolutely naturalistic in its exclusion of assumptions about non-physical ingredients in human life. But at the same time it aims, as with all Langer's philosophical writing, to provide a conceptual structure of sufficient generality to be applicable, to be workable, both within and beyond the natural sciences.

Sources: *New York Times*, 19 Jul 1985; Turner.

PETER LEWIS

Lenin, Vladimir Il'ich (pseudonym of V.I. Ul'ianov)

Russian. *b:* 10 April (22 N.S.) 1870 Simbirsk. *d:* 21 January 1924, Gorki, near Moscow. *Cat:* Marxist. *Educ:* Simbirsk gymnasium, 1879–87; briefly attended University of Kazan' in 1887 until his expulsion and exile; graduated in Law as an external student of the University of St Petersburg in 1891. *Infls:* Influenced by Marx, Engels, A. I. Herzen, N. G. Chernyshevsky, Plekhanov and Bukharin. *Appts:* Professor of Philosophy, University of Moscow, 1883–1920.

Main publications:

(1902) *Chto deliat'? Nabolevshie voprosy nashego dvizheniia*, Stuttgart (English translation, *What is to be Done? Burning Questions of our Movement*, New York: International Publishers, 1929).
(1909) *Materializm i empiriokrititsizm: kriticheskie zametki ob odnoi reaktsionnoi filosofii*, Moscow (English translation, *Materialism and Empirio-Criticism: Critical Notes Concerning a Reactionary Philosophy*, trans. David Kvitko, New York: International Publishers, 1927).
(1916) *Imperializm, kak vysshaia stadiia kapitalizma: populiarnyi ocherk*, Petrograd (English translation, *Imperialism, the Highest Stage of Capitalism: A Popular Outline*, New York: International Publishers, 1933).
(1918) *Gosudarstvo i revoliutsiia: uchenie marksizma o gosudarstve i zadachi proletariata v revoliutsii*, Petrograd (English translation, *State and Revolution: Marxist Teaching on the State and the Task of the Proletariat in the Revolution*, United Communist Party of America, 1917).
(1933) *Filosofskie tetradi* [Philosophical Notebooks], Moscow (first separate edition).
(1960–80), *Collected Works*, 47 vols, Moscow and London: Foreign Languages Publishing House, Progress Publishers and Lawrence and Wishart (English translation of the fourth Russian edition of Lenin's work).

Secondary literature:

Copleston, F. C. (1986) *Philosophy in Russia: From Herzen to Berdyaev*, Tunbridge Wells: Search Press and Notre Dame: University of Notre Dame Press, ch. 11.
Harding, N. (1977–81) *Lenin's Political Thought*, vol. 1: *Theory and Practice in the Democratic Revolution*, vol. 2: *Theory and Practice in the Socialist Revolution*, London and Basingstoke: Macmillan.
Wetter, G. A. (1958) *Dialectical Materialism: A Historical and Systematic Survey of Philosophy in the Soviet Union*, trans. Peter Heath, London Routledge & Kegan Paul, ch. 5.

The son of a school inspector, Lenin was introduced to Marxism by his elder brother Aleksandr, who was executed in 1887 for his part in a revolutionary populist plot to assassinate Tsar Alexander III. From 1893 Lenin practised as a lawyer in St Petersburg, where he became leader of the main Marxist circle. In 1895 he was arrested and imprisoned, and in 1897 exiled to Siberia. In 1900 he emigrated to Western Europe, and led the Bolshevik faction which emerged from the Second Congress of the Russian Social-Democratic Labour Party in 1903. He returned to Russia during the 1905 Revolution but again emigrated to Western Europe in 1907, where he was active in the international socialist movement and again embroiled in party strife and leadership struggles, not least with Bogdanov and Trotsky. He opposed Russia's participation in the First World War, and returned after the February Revolution, organizing the seizure of power in October 1917 with his former opponent Trotsky. The first head of state of the Soviet Union, he survived the period of civil war and Allied intervention (he was severely wounded by a Social Revolutionary in 1918), and in 1921 replaced the coercive policies of War Communism with the more liberal New Economic Policy. He died in 1924 from a stroke.

Although his earliest works criticized the petit-bourgeois economic romanticism of Russian Populism, affinities arguably remained in the emphases Lenin brought to Marxism as a political theory; notably in his rejection of 'objectivist', determinist and evolutionary versions of Marxism, his belief in the peasants' latent revolutionary potential, and the paramount role accorded in *What is to be Done?* (1902) to a tightly disciplined vanguard of professional activists in leading the masses to revolutionary consciousness and action. In his *Imperialism, the Highest Stage of Capitalism* (1916), he saw the growth of monopolies and the scramble for colonies as morbid symptoms, and justified his activist strategy in the Russian context by appealing to the uneven development of capitalism in different countries. The consequence that socialism would triumph at different times in different countries was part of his argument for the continuing post-revolutionary role of the state as an instrument of class domination (this time of the proletariat). The Leninist theory of the state was expounded in *State and Revolution* (1918).

Lenin's *Materialism and Empirio-Criticism* (1909), a strikingly polemical work replete with quotations from Russian and Western writers, was conceived in the library of the British Museum and prompted by a leadership struggle among the Bolshevik Émigrés. It defended Engels's dialectical materialism against the attempts of Bogdanov, Lunacharsky and other Bolsheviks to modernize Marxism by marrying it to the empiriocriticism of Avenarius and Mach. Lenin insisted that in denying that human experience is caused by a reality external to it, the Russian Machists were embracing subjective idealism, which inevitably termi-

nates in solipsism. Bogdanov's conflation of social consciousness and social being also undermined the Marxist distinction between class consciousness and objective social conditions (a distinction which underlay Lenin's emphasis on the role of the revolutionary activist). Lenin, by contrast, predicated his metaphysics and epistemology on the naive realism accepted by 'every healthy person who has not spent some time in a lunatic asylum or studied the science of idealist philosophers'. He equated matter with 'objective reality, which is given to man in his sensations, and which is copied, photographed and reflected by our sensations, while existing independently of them' (author's translations; see *Collected Works*, vol. 14, pp. 69, 130). Through this definition he reasserted materialism in the face of 'physical idealist' interpretations of the contemporary 'crisis in physics'. His effective identification of philosophical materialism with realism and a representationalist theory of perception was of decisive significance in Soviet philosophy and intellectual history. Equally influential was his insistence that all philosophical positions are ultimately either materialist or idealist (the 'agnosticism' of Hume and Kant being concealed idealism), and that these 'two great camps' represent antagonistic social classes. Hence the 'struggle of parties' in philosophy, or its 'partisanship' (*partiinost'*), a quality openly exhibited in Lenin's unrestrained invective against his opponents, to the dismay even of fellow Marxists like Aksel'rod (Ortodoks).

Despite the philosophical crudities of Lenin's assault on phenomenalism, he was at pains to distinguish his position from the vulgar or 'mechanical' materialism of Vogt, Büchner and Moleschott. Thought is not secreted from the brain like bile from the liver; the psychical is 'the highest product of matter' but is not reducible to it. The relationship between thought and nature is dialectical, and the dialectic in general was given greater prominence in Lenin's *Philosophical Notebooks*, a collection of notes, summaries and drafts largely dating from 1914–16, when he was in Switzerland, and unpublished until 1929–30, when they were included in a collection of his works. Most striking is the respect paid to Hegel (a full understanding of his *Logic* is held to be necessary for a proper understanding of Marx's *Capital*) and, memorably, Lenin asserts that intelligent idealism is closer than stupid materialism to intelligent materialism. Unlike Engels, he placed the law of the unity and struggle of opposites above the law of the transformation of quality into quantity: it was the heart of the dialectic, which he now considered to be the essence of Marxism; and he found support in the dialectic for his typically activist belief that 'man's consciousness not only reflects the objective world, but creates it' (*Collected Works*, vol. 38, pp. 180, 242, 276). Few Western scholars perceive in Lenin's writings anything of philosophical profundity or originality, but their influence upon and reverential treatment by one of the world's largest communities of professional philosophers is an indelible feature of the history of twentieth-century philosophy.

COLIN CHANT

Levinas, Emmanuel

French. *b:* 30 December 1905, Kaunas, Lithuania. *Cat:* Phenomenologist; theologian. *Ints:* Ethics; philosophy of religion; judaism. *Educ:* University of Strasbourg Institute of Philosophy and University of Fribourg. *Infls:* Bergson, Husserl and Heidegger. *Appts:* Professor of Philosophy, University of Paris X; University of Paris IV; Director of the École Normale Israélite Orientale.

Main publications:

(1930) *La Théorie de l'intuition dans la phénoménologie de Husserl*, Paris: Alcan (English translation, *The theory of intuition in Husserl's Phenomenology*, trans. André Orianne, Evanston: Northwestern University Press, 1973).
(1947) *De l'existent à l'existence*, Paris: Fontaine (English translation, *Existence and Existents*, trans. Alphonso Lingis, The Hague: Nijhoff, 1978).
(1949) *En découvrant l'existence avec Husserl et Heidegger*, Paris: Vrin.
(1961) *Totalité et infini*, The Hague: Nijhoff (English translation, *Totality and Infinity*, trans. Alphonso Lingis, The Hague: Nijhoff, 1969).
(1963) *Difficile liberté*, Paris: Albin Michel.
(1974) *Autrement qu'être ou au-delà de l'essence*, The Hague: Nijhoff (English transaltion, *Otherwise than Being or Beyond Essence*, trans. Alphonso Lingis, The Hague: Nijhoff, 1981).
(1982) *Éthique et infini*, Paris: Fayard (English translation, *Ethics and Infinity*, trans. Richard A. Cohen, Pittsburgh: Duquesne University Press, 1985).

Secondary literature:

Bernasconi, R and Wood, D. (1988) *The Provocation of Levinas: Rethinking the Other*, London and New York: Routledge (collection of critical essays by T. Chanter, S. Gans, J. Llewelyn, *et al.*).
Blanchot, M. *et al.* (1980) *Textes pour Emmanuel Levinas*, Paris: J. M. Place.
Cohen, R. (ed.) (1986) *Face to Face with Levinas*, Albany: State University of New York Press (collection of essays by T. de Boer, J.-F. Lyotard, R. Bernasconi, *et al.*).
Derrida, J. (1978) 'Violence and metaphysics', in *Writing and Difference*, trans. Alan Bass, London: Routledge & Kegan Paul and Chicago: Chicago University Press, pp. 79–153.
Lingis, A. (1985) *Libido: the French Existential Theories*, Bloomington: Indiana University Press.
Wyschogrod, E. (1974) *Emmanuel Levinas: the Problem of Ethical Metaphysics*, The Hague: Nijhoff.

Emmanuel Levinas was first to introduce the phenomenology of **Husserl** and the philosophy of **Heidegger** to a French audience. His philosophical method is phenomenological but the central themes of his philosophy are ethical. Through a phenomenological study of the relation of the self to other persons, Levinas argues for the primacy of the good over the true. Phenomenology, as the way to discover meaning from within our lived experience, allows himto study face-to-face human relations such as desire and love. From this point of departure, he argues that man's ethical relation to another person comes before his relation to himself (self-interest) or to the world of things (Being). For Levinas, the other person is absolutely other: beyond knowledge or thought about the being of things. Face-to-face with the other person man is obliged to put responsibility for the other before self; for this reason the relation puts man in the position of hostage. Thus Levinas puts forward an ethics of obligation and self-sacrifice dependent on a relation to the other that is beyond totalization, beyond comprehension and expression: he calls it infinite. In *Totality and Infinity* (1961), his most influential book, this infinity is presented through the perception of the face and through the obligation man is put under when in the presence of the face of another. Levinas has influenced philosophers such as Jacques **Derrida** and Jean-François **Lyotard** and the writer Maurice Blanchot. His thought is a major reference-point when philosophers consider the relation of their thought to ethics, theology and Judaism.

Sources: Catalogues of Bibliothèque Nationale, Paris and National Library of Scotland.

JAMES WILLIAMS

Lewis, David K(ellogg)

American. *b:* 28 September 1941, Oberlin, Ohio. *Cat:* Analytical philosopher of language; logician. *Ints:* Philosophy of mathematics; philosophy of mind; ethics. *Educ:* St Catherine's Society, Oxford, Swarthmore and Harvard. *Infls:* The analytical tradition, in particular Rudolf Carnap and F. P. Ramsey. *Appts:* 1966–70, Assistant Professor of Philosophy, UCLA; 1970–3, Associate Professor of Philosophy, 1973–, Professor of Philosophy, Princeton; 1983, elected to

American Academy of Arts and Sciences; 1992, elected Corresponding Fellow of the British Academy; visiting appointments and fellowships in Australia, the USA and Britain; editorial consultant to *Philosophical Papers*.

Main publications:

(1969) *Convention: A Philosophical Study*, Cambridge: Harvard University Press.
(1973) *Counterfactuals*, Oxford, Blackwell.
(1983) *Philosophical Papers*, vol. 1, Oxford: Oxford University Press.
(1986) *On the Plurality of Worlds*, Oxford: Blackwell.
(1987) *Philosophical Papers*, vol. 2, Oxford: Oxford University Press (contains bibliography to 1986).
(1991) *Parts of Classes*, Oxford: Blackwell.

Secondary literature:

Elgin, C. Z. (1992) Critical Notice of *Parts of Classes*, in *Philosophical Books* 33: 193–8.
Inwagen, P. van (1986) Critical Notice of *Philosophical Papers I*, in *Mind* 95: 246–57.
Loux, M. J. (ed.) (1979) *The Possible and the Actual: Readings in the Metaphysics of Modality*, Ithaca: Cornell University Press.
Stalnaker, Robert (1988) critical notice of *On the Plurality of Worlds*, in *Mind* 97: 117–28.

David Lewis has written on several areas of philosophy (metaphysics, mind, logic, language), but is best known for his work on counterfactuals (conditionals such as 'If kangaroos had no tails, they would topple over'). Lewis analyses such conditionals in terms of possible worlds, and in so doing espouses 'extreme modal realism'—see Robert Stalnaker's article in Loux 1979. Extreme modal realism—as it emerges from Lewis's *Counterfactuals* (1973) *On the Plurality of Worlds* (1986) and articles in the *Philosophical Papers*—is 'the thesis that the world we are part of is but one of a plurality of worlds, and that we who inhabit this world are only a few out of all the inhabitants of all the worlds' (1986, p. vii). Moreover, the claim that there is a plurality of worlds is, Lewis maintains, an existential one.

The notion of similarity between worlds functions here as a primitive and raises issues concerning, for instance, identity across worlds (Lewis's position on which has been criticized by Saul **Kripke** in 'Identity and necessity': see Moore 1993 below), but it offers Lewis a standpoint from which to treat other matters. Modality on his analysis becomes quantification (what is possible is what is the case at some world, what is necessary is what is the case at all worlds, and so on for 'the impossible' and 'the contingent'). Similarly, the articles 'Causation' and 'Events' (in 1987) analyse both phenomena in terms of counterfactuals as Lewis conceives them. Lewis's version of modal realism has, however, been criticized by, among others, P. Forrest and D. M. Armstrong (*Australasian Journal of Philosophy* 62 (1984): 164–8), and moderate modal realists such as Robert Stalnaker (see his contribution in Loux) have instead attempted to interpret 'possible worlds' in terms of states of affairs or possible histories of the world (Lewis rejects 'ersatz modal realism', as he calls this position, in chapter 3 of 1986, and replies to other criticisms in chapter 2).

In the introduction to volume 2 of *Philosophical Papers* (1987) Lewis writes that much of his work seems to advance the thesis of 'Humean supervenience ... the doctrine that all there is to the world is a vast mosaic of local matters of particular fact' (p. ix): the world is the sum of all space-time points and qualities at them—'all else supervenes on that'. Lewis's materialism motivates his contributions to the philosophy of mind (see the articles collected under that heading in volume 1 of *Philosophical Papers*, 1983), in which he has developed 'a broadly functionalist theory of mind, according to which mental states *qua* mental are realizers of roles specified in common-sense psychology' (p. xi).

Lewis's more recent concern has been with the philosophy of mathematics. In *Parts of Classes* (1991) he attempts a mereological reduction of set theory: parts of classes are subclasses (the null set not being a genuine class), and singletons (unit classes) are their mereological atoms; Lewis's axiomatization of set theory makes singletons the primitives of his theory. If, as Lewis believes, 'most of mathematics is into set theory up to its ears' (p. 58), then his structuralist treatment of set theory results in the nominalization of mathematics.

Sources: A. W. Moore (ed.) (1993) *Meaning and Reference*, Oxford; *AJP* 62, 1984; IWW; WW(Am); DAS; Burkhardt.

STUART LEGGATT

Lonergan, Bernard

Canadian. **b:** 17 December 1904, Buckingham, Quebec. **d:** 26 November 1984, Pickering, Ontario. **Cat:** Thomist. **Ints:** Epistemology; methodology; metaphysics; philosophical theology. **Educ:** Heythrop College and Gregorian University. **Infls:** Aristotle, Aquinas and Newman. **Appts:** 1953–1965, Gregorian University; 1966–70, Regis College, Toronto; 1973–83, Boston College.

Main publications:

(1957) *Insight*, London: Longman, Green & Co.; fifth edition, *Collected Works of Bernard Lonergan*, vol. 3, Toronto: University of Toronto Press, 1992.

(1967) *Collection*, edited by F. E. Crowe, New York: Herder & Herder; second edition, *Collected Works of Bernard Lonergan*, vol. 4, Toronto: University of Toronto Press, 1988.

(1968) *Verbum: Word and Idea in Aquinas*, London: Darton, Longman & Todd.

(1974) *A Second Collection*, edited by William F. J. Ryan and Bernard J. Tyrell, London: Darton, Longman & Todd.

Secondary literature:

Crowe, Frederick E. (1992) *Lonergan*, London: Geoffrey Chapman.
Lamb, Matthew L. (ed.) (1981) *Creativity and Method*, Milwaukee: Marquette University Press.
McShane, Philip (ed.) (1971–2) *Papers from the International Lonergan Congress 1970*, 2 vols, Dublin: Gill & Macmillan (vol. 2: *Language, Truth and Meaning*).
Meynell, Hugo A. (1976) *An Introduction to the Philosophy of Bernard Lonergan*, London: Macmillan; second edition, 1991.
Tracy, David (1970) *The Achievement of Bernard Lonergan*, New York: Herder & Herder.

Bernard Lonergan was the main exponent in English of what is sometimes called 'transcendental Thomism'. This emerged from a confrontation, and a partial synthesis, of some elements of Kantian method with Thomistic realism, initiated earlier in the century by Maréchal. A fundamental principle in Lonergan's philosophy is his definition of being as 'the objective of the pure desire to know'. Reality, that is, has a structure which is isomorphic with the structure of knowledge. It follows that a description and a theory of knowledge is a precondition and the foundation of metaphysics. A knowledge of knowledge leads to a knowledge of what is known, and what is known is what there is.

This methodological priority of epistemology over metaphysics was strongly contested by Thomists such as **Gilson**, for whom a philosophy that began with a study of consciousness could never escape from it and arrive at the extra-mental world. Gilson pointed to Descartes and Kant as philosophers who conspicuously failed in this respect. Transcendental Thomists, however, would claim that Kant's view that we cannot know things in themselves was a kind of failure of nerve. If Kant had exploited his own critical method to the full, he would have come to realize that the very concept of knowledge is itself intelligible and possible only on the prior assumption of real objects and properties which are objects for knowledge, and which are actually known by the knowing subject.

For Lonergan, then, philosophy begins with the attempt to know what knowing is. The very possibility of knowing what knowing is is inherent in the nature of consciousness. Knowing is a conscious activity, and consciousness is an awareness immanent in cognitional acts. The knowing of which we are aware has a threefold character: empirical, intellectual and rational. As empirical, knowing is sensing, perceiving and imagining. As intellectual, knowing involves the act of understanding and the formation of concepts. As rational, knowing culminates in affirmations of what there is. These are not three types or stages of knowing, but constitute a dynamic unity. All knowing requires a process of 'insight' (hence the title of Lonergan's most famous work), which is the name he uses for the act of understanding a set of data. Insight is exemplified in Archimedes's cry 'Eureka', and in the slaveboy in Plato's *Meno*. The early chapters of *Insight* provide a detailed analysis of the activity of knowing in mathematics, the empirical sciences and common sense.

The dynamic, historically evolving, methodologically diverse character of knowing makes it plain that reality cannot be conceived of as a static universe ruled by classical laws of physics. Lonergan describes it rather as 'emergent probability', a phrase designed to indicate that the universe functions as much by statistical probabilities as by classical laws. When reality is conceived of as the knowable, as something 'proportionate' to human cognition ('proportionate being'), it can be said to have three components: 'potency' is the component that is experienced or imagined; 'form' is the component that is known by the understanding; 'act' is the component known by the judgement of reason.

These three components can themselves be of different kinds. Our understanding of things is an understanding both of their properties and relations, and of their concrete individuality: the former is 'conjugate form' and the latter is 'central form', terms which correspond with Aristotle's accidental and substantial form. Coordinate with these we can also distinguish central and conjugate potency, and central and conjugate act. Central act is existence and conjugate act is occurrence.

Lonergan also examines practical reasoning and the possibility of ethics. He defines good as 'the object of desire'. However, one of the things that we desire is knowledge, and this desire generates a second sense of good: the good of order, as instantiated in the state, the economy or the family. Good refers here to states of affairs which are rationally and purposefully designed, willed and constructed to satisfy our desires. Good as the object of rational choice presents itself as value. On the ontological level, good refers to every kind of order and, at its limit, to the intelligibility intrinsic in being. Moral choices involve four elements: sensible and imaginative representations; practical insight; practical reflection; and decision.

One of the peculiarities of human knowing is that, although we have an unrestricted desire to know, we have a limited capacity to know. Thus, 'the range of possible questions is larger than the range of possible answers'. This consideration leads Lonergan to the postulation of transcendent being, that is to say, being that is beyond us, which is 'without the domain of man's outer and inner experience'. Transcendent being, however, must be presumed to be intelligible, and this leads to the logical possibility of an unrestricted act of understanding, whose object includes transcendent as well as proportionate being. Its object would also include self-understanding (since all knowing is, by definition, conscious). Such an understanding would be one of the characteristics of God.

The affirmation of what God is, and the affirmation that God is, are different matters. Lonergan believes that many of the

arguments for the existence of God are included in the general form: 'If the real is completely intelligible, God exists. But the real is completely intelligible. Therefore, God exists.' However, Lonergan does not think that this argument will persuade someone who was hitherto an agnostic or an atheist that God exists. Its function rather is, like that of St Anselm's proof, to demonstrate to those who already believe in God that their belief is rationally grounded and defensible. Lonergan is regarded by some as having one of the most powerful philosophical minds of the twentieth century, but he is not widely known outside Thomistic circles.

Sources: *Catholic Encyclopedia; RPL* 83, 1985.

HUGH BREDIN

Lukács, Gyorgy

Hungarian. *b:* 13 April 1885, Budapest. *d:* 1971, Budapest. *Cat:* Marxist; aesthetician; metaphysician; political philosopher; literary theorist. *Ints:* Hegel. *Educ:* Universities of Berlin and Heidelberg, and the Marx–Engels Institute in Moscow. *Infls:* Marx, Hegel, Kant, Dilthey, Weber, Rosa Luxemburg, Georges Sorel and Georg Simmel. *Appts:* Professor of Aesthetics and Cultural Philosophy, University of Budapest.

Main publications:

(1911) *Die Seele und die Formen*, Berlin: Fleischel (English translation, *Soul and Form*, trans. Anna Bostock, London: Merlin Press, 1974).
(1920) *Die Theorie des Romans*, Berlin: Paul Cassirer (English translation, *The Theory of the Novel*, trans. Anna Bostock, London: Merlin Press, 1971).
(1923) *Geschichte und Klassenbewusstsein*, Berlin: Malik Verlag (English translation, *History and Class Consciousness*, trans. Rodney Livingstone, London: Merlin Press, 1971).
(1924) *Lenin: Studie über den Zusammenhang seiner Gedanken*, Vienna: Verlag der Arbeiterbuchhandlung (English translation, *Lenin: A*

Study on the Unity of his Thought, trans. Nicholas Jacobs, London: NLB, 1970).

(1947) *A történelmi regény*, Budapest: Hungaria (English translation, *The Historical Novel*, trans. Hannah and Stanley Mitchell, Harmondsworth: Penguin, 1969).

(1947) *Goethe und seine Zeit*, Berne: Francke (English translation, *Goethe and his Age*, trans. Robert Anchor, London: Merlin Press, 1968).

(1947) *A polgár nyomában: a hetvenéves Thomas Mann*, Budapest: Hungaria (English translation, *Essays on Thomas Mann*, trans. Stanley Mitchell, London: Merlin Press, 1964).

(1948) *Der Junge Hegel*, Zurich and Vienna: Europa Verlag (English translation, *The Young Hegel*, trans. Rodney Livingstone, London: Merlin Press, 1975).

(1950) *Studies in European Realism*, trans. Edith Bone, London: Hillway.

(1958) *Wider den missverstanden Realismus*, Hamburg: Claasen (English translation, *The Meaning of Contemporary Realism*, trans. John and Necke Mander, London: Merlin Press, 1963).

(1963) *Die Eigenart des Aesthetischen*, Neuwied: Luchterhand.

(1976) *Zur ontologie des gesellschaftlichen seins*, Budapest: Magveto Kiado (English translation, *The Ontology of Social Being*, trans. David Fernbach, London: Merlin Press, 1978).

Secondary literature:

Arato, Andrew and Breines, Paul (1978) *The Young Lukács and the Origins of Western Marxism*, London: Seabury Press and New York: Pluto Press.

Gluck, Mary (1985) *George Lukács and his Generation, 1900–1918*, Cambridge: Mass.: Harvard University Press.

Heller, Agnes (ed.) (1983) *Lukács Reappraised*, New York: Columbia University Press.

Joos, Ernest (ed.) (1987) *George Lukács and his World: A Reassessment*, New York: Peter Lang.

Lichtheim, George (1970) *Lukács*, Collins.

Marcus, Judith and Tarr, Zoltan (eds) (1989) *George Lukács: Theory, Culture, and Politics*, New Brunswick, NJ: Transaction.

Zitta, Victor (1964) *George Lukács' Marxism: Alienation, Dialectics, Revolution. A Study in Utopia and Ideology*, The Hague: Martinus Nijhoff.

Lukács is generally regarded as one of the first theorists of note in what has come to be called 'Western' Marxism, a writer who made valuable contributions to several areas of Marxist theory, most notably perhaps in aesthetics. He is identified with a Hegelian approach to Marxism which was at odds with Communist Party orthodoxy for most of his lifetime. His earliest writings on aesthetics were tinged with the neo-Kantianism so fashionable in pre-First World War Central European intellectual circles, and he described himself as a 'subjective idealist' at this point in his career. From *The Theory of the Novel* (1920) onwards, however, the influence of Hegel begins to dominate. Lukács's mature intellectual development is very much tied up with the political fortunes of Marxism, and at various times he was an activist on behalf of the Communist Party in Hungary and Germany as well as holding Hungarian government posts during the Soviet Republic of 1919 and the uprising of 1956. During the 1930s and 1940s Lukács spent much of his time in Moscow, working at the Marx–Engels Institute and the Philosophical Institute of the Moscow Academy of Sciences, as well as editing various literary periodicals. On his return to Hungary after the Second World War he took up a Chair at the University of Budapest, although he was later expelled from the Communist Party for his part in the 1956 uprising and even exiled for a while. Lukács's most contentious work of Marxist theory is *History and Class Consciousness* (1923), whose Hegelian idealist bias, lukewarm commitment to materialism and generally anti-positivist sentiments scandalized the Russian Communist Party leadership in the 1920s. Lukács was later to reject the idealist dimension of this work, although Hegel remained a lifelong source of inspiration. It is Lukács's aesthetic writings that have probably done the most to build his reputation, particularly his works of literary criticism and literary theory. *Studies in European Realism* (1946), *The Historical Novel* (1937) and *The Meaning of Contemporary Realism* (1957) have all been highly influential studies, and represent some of the most successful defences of realism in the Marxist canon. A supporter of the official

Soviet aesthetic doctrine of socialist realism, Lukács nevertheless could be severely critical of its simplistic tendencies and he developed a variant form known as 'critical realism', which judged novels less in terms of their political correctness than on their ability to make plain the socio-political forces that shaped human character in any given historical period. This led to the controversial rejection on ideological grounds of the modernist tradition in literature (Kafka and Joyce, for example) in favour of approved 'critical realists' like Thomas Mann. In his late career Lukács explored the history of aesthetic theory in *The Specificity of the Aesthetic* (1963), a heavily Hegelian work centrally concerned with the issues of reflection and representation, and, finally, the ontological theories of Marx and Hegel (published posthumously in 1976. Lukács has been a highly influential figure in the Western Marxist tradition, although his dogmatic commitment to realism and dislike of modernist experimentation have drawn criticism from various quarters—most notably perhaps from the playwright Bertolt Brecht, who clashed with Lukács over the form a Marxist aesthetic should take. The impact of Lukács' brand of Hegelianized Marxism can be seen in the work of Walter **Benjamin**, the Frankfurt School, the French-Romanian theorist Lucien Goldmann and the American critic Frederic Jameson.

STUART SIM

Lyotard, Jean-François

French. *b:* 1924. *Cat:* Postmodernist; political philosopher; philosopher of language; aesthetician; culture theorist. *Educ:* University of Paris; 1971, doctorate. *Infls:* Marx, Freud, Lacan, Nietzsche and Kant. *Appts:* 1972, Professor of Philosophy, University of Paris VIII (Vincennes), 1949–59, taught at Lycées and the University of California at Irvine; founding

member of the International College of Philosophy, Paris. Held posts at various universities in the USA.

Main publications:

(1954) *La Phénoménologie*, Paris: Presses Universitaires de France, 1954 (English translation, *Phenomenology*, trans. Brian Beakley, Albany, NY: SUNY Press, 1991).

(1971) *Discours, figure*, Paris: Klinckseick.

(1974) *Économie libidinale*, Paris: Minuit (English translation, *Libidinal Economy*, trans. Iain Hamilton Grant, London: Athlone Press, 1993).

(1977) *Instructions païennes*, Paris: Galilée.

(1977) *Rudiments païens: genre dissertatif*, Paris: Union générale d'éditions.

(1979) (with Jean-Loup Thebaud) *Au Juste*, Paris: Christian Bourgeois (English translation, *Just Gaming*, trans. Wlad Godzich, Manchester: Manchester University Press, 1985).

(1979) *La Condition postmoderne*, Paris: Minuit (English translation, *The Postmodern Condition*, trans. Geoffrey Bennington and Brian Massumi, Manchester: Manchester University Press, 1984).

(1983) *Le Différend*, Paris: Minuit (English translation, *The Differend*, trans. George Van Den Abbeele, Manchester: Manchester University Press, 1988).

(1984) *Tombeau de l'intellectuel et autres papiers*, Paris: Galilée.

(1988) *Peregrinations*, New York: Columbia University Press (written in English by Lyotard).

(1988) *L'inhumain*, Paris: Galilée (English translation, *The Inhuman*, trans. Geoffrey Bennington and Rachel Bowlby, Cambridge: Polity, 1991).

Secondary literature:

Bennington, Geoffrey (1988) *Lyotard: Writing the Event*, Manchester: Manchester University Press.

Callinicos, Alex (1989) *Against Postmodernism: A Marxist Perspective*, Cambridge: Polity Press.

Dews, Peter (1987) *Logics of Disintegration: Post-structuralist Thought and the Claims of Critical Theory*, London and New York: Verso.

Readings, Bill (1991) *Art and Politics: Introducing Lyotard*, London: Routledge.

Sarup, Madan (1990) *An Introductory Guide to Post-structuralism and Postmodernism*, Hemel Hempstead: Harvester.

Sim, Stuart (1992) *Beyond Aesthetics: Confronta-
tions with Poststructuralism and Postmodernism,*
Hemel Hempstead: Harvester.

Postmodernism is a sceptically inclined form
of philosophy which calls into question the
certainties of other discourses, and Lyotard
is one of the movement's leading theorists.
Although best known for his writings on
postmodernism he has published widely in
various areas of philosophy such as philosophy of language, political philosophy and
aesthetics. His early work is in the Marxist
tradition; but in common with many left-
wing French intellectuals he turned sharply
against Marxism in the aftermath of the
1968 'évènements', and in his highly controversial study *Économie libidinale* (1974) he
staked out a provocatively post-Marxist
position which rejected the basic assumptions of Marxist methodology. This line of
development culminated in *The Postmodern
Condition* (1979), where the notion of universal theories was dismissed out of hand,
the argument being that such 'grand narratives' (for example Marxism) had lost all
credibility. Against grand narrative, with its
authoritarian connotations, Lyotard cham-
pioned the cause of 'little narrative', essentially the narrative of individual human
beings, which needed no foundational justification (Lyotard is a committed antifoundationalist). Much of his post-1968 political
thinking is structured around the idea of
specific campaigns to correct abuses of
individual freedoms. Lyotard has become
increasingly concerned with the nature and
rules of judgement in his later work, where
his line of argument tends to be that
judgement is essentially pragmatic and specific to a discourse. In Lyotard's view
discourses are incommensurable, and between any two discourses lies an unresolva-
ble area of dispute, or 'differend'. Kant is a
constant point of reference in these later
writings, where Lyotard consciously seems to
be trying to return to a pre-Marxist and
Hegelian framework of dialectical thought.

The iconoclastic sentiments of *The Postmodern Condition* struck a chord in contemporary intellectual circles and have inspired a
whole generation of cultural theorists. Reaction amongst more orthodox left-wing thinkers to Lyotard's postmodernist scepticism
has been predictably hostile.

STUART SIM

MacIntyre, A(lasdair) C(halmers)

British. *b:* 1929, Glasgow. *Cat:* Analytic
philosopher. *Ints:* Ethics; history of ethics;
Aristotle; Aquinas; Confucianism. *Educ:*
Universities of London and Manchester.
Infls: Franz Steiner, Karl Polanyi and St
Thomas Aquinas. *Appts:* Lecturer in Philo-
sophy of Religion, University of Manchester,
1951–7; Lecturer in Philosophy, University
of Leeds, 1957–61; Fellow of University
College, Oxford, 1963–6; Professor of So-
ciology, University of Essex, 1966–70; Uni-
versity Professor of Philosophy and Political
Science, University of Boston, 1972–80; W.
Alton Jones Distinguished Professor of
Philosophy, Vanderbilt University, 1982–8;
McMahon/Hank Professor of Philosophy,
University of Notre Dame, from 1988;
various other positions at Oxford, Yale,
Princeton, Brandeis University, Wellesley
College.

Main publications:

(1953) *Marxism: An Interpretation,* London:
SCMP; revised and reissued as *Marxism and
Christianity,* New York: Schocken Books,
1968.
(1955) (ed. with Antony Flew) *New Essays in
Philosophical Theology,* London: SCMP.
(1958) *The Unconscious,* London: Routledge &
Kegan Paul.
(1959) *Difficulties in Christian Belief,* London:
SCMP.
(1966) *A Short History of Ethics,* New York:
Macmillan.
(1967) *Secularization and Moral Change,* London:
Oxford University Press.

(1971) *Against the Self-Images of the Age*, London: Duckworth.

(1981) *After Virtue*, London: Duckworth.

(1987) 'The idea of an educated public', in G. Haydon (ed.) *Education and Values*, London University Institute of Education.

(1988) *Whose Justice? Which Rationality*, Notre Dame: Notre Dame University Press.

(1990) *First Principles, Final Ends and Contemporary Philosophical Issues*, Milwaukee: Marquette University Press.

(1990) *Three Rival Versions of Moral Enquiry*, Notre Dame: Notre Dame University Press.

Secondary literature:

Horton, J. and Mendus, S. (eds) (1993) *After MacIntyre*, Oxford: Polity Press.

MacIntyre, Alasdair, Dahl, Norman O., Baier, Annette and Schneewind, J. B. (1991) 'Book symposium' on *Whose Justice? Which Rationality?*, in *Philosophy and Phenomenological Research* 11: 149–78.

MacIntyre's first book, written when he was 23, tried to rescue both a purified Christianity and a purified Marxism for the modern world. He argued that, properly understood, Marxism, as the historical successor to Christianity, largely shares both its content and its function as an interpretation of human existence.

In 1955 *New Essays in Philosophical Theology*, which MacIntyre edited with Antony Flew, and which gathered together a number of essays applying the methods of conceptual analysis to specific religious issues, reinaugurated the serious study of the philosophy of religion, a subject which had been moribund in the analytical tradition for some decades.

Since the mid-1960s most of MacIntyre's work has been concerned with ethical and social theory.

In *A Short History of Ethics* (1966) he attacked the notion that moral concepts are a timeless, unchanging, determinate set. He held rather that they are embodied in, and partially constitutive of, forms of social life, and so change as social life changes. This does not mean merely that different societies have held different things to be right or good but, much more radically, that what it means to describe something as right or good may itself change; indeed, the very idea of morality is subject to change. So, to take one central case, the peculiarly moral, Kantian sense of 'ought' that characterizes much modern ethical thought—an 'ought' that expresses obligations binding on all rational beings as such, but unable to be derived logically from any factual statements—is completely absent in, for instance, the Homeric period. It arose, according to MacIntyre, in the modern period when the social roles and ideals that had originally provided a backing for it gradually dropped away. And this development explains the peculiarly intractable nature of moral disputes in the modern world, which is not a feature of all possible moralities but of one with a certain history.

MacIntyre developed in detail this diagnosis of the problems of modern morality in *After Virtue* (1981). Its central claim is that modern morality is in deep disarray. It is, he suggested, no more than the fragments of a conceptual scheme which has lost the context which once made it intelligible, and to which have been added, as a way of attempting to cope with the breakdown of the traditional moral philosophy, such moral fictions as natural rights and utility. The attempt is a failure since, for one thing, there are no such things as natural rights or utility; and, for another, this yoking of incompatible moral traditions has largely made of morality just what **Nietzsche** and various forms of emotivism have claimed that it is: the mere expression of subjective preference with no objective criteria for deciding between them.

If morality is again to make sense for us, we must, according to MacIntyre, recapture something of the Aristotelian tradition of moral philosophy. Further, given the nature of our society and its ruling liberal individualist ideas, this will not be easy. It would entail recapturing a number of ideas that are now lost. The concept of what MacIntyre calls a *practice*—a cooperative enterprise in pursuit of goods internal to that enterprise—would be essential; this, outside of the area of games, and particularly in our participation in political life, we have all but lost. So too we should need to recapture the notion of a *whole human life*, an idea lost to us now because bureaucratic modernity has seen to it that our lives have no unity. And, third, we should need to recapture the sense that what we are is largely a matter of what we have become through our history and traditions. Without these notions, morality can make little sense for us. The choice, as MacIntyre puts it, is between Nietzsche and Aristotle.

Given this analysis, a central problem is how rationally to recommend one tradition of thought as against another. MacIntyre turned to this issue in *Whose Justice? Which Rationality?* (1988) and in his Gifford Lectures, *Three Rival Versions of Moral Enquiry* (1990). The accounts of justice that we find in Aristotle and Hume—to take what are for us two of the most central examples—are, according to MacIntyre, embedded in overall systems of thought which respectively impose their own standards of rationality on them. That being so, how may we adjudicate between them? MacIntyre argues that there can be no such thing as a rational enquiry which does not adopt the standpoint of a particular tradition; this, however, need not involve any form of relativism, since the tradition from which one reasons may itself involve an absolute conception of truth. So it is with the Thomist tradition that MacIntyre recommends in these works. And it can show itself rationally superior to both the Nietzschean tradition and the tradition of post-Enlightenment ethics that we have inherited; it can solve problems that these traditions themselves must recognize to be problems, and explain why they themselves cannot do so. If the state of modernity is characterized by lack of agreement about even the most fundamental questions, what role does this

leave for the university? In 'The idea of an educated public' (1987), MacIntyre argued that the dual aim of the liberal university—to prepare students for a social role and to teach them to think for themselves—could no longer be achieved: the demise of the 'educated public', a self-conscious body of people with a common intellectual inheritance and shared standards of argument, has made it impossible. In *Three Rival Versions of Moral Enquiry* he envisages the university 'as a place of constrained disagreement, of imposed participation in conflict, in which a central responsibility of higher education would be to initiate students into conflict' (pp. 230–1). MacIntyre's work has been widely influential. Some, however, have questioned his historical interpretation; and many have not found modern moral thought to be in such comparative disarray as he suggests.

Sources: Flew; WW 1992; Becker; personal communication.

ANTHONY ELLIS

McTaggart, John McTaggart Ellis

British. *b:* 1866, London. *d:* 1925, London. *Cat:* Ontological idealist. *Ints:* Metaphysics. *Educ:* MA and LittD, Trinity College, Cambridge. *Infls:* Spinoza and Hegel. *Appts:* Fellow of Trinity College, Cambridge, 1891–1923; College Lecturer, 1897–1923.

Main publications:

(1896) *Studies in the Hegelian Dialectic*, Cambridge.
(1901) *Studies in Hegelian Cosmology*, Cambridge.
(1906) *Some Dogmas of Religion*, London: Arnold; second edition, 1930.
(1910) *A Commentary on Hegel's Logic*, Cambridge.
(1921–7) *The Nature of Existence*, 2 vols, Cambridge: Cambridge University Press.
(1934) *Philosophical Studies*, ed. S. V. Keeling, London: Arnold (papers of 1893–1923).

Secondary literature:

Broad, C. D. (1933–8) *Examination of McTaggart's Philosophy*, Cambridge.
Geach, P. T. (1979) *Truth, Love and Immortality*, London: Hutchinson.

McTaggart gave short, clear outlines of his thinking in two papers reprinted in *Philosophical Studies* (1934): early, in 'The further determination of the absolute' (1893), and late, in 'An ontological idealism' (1923). There was little change in his views during his lifetime, although he did move from a preference for a dialectical, Hegelian method towards a more directly deductive exposition. His final position is summed up in the two volumes of *The Nature of Existence* (1921–7), a detailed and comprehensive treatment of his idealist metaphysics, along with its ramifications for religion and the place of values.

McTaggart called himself as 'ontological idealist' ('all reality is spirit') although he did not regard this position as being open to 'rigid demonstration' (1921–7, SS432). He was also, unusually, an epistemological realist in that he said that knowledge was a true belief: 'and I should say that a belief was true when, and only when, it stands in a relation of correspondence to a fact' (1934, p. 273). Although he was impressed by Hegel, and has often been classed with **Bradley** as an English neo-Hegelian, his idiosyncratic form of idealism differed from Hegel and Bradley in crucial ways (see 1921–7, SS48, 52, 136). He accepted the real existence of separate individuals. He thought that individual truths could be fully true, and believed that truth consisted in a relation of correspondence between a belief and a fact. The starting-point for his idealism was not the dependence of an object on a knowing subject but 'the assertion that nothing exists but spirit' (SS52). He differed from Hegel and Bradley, too, in the clarity of his exposition and the modesty of its tone (see, for example, SS912). Broad commented unkindly that if Hegel was the prophet of

the absolute and Bradley its chivalrous knight, McTaggart was its 'devoted and extremely astute family solicitor' (Introduction to second edition of *Some Dogmas of Religion*, 1906, p. xxviii). This is less than fair, not only because McTaggart's meticulous caution is more likely to appeal to modern readers than Bradley's haphazard rhetoric, but because McTaggart's Universe, 'a substance which contains all content, and of which every other substance is a part' (1921–7, SS135), is far less metaphysically charged than Bradley's Hegelian Absolute. Although McTaggart rarely acknowledged the direct debit, his nearest philosophical ancestor was not Hegel but Spinoza: both he and Spinoza aimed at the same kind of comprehensive, deductively explained metaphysical view. He felt a sympathy with the mystical strain in Part V of Spinoza's *Ethics* (see 1906, SS247), but he also shared the reluctance of Spinoza to appeal directly to mystical experience.

The exact details of McTaggart's system will be followed by very few modern readers. There are numerous undefined terms. The reasoning, from a priori premises, is proudly deductive, allowing for only two empirical postulates: that something exists and that what is exists is differentiated (1921–7, chapter 3). There is a plurality of (spiritual) substances which together make up the Universe, but no God (SS500). McTaggart considers issues of divisibility, definition and identity to reach a conclusion that a *sui generis* relation of 'determining correspondence' must hold between wholes and parts of substances (see SS197, 202). Reality as it is has to be very different from how it seems. Space, time and physical objects are all proved to be 'unreal' (ibid., chapters 33–5). (And it is the ingenious proof of the unreality of time which remains the most widely studied part of the system.) Individual minds are substances which must be immortal (liable to metempsychosis): a point to which McTaggart attached great personal significance. Love was seen as an 'emotional quality' of souls of particular importance: an 'intense and passionate' 'species of liking' only felt by persons for each other (SS459–60). McTaggart's moral philosophy was only scantily developed. His attribution of values to states of souls and his views on the indefinability of good owe a clear debt to **Moore** (who would hardly have accepted the supporting metaphysics, including its uncompromising determinism). *The Nature of Existence* ends with Spinozistic praise of 'a timeless and endless state of love—love so direct, so intimate and so powerful that even the deepest mystic rapture gives us but the smallest foretaste of its perfection' (SS913). McTaggart's philosophy is highly individual in combining views that are often held apart: a belief in the immortality of the soul along with atheism; ontological idealism along with epistemological realism and pluralism. McTaggart is usually seen as a foil in the early development of G. E. Moore and **Russell**, who both came to differ diametrically from him after their revolt against idealism in 1898. Later readers may find that his arguments were less ridiculous that Moore and Russell portrayed them to be. His argument on the unreality of time, in particular, continues to attract some interest. Few today will accept his opinion that the 'utility of Metaphysic is to be found ... in the comfort it can give us' (1934, p. 184). He had no disciples and no successors, but he has had occasional admirers, sometimes unexpectedly; for example: 'I could not ... imagine a much more exciting and rewarding enterprise than the rational rigour combined with the satisfaction of one's deepest cravings that it seemed McTaggart offered' (M. Tanner, 'Metaphysics and music', in A. Phillips Griffiths (ed.), *The Impulse to Philosophise*, Cambridge, 1992, p. 191).

RICHARD MASON

Malcolm, Norman

American. **b:** 1911, Selden, Kansas. **d:** 1990, London. **Cat:** Analytic philosopher. **Ints:** Philosophy of language; epistemology; philosophy of mind; philosophy of religion. **Educ:** Universities of Nebraska, Harvard and Cambridge. **Infls:** G. E. Moore and Ludwig Wittgenstein. **Appts:** 1940–2, Instructor, Princeton University; 1947–50, Assistant Professor, 1950–5, Associate Professor, 1950–64, Professor of Philosophy, 1964–78, Susan Linn Sage Professor; 1979–90, Visiting Professor, Cornell University; 1990, Fellow, King's College, London.

Main publications:

(1958) *Ludwig Wittgenstein: A Memoir*, with a biographical sketch by G. H. von Wright, Oxford: Oxford University Press; second edition, with Wittgenstein's letters to Malcolm, 1984.
(1962) *Dreaming*, London: Routledge & Kegan Paul.
(1963) *Knowledge and Certainty: Essays and Lectures*, Englewood Cliffs: Prentice-Hall.
(1971) *Problems of Mind: Descartes to Wittgenstein*, New York: Harper & Row.
(1977) *Memory and Mind*, Ithaca: Cornell University Press.
(1977) *Thought and Knowledge*, Ithaca: Cornell University Press.
(1984) (with D. M. Armstrong) *Consciousness and Causality: A Debate on the Nature of Mind*, Oxford: Basil Blackwell.
(1986) *Nothing is Hidden: Wittgenstein's Criticism of His Early Thought*, Oxford: Basil Blackwell.
(1993) *Wittgenstein: A Religious Point of View?*, London: Routledge.
(1995) *Wittgensteinian Themes, Essays 1978–1989*, ed. G. H. von Wright, Ithaca: Cornell University Press.

Secondary literature:

Putnam, Hilary, (1962) *Dreaming and depth grammar*, in R. Butler (ed.) *Analytical Philosophy, First Series*, Oxford: Basil Blackwell.

Malcolm's earliest work—and possibly some of his best—minutely analysed and rejected the argument, commonly propounded by epistemologists from Hume onwards, that no empirical judgement can be known for certain to be true since future experience may always give us reason to think it false. One of the most discussed of Malcolm's works, however, was his book *Dreaming* (1962), in which he argued that dreams are not mental experiences that take place during sleep. The idea that they are such mental experiences is an incoherent theory generated by the desire to explain a phenomenon that has no (philosophical) explanation, namely that 'sometimes when people wake up they relate stories in the past tense under the influence of an impression' (p. 87). (One reason this book was so widely discussed was that it seemed to encapsulate a sort of behaviourism that was widely thought to be unavoidable given the basically Wittgensteinian foundation to which many were attracted.)

In an influential article, Malcolm argued that one version of the ontological argument for the existence of God is in fact valid—a view almost universally rejected since Kant. His argument rested upon the idea that the reality of God's existence is to be found in the 'language games' of religious believers, and that one of those 'language games' involves the concept of a God who has 'necessary existence'.

The influence of G. E. **Moore** on Malcolm is clear in his constant attempt to recall philosophers to ordinary language; and the influence of **Wittgenstein** is clear in his underlying belief that our only access to reality, whether the reality of God or of mental phenomena such as dreams, is through human linguistic practices. The influence of both is clear in his sympathy with the deliverances of common sense, and it is on these foundations of his philosophical work that most criticism of Malcolm has focused.

Sources: Passmore 1957; personal communication with Ruth Malcolm.

ANTHONY ELLIS

Mao Zedong (Mao Tse-Tung)

Chinese. *b:* 1893, Shaoshan, Xiangtang County, Hunan Province, China. *d:* 1976, Beijing. *Cat:* Marxist; political and military leader; poet. *Ints:* Social and political philosophy. *Educ:* First Normal School, Changsha, Hunan Province and briefly audited courses at University of Beijing. *Infls:* Kang Youwei, Liang Qichao, Yan Fu and Western liberal thinkers, Li Dazhao, Chen Duxiu, Marx, Lenin, Stalin, and Soviet theoreticians, Ai Siqi, and Qin Shihuang (China's first Emperor). *Appts:* Chairman, Central Executive Committee, Chinese Soviet Republic, 1931–4; Chairman, Council of People's Commissars, Chinese Soviet Republic, 1931–4; Chairman, Politburo, Chinese Communist Party, 1935–; Chairman, Standing Committee, Chinese Communist Party Politburo, 1956–76; Chairman, Revolutionary Military Council, 1945–9; Chairman, People's Revolutionary Military Council, 1954–9; Commander in Chief, People's Liberation Army, 1945–9; Chairman, National Defence Council, 1954–9; Chairman, Chinese Communist Party Central Committee, 1943–76; Chairman, People's Government Council (Head of State), 1949–58.

Main publications:

(n.d.) *Dialectical Materialism (Lecture Notes)*, Dalian: Dazhong Bookshop.
(n.d.) *Selected Writings by Chairman Mao*, n.p.
(1960) *Comrade Mao Zedong on Marxist Philosophy (Extracts)*, Urumqi: Xinjiang Qingnian Publishing House.
(1960) *Mao Zedong's Philosophical Thought*, extracts compiled by the Department of Philosophy of Peking University).
(1960–5, 1977) *Selected Works of Mao Tse-tung*, 5 vols, Beijing: Foreign Languages Press.
(1966) *Quotations From Chairman Mao*, Beijing: People's Publishing Company.
(1967) *Selected Readings*, Beijing: Foreign Languages Press.
(1968) *Selected Readings of Mao Zedong's Writings*, 2 vols, Beijing: People's Publishing House.

(1988) *Mao Zedong's Collected Annotations on Philosophy*, Beijing: Zhongyang Wenxian Research Institute.

Secondary literature:

Boorman, H. (ed.) (1970) *Biographical Dictionary of Republican China*, New York and London: Columbia University Press.

Briere, O. (1956) *Fifty Years of Chinese Philosophy 1898–1950*, London: George Allen & Unwin Ltd.

Complete Chinese Encyclopedia (1987), Philosophy Volumes, Beijing: Chinese Encyclopedia Publications.

Louie, K. (1986) *Inheriting Tradition: Interpretations of the Classical Philosophers in Communist China 1949–1966*, Hong Kong: Oxford University Press.

Schram, S. (1966) *Mao Tse-tung*, Harmondsworth: Penguin Books.

——(1989) *The Thought of Mao Tse-tung*, Cambridge: Cambridge University Press.

After early radical activity organizing peasants and students in Hunan Province, Mao turned to Marxism under the influence of Li Dazhao and Chen Duxiu, China's first major Marxist figures. He argued from a Marxist perspective for the legitimacy of seizing power by force against Bertrand **Russell**'s reformist gradualism during Russell's visit to Hunan. Mao represented Hunan at the founding meeting of the Chinese Communist Party in 1921 and entered a busy life of organizational, educational and trade union activities. He became a member of the Communist Party's Central Committee and the Director of its Organization Department in 1923. Under Comintern policy of cooperating with the Nationalists, Mao also held important posts with the Guomindang, dealing with party organization, propaganda and the peasant movement. Mao's study of the peasantry convinced him that overthrowing the landlord class was necessary for China to secure a prosperous and independent future. He recognized the crucial revolutionary potential of China's peasant population and the importance of opening the party bureaucracy to the influence of the masses. When first articulated, these views were rejected by the Party in favour of orthodox concentration on the urban proletariat as the main focus of revolutionary activity.

During the years of Party instability following the Guomindang massacre of Communists in 1927, Mao established a base in Jiangxi Province. Together with the military strategist Zhu De, he developed theories dealing with party organization and leadership and with control of population and territory. Their guerrilla and mobile warfare and popular revolutionary mobilization evaded successive campaigns organized by Guomindang leader Jiang Jieshi (Chiang Kia-shek) to crush them. In Jiangxi, Mao also had his first experience directing a major purge of those rebelling against his authority. Mao's successful application of his theoretical position increased his political power, culminating in his elevation to party leadership in 1935 as Chairman of the Politburo.

By 1934, however, Guomindang encirclement forced Mao and his followers to embark upon the Long March which, after terrible losses, ended at Yanan, Shanaxi Province. Mao's lectures in Yanan reflected years of revolutionary experience and explored many matters, including military strategy, government, philosophy, literature and art. In all cases, he argued for the primacy of politics. His integrated military and political ideas bore fruit in the Anti-Japanese War and in renewed civil war against Jiang Jieshe and the Guomindang. Mao's victory led to the establishment of the People's Republic in 1949.

As a ruler Mao veered between the cautious and flexible pragmatism of his principal colleagues and his own utopian, voluntarist populism displayed in the establishment of the communes, the Great Leap Forward and the Cultural Revolution. He broke with the Soviet Union, which provided a model of revolution so different from his own. The humiliating failure of the Great

Leap Forward threatened his position and led to the Cultural Revolution, in which Mao appealed to the populace against the Party apparatus. In the face of the resulting anarchy and violence, Mao turned to the army to restore order; but with a debilitated Party and dogmatic leadership under the Gang of Four, he spent his last years publicly revered, though in growing isolation and confusion.

In the treatment of philosophers and other intellectuals, Mao also responded to conflicting demands. Because his regime needed the cooperation of sophisticated, Western-educated figures to articulate and implement new policies, Mao included all who were not enemies in a broad front programme of New Democracy. His conception of democracy, however, was based on the doctrine of popular dictatorship, in which the party would exercise leadership through constant attention to the masses. He was contemptuous of the 'flabby liberalism' of bourgeois democracy. Mao sought to reshape the thinking of intellectuals to gain loyalty as well as consent on the model of his party rectification campaign of 1942–3. Mao provided gestures of conciliation, but also closed the universities to retrain philosophers and others in Marxist thought. He waged intense campaigns against intellectual opponents, initially the pragmatist and liberal philosopher Hu Shi. The relative latitude of the Hundred Flowers Campaign gave way to the harsh Anti-Rightist Campaign when Mao was angered by the depth of residual bitterness and opposition amongst intellectuals. A modest return to wider debate was swept away by the Cultural Revolution, during which distinguished figures were humiliated and physically attacked, with some hounded to death. Intellectuals were sent to the countryside, in some cases with their work of a lifetime destroyed.

Regarding the brutal side of his treatment of intellectuals, Mao compared himself with Qin Shihuang, China's rationalizing and unifying first Emperor. In other more positive ways, Mao aimed to sinify Marxism by placing it within the context of Chinese history, thought and literature, although he was hostile to Confucianism as the central ideology of China's feudal past.

Mao's own philosophical work took the form of lectures on dialectical materialism delivered in 1937 in Yanan. For the most part, these lectures were unimpressive summaries of Soviet texts, but two essays 'On practice' and 'On contradiction' were extracted and printed in revised form in 1950 and 1952. 'On practice' discusses Marxist epistemology and the relations between theory and practice. The theme of seeking the truth from the facts derives from ancient Chinese sources and was used to combat the Moscow-educated dogmatists who challenged Mao's authority. More original was 'On contradiction', an exploration of dialectics drawn theoretically from ancient yin-yang doctrines as well as from Hegel and Marx and practically from Mao's understanding of Chinese society. The claim that contradictions would continue to arise in society even after the establishment of socialism supported Mao's doctrine of permanent revolution. His distinction between antagonistic and non-antagonistic contradictions allowed room for discussion rather than violence as a response to some controversies. His voluntarism was supported by the claim that at times superstructure, theory and relations of production took priority in determining social developments. 'On practice' and 'On contradiction' became major elements in Mao Zedong Thought, studied and emulated throughout China. Their dogmatic use undermined the doctrines of voluntarist flexibility, respect for the facts and the concrete appropriation of China's complex history within universal Marxist thought.

NICHOLAS BUNNIN

Marcel, Gabriel

French. *b:* 1889, Paris. *d:* 1973, Paris. *Cat:* Neo-Socratic and theistic existentialist; playwright and musician. *Ints:* The phenomenology of the human existence; metaphysical reality; ethics. *Educ:* The Sorbonne, Paris; 1908, doctoral thesis on 'The Metaphysical Ideas of Coleridge and their Relationship to the Philosophy of Schelling'. *Infls:* Karl Jaspers and Roman Catholicism. *Appts:* 1912–40, taught intermittently at various secondary schools in Verdôme, Paris and Sens; worked for the Red Cross in the Second World War; 1929, converted to Roman Catholicism; undertook numerous European lecture tours, including the Gifford Lectures in 1949–50.

Main publications:

(1927) *Journal métaphysique* (1913–23), Paris: Gallimard (English translation, *Metaphysical Journal*, trans. Bernard Wall, Chicago: Regnery, 1952).

(1935) *Être et avoir*, Paris: Aubier (English translation, *Being and Having*, trans. Katherine Farrer, New York: Harper & Brothers, 1949).

(1945) *Homo Viator: Prolégomènes à une métaphysique de l'espérance*, Paris: Aubier (English translation, *Homo Viator: Introduction to a Metaphysic of Hope*, trans. Emma Crawford, Chicago: Regnery, 1951; reprinted, New York: Harper & Row, 1962).

(1945) *La Métaphysique de Royce*, Paris: Aubier.

(1949–50) *Le Mystère de L'être* (The Gifford Lectures) (English translation in 2 vols, *The Mystery of Being*: 1. *Reflection and Mystery* (1949); 2. *Faith and Reality* (1950), trans. G. S. Fraser and R. Hague, Chicago: Regnery).

(1955) *The Decline of Wisdom*, New York: Philosophical Library.

(1963) *The Existential Background of Human Dignity*, Cambridge: Mass.: Harvard University Press.

Secondary literature:

Gilson, Étienne (ed.) (1947) *Existentialisme chrétien: Gabriel Marcel*, Paris: Plon (essays in honour of Marcel, including his reply, 'Regard en arrière', trans. in *The Philosophy of Existence*, London: The Harvill Press, 1948).

Hammond, Julien (1992) 'Marcel's philosophy of human nature', *Dialogue* 35, 1: 1-5.

Schilpp, Paul A. (ed.) (1994) *The Philosophy of Gabriel Marcel*, La Salle: Open Court.

Troisfontaines, Roger (1953) *De l'Existence à l'Être*, 2 vols, Paris (concordance and bibliography).

Marcel's philosophy is discursive and unsystematic: the expression of a reflective exploration rather than a record of conclusions reached. His intention is to reveal a metaphysical reality and his starting-point is the human situation, the experience of being-in-the-world. The mainspring of his thought is the claim that the human person is, *au fond*, a participant in, rather than a spectator of, reality and the life of the world; a being that ultimately cannot be encompassed to become an object of thought.

Marcel described himself as Socratic and questioning rather than as an existentialist. He repudiated idealism because of the 'way in which [it] overrates the part of construction in sensual perception', and he was repelled by philosophies that deployed special terminologies or proceeded by assuming that reason, properly exerted, could achieve a total grasp of reality. 'Reality', he wrote, 'cannot be summed up.' Immediate, personal experience is the touchstone of all his enquiries, and in this he resembles the avowedly existentialist thinkers even though he emphasized personal transcendence and human relationships rather than the existential freedom and autonomy traditionally associated with existentialism. He developed a phenomenology of his own that owed nothing to **Husserl**.

Marcel distinguished two kinds of consciousness, 'first reflection' and 'second reflection'. In first reflection a person might mentally stand back from, say, a direct relationship of friendship, in order to describe and objectify it. This, according to Marcel, is to separate oneself from the relationship and to treat it as a 'problem' in need of explanation. In 'second reflection' the immediacy of the relationship is restored, but additionally there is an awareness of participation in Being: the recognition that we inhabit a 'mystery'; that it is not our prime task to separate ourselves and objectify this condition and that 'Having', that sense of owning one's body, talents, abilities, must be transformed into 'Being'.

On the basis of this analysis Marcel conducts an investigation into a range of concepts, including incarnation, fidelity, hope, faith, love and *disponibilité* (availability). In being *disponible* a person is receptive to others, is fully present and responsive to them and, through this kind of intersubjectivity, affirms a mutual participation in Being.

A summary of Marcel's ideas conveys little of his thought's philosophical penetration, which is achieved by detailed and vivid phenomenological enquiry rather than by the orderly presentation of proofs. His dramatic and other writings powerfully complement the major themes of the philosophy.

Sources: *PI.*

DIANÉ COLLINSON

Marcuse, Herbert

German. **b:** 19 July 1898, Berlin. **d:** 30 July 1979, Munich. **Cat:** Critical theorist. **Ints:** History of philosophy; social philosophy; psychoanalytic theory. **Educ:** Philosophy at Berlin and Freiburg (doctorate 1923); further study in Freiburg, 1929–32, with Husserl and Heidegger; left after his relations with Heidegger deteriorated. **Infls:** Husserl, Heidegger, Adorno, Horkheimer, Hegel, Marx and Freud. **Appts:** Member of Institut für Sozialforschung, from 1933; exile in Geneva, New York and California; Section Head, Office of Strategic Services, 1942–50; Professor of Philosophy, Brandeis University, 1954–67; Professor of Philoso-

phy, University of California at Santa Barbara, 1967.

Main publications:

(1928) 'Beiträge zu einer Phänomenologie des historischen Materialismus', *Philosophische Hefte*: 45–68.

(1932) *Hegels Ontologie und die Grundlegung einer Theorie der Geschichtlichkeit*, Frankfurt: V. Klostermann (English translation, *Hegel's Ontology and the Theory of Historicity*, Seyla Benhabib, Cambridge, Mass.: MIT Press, 1987).

(1936) (with Erich Fromm and Max Horkheimer) *Studien über Autorität und Familie*, Paris: F. Alcan.

(1941) *Reason and Revolution. Hegel and the Rise of Social Theory*, New York: Oxford University Press; second edition, Boston: Beacon Press, 1960.

(1955) *Eros and Civilization: A Philosophical Inquiry into Freud*, Boston: Beacon Press.

(1964) *One Dimensional Man: Studies in the Ideology of Advanced Industrial Society*, Boston: Beacon Press.

(1964) *Soviet Marxism: A Critical Analysis*, Boston: Beacon Press; new edition, Harmondsworth: Penguin, 1971.

(1965) *Kultur und Gesellschaft*, 2 vols, Frankfurt: Suhrkamp.

(1965) (with Robert P. Wolff and Barrington Moore Jr) *A Critique of Pure Tolerance*, Boston: Beacon Press.

(1968) *Negations: Essays in Critical Theory*, Boston: Beacon Press.

(1968) *Psychoanalyse und Politik*, Frankfurt: Europäische Verlagsanstalt.

(1968) (with others) *Aggression und Anpassung in der Industriegesellschaft*, Frankfurt: Suhrkamp.

(1969) *An Essay on Liberation*, Boston: Beacon Press.

(1969) *Ideen zu einer kritischen Theorie der Gesellschaft*, Frankfurt: Suhrkamp.

(1970) *Five Lectures: Psychoanalysis, Politics and Utopia*, trans. Jeremy J. Shapiro and Shierry M. Weber, Boston: Beacon Press.

(1972) *Counterrevolution and Revolt*, Boston: Beacon Press.

(1973) *Studies in Critical Philosophy*, Jois de Bres, Boston: Beacon Press.

(1975) *Zeit-Messungen. Drei Vorträge und ein Interview*, Frankfurt: Suhrkamp.

(1977) *Die Permanenz der Kunst. Wider eine bestimmte marxistische Ästhetik: Ein Essay*, Munich: Hanser.

(1978) *The Aesthetic Dimension: Towards a Critique of Marxist Aesthetics*, Boston: Beacon Press.

(1978–) *Schriften*, Frankfurt: Suhrkamp.

(1980) *Das Ende der Utopie. Vorträge und Diskussionen in Berlin 1967*, Frankfurt: Verlag Neue Kritik.

Secondary literature:

Breuer, Stefan (1977) *Die Krise der Revolutionstheorie. Negative Vergesellschaftung und Arbeitsmetaphysik bei Herbert Marcuse*, Frankfurt: Syndikat Autoren- und Verlagsgesellschaft.

Brunkhorst, Hauke and Koch, Gertrud (1987) *Herbert Marcuse zur Einführung*, Hamburg: Junius.

Claussen, Detlev (1981) *Spuren der Befreiung— Herbert Marcuse. Eine Einführung in sein politisches Denken*, Darmstadt: Luchterhand.

Habermas, Jürgen (ed.) (1968) *Antworten auf Herbert Marcuse*, Frankfurt: Suhrkamp.

——(1978) *Gespräche mit Herbert Marcuse*, Frankfurt: Suhrkamp.

Jansohn, Heinz (1971) *Herbert Marcuse: Philosophische Grundlagen seiner Gesellschaftskritik*, Bonn: Bouvier.

Katz, Barry (1982) *Herbert Marcuse and the Art of Liberation: An Intellectual Biography*, London: New Left Books.

Kellner, Douglas (1984) *Herbert Marcuse and the Crisis of Marxism*, London: Macmillan.

MacIntyre, Alasdair (1970) *Marcuse*, Glasgow: Fontana.

Mattick, Paul (1972) *Critique of Marcuse: One-Dimensional Man in Class Society*, London: Merlin.

Roth, Roland, *Rebellische Subjektivität. Herbert Marcuse und die neuen Protestbewegungen*, Frankfurt and New York: Campus.

Stark, Franz (ed.) (1971) *Revolution oder Reform. Herbert Marcuse und Karl Popper. Eine Konfrontation*, Munich: Kösel (English translation, *Reform or Revolution: A Confrontation Between Herbert Marcuse and Karl Popper*, trans. Michael Aylway and A. T. Ferguson, Chicago: New University Press, 1976).

Wolff, Kurt H. and Moore Jr, Barrington (eds) *The Critical Spirit: Essays in Honor of Herbert Marcuse*, Boston: Beacon Press.

Of the core members of the Frankfurt School, Marcuse was both the most actively political and the most concerned with a directly philosophical engagement with classical Marxism and with the phenomenology of his teachers **Husserl** and **Heidegger**. Marcuse's early work in particular is strongly marked by the attempt to fuse Marxist and phenomenological insights, a central feature of later existentialist Marxism in France and of praxis philosophy in Yugoslavia. Along with Marxism and phenomenology, the third element—already prominent in the 1930s in Marcuse's many essays in the Institute's journal, the *Zeitschrift für Sozialforschung*, and in his contribution to its joint project on authority and the family—was Freudian theory. His postwar work was dominated by a reworking of themes in Marx (especially the analysis of alienation in the 1844 manuscripts) and Freud, in an ambitious theory of human emancipation. Together, *Eros and Civilization* (1955) and *One Dimensional Man* (1964) made Marcuse the paradigmatic thinker of the New Left across North America and Western Europe in the late 1960s and into the 1970s—a role which surprised but did not disturb him. Although the empirical analysis in *One Dimensional Man* can be questioned, and it now appears in some ways as a left variant of the theories of industrial society prominent in the 1950s and 1960s, it remains a brilliant attempt at a philosophical diagnosis of the times.

WILLIAM OUTHWAITE

Maritain, Jacques

French. **b:** 18 November 1882, Paris. **d:** 28 April 1973, Toulouse. **Cat:** Thomist. **Ints:** All areas of philosophy. **Educ:** University of Sorbonne, Collège de France and University of Heidelberg. **Infls:** Bergson, Aquinas, Charles Péguy and Léon Bloy. **Appts:** 1914–40, Institut Catholique, Paris; 1948–60, Princeton.

Main publications:

(1920) *Art et scolastique*, Paris: Librairie de L'Art Catholique; third edition, 1935 (English translation, *Art and Scholasticism*, London: Sheed & Ward; New York: Charles Scribner's Sons, 1930).

(1932) *Distinguer pour unir, ou les degrès du savoir*, Paris: Desclée de Brouwer; eighth edition, 1963 (English translation, *The Degrees of Knowledge*, London: G. Bles; New York: Charles Scribner's Sons, 1959).

(1934) *Sept leçons sur l'être et les premiers principes de la raison spéculative*, Paris: Pierre Téqui (English translation, *A Preface to Metaphysics*, London and New York: Sheed & Ward, 1939).

(1942) *Les Droits de l'homme et la loi naturelle*, New York: Editions de la Maison Française; Paris: Paul Hartmann, 1947 (English translation, *The Rights of Man and Natural Law*, New York: Charles Scribner's Sons, 1943; London: G. Bles, 1944).

(1947) *Court Traité de l'existence et de l'existant*, Paris: Paul Hartmann (English translation, *Existence and the Existent*, New York: Pantheon Books, 1948).

(1947) *La Personne et le bien commun*, Paris: Desclée de Brouwer (English translation, *The Person and The Common Good*, New York: Charles Scribner's Sons; London: G. Bles, 1948).

(1953) *Creative Intuition in Art and Poetry*, New York: Pantheon Books; London: Harvill Press, 1954.

Secondary literature:

(1972) *The New Scholasticism* 46: 118–28 (bibliography, excluding articles up to 1961).

Allard, Jean-Louis (ed.) (1985) *Jacques Maritain*, Ottawa: University of Ottawa Press.

Hudson, Deal W. and Mancini, Matthew J. (eds) (1987) *Understanding Maritain*, Macon, Ga.: Mercer University Press.

Knasas, John F. X. (ed.) (1988) *Jacques Maritain: The Man and his Metaphysics*, Notre Dame, Ind.: University of Notre Dame Press.

Phelan, Gerald B. (1937) *Jacques Maritain*, New York: Sheed & Ward.

Redpath, Peter A. (ed.) (1992) *From Twilight to Dawn: The Cultural Vision of Jacques Maritain*, Notre Dame, Ind.: University of Notre Dame Press.

Rover, Thomas Dominic (1965) *The Poetics of Maritain*, Washington, DC: The Thomist Press.

Jacques Maritain was one of the most significant and influential Thomistic philosophers of the first half of the twentieth century. It is possible to regard him as a conservative and orthodox Thomist, more like Garrigou-Lagrange than like apparently more radical transcendental Thomists such as Maréchal and Lonergan. However, his philosophical subtlety and insight raised him far above his more pedestrian contemporaries, and his genius was supported, rather than suppressed or distorted, by the Thomistic framework within which he worked.

Maritain's epistemology and his metaphysics can conveniently be dealt with together. The act of knowledge, he states, begins in the encounter between an intellect and sensible realities. These realities, however, are envisaged by the intellect in one of two ways. In one way, the intellect concentrates upon observable and measurable phenomena; and being as such, though it is the metaphysical foundation of phenomena, is ignored. This is the perspective adopted by the empirical sciences. In the other way, which Maritain calls the way of common sense, sensible realities are either apprehended unreflectively or, if reflectively, by a mental process of progressive abstraction and classification, culminating in a concept of being which has a universal extension but little or no intension: 'being' then becomes an empty concept. This perspective, if divested of all connection with reality, is the starting-point of logic and mathematics.

Common-sense knowledge, however, can also generate an intuition of being *qua* being, and this intuition is the beginning of metaphysics. The object of such an intuition (which he variously called abstractive intuition, eidetic intuition and eidetic visualization) is being in all its richness and plenitude, the exploration of which is a lifetime's work. The intuition is intellectual in character, and thus unlike Bergsonian intuition. Also, it is not given to everyone to have it. It is, in fact, 'a sublime and exceedingly rare mental endowment', a 'gift bestowed upon the intellect', a kind of intuition never experienced, for instance, by Kant.

Maritain believed that, by reflecting both upon being, the object of the intuition, and also upon the concept of being which the intuition brings forth in our minds, the metaphysician can progressively clarify and formulate various properties and principles of being. Thus he will observe the distinctness of essence and existence. Again, he will find that he is able to apprehend being under different aspects. In one aspect, he sees that being possesses the attribute of unity. In another aspect, being as an object of thought, he sees its truth. Being as an object of love and will possesses goodness. In this way, the metaphysician comes to formulate the transcendental attributes of being: its unity, truth and goodness.

Reflection on being, and our intuitive concept of it, also produce the first principles of reason. Thus, being as something given to the mind, and being as something affirmed by the mind, come together as subject and predicate of the judgement 'being is being', the principle of identity (whose logical counterpart is the principle of non-contradiction). This principle is not a tautology, but an expression of the energy of existence, of the affluence and luxury of being. The principle of sufficient reason, that 'everything which is, to the extent to which it is, possesses a sufficient reason for its being', follows from reflection on the fact that being and intellect are connatural, or made for one another. It also induces reflection on the distinction between dependent existence and existence *a se*, and thus leads us to the idea of a Divine Being.

Maritain's social and political philosophy was a response to the cataclysmic events of the 1930s and 1940s, and was in essence a defence of liberal democracy against the two extremes of totalitarianism and individualist utilitarianism. At the heart of his thinking is a distinction between the individual and the person. The concept of the individual is opposed to the concept of the universal. An individual is a instantiation of humanity in a particular living body. Since all matter has a kind of 'avidity' for being, an individual seeks an egotistical absorption of everything into itself. It also is disposed to change and dissolution. Personality, in contrast, refers to the spiritual identity of human beings. It has two characteristics: first, persons have a wholeness and independence, a possession of their own existence, such that their actions aim to perfect and realize themselves; and second, the spiritual nature of persons disposes them to be open to others and otherness, to engage in communication, love and friendship.

Both individuality and personality generate the urge to live in society, and have an influence on social organization and social justice. As individuals, we look to society for the satisfaction of our material needs. As persons, however, we seek out other people in love and friendship. It is on the latter level that Maritain explains his conception of the common good, which is one of his fundamental socio-political principles and the foundation, in his view, of true democracy. The common good is not the same as a collection of individual goods, in the utilitarian manner. Neither is it the same as the public good, if by this is meant the good of a social collective regarded as something distinct from the good of its members. The common good is, rather, the good of 'a multitude of persons', and that is to say, the good of each person individually which is, simultaneously, the good of the society of persons taken as a whole.

The good in question is the good of persons, and thus pertains to spiritual and cultural development. A necessary precondition for this is personal freedom, and this implies the progressive freeing of humanity from economic bondage and totalitarian repression. It also justifies the traditional values in social and political theory: progress, human dignity, equality, democracy and morality in public life.

Maritain's aesthetics, or rather his philosophy of art, exploits the notion of 'creative intuition'. This is a type of intuition which originates in the preconscious or unconscious mind: not the Freudian unconscious of instinct and repressed desire, but a preconscious which underlies and provides the energy for intellection. In some people, 'privileged or ill-fated', preconscious energies are productive and formative, or in short, creative.

Creative intuition is cognitive, although it is a non-conceptual or preconceptual form of knowledge. What it reveals is both the subjectivity of the artist and, simultaneously, the reality of things with which his subjectivity is connatural. Realities are grasped in their singularity rather than their essence, but their very singularity is emblematic of the universe of things to which they belong. A work of art is therefore a sign both of the universe at large and of the subjective universe of the artist. Maritain's works no longer receive the attention that they attracted during his lifetime, and his type of Thomism is not at present fashionable. It remains to be seen whether his influence can equal his stature.

Sources: DFN; EF; WWW; *RPL* 71, 1973.

HUGH BREDIN

Meinong, Alexius (von)

Austrian. **b:** 17 July 1853, Lemberg (now Lvov). **d:** 27 November 1920. **Cat:** Metaphysician. **Ints:** Philosophy of mind; perception. **Educ:** Studied at University of Vienna, first History with subsidiary Philosophy (graduating 1874), then, via the Law School, Philosophy. **Infls:** Hume, Kant, Schopenhauer, Brentano, Carl Menger, Russell and several of his own students. **Appts:** Taught at Vienna, 1878–82, and then Graz, becoming full Professor, 1889; founded first laboratory for experimental pyschology in Austria at Graz, 1894.

Main publications:

(1877, 1882) *Hume-studien*: I, *Zur Geschichte und Kritik des modernen Nominalismus*, II, *Zur Relationstheorie*, in *Sitzungsberichte der philosophisch—historischen Klasse der Kaiserlichen Akademie der Wisenschaften*, vols 78, 101, Vienna (see 1966 for translations).

(1885) *Über philosophische Wissenschaft und ihre Propädeutik*, Vienna: A. Holder.

(1894) *Psychologisch-ethische Untersuchungen zur Werth-Theorie*, Graz: Leuschner & Lubensky.

(1896) 'Über die Bedeutung des Weberschen Gesetzes. Beiträge zur Psychologie des Vergleichens und Messens', in *Zeitschrift für Psychologie und Physiologie der Sinnesorgane* 11.

(1899) 'Über Gegenstande höherer Ordnung und deren Verhältniss zur inneren Wahrnehmung', in *Zeitschrift für Psychologie und Physiologie der Sinnesorgane*, 21.

(1902) *Über Annahmen*, Leipzig: J. A. Barth (see 1910).

(1904) 'Über Gegenstandstheorie', in A. Meinong (ed.), *Untersuchungen zur Gegenstandstheorie und Psychologie*, Leipzig: J. A. Barth (English translation, 'The theory of objects', trans. I. Levi, R. B. Terrell and R. M. Chisholm, in R. M. Chisholm (ed.), *Realism and the Background of Phenomenology*, Glencoe, Ill.: Free Press, 1960.

(1906) 'Über die Erfahrungsgrundlagen unseres Wissens', in *Abhandlungen zur Didaktik und Philosophie der Naturwissenschaften* Sonderabdruck der *Zeitschrfit für den physikalischen und chem ischen Unterricht* 1.

(1906) 'Über die Stellung der Gegenstandstheorie im System der Wissenschaften, in Zeitschrift für Philosophie und philosophische Kritik 129.

(1910) *Über Annahmen*, second edition, considerably revised, Leipzig: J. A. Barth (English translation, *On Assumptions*, trans. J. Heanue, Berkeley, Cal.: University of California Press, 1983; editor's introduction includes details of how 1910 differs from 1902).

(1915) *Über Möglichkeit und Wahrscheinlichkeit*, Leipzig: J. A. Barth.

(1917) 'Über emotionale Präsentation', in *Sitzungsberichte der Akademie der Wissenschaften in Wien*, Philosophisch-historischen Klasse 183 (English translation, *On Emotional Presentation*, trans. M.-L. Schubert Kalsi, Evanston, Ill.: Northwestern University Press, 1972).

(1918) 'Zum Erweise des allgemeinen Kausalgesetzes', in *Sitzungsbericht der Akademie der Wissenschaften in Wien*, Philosophich-historischen Klasse 189.

(1920) 'Selbstdarstellung', in *Gesaumtausgabe* (1968–78), vol. 7 (partial English translation, in

R. Grossman, *Meinong*, London: Routledge & Kegan Paul, 1974.

(1923) *Zur Grundlegung der allgemeinen Werttheorie* (in place of second edition of 1894), Graz: Leuschner & Lubensky.

(1966) K. F. Barber, *Meinong's Hume Studies*, University Microfilms, Michigan: Ann Arbor (translation with commentary of 1877 and parts of 1882).

Collected editions:

(1913–14) *Gesammelte Abhandlungen*, Leipzig: J. A. Barth.

(1968–78) *Alexius Meinong Gesamtausgabe*, 8 vols, Graz: Akad. Druck- und Verlagsanstalt (vol. 7 includes full bibliography).

Secondary literature:

Chisholm, R. M. (1982) *Brentano and Meinong Studies*, Amsterdam: Rodopi.

Findlay, J. N. (1933) *Meinong's Theory of Objects*, Oxford: Clarendon Press; second expanded edition, 1963.

Grazer Philosophische Studien 25–6 (1985–6) (contains several articles on Meinong).

Grossmann, R. (1974) *Meinong*, London: Routledge & Kegan Paul.

Lambert, K. (1983) *Meinong and the Principle of Independence*, Cambridge: Cambridge University Press.

Radakovic, K., Tarouca, S. and Weinhandl, F. (eds) (1952) *Meinong-Gedenkschrift*, vol. 1, Graz: 'Styria' Steirische Verlagsanstalt.

Russell, B. (1904) 'Meinong's theory of complexes and assumptions', *Mind*.

Schubert Kalsi, M. L. (1987) *Meinong's Theory of Knowledge*, Dordrecht: Nijhoff (includes biographical note and discussions of Brentano's influence on Meinong and Meinong's on Chisholm).

After his initial study of history Meinong entered philosophy via its own history, working on his own on Kant for the subsidiary subject in his first degree, and then, at **Brentano**'s suggestion, on Hume. He soon turned to pure philosophy, though in his early years combining it, as was almost inevitable then, with psychology, setting up the first Austrian experimental laboratory in psychology, in Graz, where he worked from 1882, being almost completely blind for his last fifteen years or so. His experimental work was on psychology of perception, but he gradually emancipated himself from 'psychologism', the attempt to solve philosophical problems by irrelevant empirical or introspective methods. Here as elsewhere he worked in parallel with **Frege** and **Husserl**, though apparently without any mutual influence. Nevertheless he insisted that psychology must not be abandoned altogether. Like a good phenomenologist he insisted on 'inner experiences' as a, if not the, subject matter for philosophy (1968–78, vol. 7, p. 11, written in 1920), and in 1912 wrote an article entitled 'For psychology and against psychologism in general value theory' (*Logos* III, 1912, reprinted in vol. 3 of *Alexius von Meinong Gesamtausgabe* (1968–78).

Meinong was unfortunate in living too early to be flung out of Austria by Hitler, so that he could not join the many German-speaking philosophers in exile who wrote in English. Apart from a single page in *Mind* (1879, reprinted in 1968–78, vol. 7) he wrote exclusively in German, and, despite the better fate of Mach and Frege, that may be partly why he has never achieved the popularity in Anglophone philosophy of Moore and Russell, with whom he has considerable philosophical kinship. Only recently, after the pioneering efforts of J. N. Findlay and R. M. **Chisholm** and others, have translations started appearing.

The one thing everybody knows about Meinong is that he had a jungle, providing rich nutrient for all manner of strange beasts, from the golden mountain to the round square. Recently, however, the lushness of its vegetation has come under more sceptical scrutiny (Grossman 1974; N. Griffin in *Grazer Philosophie Studien*, 1985–6). The issue is complex. Meinong does talk in a jungly sort of way, and apart from being and subsistence we are asked to accept, at various times, quasi-being, pseudo-existence and 'outside-of-being-ness' (*Aussersein*, variously translated, but often and perhaps best left untranslated). If we are to talk about something, he thinks, there must in some sense be something there to talk about. But in what sense? Every thought must have an object (*Gegenstand*), which Meinong then treats as an entity (Grossman (1974) translates *Gegenstand* as 'entity', but this seems question-begging and breaks the link with thought). Some objects are real (*wirklich*): roughly, those that are perceptible and in space and time. These also subsist (*bestehen*), but some objects merely subsist and are not real, though they still have being (*Sein*); they are higher-order objects and presuppose objects of the lowest order, which one can say 'with a grain of salt'—one of Meinong's favourite expressions—they have as parts; a stock example is the difference between red and green, although the assignment of objects in general to the different orders is a complex matter. Some objects, however, neither exist nor subsist, such as the golden mountain and the existence of the golden mountain, although we can think of them and they have properties or 'being so' (*Sosein*): the golden mountain is golden.

Meinong now faces a problem because of the principle that higher-order objects presuppose lower-order ones. But how can the perfectly good higher-order object, the non-existence of the golden mountain, subsist if its presupposed lower-order object, the golden mountain, does not? At first he toyed with a shadowy third kind of being, or 'quasi-being', which would belong to every object, i.e. anything at all, however absurd or contradictory. 'There are objects of which it is true that there are no such objects', as he puts it with conscious paradox (1904, translation p. 83), thereby raising questions about quantification that have similarly engaged Frege, **Russell** and **Quine**. This does indeed suggest the jungle, and he later said that it betrayed the same 'prejudice in favour of the actual' (or real) that he had sought to oppose by a third alternative to existence and subsistence (1910, translation pp. 159, 170). But his main objection was that being of universal application it would have no significance, and his later solution was 'the

Aussersein of the pure object' (1904, translation pp. 83–6). The point, in effect, is to abandon the need to specify an ontological status for the basic objects of thought. But alas! *Aussersein* itself ends up as something 'being-like' (*seinsartiges*), which does not after all apply universally: the round square has it only in a qualified way, and things even more defective, like the paradoxical Russell class, not at all (1917, chapter 2; cf. Heanue's introduction to his translation of 1910, pp. xxx–xxxi; Griffin, in *Grazer Philosophische Studien* 1985–6, draws some interesting implications regarding modern 'paraconsistent' logic).

Meinong regards all this as a new philosophical subject, the theory of objects, an a priori science of objects in general; so far, he thinks, mathematics is the only part of this theory which has been developed. It goes beyond metaphysics, which is, or should be, an empirical science studying everything which can be known empirically (1904, translation pp. 109–10 especially). Facts about what exists can only be known empirically, whereas all other facts are knowable only a priori (1910, translation p. 61). This claim, however, to see a new rival to metaphysics has not been generally accepted.

In escaping from psychologism Meinong went beyond Brentano by distinguishing (along with Twardowski and Husserl but with greater insistence) the object and the content of a thought or experience (e.g. 1917, chapter 7), and also by distinguishing 'assumptions' or 'supposals' (*Annahmen*) as intermediate between judgements and ideas or representations (*Vorstellungen*)—a topic to which he devoted a whole book, although he has been accused (by C. D. Broad reviewing 1910 in *Mind*, 1913) of conflating assuming (or just pretending) a proposition is true with merely entertaining it (does 1910—translation p. 254—counter this?). But judgements etc. are not the propositions or states of affairs they are of. Meinong calls these 'objectives' (*Objektive*), a rather wider term (1910, translation pp. 75–6). Objectives form a special class of objects, distinguished as essentially being positive or negative, the (in German) rather harsh term *Objekt* then being introduced for other objects. Finally he applies these various notions, or analogues of them, to develop theories of emotional and conative, as well as cognitive, mental processes and their objects, and develops an objectivist theory of values. Apart from his widespread role as an Aunt Sally of ontological profligacy, Meinong influenced the 'critical realism' of Dawes Hicks and others, and philosophers currently better known such as **Ryle** and Chisholm. Some of the ideas touched on in the last paragraph show a considerable kinship with, if less direct and overt influence on, the later theories of speech acts and the currently popular investigations into content. (See also Findlay, in Radakovic *et al.* (eds) 1952.)

Sources: *PI;* Passmore 1957; Edwards; personal communication with Prof. P. Simons.

A. R. LACEY

Merleau-Ponty, Maurice

French. *b:* 1908, Rochefort-sur-mer, France. *d:* 1961. *Cat:* Phenomenologist. *Ints:* Epistemology; philosophy of language; aesthetics. *Educ:* After a brilliant student career at various lycées and the École Normale Supérieur (1926–30), Merleau-Ponty gained his agrégation in 1931. *Infls:* Descartes, Husserl, Sartre and empirical psychology. *Appts:* Taught in a number of lycées before the Second World War; served in the French army during the war; professorships at Lyon, the Sorbonne and finally the Collège de France; Coeditor, with Sartre and de Beauvoir, of *Les Temps Modernes.*

Main publications:

(1942) *La Structure du comportement*, Paris: PUF.
(1945) *Phénoménologie de la perception*, Paris: NRF Gallimard.

(1947) *Humanisme et terreur*, Paris: Gallimard.
(1948) *Sens et non-sens*, Paris: Nagel.
(1953) *Eloge de la philosophie*, Paris: NRF Gallimard.
(1955) *Les Aventures de la dialectique*, Paris: Gallimard.
(1960) *Signes*, Paris: NRF Gallimard.

Secondary literature:

Dillon, M. C. (1988) *Merleau-Ponty's Ontology*, Bloomington: Indiana University Press.
Edie, J. M. (1987) *Merleau-Ponty's Philosophy of Language*, Lanham: University Press of America.
Madison, G. B. (1973) *La Phénoménologie de Merleau-Ponty*, Paris: Klincksieck.
Robinet, A. (1970) *Merleau-Ponty*, Paris: PUF.
Spiegelberg, H. (1969) *The Phenomenological Movement*, vol. II, second edition, The Hague: Martinus Nijhoff.
Tilliette, X. (1970) *Merleau-Ponty*, Paris: Seghers.

Merleau-Ponty has been presented both as a phenomenologist and as an existentialist, but a study of his thought reveals the limited utility of general labels of this kind. Whilst he was the first French thinker to use the term 'phenomenology' in the title of a major work and to identify philosophy with phenomenology, he does not rely greatly on the methods of **Husserl**; and equally, although he shares many of the concerns of his friend **Sartre**, Merleau-Ponty disagrees with the latter on such fundamental issues as the extent of human freedom. He argues that experience is shot through with pre-existent meanings, largely derived from language and experienced in perception.

Merleau-Ponty arrived at these views gradually, beginning from a prolonged and extensive study of the psychology of perception. His first significant work, *La Structure du comportement* (1942) is essentially a critique of the major psychological theories of perception of the time, notably behaviourism and Gestalt theory (as put forward by Köhler). Merleau-Ponty denied that there is a causal relationship between the physical and the mental, and he therefore finds the behaviourist account of perception, entirely in terms of causation, unacceptable. Gestalt theory he finds not false but not developed sufficiently to do justice to the facts of perception. His general conclusion is that a new approach is needed if perception is to be properly understood.

This new approach is his version of phenomenology, and its application to perception is the subject of his second and most important work, *Phénoménologie de la perception* (1945). The fundamental premise of this work is that of the primacy of perception: our perceptual relation to the world is *sui generis*, and logically prior to the subject–object distinction. Theories of perception which deny this are rejected in the opening chapters of the work: for example, all sense-data theories are dismissed, since they attempt to reconstruct experience by using artificial abstractions which presuppose the subject–object dichotomy. By contrast Merleau-Ponty goes on to explore the phenomenal field by using a much expanded notion of Gestalt. It is argued that the elements of Gestalts are both inherently meaningful and open or indeterminate.

One of the most original features of this phenomenology is his theory of the role of the body in the world as perceived (*le monde perçu*), an area of thought he develops at much greater length than does Sartre. Merleau-Ponty contends that a number of the most fundamental features of perception are a result of our physical incarnation: our perception of space is conditioned by our bodily mode of existence; or again, we regard perceived things as constant because our body remains constant. Further, Merleau-Ponty contends that perception is a committed (*engagé*) or existential act, not one in which we are merely passive. We discover meanings in the world, and commit ourselves, without complete logical justification, to believing in its future.

The concluding section of the work draws out some important consequences of these views, firstly concerning Cartesianism. As with Husserl, Merleau-Ponty's thought to some extent defines itself by reference to that of Descartes. Merleau-Ponty is logically bound to deny that Cartesianism is acceptable, and this he does. The Cartesian presupposition of a distinction between meditating ego and transcendent cogitata is incompatible with the thesis of the primacy of perception, and thus Merleau-Ponty classifies the cogito of the second *Meditation* as a merely 'verbal cogito'. He replaces it with a 'true cogito' of the form 'there is a phenomenon; something shows itself'. Put in metaphysical terms, the fundamental category revealed by Merleau-Ponty's philosophy is what he terms 'being-in-the-world' (*être-au-monde*). The subjective and the objective are facets of this prior, embracing structure.

This thesis conditions his analysis of time, in which he argues that the notions of time and subjectivity are mutually constitutive. Time is not a feature of the objective world, but is a dimension of subjectivity: past and future appear in our present and can only occur in a temporal being. Time is more than the form of the inner life, and more intimately related to subjectivity than is suggested by regarding it as an attribute or property of the self. To analyse time, Merleau-Ponty contends, is to gain access to the complete structure of subjectivity.

In the final pages of the *Phenomenology of Perception* Merleau-Ponty discusses the nature and limits of human freedom, a theme developed further in the political works, *Humanisme et terreur* (1947) and *Les Aventures de la dialectique* (1955). He rejects the Sartrean doctrine that we are condemned to be (absolutely) free, replacing it with his own view that we are condemned to meaning. Experience comes ready furnished with meanings, and so although we are free to make choices the field of freedom is accordingly circumscribed. These meanings are conveyed by a number of social institutions, but above all by language. As he puts it in his discussion of the cogito: 'Descartes, and a fortiori his reader, begin their meditation in what is already a universe of discourse' (*Phenomenology of Perception*, p. 401). Unsurprisingly, it was to a consideration of the role of language as a vehicle for intersubjectivity that Merleau-Ponty turned in his final years, but he did not live to work out a complete theory.

Merleau-Ponty also developed an interest in aesthetics, especially of the visual arts. This follows from his theory of the primacy of perception: he found in painting a fuller appreciation of our special perceptual relation with the world than in science or in philosophies which analyse perception in terms of the primacy of the subject–object distinction.

ROBERT WILKINSON

Moore, G(eorge) E(dward)

British. *b:* 1873, London. *d:* 1958, Cambridge, England. *Cat:* Analytic philosopher. *Ints:* Epistemology; moral philosophy. *Educ:* University of Cambridge University, 1892–6. *Infls:* J. M. E. McTaggart and Bertrand Russell. *Appts:* Lecturer in Philosophy at University of Cambridge, 1911–25, Professor of Mental Philosophy and Logic, 1925–39, University of Cambridge; Editor of *Mind*, 1921–47; Fellow of the British Academy, 1918; Order of Merit, 1951.

Main publications:

(1903) *Principia Ethica*, Cambridge: Cambridge University Press.
(1912) *Ethics*, London: Williams & Norgate.
(1922) *Philosophical Studies*, London: Routledge & Kegan Paul.
(1953) *Some Main Problems of Philosophy*, London: George Allen & Unwin.
(1959) *Philosophical Papers*, London: George Allen & Unwin.
(1962) *Commonplace Book, 1919–1953*, London: George Allen & Unwin.

(1986) *G. E. Moore: The Early Essays*, Philadelphia: Temple University Press.
(1991) *The Elements of Ethics*, Philadelphia: Temple University Press.

Secondary literature:

Ambrose, Alice and Lazerowitz, Morris (eds) (1970) *G. E. Moore: Essays in Retrospect*, London: George Allen & Unwin.
Klemke, E. D. (ed.) (1969) *Studies in the Philosophy of G. E. Moore*, Chicago: Quadrangle Books.
Schilpp, P. A. (ed.) (1968) *The Philosophy of G. E. Moore*, third edition, Open Court: La Salle.

When Moore was a student the idealism of such philosophers as **Bradley** and Bosanquet was dominant in British philosophy. It is no surprise, then, that Moore's earliest published work shows considerable sympathy with this movement. However, his famous 1903 paper 'The refutation of idealism' (*Mind* 12, 1903) marked a break with it, and his work over the next few years, along with that of Bertrand **Russell**, was a sustained criticism of the idealist movement. This work is often thought to put Moore squarely in the empiricist camp, and much of it is certainly an attempt to clarify an empiricist epistemology. However, the limits of this empiricism are clearly visible in his ethical work, where he held that goodness was a non-natural, irreducible property, the object of direct, non-sensory knowledge.

Much of Moore's later work was concerned with the scepticism that characterized the empiricist movement from Hume to Russell. In opposition to this, he defended the view that most of the things that we think we know we really do know. This gave rise to the popular image of Moore as the philosopher of plain common sense.

There is, however, little to sustain that image in Moore's first published book, *Principia Ethica* (1903). It defended a consequentialist theory of ethics, holding that the fundamental concept of ethics is the good, and that right actions are those which maximize the good. A popular version of such a theory is the utilitarianism of Mill and Bentham, the doctrine that marries consequentialism with hedonism, and holds that the right action is always that which maximizes happiness. Moore, however, ferociously rejected the hedonism that he found in utilitarianism and held instead that goodness is to be found in a number of different things, but preeminently in the experience of personal affection and the contemplation of beauty. (This aspect of his philosophy strongly influenced the Bloomsbury Group, of which he was a member.) He held that it is impossible to give any *argument* as to what are the ultimate goods; it is self-evident, and we know *directly*, without argument, what they are. What actions will maximize the good could not be directly known, however; this is a matter of calculation, and so Moore rejected the type of intuitionism which held that we could directly know, without argument or calculation, what are the right acts or the correct moral rules.

That 'the fundamental principles of Ethics must be self-evident' (1903, p. 143) Moore thought followed from a more basic claim: the fundamental principles of ethics cannot be inferred from any further principles; they are true, but there is no *reason why* they are true. This view was part of what was to become the most influential aspect of *Principia Ethica*: its attack on naturalism in ethics. Moore was never completely clear just what he had in mind by talking of naturalism, and he gave a number of different explanations. But we may say that it was, in a general way, any attempt to reduce evaluative notions to non-evaluative ones. The attempt to do so Moore baptized 'the Naturalistic Fallacy', and it seemed to Moore, and to many others, that it followed from his diagnosis that ethical propositions could not be inferred in any way from non-ethical ones. A concern with this issue dominated moral philosophy in the English-speaking world for more than half a century following the publication of Moore's

book. Many thought that Moore's argument had captured the essential autonomy of ethics. Others, however, thought that it rendered ethics a suspect endeavour, since it seemed to put it largely beyond the pale of rational argument.

Moore's subsequent writing on ethics had nothing like the influence of *Principia Ethica*. His *Ethics* (1912) was a minute statement of utilitarianism, and an equally minute examination of some objections to it. It defends a consequentialist position, though mainly by asserting that it is self-evidently correct, a type of argument that has had little force against generations of philosophers who thought that it is self-evidently incorrect.

Once he had broken with the idealist tradition, Moore's dominating concern was to understand the nature of sense data and their relation to the material world. Outside of ethics, it is his work in this general area that was most influential. He began this in a series of lectures given in 1910–11 (*Some Main Problems of Philosophy*, 1953), and his very last works still show a concern with the problem. Roughly speaking, sense data might be thought to be identical with material objects, which would yield a theory of perception often known as direct realism; or they might be thought to be separate, mental entities which represented material objects (the representative theory of perception); or it might be that there are no material objects independent of our sense data, and that to know a proposition about a material object is merely to know that if certain conditions were satisfied then certain sense data would be experienced (phenomenalism). Moore analysed these types of theory, over and over again, in enormous detail in such articles as 'A defence of common sense' (1925; reprinted in *Philosophical Papers*, 1959) and 'Proof of an external world' (1939; reprinted in *Philosophical Papers*).

These papers, like nearly all of Moore's work, are characterized by an obsessive concern simply to be clear about just what philosophers have *meant* when they have made such typically philosophical claims as that we can never really know anything about the external world, or that time or space is unreal. The painstaking analysis in such papers gave rise to the popular view that analysis was an end in itself for Moore, but this was not so. He saw it merely as the necessary groundwork for arriving at the truth.

Moore did not arrive speedily at many philosophical truths: about the relation of sense data to external objects, for instance, he did not form a view until 1953 and even then he did no more than reject direct realism. On the question of whether we could have knowledge of the external world, however, Moore formed an opinion very early. In his 1905–6 lecture 'The nature and reality of objects of perception' (*Philosophical Studies*, 1922), Moore submitted to inordinately detailed examination the meaning of the question whether we can have any knowledge of the external world. In *Some Main Problems of Philosophy* (1953) he began to work towards an answer, one which, in one way or another, he held to for the rest of his life: surely, the claim that I know some things about the external world is more certain than any argument that might be given to show it wrong. His position found its most famous exposition on the occasion when, in a British Academy lecture ('Proof of an external world', published in *Proceedings of the British Academy* 25), he claimed to disprove the proposition that we cannot know the existence of external objects by pointing out to the audience his two hands. This typified what came to be thought of as the characteristic Moorean 'appeal to common sense'.

There has been much debate as to what force—if any—this argumentative strategy had. To some, it has seemed that Moore was doing no more than merely denying what philosophers have given *arguments* for. Others have thought that he was trying to show that such philosophical claims violated the rules of ordinary language. It is fair to say that Moore himself was never clear in his own mind just what was the force of his arguments. Whatever their precise force, however, they had enormous influence, transforming the face of epistemology.

Moore was not a great prose stylist, once guilelessly writing an 82-word sentence in which 46 of the words are 'so' or 'and'. His writing, however, always aspired to, and usually achieved, a remarkable simplicity and clarity.

Sources: Passmore 1957; Flew; *The Times*, 25 Oct 1958, p. 10.

ANTHONY ELLIS

Murdoch, (Jean) Iris

Irish. *b:* 15 July 1919, Dublin. *Cat:* 'I might describe myself as a Wittgensteinian neo-Platonist!'. *Ints:* Moral philosophy; Plato; religion; metaphysics. *Educ:* MA, Somerville College, Oxford; Newnham College, Cambridge. *Infls:* Plato, Wittgenstein, Sartre and Weil. *Appts:* Fellow of St Anne's College, Oxford, from 1948.

Main publications:

(1953) *Sartre, Romantic Rationalist*, Cambridge: Bowes & Bowes; second edition, *Sartre, Romantic Realist*, 1980.
(1970) *The Sovereignty of Good*, London: Routledge & Kegan Paul.
(1977) *The Fire and the Sun*, Oxford.
(1986) *Acastos*, London: Chatto & Windus.
(1992) *Metaphysics as a Guide to Morals*, London: Chatto & Windus.

Secondary literature:

Begnal, K. (1987) *Iris Murdoch A Reference Guide*, Boston: G. K. Hall.

Iris Murdoch's philosophical works have been few in comparison with her many novels, although she herself might see little distinction between the genres: 'It may be that the best model for all thought is the creative imagination' (1992, p. 169). The views in almost all her philosophical writings are recapitulated and elaborated in *Metaphysics as a Guide to Morals* (1992). Ruminative in pace, discursive in style and intuitive in the flow of its arguments, this wide-ranging treatise is at the farthest point from conventional academic exposition. It must be ironic that a work written in this way might well turn out to be seen as one of the finest and most original examples of philosophy produced in twentieth-century Britain.

Murdoch has always stood apart from analytical orthodoxy. Plato has been her model and prime inspiration. *Metaphysics as a Guide to Morals* makes no effort to argue basic Platonic premises which a more cautious author would have felt some need to defend. ('A work of art is of course not a material object, though some works of art are bodied forth by material objects so as to seem to inhere in them' is asserted without argument on p. 2.) The Platonic themes she has pursued have been largely those of the *Phaedrus* and of the *Republic*: the soul; the indispensability of metaphor; the motivation for the search for truth (Eros, to her and Plato); the reality of the good; the relations between art, truth, the good and God.

One of her starting-points has been opposition to a view of the self which she identifies in both **Sartre** and **Wittgenstein**: a view that left morality to be located only in the rightness of discrete choices, displacing goodness, character and virtue—'The agent, thin as a needle, appears in the quick flash of the choosing will' ('On "God" and "Good"', in *The Sovereignty of Good*, 1970, p. 53). She has maintained a confidence in the solidity and continuity of the self (or the *soul*, as she prefers it): 'What goes on inwardly in the soul is the essence of each man, it's what makes us individual people. The relation between that inwardness and public conduct *is morality*' ('Art and Eros: a dialogue about

art', in *Acastos*, 1986, p. 31). She writes of 'our confidence in our own inner life of thought and judgment and in our real existence as individual persons capable of truth' (1992, p. 221): 'no theory can remove or explain away our moral and rational mastery of our individual being' (p. 213). This anti-existentialist confidence is realized interestingly in her fiction. One of her characters says: 'one is responsible for one's actions, and one's past does belong to one. You can't blot it out by entering a dream world and decreeing that life began yesterday. You can't make yourself into a new person overnight' (*The Black Prince*, Harmondsworth: Penguin, 1975, p. 359).

Against **Derrida** (whom she classes as a 'structuralist') she argues for a clear, strong view of truth: 'the truth, terrible, delightful, funny, whose strong lively presence we recognise in great writers' (1992, p. 215). Her argument is a transcendental one: 'We must check philosophical theories against what we know of human nature (and hold on to that phrase too) ... Language is meaningful, *ergo* useful, it performs its *essential* task, through its ability to be truthful' (p. 216).

Truth, reality and the good are linked in her work as they are in the *Republic*, except that, for her, a vision of the real is not the preserve of the mathematically educated elite, as it was Plato: 'We find out in the most minute details of our lives that the good is the real. Philosophy too can attend to such details' (p. 430). As with Plato, visual imagery is central (and also the imagery of *attention*, from Simone **Weil**): 'Looking can be a kind of intelligent reverence. Moral thinking, serious thinking, is clarification (visual image). The good, just, man is lucid' (p. 463). We *see* reality; a truthful view of it shows us the good, and 'The sovereign Good is ... something which we all experience as a creative force' (p. 507).

Much of her thinking has been devoted to the value and danger of art. (Her interpretations of Plato on these themes are in *The Fire and the Sun* and in 'Art and Eros', in *Acastos*.) Good art, she believes, 'shows us how difficult it is to be objective by showing us how differently the world looks to an objective vision' (1970, p. 86).

Metaphysics as a Guide to Morals includes extended reflections on the value in ontological arguments. Murdoch wrote earlier that 'God was (or is) a *single perfect transcendent non-representable and necessarily real object of attention*; and ... moral philosophy should attempt to retain a central concept which has all these characteristics' ('On "God" and "Good"', in 1970, p. 55). Yet 'to speak of "religious language" as something specialised, supposed to be expressive rather than referential, is to separate religion from the truth-seeking struggle of the whole of life' (1992, p. 418).

Clarity of vision must be matched by clarity of language. To achieve this remains one of the roles of philosophy:

We must ... preserve and cherish a strong truth-bearing everyday language, not marred or corrupted by technical discourse or scientific codes; and thereby promote the clarified objective knowledge of man and society of which we are in need as citizens, and as moral agents

(p. 164).

And:

The task of philosophy is not less but more essential now, in helping to preserve and refresh a stream of meticulous, subtle, eloquent ordinary language, free from jargon and able to deal clearly and in detail with matters of a certain degree of generality and abstraction. We cannot see the future, but must fear it intelligently

(p. 211).

She writes that she has been wanting to put the argument of Plato 'into a modern context as background to moral philosophy, as a bridge between morals and religion, and as relevant to our new disturbed understanding of religious truth' (p. 511). Her thought must be unique as a creative reimagining of Plato in the late twentieth century.

RICHARD MASON

Nietzsche, Friedrich

German. *b:* 15 October 1844, Rocken. *d:* 25 August 1900, Weimar, Germany. *Cat:* Post-Kantian philosopher. *Ints:* Ontology: epistemology; Greek and Christian thought; theory of values; nihilism; aesthetics; cultural theory. *Educ:* 1858–64, received a primarily classical education at the renowned Pforta school; after a brief spell at the University of Bonn, where he intended to study Philology and Theology, went to the University of Leipzig to study Philology under Ritschl. *Infls:* Ancient Greek thought, particularly Heraclitus, Plato and Socrates; Montaigne, Spinoza, Lichtenberg, La Rochefoucauld, Schopenhauer, Wagner, F. Lange, Kuno Fischer and Emerson. *Appts:* 1869–79, taught philosophy, University of Basel (increasing ill-health and disillusion with academic life prompted his resignation); 1879–, survived on a sparse pension, living ascetically and wandering restlessly, mainly between Sils Maria in the Ober-Engadine, Nice and Turin; 1889, collapsed, was taken back to Germany and died soon after.

Main publications:

The now authoratative edition of Nietzche's collected works is the *Nietzsche Werke: Kritische Gesamtansgabe* (KGW), 30 vols, ed. Giorgio Colli and Mazzino Montinari, Berlin: de Gruyter, 1967–78.

(1872) *Die Gebürt der Tragödie* (English translation, *The Birth of Tragedy*, trans. W. Kaufmann, New York: Viking Press, 1954).

(1873–6) *Unzeitgemässe Betrachtungen*; Bd I, *David Strauss, der Bekenner und Schriftsteller,*

1873; Bd 2, *Vom Nutzen und Nachteil der Historie für das Leben*, 1874; Bd 3, *Schopenhauer als Erzieher*, 1874; Bd 4, *Richard Wagner in Bayreuth*, 1876 (English translations, *Untimely Meditations*: no. 1, *David Strauss, the Confessor and Writer*; no. 2, *On the Uses and Disadvantages of History for Life*; no. 3, *Schopenhauer as Educator*; no. 4, *Richard Wagner in Bayreuth*, trans. R. J. Hollingdale, Cambridge: Cambridge University Press, 1983).

(1878–80) *Menschliches, Allzumenschliches*, Bd 1, 1878, Bd 2, *Vermischte Meinungen und Sprüche*, 1879, *Der Wanderer und sein Schatten*, 1880 (English translation, *Human All Too Human*, including 'Assorted maxims and opinions' and 'The wanderer and his shadow', trans. R. J. Hollingdale, Cambridge: Cambridge University Press, 1986).

(1881) *Die Morgenröthe* (English translation, *Daybreak*, trans. R. J. Hollingdale, Cambridge: Cambridge University Press, 1982).

(1882) *Die fröhliche Wissenschaft*, Abt. V 343–83, 1887 (English translation, *The Gay Science*, trans. W. Kaufmann, New York: Vintage Press, 1974).

(1883–5) *Also sprach Zarathustra*, Abt. 1 & 2, 1883, Abt. 3, 1884, Abt. 4, 1885 (English translation, *Thus Spoke Zarathustra*, trans. R. J. Hollingdale, Harmondsworth: Penguin Classics, 1969).

(1886) *Jenseits von Gut und Böse* (English translation, *Beyond Good and Evil*, trans. W. Kaufmann, New York: Vintage Press, 1966).

(1887) *Zur Genealogie der Moral* (English translation, *On the Genealogy of Morals*, trans. W. Kaufmann and R. J. Hollingdale, New York: Vintage Press, 1968).

(1888) *Der Fall Wagner* (English translation, 'The case of Wagner', trans. W. Kaufmann, in *The Portable Nietzsche*, ed. W. Kaufmann, New York: Viking Press, 1954).

(1889) *Die Götzen-Dämmerung* (English translation, *The Twilight of the Idols*, trans. R. J. Hollingdale, Harmondsworth: Penguin Classics, 1968).

(1895) *Der Antichrist* (English translation, *The Anti-Christ*, trans. R. J. Hollingdale, Harmondsworth: Penguin Classics, 1968).

(1895) *Nietzsche contra Wagner* (English translation, 'Nietzsche against Wagner', trans. W. Kaufmann, in *The Portable Nietzsche*, ed. W. Kaufmann, New York: Viking Press, 1954).

(1908) *Ecce Homo* (English translation, *Ecce Homo*, trans. W. Kaufmann, New York: Vintage Press, 1968).

Two of Nietzsche's important early essays, 'Philosophy in the tragic age of the Greeks' (1872–5) and 'Truth and lies in a nonmoral sense' (1873) appear in translation by D. Brezeale in *Philosophy and Truth: Selections from Nietzsche's Notebooks of the Early 1870s*, Atlantic Highlands, NJ: Humanities Press, 1979. A substantial quantity of Nietzsche's later, most philosophically provocative unpublished notes appear in the posthumous and ill-named collection *Der Wille zur Macht* (*Samtliche Werke*, Bd IX), edited by Baeumler, Stuttgart: Kröner, 1965 (English translation, *The Will to Power*, trans. W. Kaufmann and R. J. Hollingdale, London: Weidenfeld & Nicolson, 1969).

Secondary literature:

Allison, D. (ed.) (1977) *The New Nietzsche, Contemporary Styles of Interpretation*, New York: Dell Publishing Co.

Ansell Pearson, K. (1991) *Nietzsche and Modern German Philosophy*, London: Routledge.

Deleuze, G. (1983) *Nietzsche and Philosophy*, London: Althone Press.

Heidegger, M. (1979–82) *Nietzsche*, ed. and trans. D. Krell, 4 vols, New York: Harper Row.

Janz, Otto (1978) *Friederich Nietzsche*, 3 vols, Munich: Carl Hanser Verlag (probably the most reliable and scholarly biography).

Nehemas, A. (1985) *Nietzsche: Life as Literature*, Cambridge, Mass.: Harvard University Press.

Schacht, R. (1983) *Nietzsche*, London: Routledge.

Schrift, A. (1990) *Nietzsche and the Question of Interpretation*, London: Routledge.

The enigma of Friedrich Nietzsche, one of twentieth-century Europe's most influential philosophers, does not lie in the now well-documented politically motivated abuse of his writings by his sister Elizabeth Forster-Nietzsche but in the fact that his philosophy is simultaneously familiar and remote. The post-structuralist genealogical stratagems of Michel **Foucault** and **Derrida**'s dissolution of fixed meaning make Nietzsche's nihilism and perspectivism strangely familiar. Yet that familiarity is disconcerting, for Nietzsche's voice also speaks in the now unfamiliar philosophical languages of Schopenhauer, Lange, Spir and Teichmuller.

Nietzsche's notoriety rests upon such singular doctrines as the will to power, the eternal recurrence, nihilism and the announcement of God's death, iconoclastic expression, mastery of aphoristic form, and a deployment of contradiction and inconsistency which for many compromised his philosophical status. Nietzsche's reception is now an autonomous field of study and recent scholarship has come to question the 'received' view of him as an unorganized thinker, suggesting that his written *corpus* gains its coherence in its very plurality. His responses to nihilism and to art's relation to existence clearly vary but the questions to which his different responses are an answer are invariably the same.

Nietzsche's early university experiences set his lifelong philosophical preoccupations: first, interpreting Ancient Greek culture as a response to the existential problematic of finitude; second, pursuing the philosophical and cultural consequences of post-Kantian metaphysical scepticism; and third, maintaining intellectual integrity whatever the cost. His thought is an instance of a *Lebensphilosophie*: philosophy without experience is empty and experience without philosophy is blind. A combination of his knowledge of Greek thought, his discovery of Schopenhauer and a reading of the history of philosophy by Kuno Fischer established his primary philosophical *Leitmotifen*. First, reality is an endless Becoming (*Werden*). Second, as instrumentalist devices language and reason reflect the world not as it is but how our needs require us to perceive it. Third, within religion, ethical codes and scientific practice humanity has institutionalized its values, projected and mistaken them as aspects of being-in-itself. Fourth, the existential predicament is grasped as the imminent risk of having one's belief in reason as a criterion of truth and reality exploded by the unintelligibility of flux and of having, as a consequence, to stare into the presence of nihilism. And, fifth, there is the question of how one can live with a knowledge of the latter abyss. When read as a continuous response and reappraisal of thse *Leitmotifen*, the alleged inconsistencies of Nietzsche's thinking virtually vanish.

Artistenmetaphysik is the name Nietzsche gives to his first response to these *Leitmotifen* as expressed within *The Birth of Tragedy* (1872) and the *Untimely Meditations* (1873–6). Combining an assumed universal existential predicament with the hermeneutical axiom of looking at one's own through the eyes of the foreign, he contends that the relevance of Greek aesthetic practice lies in its transformation of the existential predicament without recourse to otherworldly metaphysics. The Dionysian arts of music and drama do so by ecstatically succumbing to flux, the Apollonian plastic arts by deliberately denying the actuality of becoming with the illusion of timeless beauty, and tragic drama by reconciling its audience to the horror of every open finitude with a closed and graspable image of it.

The *Artistenmetaphysik* is an inverted Platonism: metaphysical truth is vacuous whilst art as living within appearance is understood as the means of suppressing awareness of the futility of existence. Socratic reasoning is attacked for atrophying the aesthetic impulse. By positing the illusion of an intelligible world of Being, the desire to create a reality according to our needs is negated. Nietzsche was haunted by the question: what creative resources will European thought retain if the Socratic faith is rendered empty and nihilism looms?

The 'experimentalist' phase of Nietzsche's thinking—*Human All Too Human* (1878–80), *Daybreak* (1881) and *The Gay Science* (1882)—exposes the shortcomings of this aesthetic. As all illusions are temporary, Apollonian aesthetics can only exacerbate the existentialist predicament. The loss of its spell will make the return to Dionysian actuality even more painful. The *Artistenmetaphysik* entails a needlessly pessimistic view of becoming. Finitude *per se* is not the problem, but our evaluation of it. Accordingly, Nietzsche's *experimentalische Denken* criticizes religious and moral systems which alienate individuals from actuality by perpetrating the illusion of fixed truths. Art is condemned for beautifying such truths and extending their influence subsequent to the collapse of their supporting beliefs. Experimentalism quests for both historical and non-European exemplars of 'this-worldly' lifestyles which promote values affirming rather than denying the existential predicament. Yet this experimentalism requires what it criticizes, namely, the imaginative capacity to speculate about what is not seen but might be the case, an imaginative capacity which is condemned in art as capable of estranging one from actuality. In addressing this problem, *Thus Spoke Zarathustra* (1883–5) announces Nietzsche's final phase of thinking, which centres around the notions of the will to power, radical nihilism, perspectivism and the eternal recurrence. Within *Thus Spoke Zarathustra* notions of existential alienation, willing, becoming and creativity are fused into a unified monistic ontology in which artistic creativity becomes the transforming vehicle of mankind's being as a mode of becoming. Pain, suffering and contradiction are no longer seen as objections to existence but as an expression of its actual tensions. This does not rid the individual of his suffering but transforms his evaluation of it. In Nietzsche's thinking the importance of the creative individual lies in his being an embodiment of the life-transforming process which constitutes all becoming.

In subsequent writings, the will to power is developed into a Leibniz-like monadology without the latter's central organizing principle. Within this ontology of flux, inanimate and animate beings are presented as different densities of *Kraftzentren* (power centres) combining and interchanging for the sake of the greater power, i.e. unhindered activity. This account of becoming is the ground both of Nietzsche's repudiation of unchanging things and selves and of his affirmation of perspectivism: the world does not exist apart from the totality of perspectival interactions which make it up. This *Interpretationsphilosophie* operates both as critical hermeneutic and as an aesthetic prescription for the new *Weltanschauung*. If there is no absolute truth or ground, the question arises as to what values prompt a belief in their existence. The absence of meaning-in-itself is no cause for pessimism since it liberates us from the canons of culturally transmitted meaning to the end of creating our own purposes and values. The dynamic is that of having to overcome the need for received meaning (Nietzsche's definition of weakness) in order to take responsibility for legislating one's own (his definition of strength). The eternal recurrence gains its ethical force in this context for, as well as being a hypothesis about how within infinite time endless but numerical finite configurations of energy must repeat themselves, it also serves as an existential prohibition. Without taking on the creative responsibility for one's perspective one is eternally condemned to a repetition of the same disillusionment, as adopted faith after faith is broken within the vortex of the abyss. Art as the means of projecting meaning and value into existence thereby returns to pride of place within Nietzsche's analysis of the existential predicament. Despite the enormous impact of Nietzsche's thought upon European art and literature, his philosophical reception continues to be distorted by the ideological consequences of his sister's politically inspired editorial meddling and its strange legitimization by Marxist intellectuals desirous of perpetuating the myth of Nietzsche as a philosophical precursor of fascism. What is not in question, however, is that the piety of his metaphysical nihilism and his endeavour to contemplate existence without recourse to religious apologetics affects the direction of Heideggerian thought and, because of that, subsequently shapes French post-structuralism and deconstruction. In its account of disclosive meaning, hermeneutics now assumes what Nietzsche's aphoristic devices demonstrate. As words can communicate as clearly through the unsaid as through the said, the aphoristic rather than the systematic style is better suited to invoking the unstated realms of thought behind assertions. Nietzsche's major contribution to this sea-change in twentieth-century European philosophical sensibility is only now beginning to receive the acknowledgement it truly merits.

NICHOLAS DAVEY

Nishida, Kitaro

Japanese. *b:* 1870. *d:* 1945. *Cat:* Zen philosopher. *Infls:* Profoundly influenced by the Zen Buddhist canon, the negative theology of Nicholas of Cusa, French positivism, Bergson, William James, Fichte and Hegel. *Appts:* 1901, *koji* (lay Zen practitioner); Professor of Philosophy and Religion, former Imperial Kyoto University.

Main publications:

(1911) *An Inquiry into the Good* (English translation, M. Abe and C. Ives, New Haven, CT and London: Yale University Press, 1990).
(1915) *Thought and Experience*; extended in 1937.
(1917) *Intuition and Reflection in Self-consciousness* (English translation, V. H. Viglielmo, Y. Takeuchi and J. S. O'Leary, Albany: State University of New York Press, 1987).
(1923) *Art and Morality* (English translation, D. A. Dilworth and V. H. Viglielmo, Honolulu: University of Hawaii Press, 1973).
(1927) *From the Actor to the Seer.*
(1930) *The Self-consciousness of the Universal.*
(1932) *The Self-determination of Nothingness.*
(1933–4) *Fundamental Problems of Philosophy* (English translation, D. A. Dilworth, Tokyo: Sophia University, 1970).
(1933–45) *Philosophical Essays*, 3 vols.
(1945) *The Logic of the Place of Nothingness and the Religious World-view* (English translation, *Last Writings: Nothingness and the Religious World-view*, D. A. Dilworth, Honolulu: University of Hawaii Press, 1987).
(1947–53) *Complete Works*, 18 vols, Tokyo.

Secondary literature:

Collinson, D. and Wilkinson, R. (1994) *Thirty-Five Oriental Philosophers*, London: Routledge.
Nishitani, Keiji (1991) *Nishida Kitaro*, trans. J. W. Heisig and Yamamoto Seisaki, Oxford: Yale University Press.
Toratoro, Shimonura (1960) *Nishida Kitaro and Some Aspects of his Philosophical Thought*, Tokyo.
Yoshinori, Takeuchi (1982) 'The philosophy of Nishida', in Frederick Franck (ed.) *The Buddha Eye*, New York: Cross Road.
Waldenfels, Hans (1980) *Absolute Nothingness: Foundations for a Buddhist–Christian Dialogue*, trans. J. W. Heisig, New York: Paulist Press.

Kitaro Nishida is esteemed as the first modern Japanese 'philosopher' in the European sense and is primarily associated with the founding of the 'Kyoto School' of philosophy. Through his role in that school Nishida had a seminal influence upon such contemporary Japanese philosophers as Abe Masao, Yoshinori Takeuchi, Hajime Tanabe but particularly upon the two greatest twentieth-century disseminators of Japanese thought in the West, D. T. Suzuki and Keiji **Nishitani**.

Perhaps the respective courses of European and Japanese thought are now so propitiously aligned that the importance of Nishida's philosophical achievement can be appreciated outside Asia. Since the epoch-making work of **Nietzsche** and **Heidegger**, much continental European philosophy has attempted to resolve the challenge of nihilism by articulating the nature of existence and existential experience without recourse to metaphysical dogma or a philosphical language tainted by the traditional categories of metaphysics. Such an undertaking is a particularly difficult one as European thought lacks what Buddhist tradition has long possessed, namely an experimental analytic capable of theorizing nothingness. On the other hand, the situation faced by many Japanese religious thinkers after the Meiji restoration of 1868 was to capitulate to the increasing influences of European norms of thought, to become outright nationalist reactionaries or to utilize the conceptual artillery of European philosophy as a means of bringing into communicable clarity for

Japanese and European readers alike the undogmatic but elusive insights of Zen philosophy. Nishida made the last path his own and offered to European philosophy a profoundly non-nihilistic Zen view of nihility rendered in Western philosophical terms.

The confrontation of Buddhist thought and Western philosophy in Nishida's work involves a characteristic conceptual and experiential transposition. Whereas Christianity and Western metaphysics might be disadvantaged by holding the absolute (God) to be above both immediate expression and experience, they have the advantage of a conceptual framework which can cognize the transcendent. Conversely, Zen philosophy is advantaged by regarding the absolute (i.e. reality 'as it is') to be amenable to immediate experience, while it lacks the conceptual artillery to grapple with that which lies beyond immediate expression. Nishida attempts a fusion of the positive aspects of both European and Zen tradition by suggesting that the Zen experiential intuition of absolute nothingness (*zettai mu*) can be conceptually articulated via Nicholas of Cusa's negative concept of God: it is never that which can be stated of it for it is always more than that; it is what it is not stated to be.

Nishida's invocation of absolute nothingness or emptiness (*sunyata*) should not be understood within the customary polarities of being and non-being, affirmation and denial. *Zettai mu* encompasses both the immanent simultaneity of all coming into being (*creatio ex nihilo*) and of all passing away. It is close to what the existential metaphysics of Nietzsche and Heidegger would render as the 'being' of all becoming. Rather than calling it Being, Nishida names the absolute 'nothingness' on the grounds that were the absolute an absolute Being, all potentialities would be realized and the infinity of coming into being and passing away would be denied. *Zettai mu* allegedly preserves that potentiality, offering to Western thought the possibility of an existentially affirmative nihilism. It fell to Nishitani,

one of Nishida's most talented successors, to work out the philosophical implications of such a mode of thought.

NICHOLAS DAVEY

Nishitani, Keiji

Japanese. *b:* 27 February 1900. *d:* 1991. *Cat:* Zen philosopher; philosopher of religion. *Educ:* Schooled in Ishikawa Prefecture and Tokyo; in 1924 graduated in Philosophy from Kyoto University. *Infls:* Meister Eckhart, Nietzsche, Dostoyevsky, Kierkegaard, Heidegger, Emerson, Carlyle, St Francis, Nishida, Sosseki, Hakuin and Takuan. *Appts:* 1926, Lecturer in Ethics and German, Kyoto Imperial College; 1928, Lecturer, Buddhist Otani University; 1935, Professor of Religion, Kyoto Imperial University; 1936–9, studied with Heidegger in Freiburg, Germany; 1955–63, Chair of Modern Philosophy, Kyoto State University.

Main publications:

(1940) *The Philosophy of Fundamental Subjectivity*, Tokyo.
(1946) *Nihilism*, Tokyo (English translation, *The Self-Overcoming of Nihilism*, trans. G. Parkes and Setsuko Aihara, Albany, NY: State University of New York Press, 1990).
(1948) *Studies in Aristotle*, Tokyo.
(1949) *God and Absolute Nothingness*, Tokyo.
(1961) *What is Religion?*, Tokyo (English translation, *Religion and Nothingness*, trans. Jan Van Bragt, London: California University Press, 1982).
(1992) 'The awakening of self in Buddhism', 'The I–thou relation in Zen Buddishm', and 'Science and Zen', in Frederick Franck (ed.) *The Buddha Eye: An Anthology of the Kyoto School*, New York: Cross Road, pp. 22–30, 47–60 and 111–37 respectively.

Secondary literature:

Parkes, Graham (ed.) (1991) *Nietzsche and Asian Thought*, Chicago: University of Chicago Press;

see pp. 13, 18, 106–11, 195–9, 213 (useful on Nishitani and excellent on Japan's assimilation of German philosophy).

Van Bragt, Jan (1961) 'Introductory essay' to *Religion and Nothingness*, London: California University Press.

Waldenfels, Hans (1980) *Absolute Nothingness: Foundations for a Buddhist-Christian Dialogue*, trans. J. W. Heisig, New York: Paulist Press (contains substantial bibliography of Nishitani's published articles).

Nishitani was a leading figure in the Kyoto School of Japanese philosophy, a non-sectarian Zen Buddhist philosopher profoundly concerned with interconnecting, first, Christian and Buddhist ethics and, second, the Buddhist ontology of *sunyata* (emptiness) with European ontologies of nothingness (nihilism). A student of Martin **Heidegger** from 1936–9, significantly he attended the latter's lectures on **Nietzsche** and nihilism at Freiburg University. One of the most outstanding non-European commentators on both the mystical tradition in German theology and the works of Kierkegaard, Nietzsche and Heidegger, Nishitani was also a renowned translator into Japanese, one of his principal achievements being the translation of Schelling's *Essence of Human Freedom*.

The hermeneutic axiom 'questioning one's own from the perspective of the foreign' describes Nishitani's lifelong preoccupation with nineteenth- and twentieth-century European existentialist thought as offering a means to articulating and philosophically reappropriating the central conceptions of Zen thought. Nishitani commenced his philosophical career exclusively preoccupied with thinkers of the continental European existential and phenomenological tradition. Not until his discovery of the philosophy of Nishida did Nishitani, far from abandoning his former interests, see them as a means to reengage with the Zen tradition of religion and philosophy. Like Nishida, Nishitani focuses primarily upon the problem of nihilism and Zen's capacity to accept and yet positively transform an ontology of nothingness. Some brief contextual remarks will illuminate the circumstances appertaining to Nishitani's fusion of aspects of European with Zen philosophical tradition.

Japanese cultural tradition tends not to attribute to individualism the same value as Occidental culture. Although unusual for a Japanese, it was not personally inappropriate that after the death of his father and the onset of a serious tubercular affliction the young Nishitani should turn in his sense of hopelessness and despair to arch-European analysts of the suffering individual consciousness, namely, Nietzsche, Kierkegaard, Dostoevsky and Heidegger. And yet despite their unJapanese individualism, key elements in these thinkers made them curiously accessible to Nishitani. The aesthetical-existential dimension of Japanese tradition emphasizes the aesthetic as the meaningfully sensed and emotionally appropriated and the existential as that which affects the very substance of one's personal being. A terser summary of Nietzsche's and Heidegger's aspirations for philosophy could not be found. Their high regard for aesthetic intuitions of the meaningfully 'disclosed' irrespective of volition is clearly paralleled in the Japanese understanding of the aesthetic. Furthermore, the highly indeterminate character of the Japanese language, which lends itself to allegory and allusion, finds a curious resonance in the styles of Nietzsche and Heidegger, who more often than not convey their meaning not by the utterance of pure statements but by allowing the unspoken reservoirs of meaning behind the said to be resonated by what is said. Given such hermeneutical 'crossovers', it is perhaps not so surprising that Nietzsche's and Heidegger's examination of nihility should profoundly strike Nishitani's philosophical imagination, nor that he should be able to offer such a lucid and pertinent critique of their analysis as he does, but from the philosophical perspective of Zen Buddhism.

The underlying motif of Nishitani's

thinking is religious in the special Zen sense of refusing to distinguish between the religious and philosophical quest. When Nishitani writes that religion is the existential exposure of the problematic which is contained in the usual mode of self-being, so would he equally accept Tillich's assertion that the proper role of philosophy is to advance existential interests, to existentialize humanity's mode of being. The transition from 'the usual mode of self-being' to 'fully existentialized human existence' is in Nishitani's terms the journey from the Great Doubt (*taigi*) to the Great Affirmation, from the traumatic discovery of the emptiness of self-centred being to the ecstatic insight that such a loss of (illusory) selfhood is a condition of realizing what was in fact always the case: that one is neither set apart from nor set against the universe but intertwined with *all* of its aspects.

The presuppositions of this transformative argument are eightfold. First, all things are becoming (*shojo*: perpetually coming to be and passing back into extinction) as they are nothing (*mu*) or lack an essence. Second, the world is therefore an emptiness (*sunyata*). Third, the things which make up the world must be considered not as stable identities but as fields of force or energy, the character of which perpetually change according to mutual density and proximity. Fourth, Nishitani equates this Nietzschean ontology with the Buddhist notion of 'networks of causation' (*pratitya-samutpada*), thereby linking the Sanskrit conception of *karma* (the interdependence of all things) with Nietzsche's *amor fati*. Fifth, adapting the *Heart Sutra*'s contention that the 'hindrance of ignorance' is the principal cause of suffering, Nishitani contends *pace* Nietzsche that egoistic self-preoccupation, the fictions of pyschology and the 'metaphysics of grammar' prevent us from seeing that 'self that is not a self', namely the 'original self' which has its ecstatic 'home-ground' in the interconnectedness of

all those fields which constitute *sunyata*. Sixth, Nishitani then embarks upon a critique of Western technology not so much because it presupposes the fiction of the self as detached cognitive subject but because mechanistic explanation renders redundant the very subject which it supposedly serves: 'at the basis of technological thought lies the ... "dehumanization" of humanity ... With regard to a human being, the dimension out of which a "thou" confronts an "I" is completely erased'. Seventh, what Nishitani fears within the process of 'dehumanization' is the irrevocable appearance of what Nietzsche would call 'passive nihilism'. Technology's subversion of the existential 'why?' with the purposeless 'how' of mechanistic explanation suggests that the ultimate 'for-the-sake-of-which' may be for the sake of nothing at all. Western science and philosophy thus lead for Nishitani to the crisis of nihilistic despair. However, eighth, the Japanese term for crisis none the less also implies an opportunity and it is at the moment of the Great Doubt that Nishitani comes into his own.

Nietzsche's solution to passive nihilism is active nihilism. If there are no meanings in themselves, not only can the world not be condemned as meaningless (passive nihilism) but we are free to create our own meanings and perspectives (active nihilism). Nishitani correctly perceives that Nietzsche's active nihilism requires that one pass through passive nihilism. That, however, implies that active nihilism cannot fully overcome its passive forerunner since the act of creating 'new' values presupposes precisely the gulf between subject and world which sets the oppositional basis for the problem of passive nihilism in the first place.

Having exposed the *cul de sac* in the Western analysis of nihilism, Nishitani turns back via Nishida to the Zen tradition but armed with European philosophical techniques capable of rendering into reasonable and meaningful words the wordless wisdom of Zen. The result of that return is that nihilism can be made to overcome itself. For Nishitani, 'religion is an existential exposure to the problematic in the usual mode of self-being'. Within Buddhist dialectics, the Great (philosphical) Doubt can transform itself into the Great (religious) Affirmation. Returning to the concept of essenceless networks of causation, Nishitani remarks:

> On that field of emptiness, each thing comes into its own and reveals itself in a self-affirmation, each in its own possibility and *virtus* of being. The conversion to and entrance to that field means, for us men, the fundamental affirmation of the being of all things, and at the same time of our own existence. The field of emptiness is nothing but the field of the great affirmation.

One could not be more removed from Nietzsche's active nihilism than here, for whereas the latter distances the creative individual from those who cannot overcome the rancours of passive nihilism, Nishitani's position offers via 'the waters of nihilism' an ecstatic reconciliation of the 'empty' or 'purified' self with all other beings that constitute the 'field of emptiness' that is the world. Nishitani's philosophical mission is undoubtedly rendered all the more difficult because of his standing both within and without his tradition, and yet precisely because he attempts to 'question his own through the eye of the foreign' we—the European foreigner—obtain an extraordinary 'eye into our own'.

NICHOLAS DAVEY

Nozick, Robert

American. **b:** 16 November 1938, Brooklyn. **Cat:** Political philosopher; epistemologist. **Ints:** Political philosophy; epistemology. **Educ:** Columbia University, BA 1959; Princeton University, AM 1961, PhD 1963, with dissertation on 'The Normative Theory of Individual Choice'. **Infls:** Locke, Rawls, Hempel, Vlastos, Morgenbesser. **Appts:** Taught at Princeton, 1962–5; Fullbright Scholar, University of Oxford, 1963–4; taught at Harvard, 1965–7, and at Rockefeller University, 1967–9; Professor of Philosophy, Harvard, 1969–85, from 1985, Arthur Kingsley Porter Professor of Philosophy; Woodrow Wilson National Fellowship, 1959–60; Fellow at Van Leer Jerusalem Foundation 1976–7; Fellow of Center for Adanced Study in Behavioral Sciences, Palo Alto, 1971–2; Rockefeller Foundation Fellowship, 1979–80; National Endowment of Humanities Fellowship, 1987–8; Fellow of American Academy of Arts and Sciences, 1984–; Honorary AM, Harvard, 1969; Honorary DHumLitt, Knox College, 1983.

Main publications:

(1968) 'Moral complications and moral structures', *Natural Law Forum.*
(1969) 'Newcomb's problem and two principles of choice', in N. Rescher (ed.), *Essays in Honour of Carl G. Hempel*, Dordrecht: Reidel (this article introduced the problem to the philosophical world).
(1974) *Anarchy, State, and Utopia*, Oxford: Blackwell (received National Book Award 1975).
(1981) *Philosophical Explanations*, Oxford: Oxford University Press (received Ralph Waldo Emerson Award 1982; as well as epistemology this book treats metaphysics, philosophy of mind and ethics).
(1989) *The Examined Life*, New York: Simon & Schuster.
(1990) (ed.) *Harvard Dissertations in Philosophy, 1930–1988* 20 vols, New York: Garland Press.
(1990) *The Normative Theory of Individual Choice*, New York: Garland Press (reprint of 1963 PhD dissertation).
(1993) *The Nature of Rationality*, Princeton, NJ: Princeton University Press.

Secondary literature:

Block, W. (1980) 'On Robert Nozick's "On Austrian methodology"', *Inquiry.*

Campbell, R. and Sowden, L. (eds) *Paradoxes of Rationality and Cooperation*, Vancouver: UBC Press (reprints 1969 article with discussions).

Capaldi, N. (1984) 'Exploring the limits of analytic philosophy: a critique of Nozick's *Philosophical Explanations*', *Interpretation*.

Corlett, J. A. (ed.) (1991) *Equality and Liberty: Analysing Rawls and Nozick*, New York: St Martin's Press, London: Macmillan.

Dancy, J. (1985) *An Introduction to Contemporary Epistemology*, Oxford: Blackwell.

Elster, J. and Moene, K. O. (eds) (1989) *Alternatives to Capitalism*, New York: Cambridge University Press.

Journal of Libertarian Studies, 1977 (has several relevant articles).

Machan, T. R. (1989) *Individuals and Their Rights*, La Salle, Ill: Open Court.

Moffatt, R. C. L. (ed.) (1978) '"Minimal government" in theory and practice', in *Personalist* (October issue, devoted to Nozick).

Narveson, J. (1988) *The Libertarian Idea*, Philadelphia: Temple University Press.

Nielsen, K. (1985) *Equality and Liberty: A Defence of Radical Egalitarianism*, Totowa, NJ: Rowman & Allanfeld.

Noonan, H. W. (1985) 'The closest continuer theory of identity', *Inquiry*.

Paul, J. (ed.) (1981) *Reading Nozick: Essays on Anarchy, State, and Utopia*, Totowa, NJ: Rowman & Littlefield.

Political Theory, 1977 (contains some relevant articles).

Sampson, G. (1978) 'Liberalism and Nozick's "minimal state"', *Mind* (cf. discussion by J. R. Danley in *Mind*, 1979).

Schaefer, D. (1984) 'Libertarianism and political philosophy: a critique of Nozick's *Anarchy, State, and Utopia*', *Interpretation*.

Wolff, J. (1991) *Robert Nozick: Property, Justice and the Minimal State*, Cambridge: Polity Press.

Nozick has made notable contributions to both political philosophy and epistemology. His most famous work, *Anarchy, State, and Utopia* (1974), propounds an extreme libertarian position. Starting from the inviolability of certain rights he claims that justice is not a matter of achieving a certain end-state nor a pattern of distribution but rests on entitlement: given certain rules of acquisition in a Lockean 'state of nature', and certain rules of transfer by contract or gift, 'whatever arises from a just situation by just steps is itself just' (p. 152). A 'minimal state' is envisaged as hypothetically developing from the state of nature, limited to 'protecting all its citizens against violence, theft, and fraud, and to the enforcement of contracts, and so on' (p. 26), and Part II claims that no further development of the state can be justified. However, an important principle of rectification is implied, and may involve some redistribution in actual societies, though without 'introduc[ing] socialism as the punishment for our sins' (p. 153), and some features are later modified (for example, see *The Examined Life* (1989), chapter 3, on inheritance). Critics have asked, inter alia, whether he succeeds in steering between anarchism and the more extensive state, whether he relies overmuch on moral behaviour, whether his doctrine of entitlement is adequately founded, especially the rules of acquisition, and whether he can avoid supplementing rights with other considerations.

In epistemology Nozick analyses knowledge in terms of 'tracking' the truth (*Philosophical Explanations*, chapter 3): one knows a truth if one believes it, would not believe it were it false, but would believe it were it true. He uses this to deal with scepticism, but it has controversial features: for example, that one can know a conjunction while not knowing (but merely believing) one of its conjuncts (p. 228).

Nozick's latest book, *The Nature of Rationality* (1993), starts by exploring the rationale of acting on principle and then introduces the notion of symbolic utility, i.e. the value of something as a symbol, a notion he had used in *The Examined Life* (pp. 286ff) to moderate some of the conclusions of *Anarchy, State, and Utopia*. As well as offering further views on Newcomb's problem (compare the 1969 article), he develops a theory of rational belief (although one might wonder whether he here satisfactorily distinguishes belief from acceptance), and emphasizes throughout the role of evolution in determining why we have the intuitions we have, especially when, as with the Euclidean nature of space, these intuitions are not strictly true (p. 105).

Sources: IWW 1993–4; WW(Am) 1992–3; *PI*; personal communication.

A. R. LACEY

Ortega y Gasset, José

Spanish. **b:** 1883, Madrid. **d:** 1955, Madrid. **Cat:** Ratio-vitalist. **Educ:** Educated at the University of Madrid and then in Germany. **Appts:** Began his career as a neo-Kantian; he began to develop his own ideas from 1910 onwards as Professor of Metaphysics at Madrid, a position he retained until forced into exile by the Civil War and the Second World War; returned to Madrid in 1948, founding, with Julián Mariás, the Institute of Humanities.

Main publications:

All in *Obras completas*, 12 vols, Madrid: Alianza/Revista de occidente, 1983:
(1912) *Meditaciones del Quijote*.
(1921) *España invertebrada*; revised 1922 and 1934.
(1925) *La deshumanizacion del arte*.
(1930) *La rebelión de las masas*.
(1932–3) *Unas lecciones de metafísica* (published 1966).
(1935) *Historia como sistema*.
(1940) *Ideas y creencias*.
(1958) *La idea de principio en Leibniz y la evolución de la teoría deductiva* (posthumous).

Secondary literature:

Borel, J. (1959) *Raison et vie chez Ortega y Gasset*, Neuchâtel: La Baconnière.
Garagorri, P. (1970) *Introducción a Ortega*, Madrid: Alianza Editorial.
Guy, A. (1969) *Ortega y Gasset*, Paris: Seghers.
Mariàs, J. (1960) *Ortega y Gasset: circumstancia y vocación*, Madrid: Revista de Occidente.

Ortega is a figure of the first importance in the recent intellectual history of his country, both as a writer and as editor of the *Revista de Occidente*, a periodical and a series of books through which modern European ideas were transmitted to Spain. Ortega's own extensive writings range over history, politics, aesthetics and art criticism as well as the history of philosophy, metaphysics, epistemology and ethics. They are written in lucid Castilian, by a master of the language, making Ortega a considerable stylist as well as an important thinker.

After a youthful period as a neo-Kantian, Ortega began to develop his own ideas in the *Meditaciones del Quijote* (1914), and the lines of thought adumbrated there are worked out in his major philosophical works thereafter, culminating in the incomplete, posthumously published *La idea de principio en Leibniz* (1958), on which Ortega was working at the time of his death. Ortega referred to his own mature philosophy as 'ratio-vitalist', a term he uses regularly from the early 1920s onwards.

Ortega's metaphysics begins with a critique of both realism and idealism. The former takes the world or objects to be the ultimate reality, while the latter gives priority to the self. Neither view is acceptable, since there is a further category logically prior to both that of self and that of thing, and this ultimate category is life: 'I am not my life. This, which is reality, is made up of me and of things. Things are not me and I am not things: we are mutually transcendent, but both are immanent in that absolute coexistence which is life' (1932–3, XIII). Further, although the life of an individual is given to them, each person must work unceasingly to preserve it. We are in continual danger of catastrophe, and to avoid it is our ceaseless endeavour. As he often says, 'Life is a task' ('La vida es quehacer'). Our chief asset in this struggle is reason. By 'reason' he does not mean pure intellection or a capacity for abstract thought, but more broadly, 'any intellectual action which puts us in contact with reality, by means of which we knock against the transcendent' (i.e. things; 1935,

IX). This is the 'vital reason' (*razon vital*) which gives his thought its name.

This philosophy contains markedly existentialist elements. Ortega contended that the natural sciences had made no progress with regard to understanding human affairs. The reason for this is that science presupposes that nature is fixed or immutable (an assumption he refers to as the 'gigantic arbitrariness of Parmenides'), whereas human beings have no fixed nature. A human being is not a thing but a drama, and nature is merely a transitory label we fix to what we encounter in our lives: 'Man is the being who makes himself' (1935, VII). Ortega's principal ethical injunction, to live an authentic life, is grounded directly on this view. Like **Sartre**, Ortega regards human beings as condemned to be free. At each moment many possibilities are open to us, and we must choose between them. Freedom is not an activity exercised by a being with a fixed nature. To be free means to lack a constitutive identity.

Science rests on 'Eleatic' assumptions of the fixed character of nature. To deal with the affairs of human beings, who lack a fixed nature, a different sort of discipline is necessary and this is history. Life is the fundamental reality, and history is the systematic science of life. We are what has happened to us, both as individuals and as a species, and human affairs are only understandable by understanding their history. Further, history, like all knowledge, is something that we make in our struggle to survive, not a dispassionate discovery of truth. All our intellectual discoveries are elements in what Ortega calls perspectives, views of the world which ineluctibly involve an individual point of view. The only false perspective is one which claims to transcend a point of view and be absolute.

Politically, Ortega favoured a form of aristocracy, his views resting on his theories of the nature of life combined with a firm belief in natural inequalities of ability between people. Life is a struggle, and

culture is insecure, needing constant attention and modification if it is not to collapse. Most human beings are incapable of the creativity and foresight needed to maintain culture, and revolutions by the masses are merely goalless protests which threaten to destroy culture. Culture is maintained by an intellectual aristocracy, who take care, however, to avoid involvement in the day-to-day activity of government, which is tedious and degrading. For the rest of the time, they should occupy themselves with what Ortega regarded as the 'exact fantasies' of philosophy, mathematics or science, games invented to allay the boredom of humdrum existence. These ideas were developed by Ortega over a long period, from *La rebelión de las masas* (1930) until his death: they are still under elaboration in this final work, *La idea de principio en Leibniz*.

ROBERT WILKINSON

Peirce, Charles S(anders)

American. **b:** 10 September 1839, Cambridge, Massachusetts. **d:** 14 April 1914, Milford, Pennsylvania. **Cat:** Physicist; logician; philosopher of science; pragmatist philosopher. **Ints:** Logic; philosophy of science. **Educ:** Harvard University, BA in Physics, 1859, MA 1862, BS in Chemistry, 1863. **Infls:** Duns Scotus, Kant and Boole. **Appts:** 1861–91, Physicist and Astronomer, United States Coast and Geodetic Survey; 1864–5, Lecturer, Philosophy of Science, Harvard University; 1867–72, Assistant Director, Harvard Observatory; 1879–84, Lecturer in Logic, Johns Hopkins University.

Main publications:

(1868) 'Questions concering certain faculties claimed for man', *Journal of Speculative Philosophy* 2: 103–114; reprinted in *CP* 5: 135–55.
(1868) 'Some consequences of four incapacities', ibid. 2: 140–57; reprinted in *CP* 5: 156–89.

(1869) 'Grounds of validity of the laws of logic: further consequences of four incapacities', ibid. 2: 193–208; reprinted in *CP* 5: 190–222.

(1877) 'The fixation of belief', *Popular Science Monthly* 12: 1–15; reprinted in *CP* 5: 223–47.

(1878) 'How to make our ideas clear', ibid. 12: 286–302; reprinted in *CP* 5: 248–71.

(1878) 'The doctrine of chances', ibid. 12: 604–15; reprinted in *CP* 2: 389–414.

(1878) 'The probability of induction', ibid. 12: 705–18; reprinted in *CP* 2: 415–32.

(1878) 'The order of nature', ibid. 13: 203–17; reprinted in *CP* 6: 283–301.

(1878) 'Deduction, induction, and hypothesis', ibid. 13: 470–82; reprinted in *CP* 2: 372–88.

(1891) 'The architecture of theories', *The Monist* 1: 161–76; reprinted in *CP* 6: 11–27.

(1892) 'The doctrine of necessity examined', ibid 2: 321–37; reprinted in *CP* 6: 36–45.

(1892) 'The law of mind', ibid. 2: 533–59; reprinted in *CP* 6: 86–113.

(1892) 'Man's glassy essence', ibid. 3: 1–22; reprinted in *CP* 6: 155–75.

(1982–) *Writings of Charles S. Peirce. A Chronological Edition*, ed. Max H. Fisch, *et al.*, Bloomington: Indiana University Press.

Collections:
(1931–5) *The Collected Papers of Charles Sanders Peirce*, vols 1–6, ed. Charles Hartshorne and Paul Weiss, Cambridge, Mass.: Harvard University Press. (Cited below as *CP* followed by volume and page numbers.)

(1959) *The Collected Papers of Charles Sanders Peirce*, vols 7–8, ed. Arthur Burks, Cambridge, Mass.: Harvard University Press. (Cited below as *CP* followed by volume and page numbers.)

Secondary literature:

Feibleman, J. K. (1946) *An Introduction to Peirce's Philosophy, Interpreted as a System*, New York: Harper & Brothers.

Murphey, M. G. (1961) *The Development of Peirce's Philosophy*, Cambridge, Mass.: Harvard University Press.

Thompson, M. (1953) *The Pragmatic Philosophy of C. S. Peirce*, Chicago: University of Chicago Press.

The son of Benjamin Peirce, the most eminent American mathematician in the nineteenth century and a Harvard professor, Charles Peirce began his career as a physicist with the United States Coast and Geodetic Survey, of which his father was superintendent. As a working scientist he was a pioneer in the effort to map our galaxy, publishing in 1878 *Photometric Researches*. In the 1870s he was one of the major participants in the Metaphysical Club in Cambridge, Massachusetts. This informal group included William **James**, Oliver Wendell Holmes and Chauncey Wright, and is the alleged birthplace of American pragmatism. After his resignation from the Geodetic Survey in 1891, Peirce lived in Arisbe near Milford, Pennsylvania. Living in poverty, he wrote and occasionally lectured for the rest of his life. William James often came to his assistance, providing funds and arranging for his lectures.

A series of three articles in the *Journal of Speculative Philosophy* in 1868–9 launched Peirce as a philosopher who rejected the foundationalism, intuitionism, introspectionism and egoism prevalent in modern philosophy since Descartes. In this series of articles Peirce contended that scepticism could not be employed wholesale to beliefs in general, as Descartes had proposed, nor could it be used to establish beliefs that were absolutely certain, since every belief was fallible. Further, he denied that introspection was a means of internal observation of private mental states, and contended that all knowledge of mind is inferred from external observation. He therefore denied that the human mind has the capacity of intuition to grasp clear and distinct ideas as certain truths. Inquiry, he maintained, is a social and not a private enterprise. He also depicted thinking as essentially the interplay of signs, generalizing even that the individual human mind is but a sign. From 1877 to 1878 a series of six articles in the *Popular Science Monthly* established Peirce as a pioneer in the philosophy of science. The series is most famous for Peirce's enunciation of the principle of pragmatism, stated in the second article without use of the word, as the following rule for the clarification of ideas: 'Consider what effects, which might conceivably have practical bearings, we conceive the object of our conception to have. Then, our conception of these effects is the whole of our conception of the object' (*CP* 5: 258). When in 1898 James used the term 'pragmatism', inspiring an international philosophical movement, he cited Peirce's formula. Displeased by James's psychologizing of a logical principle, and by his transformation of a methodological rule into a metaphysics wedded to nominalism, Peirce renamed his principle 'pragmati*c*ism'—a word 'ugly enough to be safe from kidnappers' (*CP* 5: 277). Many of Peirce's most influential ideas were presented in the *Popular Science* articles: his conception of belief as a habit of action; his conception of enquiry as the process of fixing belief; his emphasis on the scientific method as the only reliable method of fixing belief; his doctrine of fallibilism—namely, that no belief is absolutely certain; his conceptions of truth as the opinion that the unlimited community of scientific enquirers is fated to reach and of reality as the object of that opinion; his conception of natural law as statistical, and hence the doctrine of chances; his discovery of the role of hypothesis in scientific inquiry, which he called abduction to distinguish it from induction and deduction. Peirce's philosophical investigations anticipated major developments not only in pragmatism and the philosophy of science, but also in symbolic logic and the theory of signs. His writings on formal logic, many of them posthumously published, presage the subsequent rise of symbolic logic, and his work on the theory of signs, which he named 'semiotic', remains in the forefront of current research. In his logical investigations Peirce had discovered three fundamental kinds of relations: one-term (monadic), two-term (dyadic) and three-term (triadic), all other kinds of relations being resoluble into these three, but none of the three being reducible further. Meaning, the sign-relation, he found to be a triadic relation, its three terms being the sign, the object and the interpretant. The three kinds of relations are the key to Peirce's basic set of categories: Firstness (Quality), Secondness (Relation) and Thirdness (Generality). In a series of five articles that appeared in *The Monist* in 1891–3, Peirce undertook to erect a system of metaphysics, a 'cosmogonic' philosophy, by drawing upon the principles and concepts of the sciences. Peirce argued for tychism (the doctrine of objective chance), synechism (the doctrine of continuity) and agapism (the doctrine of evolutionary love). He also identified his categories of firstness, secondness, and thirdness phenomenologically and psychologically as feeling, resistance, and conception. Drawing upon the principles and conceptions of the special sciences, he sketched a cosmogonic philosophy of evolutionary idealism. Peirce maintained that philosophy is a science. During his life he made several attempts to classify the sciences and place philosophy within the classification. The theme threading his various efforts is that the sciences be ranked according to the generality of their principles and conceptions, so that the more general be at the top of the hierarchy, those lying below being less general yet depending upon the higher for some of their general principles. Hence all sciences are divided into three classes in descending order: sciences of discovery, sciences of review and practical sciences. Philosophy is located in the sciences of discovery, which are ranked in descending order: mathematics, philosophy (coenoscopy) and the special sciences (ideoscopy). Philosophy, moreover, is subdivided in descending order as phenomenology (phaneroscopy), normative science (including ethics, esthetics, logic) and metaphysics. Peirce never completed his lifework, but he left at his death a welter of papers, which his widow sold to the Harvard University Department of Philosophy. These papers have proved to be a treasure-trove for philosophical scholars. *The Transactions of the Charles S. Peirce Society*, founded in 1964 and edited by Peter Hare and Richard S. Robin, is a journal that, in quarterly publication, presents articles and reviews on Peirce and Peirce scholarship.

Sources: DAB: Edwards; EAB.

ANDREW RECK

Piaget, Jean

Swiss. *b:* 1896, Neuchâtel, Switzerland. *d:* 1980, Geneva. *Cat:* Developmental psychologist. *Ints:* Child development, especially cognitive; epistemology. *Educ:* University of Neuchâtel, PhD on biology of land molluscs; University of Zurich, psychology; Sorbonne University, psychology, logic, philosophy of science. *Infls:* Philosophical influences: Kant, André Lalande and Léon Brunschvieg. Psychological influence: Alfred Binet. *Appts:* 1921, Director of Studies, Institut J.-J. Rousseau (now Institut des Sciences de l'Education), Geneva (1932, Codirector); 1925, Professor of Philosophy, University of Neuchâtel; 1929, Professor of the History of Scientific Thought, University of Geneva; 1940, Professor of Experimental Psychology, Director of the Psychological Laboratory, Geneva; 1955, Professor of Psychology, Sorbonne, and Director, Centre International de l'Epistémologie Génétique, Geneva.

Main publications:

(1924) *Le Langage et la pensée chez l'enfant*, Paris: Delachaux & Niestle (English translation, *The Language and Thought of the Child*, trans. M. Warden, London: K. Paul, Trench, Trubner & Co., 1926; second edition, trans. M. Gabain, 1932).

(1924) *Le Jugement et la raisonnement chez l'enfant*, Paris: Delachaux & Niestle (English translation, *Judgement and Reasoning in the Child*, trans. M. Warden, London: Routledge & Kegan Paul, 1928).

(1930) *The Child's Conception of Physical Causality*, trans. M. Grabin, London: Routledge & Kegan Paul (originally published 1927).

(1936) *The Origin of Intelligence in the Child*, London: Routledge & Kegan Paul, 1953; New York: International Universities Press, 1966.

(1937) *The Child's Construction of Reality*, London: Routledge & Kegan Paul, 1955; New York: Basic Books, 1954.

(1941) (with A. Szeminska) *La Genèse du nombre chez l'enfant*, Paris (English translation, *The Child's Conception of Number*, trans. C. Gattegno and F. M. Hodgson, London: Routledge & Kegan Paul, 1952).

(1941) (with Barbel Inhelder) *The Child's Construction of Quantities*, London: Routledge & Kegan Paul and New York: Basic Books, 1974.

(1974) *Experiments in Contradiction*, London: Routledge & Kegan Paul; New York: Norton.

(1974) *The Development of Thought*, London: Routledge & Kegan Paul; New York: Norton.

Secondary literature:

Boden, M. A. (1979) *Piaget*, Brighton: Harvester Press and London: Fontana Paperbacks; New York: Viking Press, 1980.

Flavell, J. H. (1963) *The Developmental Psychology of Jean Piaget*, Princeton, NJ: Van Nostrand (includes full bibliography up to 1963).

Hundert, E. M. (1989) 'The child's construction of reality', ch. 4 of *Philosophy, Psychiatry and Neuroscience*, Oxford: Clarendon Press.

Piaget's theory of cognitive development in children, genetic epistemology, has become widely influential in psychology and education. The key insight of genetic epistemology is that our cognitive abilities, in particular our grasp of basic physical concepts and logical operations, are not 'given' but acquired in a series of developmental stages through interaction with the environment. Originally a biologist, Piaget became interested in developmental psychology during his time in Paris. Extending Binet's work on IQ testing, he was struck by the difficulty found by many children as old as eight in following apparently straightforward syllogisms. Children, it seemed to him, lacked certain logical capacities which as adults we take for granted. Working initially by talking with children, including his own, he went on to develop a series of ingenious experiments by which he was able to map out the stages through which these capacities are acquired.

Piaget proposed four main stages (each with a number of substages): sensorimotor, preoperational, concrete operational and formal operational. The order, though not the duration, of these stages is fixed. The sensorimotor stage lasts from birth up to about age 4. The new born-infant has no ability to organize its world. It has a number of inborn reflexes—grasping, sucking, following a moving object—through which it operates on its environment. The experiences generated by these reflex activities allow the child to build up rudimentary conceptions of space and time, of the distinction between the self and the world, and of the independent existence of objects. Piaget observed, for instance, that up to about eight months, a baby loses interest in a toy if it is hidden. The toy, he claimed, simply ceases to exist. The baby has to learn through repeated experiences that objects continue to exist even when we are not directly aware of them. At the sensorimotor stage, the child's world is a world of 'pictures emerging from nothingness at the moment of action, to return to nothingness at the moment when the action is finished' (Piaget 1937: 43).

The sensorimotor stage is followed by the preoperational stage (when language is acquired) and the 'concrete operations period', which together last up to young adolescence. During this period the child gradually ceases to depend on immediate perception and develops the capacity for logical thinking. Piaget found, for example, that a young child shown pairs of sticks of unequal length is unable to infer from separate perceptions 'A longer than B' and 'B longer than C' that A is longer than C. Again, in a series of famous 'conservation experiments', he showed that children had to learn the principle of invariance. In one experiment the child is first shown two identical glasses with equal amounts of water in them, A and B; the water from B is then poured into a third glass, C, which is thinner,

the level of the water thus ending up higher. The child's response to this, up to about eight years, is typically to claim that the amounts of water in A and B are equal, but that there is more water in C than A.

The last developmental stage, corresponding broadly with adolescence, is the 'formal operations period'. This is the least studied of Piaget's stages. It involves the emergence of the ability for 'scientific' thinking, the key to which is the ability to isolate relevant causes. This in turn, Piaget claimed, required the ability not only for logical thinking but also for second-order reflection on one's own thought processes.

Although Piaget's work was largely observational and experimental, he read widely in philosophy as a young man and throughout his life remained actively interested in the philosophical implications of his findings. He considered himself to be concerned with the traditional problems of the theory of knowledge while at the same time regarding these as biological problems. The 'reality' with which epistemology is concerned is the environment in which organisms live. Hence the 'problem of the relation between thought and things ... becomes the problem of the relation of an organism to its environment' (Piaget 1930, p. 129). If we study this relationship not as it *is* but as it *comes to be*, we have indeed a genetic epistemology.

To the extent that he was concerned with the constructive aspects of mind, Piaget was a Kantian. He considered himself 'very close to the spirit of Kantianism' and wrote of 'The child's construction of reality'. However, where Kant posited a priori cognitive structures necessary for the organization of experience, Piaget posited inherited modes of functioning by means of which, through interaction with the environment, cognitive structures were developed. These modes of functioning were no more than the simple reflex activities of the sensorimotor stage, which, by 'generalization' and 'differentiation', led ultimately to the emergence of the power of abstraction and other high-level cognitive functions. There was also, as Hundert (1989) has pointed out, a (largely unacknowledged) Hegelian component to Piaget's thinking. In addition to 'assimilation', a Kantian construction of reality by the mind, cognitive development depended on 'accommodation', a Hegelian adaptation of the mind to reality. With the possible exception of psychoanalysis, Piaget's genetic epistemology, though still controversial, has been the single most important influence on modern developmental psychology. The dependence of cognitive development on active exploration of the environment is a cornerstone of educational theory and practice. His philosophy has been much criticized. He has been accused of the 'genetic fallacy' of confusing the (psychological) origins of logical structures with their (formal) properties. It has been said that his developmental stages are, merely, logically necessary: second-order reflection presupposes first-order reflection, for instance. Yet the empirical psychology he helped to found is philosophically significant: it gives substance to philosophical speculation (there *is* no *tabula rasa*, for instance; the concepts of 'self' and 'other' really *are*, as Kant supposed, mutually dependent); and it is antifoundational, the a priori itself being shown to be rooted not just in experience, but, ultimately, in primitive sensorimotor reflexes.

Sources: Harré & Lamb.

K. W. M. FULFORD

Popper, Karl Raimund

Austrian-British. *b:* 28 July 1902, Himmelhof, Vienna. *d:* 17 September 1994. *Cat:* Philosopher of science; political philosopher. *Ints:* Epistemology. *Educ:* Studied at University of Vienna and (after its foundation in 1925) the Pedagogic Institute, 1919–28 (Maturas 1922 and 1924); PhD, 'Zur Methodenfrage der Denkpsychologie', 1928); also training as cabinet-maker and teacher in Mathematics and Science (with qualifying thesis on 'Axiome, Definitionen und Postulate der Geometrie', 1929) and working as social worker and then schoolteacher. *Infls:* Hume, Kant, Fries, Laplace, K. Büchler, H. Gomperz, Bolzano, Einstein, Bohr, R. Lammer, Tarski, V. Kraft, J. Kraft, Carnap, Feigl and von Mises. *Appts:* Taught at Canterbury University College, New Zealand, 1937–46, and London School of Economics, 1947–69, holding Chair in Logic and Scientific Method from 1949; FBA 1958; knighted for services to philosophy, 1964; FRS 1976; CH 1982.

Main publications:

A number of Popper's books were conceived or written many years before they were published, and they were often revised and expanded in later editions.

(1934) *Logik der Forschung*, Vienna: Springer.

(1945) *The Open Society and Its Enemies*, London: Routledge.

(1950) 'Indeterminism in quantum physics and in classical physics', *British Journal for Philosophy of Science*.

(1957) *The Poverty of Historicism*, London: Routledge & Kegan Paul; Boston, Mass.: Beacon Press (revised version of three articles originally published separately in 1944–5).

(1959) *The Logic of Scientific Discovery*, London: Hutchinson; New York: Basic Books (translation of revised and expanded version of *Logik der Forschung* 1934).

(1959) 'The propensity interpretation of probability', *British Journal for Philosophy of Science*.

(1972) *Objective Knowledge: An Evolutionary Approach*, Oxford: Clarendon.

(1974) 'Replies to my critics', in P. A. Schilpp (ed.), *The Philosophy of Karl Popper*, La Salle, Ill.: Open Court.

(1977) (with Sir J. C. Eccles) *The Self and Its Brain: An Argument for Interactionism*, Berlin: Springer International.

(1979) *Die beiden Grundprobleme der Erkenntnistheorie*, ed. T. R. Hansen, Tübingen: J. C. B. Mohr (Paul Siebeck).

(1982) *The Open Universe: An Argument for Indeterminism*, ed. W. W. Bartley III, London: Hutchinson; Totowa, NJ: Rowman & Littlefield.

(1982) *Quantum Theory and the Schism in Physics*, ed. W. W. Bartley III, London: Hutchinson; Totowa, NJ: Roman & Littlefield.

(1983) *Realism and the Aim of Science*, ed. W. W. Bartley III, London: Hutchinson; Totowa, NJ: Rowman & Littlefield (this and the previous two titles form (with additions) volumes I, II, and III respectively of *Postscript: After Twenty Years* in proof since 1957 but never published).

(1986) *Unended Quest: An Intellectual Autobiography*, London: Fontana (extracted from P. A. Schilpp (ed.), *The Philosophy of Karl Popper*, La Salle: Open Court, 1974).

(1990) *A World of Propensities: Two New Views on Causality* and *Towards an Evolutionary Theory of Knowledge*, Bristol: Thoemmes.

Collected editions:

(1963) *Conjectures and Refutations: The Growth of Scientific Knowledge*, London: Routledge & Kegan Paul; New York: Basic Books (essays and lectures).

(1983) D. Miller (ed.) *A Pocket Popper*, London: Fontana; reprinted as *Popper Selections*, Princeton: Princeton University Press, 1985.

(1984) *Auf der Suche nach eine besseren Welt*, Munich and Zurich: Piper (English translation, *In Search of a Better World: Lectures and Essays from Thirty Years*, London and New York: Routledge, 1992).

Secondary literature:

Bambrough, R. (ed.) (1967) *Plato, Popper and Politics: Some Contributions to a Modern Controversy*, Cambridge: Heffer.

Bunge, M. (ed.) (1964) *The Critical Approach to Science and Philosophy*, Glencoe, Ill,: Free Press; London: Collier-Macmillan.

Burke, T. E. (1983) *The Philosophy of Popper*, Manchester: Manchester University Press.

Currie, G. and Musgrave, A. (eds) (1985) *Popper and the Human Sciences*, Dordrecht: Nijhoff.

De Vries, G. J. (1952) *Antisthenes Redivivus: Popper's Attack on Plato*, Amsterdam: North-Holland.

Levinson, P. (ed.) (1982) *In Pursuit of Truth: Essays on the Philosophy of Karl Popper on the Occasion of his Eightieth Birthday*, New York: Humanities Press.

Levinson, R. B. (1953) *In Defence of Plato*, Cambridge, Mass.: Harvard University Press.

Magee, B. (1973) *Popper*, London: Fontana.

——(1985) *Philosophy and the Real World: An Introduction to Popper*, La Salle, Ill.: Open Court.

O'Heart, A. (1980) *Karl Popper*, London: Routledge & Kegan Paul.

Schilpp, P. A. (ed.) (1974) *The Philosophy of Karl Popper*, La Salle, Ill.: Open Court.

Wilkins, B. T. (1978) *Has History Any Meaning? A Critique of Popper's Philosophy of History*, Hassocks: Harvester.

Williams, D. E. (1978) *Truth, Hope, and Power: The Thought of Karl Popper*, Toronto, Buffalo and London: Toronto University Press.

Popper did not become a professional philosopher until his mid-thirties, after publishing the first version of the book by which he is most well known, *Logik der Forschung* (1934), and did not seem to think much of professional philosophers in general, at least to judge by his thoughts round his ninetieth birthday (*Sunday Times*, 12 July 1992). But he had been concerned with philosophical problems at least since the age of 17, when he first raised and solved the problem of demarcating science from non-science, and this and the problem of induction occupied much of his attention over the next few years (see *Conjectures and Refutations*, 1963). His official studies, however (when he was not training to be a cabinet-maker), were in science and mathematics and in psychology, especially child psychology, which brought him to his teacher Karl Büchler, and Alfred Adler and Heinrich Gomperz, among others. As a Jew, however, an academic, or indeed any, career in Austria was not going to be possible for him, and after being invited to lecture in England on the strength of his book he passed via New Zealand (at a time when academic research was strangely frowned upon there: see 1986, p. 119) to his final academic home in London. An incidental interest lay in music, where he had interesting ideas on the genesis of polyphony (ibid., SS12), and has had music of his own performed recently (*Sunday Times*, 12 July 1992).

Popper's philosophy is summed up in the title of one of his books: *Conjectures and Refutations* (1963). His contact with the Vienna Circle (although he was never invited to formal membership) and with psychology as studied in Vienna, as well as a reading of Hume and Kant, convinced him that two basic, and connected, sins are psychologism and inductivism. The quest for justification of our theories seems to lead to either an infinite regress or a basis in pure experience, whether this is regarded as underlying all statements (as Fries held a century earlier) or as represented by epistemologically privileged statements, as with the Vienna Circle. But no such basis exists (*The Logic of Scientific Discovery*, 1959, SSSS25–6)—as indeed is now widely accepted. His teacher Büchler had divided language into three functions, expressive, communicative and descriptive, but Popper added a fourth: argumentative, claiming that this showed 'the priority of the study of logic over the study of subjective thought processes' (1986, p. 77)—which incidentally convinced him that there were no such things as conditioned reflexes (ibid.). Inductivism, the view that statements or theories can be given positive support inductively, raises 'Hume's problem' (see 1972, p. 85), which Popper claimed to solve, by showing that scientific theories are indeed immune to verification, or to positive confirmation, but are open to falsification. Induction itself in fact he generally regarded as not only invalid but never actually used (although *The Logic of Scientific Discovery* (pp. 52–3) seems to relax this latter claim).

Falsifiability brings us to the hub of Popper's philosophy. Many readers at first thought that he was simply substituting falsifiability for the verifiability of the Vienna Circle as the criterion for meaningfulness. He since emphasized time and again that this was not so, and the point was taken. Falsifiability provides, by what he admitted is 'a proposal for an agreement or convention' (ibid., p. 37), a way of distinguishng empirical scientific statements from pseudoscience like astrology, or else, as he later decided, from metaphysics (1986, p. 41), which is not necessarily meaningless, for the negation of a falsifiable universal statement (like 'All swans are white') will not itself be falsifiable but is hardly meaningless. Also metaphysical statements, on this criterion, can provide a useful stimulus for science, as with atomism and the corpuscular theory of light (1963, pp. 257–8).

The proper procedure for science is to set up hypotheses designed to be as falsifiable as possible, and then test them by reference to 'basic statements', i.e. those whose form makes them potential falsifiers of the hypothesis, as 'There is a black swan here now' would, if accepted, falsify 'All swans are white'. The basic statements themselves must be falsifiable (hence the importance of adding 'here now' in the above example), and the regress that threatens is stopped when we reach ones we all *decide* to accept—we should not regard them as certain or established, as verificationists regard their basic statements. The need for decision on when to stop testing opens the way to abuse by 'conventionalist strategems', or 'immunization' as he later called it (1972, p. 30), but conventionalism can be avoided (*The Logic of Scientific Discovery*, pp. 108–9). One of the most controversial features of Popper's system is his replacement of confirmation (in the sense of positive support) by 'corroboration', which a hypothesis acquires by surviving severe tests (see ibid., p. 251, n.1): can he really avoid inductivism? Popper insisted at one point that an appraisal must be synthetic, not tautological, but he also insisted that we can never make any hypothesis more probable, in the sense of 'more likely to be true'. How then can saying that a hypothesis is corroborated go beyond saying simply that it *has* passed certain tests? Any attempt to *appraise* it *in the light of* this seems ruled out, and 'if corroborated then appraised' becomes tautological (see especially ibid., p. 251, n. 1, SSSS81–2, pp. 418–19, and 1972, p. 19, SSSS23–4 (answering Salmon on this—but what are we to make of 'good reason(s)' at p. 81, line 7 up, p. 91, line 1?).) Elsewhere, though in a different context, he agreed that a fresh requirement he introduced may indeed involve 'a whiff of verificationism' (1963, p. 248, n.31).

Although for Popper we cannot show our theories to be 'likely to be true', we can show them to have 'likeness to the truth' 'verisimilitude', a notion he introduced in *Conjectures and Refutations* (1963) or shortly before, encouraged by **Tarski's** rehabilitation, as Popper saw it, of the notion of truth (*The Logic of Scientific Discovery*, p. 274, n. 1; 1963, pp. 223–37). A falsified theory can, however, still be useful, as is Newton's.

Epistemology, Popper thought, should study not subjective acts of knowing but objective things known (1972, chapter 3), which belong to the third of the three 'worlds' he postulates, physical objects and subjective states inhabiting the other two (1986, SS38; 'Replies to my critics', 1974, SS21; *The Open Universe*, 1982, Addendum I).

Somewhat analogous to falsifiability is the 'negative utilitarianism' Popper developed in his other main work, *The Open Society and its Enemies* (1945), stressing the need to minimize evil rather than maximize good, which can lead to counterproductive utopianism. In this connection he strongly criticized Plato, Hegel and Marx, and with them the appeal to essentialism and definitions, provoking strong defences of Plato (1952, 1953), to which an Addendum to the 1962 edition of *The Open Society and its Enemies* replies. In similar vein *The Poverty of Historicism* (1957) attacks historicism, the view that there are laws or patterns in history that the social sciences should aim to predict, and which combines the 'naturalistic' approach of physical science with the 'anti-naturalistic' *Verstehen* approach.

Topics omitted here include: mind and body (1977), indeterminism (1950, revised in *The Open Universe*, 1982; 1972, chapter 6); propensities (the 1959 article, included in *Philosophy and Physics*, 1974, and in 1990).

Sources: Interview by Lesley White, *Sunday Times*, News Review, 12 Jul 1992, p. 8; Edwards.

A. R. LACEY

Putnam, Hilary

American. **b:** 31 July 1926, Chicago, Illinois. **Cat:** Philosopher of mathematics. **Ints:** Philosophy of mind; philosophy of science; philosophy of language. **Educ:** University of Pennsylvania, BA 1948; University of California at Los Angeles, PhD (supervisor Hans Reichenbach), 1952. **Infls:** William James, C. S. Peirce, John Dewey, Rudolf Carnap and Ludwig Wittgenstein. **Appts:** Northwestern University, Princeton University; Professor of the Philosophy of Science, MIT, 1961–5; Professor of Philosophy, Harvard University, 1965–76; Walter Beverley Pearson Professor of Mathematical Logic, 1976–; President, American Philosophical Association, 1976; President, Association of Symbolic Logic, 1980.

Main publications:

(1960) 'Minds and machines', in Sidney Hook (ed.), *Dimensions of Mind*, Albany, NY: SUNY Press.
(1967) 'Mathematics without foundations', *Journal of Philosophy* 64.
(1972) *Philosophy of Logic*, London: Allen & Unwin.
(1975) 'The meaning of meaning', in Keith Gunderson (ed.) *Language, Mind and Knowledge*, Minnesota Studies in the Philosophy of Science, vol. VII, Minneapolis: University of Minnesota Press.
(1975) *Mathematics, Matter and Method*, Philosophical Papers, vol. 1, Cambridge: Cambridge University Press.
(1975) *Mind, Language and Reality*, Philosophical Papers, vol. 2, Cambridge: Cambridge University Press.
(1978) *Meaning and the Moral Sciences*, London: Routledge.
(1980) 'Models and reality', *Journal of Symbolic Logic* 45.
(1981) *Reason, Truth and History*, Cambridge: Cambridge University Press.
(1982) *Renewing Philosophy*, Cambridge, Mass.: Harvard University Press.
(1983) *Realism and Reason*, Philosophical Papers, vol. 3, Cambridge: Cambridge University Press.
(1987) *The Many Faces of Realism*, La Salle: Open Court.

(1988) *Representation and Reality*, Cambridge, MA: MIT Press.

Secondary literature:

Clark, P. and Hale, B. (eds) (1994) *Reading Putnam*, Oxford: Basil Blackwell.

Hilary Putnam is a philosopher who manifests a unique blend of technical skill and breadth of interest. Early in his career he made significant contributions to the philosophy of mathematics and the application of logic to quantum theory. Elsewhere, his best-known writings have covered topics in the philosophy of mind, meaning and the contemporary debates about realism.

It is no surprise, therefore, that Putnam's discussions of the problems of meaning are intimately related to the positions he has taken, and frequently abandoned, on some of the central philosophical questions. He formerly espoused a form of realist position, which he later described disparagingly as 'metaphysical realism' which he characterized in terms of two basic theses: (i) that there is a determinate and mind-independent world; and (ii) that there is ultimately one 'true' theory of this world which is the goal of scientific investigation.

Where meaning is concerned, the focus of much debate has been the thesis that meaning determines reference. Putnam has contended that theories which endeavour to reduce meaning to mental states or inner processes are manifestly unsatisfactory. Deploying what has become one of the more shop-worn of philosophical fictions, he asks us to imagine two planets which differ only in the fact that one has water and the other a superficially indistinguishable fluid with fundamentally different chemical constituents. On the first planet there is an individual who speaks English; on the second planet another individual who speaks a language indistinguishable syntactically and phonetically from English. Neither of these individuals can be distinguished in terms of their utterances about the local fluid they experience: they produce identical utterances featuring the word 'water'. Putnam's point is that the word cannot mean on the lips of the first individual what it does when uttered by the second individual, because in each case there is a different fluid being referred to. So the locus of meaning cannot be 'in the mind', or if it is, it cannot determine what is being referred to in the world beyond the skull. But even granted at this point, a truth-conditional account would not be sufficient to pin down reference either. For this reason Putnam urged a shift down from the level of the sentence to the level of terms or referring expressions. So how does one fix the meaning of such terms? One familiar solution, rejected by Putnam, is the one according to which both proper names and kind terms are to be construed as abbreviated descriptions or clusters of such.

Instead, Putnam exploits the idea, due to Saul **Kripke**, of the 'rigid designator', an expression which retains the same reference in 'all possible worlds'. So a term like 'Kripke' would refer essentially to that individual, whereas the expression 'The author of *Naming and Necessity*' would not. Pursuing this approach with regard to kind terms, for example 'gold', 'copper', etc., Putnam would maintain that these 'rigidly' designate the particular metals whose fundamental constitution is the object of scientific investigation. He does, however, point out that reference can be secured by descriptions, amounting in effect to stereotypes, based on the more overt characteristics of the substances described, and this is the common currency of ordinary communication. Meaning, after all, has a social dimension and cannot be exclusively a matter of what goes on inside individual heads. As he abandoned realism, so Putnam shifted his ground on the relation between reference and meaning: the ability to understand language does not require what realism demands, namely that there is some secure 'match' between language and 'the world'. Thus has he moved to a more verificationist stance on meaning.

Of all the positions that Putnam has rejected, one of the most significant in late twentieth-century philosophy is functionalism. Formerly its leading exponent, he later considered it to be fatally flawed. Briefly, functionalism in the philosophy of mind is the thesis that psychological states, for example 'believing that snow is white', 'hoping that functionalism is true', are essentially computational states of the brain. Human psychology, therefore, is merely the software of the brain-computer. Putnam originally endeavoured to characterize functionalism in terms of Turing machine states, but one consequence of meaning not being in the head is that it is not possible to individuate concepts or beliefs without reference to the environment (including the social environment) of the cognitive agent. Putnam views the whole strategy of looking for some non-intentional characterization of the mental as misconceived, and the attempt to assign one kind of computational state to each kind of 'propositional attitude' as naive. Together with this goes his general rejection of a scientism which he saw as infecting philosophy, and his increasing preoccupation with normative issues. Putnam's influence may be measured in the lively debates he has conducted both against representatives of the realism he rejected on the one hand, and positions like that of Richard **Rorty**, which he regards as self-defeatingly relativistic.

Sources: See secondary literature.

DENIS POLLARD

Quine, W(illard) V(an) (Orman)

American. **b:** 25 June 1908, Akron, Ohio. **Cat:** Logician. **Ints:** Philosophy of language; mathematical logic; epistemology; philosophy of science. **Educ:** Oberlin College, Ohio; Harvard University, PhD 1932; University of Oxford. **Infls:** Rudolf Carnap, C. I. Lewis, Bertrand Russell, H. M. Sheffer and Alfred Tarski. **Appts:** 1936–78, first Instructor, then Associate Professor, Professor and eventually Peirce Professor of Philosophy at Harvard University; 1978–, Professor Emeritus, Harvard.

Main publications:

(1934) *A System of Logic*, Cambridge, Mass.: Harvard University Press.
(1940) *Mathematical Logic*, New York: Norton.
(1941) *Elementary Logic*, Boston: Ginn.
(1950) *Methods of Logic*, New York: Holt.
(1953) *From a Logical Point of View: 9 Logico-Philosophical Essays*, Cambridge, Mass.: Harvard University Press.
(1960) *Word and Object*, Cambridge, Mass.: MIT Press.
(1963) *Set Theory and Its Logic*, Cambridge, Mass.: Harvard University Press.
(1966) *The Ways of Paradox and Other Essays*, New York: Random House.
(1966) *Selected Logic Papers*, New York: Random House.
(1969) *Ontological Relativity and Other Essays*, New York: Columbia University Press.
(1970) *Philosophy of Logic*, Englewood Cliffs, NJ: Prentice-Hall; second edition, Cambridge, Mass.: Harvard University Press, 1986.
(1974) *The Roots of Reference*, La Salle, Ill.: Open Court.
(1978) (with J. S. Ullian) *The Web of Belief*, New York: Random House.
(1981) *Theories and Things*, Cambridge, Mass.: Harvard University Press.
(1987) *Quiddities: An Intermittently Philosophical Dictionary*, Cambridge, Mass.: Harvard University Press.
(1990) *Pursuit of Truth*, Cambridge, Mass.: Harvard University Press.

Secondary literature:

Barrett, R. B. and Gibson, Roger F. (eds) (1990) *Perspectives on Quine*, Oxford: Blackwell.
Davidson, D. and Hintikka, J. (eds) (1969) *Words and Objections: Essays on the Philosophy of W. V. O. Quine*, Dordrecht: Reidel.
Dilham, Ilham (1984) *Quine on Ontology, Necessity and Experience: A Philosophical Critique*, London: Macmillan.
Gibson, Roger F. (1982) *The Philosophy of W. V. Quine*, Tampa: University Presses of Florida.

——— (1988) *Enlightened Empiricism: An Examination of W. V. Quine's Theory of Knowledge*, Tampa: University of S. Florida Press.

Gochet, Paul (1986) *Ascent to Truth: A Critical Examination of Quine's Philosophy*, Munich: Munich Verlag.

Hahn, L. E. and Schilpp, P. A. (eds) (1986) *The Philosophy of W. V. Quine*, Peru, Ill.: Open Court.

Hookway, Christopher (1988) *Quine*, Cambridge: Polity Press.

Kirk, R. (1986) *Translation Determined*, Oxford University Press.

Shahan, R. W. and Swoyer, C. (eds) (1979) *Essays on the Philosophy of W. V. Quine*, Norman, Ok.: University of Oklahoma Press, and Hassocks, Sussex: Harvester (includes bibliography).

Quine's influence on analytic philosophy has been profound and wide-ranging. His early contribution to logic amounted to a substantial modification of the **Russell–Whitehead** system of *Principia Mathematica*, but like Russell he remained loyal to the idea of extensional two-valued logic, evincing a considerable scepticism about the very notion of alternative logics, especially those constructed to accommodate modal concepts like those of necessity and possibility.

Quine was himself influenced by logical positivism, but even while reacting to it, he preserved a strong empiricist orientation. He shared with the positivists the view that science is the only source of knowledge. There is no 'first philosophy' of the type envisaged by traditional philosophers. Espousing a broad naturalism, Quine saw philosophy as part of science, in effect as natural science's reflection on itself. He was particularly concerned with the application of this naturalistic perspective to language. In a famous paper ('Two dogmas of empiricism', in 1953) he mounted an assault on analyticity and the whole notion of 'truth by virtue of meaning'. At issue was the positivist verification principle, according to which analytic statements were characterized as those which were 'verified' by all experiences or observations. He further argued that attempts to define analyticity were circular, involving equally problematic notions like that of synonymy or sameness of meaning, and that verification could not be applied to individual statements in isolation. Quine thus embraced a holistic view in which our beliefs confronted experience, not individually, but as an entire body. Predictions which turned out to be false would entail a revision of the overall system, but this would not dictate exactly how the adjustments were to be made.

Quine, therefore, had a strong aversion to intensional notions such as those of 'meaning', 'property' or 'proposition', seeing them as having no legitimate role in a proper semantic or psychological theory. One upshot of his attack on analyticity and meaning was that there were no 'objective' relations of synonymy or sameness of meaning, and hence all translation was indeterminate. This thesis of the 'indeterminancy of translation' entails that the linguistic behaviour of language speakers is consistent with incompatible but equally coherent schemes or 'manuals' of translation that might be constructed. There is no 'fact of the matter' as to the meaning of a speaker's utterances. Given that, on Quine's view, there are no meanings or analytic truths, then there is an immediate and radical implication for philosophy itself: there is no role for philosophy as an activity exclusively or predominantly concerned with a priori theorizing about 'concepts' or 'meanings'.

Quine sought to extend his programme by naturalizing epistemology, providing a heavily behaviouristic account of the relation of beliefs and theories to sensory input. Quine appeals to the fact that we do, after all, learn language not only from the non-human world, but from other human beings, and that acquiring such language understanding is a matter of bringing one's own speech behaviour into line with that of others in one's particular language community.

Quine is also justly renowed for his discussion of ontological commitment, commenced in the seminal paper ('On what there is', in Quine 1953). Without exaggeration it can be said that this paper generated a vast secondary literature devoted to questions of ontology and reference. The question for Quine is how one determines the ontological commitments of a theory (or a person's body of beliefs about what exists). Natural language is unhelpful in this regard, since it has many different ways of expressing such commitments, i.e. there is no one readily identifiable syntactic device serving the purpose. Furthermore, speakers of natural language talk prima facie about all manner of things: their sentences contain names of nonentities, there are definite descriptive phrases which do not always have the function of referring to objects. Quine's recommendation was that ontological disputes could be clarified by resort to logic, and more specifically the device of quantification. This would mean that, in the technical thought logical idiom, ontological commitment would be expressed by means of what is standardly known as the 'existential' quantifier (informally expressed by 'There is ...' or 'There exists'). Thus someone could express their ontological commitment by saying things of the form 'There are Xs', where 'X' indicates the kinds of entity to which the person is committed. This is the basis for Quine's famous slogan that 'To be is to be the value of a bound variable' (that is, a variable bound by the existential quantifier).

Critics pointed out that there are at least some uses of 'There is' and related expressions in natural language which do not plausibly carry ontological commitment, e.g. 'there are several ways of dealing with this problem', but which, if subjected to the technical regimentation Quine recommends, would involve such commitment. Quine's indeterminacy thesis has implications for his account of ontological commitment: if there is no ultimate fact of the matter about what exactly someone is saying or what entities they are referring to in their utterances, then what a speaker if ontologically committed to becomes relativized to the particular manual or scheme of translation used to interpret their utterances.

For all the relativistic overtones of his approach, Quine has commitments of his own, not least of which is his physicalism, his view of physics as the basic science to which all other 'lesser' sciences should be in principle reducible. Despite a pronounced leaning towards nomalism, he reluctantly feels he has to countenance one category of abstract entity-sets. Science needs mathematics, and while one might dispense with many of the apparent 'entities' of mathematics such as numbers, no mathematics adequate for physical science can be sustained without sets. As always, Quine's ultimate justification for his stances is essentially pragmatic, and his own outlook represents yet another twist to the story of American pragmatism in philosophy.

Quine's views have been the focus of many debates: with Rudolf **Carnap** and Jerrold Katz on the notion of analyticity, and with Ruth Marcus Barcan and others on the question of modality and the possibility of modal logics. He had a significant influence on Donald **Davidson**, his holism has been questioned, perhaps most forcefully by Jerry Fodor, and despite his own logical stance, he has inspired much work on the development of logics tolerating reference to nonentities, at least some of which have put in question his coupling of the notions of existence and quantification.

Sources: Edwards; Turner; Quine, W. V. O. *The Time of My Life: An Autobiography*, Cambridge, Mass.: MIT Press, 1985.

DENIS POLLARD

Ramsey, Frank Plumpton

British. **b:** 22 February 1903, Cambridge, England. **d:** 19 January 1930, Cambridge. **Cat:** Philosopher of mathematics; logician. **Educ:** 1923, graduated in Mathematics, Trinity College, Cambridge; 1924–6, Fellowship at King's College, Cambridge. **Infls:** Wittgenstein, Russell and Keynes. **Appts:** 1926–30, University Lectureship in Mathematics, University of Cambridge.

Main publications:

(1931) *The Foundations of Mathematics and Other Logical Essays*, ed. Richard B. Braithwaite, London: Routledge.
(1978) *Foundations: Essays in Philosophy, Logic, Mathematics and Economics*, ed. D. H. Mellor, London: Routledge.
(1991) *Frank Plumpton Ramsey on Truth*, ed. N. Rescher and U. Majer, Dordrecht: Kluwer.

Secondary literature:

Mellor, D. H. (1980) *Prospects for Pragmatism*, Cambridge: Cambridge University Press.
Ryle, G. (1950) *'If', 'so', and 'because'*, in M. Black (ed.), *Philosophical Analysis*, Ithaca: Cornell University Press.
Sahlin, Nils-Eric (1990) *The Philosophy of F. P. Ramsey*, Cambridge: Cambridge University Press.

Son of an eminent mathematician and President of Magdalene College, and brother of Arthur Michael who became Archbishop of Canterbury, Ramsey had a short but nevertheless outstanding career at Cambridge where he made important contributions to logic and philosophy. He wrote highly original papers on the foundations of mathematics, probability, theory of knowledge, philosophy of science and economics. His early essays, 'The foundation of mathematics' (written in 1925) and 'Mathematical logic' (written in 1926) revealed the influence of **Wittgenstein**'s *Tractatus Logico-Philosophicus* and **Russell** and **Whitehead**'s *Principia Mathematica*. Ramsey accepted Russell and Whitehead's logicist objective of deriving mathematics from logic, but sought to do so without collapsing into the paradoxes which Russell had tried to resolve with the theory of types. Thus Ramsey introduced a

notion of 'predicative functions'—that is, truth functions which allow many arguments—which was derived from Wittgenstein.

Later papers revealed a development of Ramsey's thought towards pragmatism and intuitionism with regard to the problem of truth, although he maintained that a pragmatic theory of truth was actually a supplement to the correspondence theory, rather than a rival. Thus in 'General propositions and causality' (written in 1929) he argued that general propositions—for example 'All men are mortal'—are not strictly speaking propositions with truth functions which can be determined as either true or false. Instead, he argued, they represent the kind of proposition which it is reasonable or unreasonable to maintain. Thus to hold that 'All men are mortal' is to reasonably expect that all men we meet in the future will be mortal. General propositions do not make definite statements about objects, he maintained. Most of Ramsey's essays were published posthumously. In the Introduction to his collection of essays in 1931 Braithwaite said that Ramsey's premature death 'deprives Cambridge of one of its intellectual glories and contemporary philosophy of one of its profoundest thinkers'.

DAVID LAMB

Rawls, John

American. **b:** 21 February 1921, Baltimore. **Cat:** Social contract theorist. **Ints:** Moral and political philosophy; philosophical analysis. **Educ:** Princeton University. **Infls:** Social contract theorists such as Rousseau and Hobbes. **Appts:** Assistant Professor, Cornell University; John Cowles Professor of Philosophy, Harvard, from 1976.

Main publications:

(1958) 'Justice as fairness', *Philosophical Review*, 67: 164.
(1971) *A Theory of Justice*, Cambridge, Mass.: Belknap Press and Oxford University Press.
(1993) *Political Liberalism*, New York: Columbia University Press.

Secondary literature:

Barry, Brian (1973) *The Liberal Theory of Justice: A Critical Examination of the Principal Doctrines in 'A Theory of Justice' by John Rawls*, Oxford: Clarendon Press.
Blecker, H. Gene and Smith, Elizabeth H. (1980) *John Rawls' Theory of Social Justice: An Introduction*, Athens: Ohio University Press.
Chandran, Kukathas and Pettit, Philip (1990) *Rawls: A Theory of Justice and its Critics*, Cambridge: Polity.
Daniels, Norman (ed.) (1975) *Reading Rawls: Critical Studies in Rawls' 'A Theory of Justice'*, Oxford: Blackwell.
Hart (1972–3) 'Rawls on liberty and its priority', *University of Chicago Law Review*.
Martin, Rex (1985) *Rawls and Rights*, Lawrence, Kansas: University Press of Kansas.
Pogge, Thomas (1989) *Realizing Rawls*, Ithaca, NY: Cornell University Press.
Wolff, Robert Paul (1977) *Understanding Rawls: A Reconstruction and Critique of 'A Theory of Justice'*, Princeton University Press.

In his book *A Theory of Justice* (1971) Rawls is concerned with discovering the principles which any society must have if it is to be just. In order to arrive at these principles he uses the hypothetical device of placing actors behind a veil of ignorance. Each actor in this hypothetical situation has no knowledge of his place in society, his class or social status, his psychological inclinations, his intelligence and strengths, the particulars of his rational plan of life, the economic and political situation of his society, the level of cultural attainment of his society and the generation to which he belongs (p. 137). Denial of such information to the actors, according to Rawls, will allow them to arrive at principles that are not evaluated purely on the basis of circumstances specific to the actors. The actors in the original position, however, understand political affairs, principles of economic theory, the basis of social organization and the laws of human psychology (pp. 137–8). They are also assumed to act with a sense of rational self-interest and to be capable of a sense of justice (i.e. acting on the agreed principles) (pp. 140–5).

According to Rawls the parties in the original position will arrive at the following two principles: First Principle: Each person is to have an equal right to the most extensive total system of equal liberties compatible with a similar system of liberty for all. Second Principle: Social and economic inequalities are to be arranged so that they are both: (i) to the greatest benefit of the least advantaged, consistent with the just savings principle; and (ii) attached to offices and positions open to all under conditions of fair equality of opportunity (p. 302).

According to Rawls liberty, the first principle, is to have 'lexical' priority in that the first principle must be satisfied before the second principle is considered (see Hart 1972–3, p. 534 for a critical account, and Barry 1973).

Although Rawls is correct in stressing the importance of liberty one cannot but raise others, the following questions. Will the original position always yield the two Rawlsian principles? Could it not, for instance, yield education as a basic principle? Do the actors, ignorant of their society's economic and political development, have sufficient information to arrive at the two principles? Or, do the actors agree on these principles because they happen to be just in themselves?

Sources: DAS.

INDIRA MAHALINGAM CARR

Ricoeur, Paul

French. *b:* 27 February 1913, Valence, Drôme, France. *Cat:* Hermeneutics. *Ints:* Phenomenology; existentialism; literary theory; Biblical studies. **Educ:** Philosophy, Universities of Rennes and Paris. **Infls:** Jaspers, Marcel, Husserl, Heidegger, Gadamer and Freud. **Appts:** Professor of Metaphysics, Universities of Paris IV and Paris X; Dean of Faculty, University of Paris X; John Nuveen Professor Emeritus, University of Chicago.

Main publications:

(1950) *Philosophie de la volonté. I. Le volontaire et l'involontaire*, Paris: Aubier (English translation, *Freedom and Nature: The Voluntary and the Involuntary*, trans. E. V. Kohak, Evanston: Northwestern University Press).

(1955) *Histoire et vérité*, Paris: Seuil (English translation, *History and Truth*, trans. C. A. Kelbley, Evanston: Northwestern University Press, 1965).

(1960) *Philosophie de la volonté. Finitude et culpabilité. I. L'homme faillible*, Paris: Aubier (English translation, *Fallible Man*, trans. C.A. Kebley, Chicago: Henry Regnery, 1965).

(1960) *Philosophie de la volonté. Finitude et culpabilité. II. La symbolique du mal*, Paris: Aubier (English translation, *The Symbolism of Evil*, New York: Harper & Row, 1967).

(1965) *De l'interprétation. Essai sur Freud*, Paris: Seuil (English translation, *Freud and Philosophy: An Essay on Interpretation*, trans. D. Savage, New Haven: Yale University Press).

(1969) *Le Conflit des interprétations. Essais de l'herméneutique*, Paris: Seuil (English translation, *The Conflict of Interpretations: Essays in Hermeneutics*, Evanston: Northwestern University Press, 1974).

(1975) *La Métaphore vive*, Paris: Seuil (English translation, *The Rule of Metaphor: Multi-Disciplinary Studies of the Creation of Meaning in Language*, trans. R. Czerny et al., Toronto: University of Toronto Press, 1978).

(1983) *Temps et récit, Tome I*, Paris: Seuil (English translation, *Time and Narrative, Vol. I*, trans. K. McLaughlin and D. Pellauer, Chicago: University of Chicago Press, 1984).

(1984) *Temps et récit. Tome II. La Configuration dans le récit de fiction*, Paris: Seuil (English translation, *Time and Narrative, Vol. II*, trans. K. McLaughlin and D. Pellauer, Chicago: University of Chicago Press, 1988).

Secondary literature:

Bourgeois, P. (1990) *Traces of Understanding: A Profile of Heidegger's and Ricoeur's Hermeneutics*, Amsterdam: Rodopi Wurzburg.

Klemm, D. (1983) *The Hemeneutical Theory of Paul Ricoeur: A Constructive Analysis*, London and Toronto: Associated Universities Presses.

Reagan, C. (ed.) (1979) *Studies in the Philosophy of Paul Ricoeur*, Athens, OH: Ohio University Press.

Stevens, B. (1991) *On Paul Ricoeur*, London: Routledge.

——(1991) *L'Apprentissage des signes: Lecture de Paul Ricoeur*, Dordrecht: Kluwer.

The first stage in Paul Ricoeur's thought, reinforced by his study of the works of **Jaspers** in a prisoner of war camp in Germany during the Second World War, is existentialist. This existentialist basis then shifts towards phenomenology and the philosophies of **Husserl** and **Heidegger**— Ricoeur translated the first volume of Husserl's *Ideen* into French. After phenomenology, or more precisely from within phenomenology, his thought proceeds to a philosophical hermeneutics, the proper term for Ricoeur's mature philosophy. Philosophical hermeneutics studies the diverse structures through which meaning can be brought to the subject, structures such as culture, religion, society and language: it owes much to phenomenological study of experience but at the same time offers a powerful critique of the foundations of traditional phenomenology. Philosophical hemeneutics brings together two strands of hermeneutics corresponding to two of Ricoeur's main interests: Biblical interpretation and the philosophical question of textual interpretation as found in Schleiermacher, **Dilthey**, Heidegger and **Gadamer**. Here, the self-transparent autonomous sujectivity at the foundation of phenomenology is replaced by the need to interpret meaning as carried by various structures. For Ricoeur the meaning carried by structures such as texts cannot be known absolutely and thus the subject cannot claim to absolute knowledge or self-knowledge. If the central question for philosophical hermeneutics is that of meaning then its guiding principle is that the many sources of meaning cannot be reconciled into a single account or discourse. Ricoeur's work is the attentive study of these various discourses and of how they impinge on the subject and undo any attempt to bring them together into one. Ricoeur's work is important in debates on phenomenology, existentialism, hermeneutics, critical theory, deconstruction and poststructuralism. It offers a philosophy that mediates between the traditional position put forward by philosophers such as Gadamer in hermeneutics and Husserl in phenomenology and the poststructuralist critiques of those positions as encountered in the work of **Derrida** or **Lyotard** (both of whom studied with Ricoeur).

Sources: Catalogues of Bibliothèque Nationale, Paris and National Library of Scotland.

JAMES WILLIAMS

Rorty, Richard McKay

American. **b:** 4 October 1931, New York. **Cat:** Post-analytical, hermeneutical, pragmatist. **Ints:** Nature and history of philosophy; metaphysics. **Educ:** BA, Chicago, 1949; MA, Chicago, 1952; PhD, Yale, 1956. **Infls:** Dewey, Heidegger, Sellars, Wilfred S. and Wittgenstein. **Appts:** Yale, 1954–6; Wellseley, 1958–61; Princeton, 1961–82; Virginia, 1982–; many visiting appointments.

Main publications:

(1967) *The Linguistic Turn*, Chicago: University of Chicago Press.
(1979) *Philosophy and the Mirror of Nature*, Princeton: Princeton University Press.
(1982) *Consequences of Pragmatism*, Minnesota: University of Minnesota Press (papers of 1972–80).
(1989) *Contingency, Irony, and Solidarity*, Cambridge: Cambridge University Press.

(1991) *Essays on Heidegger and Others*, Cambridge: Cambridge University Press (papers of 1983–9).
(1991) *Objectivity, Relativism, and Truth*, Cambridge: Cambridge University Press (papers of 1983–9).

Secondary literature:

Hall, David L. (1993) *Richard Rorty: Prophet and Poet of the New Pragmatism*, Ithaca: SUNY Press.
Malachowski, A. R. (ed.) (1990) *Reading Rorty*, Oxford: Blackwell.
Saatkamp, H. J. (ed.) (1995) *Rorty and Pragmatism: The Philosopher Responds to His Critics*, Vanderbilt.
West, C. (1989) *The American Evasion of Philosophy*, London: Macmillan (contains a critical version of Rorty's development, chapter 5, pp. 194–210).

Rorty's first book, *The Linguistic Turn* (1967), contained a long introduction on the 'Metaphilosophical difficulties of linguistic philosophy' which signalled many of his reservations about the analytical-linguistic tradition (from which he originated), as well as revealing his interest in the nature and place of philosophy.

His large international reputation was founded by *Philosophy and the Mirror of Nature* (1979), which (like the work of **Wittgenstein**) offered a comprehensive aetiology for the problems in current philosophy. (But, unlike Wittgenstein, Rorty provides a good deal of historical analysis in support of his views.)

According to Rorty, the mind, as a subjective mirror of objective, external nature, has been a persuasive and dominating presence in Western thought, at least from the time of its most famous 'invention' by Descartes. A polarity between mind and nature, he believed, lay behind the very statement of the standard problems of epistemology. And that polarity was only restated in a variant form when the mind (regarded as a theatre for representations) was replaced, in the twentieth century, by language, and when the problems of epistemology were recast as problems of (linguistic) reference.

Rorty has always been acutely self-conscious about the nature of philosophical activity, and *Philosophy and the Mirror of Nature* included theorizing about the role and status of both past (often erroneous) and future (redirected) philosophizing as an element in its wider diagnosis. Philosophy's prestigious role as elitist cultural criticism, Rorty thought, was a consequence of the privileged terrain of the mind (later, language) as a courtroom where the philosopher could arbitrate on the acceptability of claims to knowledge (later, meaningfulness), often on the basis of 'foundationalist' theorizing, and sometimes with pretensions of being outside history. The historical dismantling of the mind removed the privileged status of philosophy. Philosophical problems had to be seen as intrinsically non-timeless, given that no one could expect to produce a finally correct, purely philosophical question and answer. What was left, Rorty thought in Part III of *Philosophy and the Mirror of Nature*, could be seen by use of Oakeshott's notion of the *conversation of mankind*:

> To see keeping a conversation going as a sufficient aim of philosophy, to see wisdom as consisting in the ability to sustain a conversation, is to see human beings as generators of new descriptions rather than beings one hopes to be able to describe accurately.
>
> (p. 378)

He pointed towards what he thought to be the less dogmatic, less problem-solving tenor of the hermeneutical tradition as a way forward. Philosophy, in any case, could be seen as a 'literary genre' (Introduction to *Consequences of Pragmatism*, 1982, p. xiv)—a thought personified by his transition at that time from a Chair in Philosophy to one in Literature (then, later, in Humanities).

His view of philosophy as literature receives some incidental support from his own admirable style of writing: plain, lucid and often witty.

His work since 1979 has pursued themes initiated in *Philosophy and the Mirror of Nature*, branching into an increasingly elaborated dialogue with critics and commentators.

(1) If philosophers' truth cannot be pure and timeless it can at least have some pragmatic value. Rorty is a frank pragmatist about truth, identifying himself as clearly in the tradition of **James** and **Dewey**. This was much debated in the 1980s, with not much progress beyond the positions staked out by James and **Russell** before 1910.

(2) Rorty portrayed the representational mind as a source of problems underlying apparently opposed philosophical positions. That procedure could stand as a clear model of deconstructionist *unmasking*. He saw his own approach as post-analytical, closer to the approaches adopted in current continental European philosophy. He traced out a history of influences leading towards his thinking, from **Nietzsche** through **Heidegger**. This history has been the subject of much debate, like his history of earlier philosophy in *Philosophy and the Mirror of Nature*. His work on **Derrida** has created an obvious comparison with his own view of 'philosophy as a kind of writing'.

(3) As an anti-foundationalist, anti-essentialist work, *Philosophy and the Mirror of Nature* (like the *Philosophical Investigations* of Wittgenstein) presented a remarkably essentialist story about the origin of philosophical problems and the place of philosophy. (Rorty, though, has not yet tested his thinking against what is apparently the most extremely non-historical territory: the traditional problems in the philosophy of mathematics.) The thought that this story might be a narrowly North American and European one was put to Rorty with some force at the Inter-American Congress of Philosophy at Guadalajara in 1985. There, his notion of

philosophy as *play* (a provocative extrapolation of *conversation*) was subject to sharp criticism by Latin American philosophers who had been in touch with a different European tradition of philosophy as radical political critique (see *Proceedings and Addresses* of the American Philosophical Association, vol. 59, no. 5, June 1986, pp. 747–59).

Contingency, Irony, and Solidarity (1989) pursues the themes developed and discussed in the decade after *Philosophy and the Mirror of Nature*, but with a wider political understanding. ('We Western liberal intellectuals should accept the fact that we have to start from where we are' ('Solidarity or objectivity?' (1985), in *Objectivity, Relativism, and Truth*, 1991). Rorty's views were prominent in debates over the social and cultural position of philosophy which raged in American academe through the 1980s. He created for himself a problem of combining an estimation of any reasoned attitude as a contingent choice of language with his own professed liberal preferences. His solution was a form of conscious ('ironic') self-consciousness: 'the citizens of my liberal utopia would be people who had a sense of the contingency of their language of moral deliberation, and thus of their community' (p. 61). A way of life could not be founded on a story based on truths about the human condition (as discovered by philosophers). It might be grounded in stories, but they would be ones told in drama, in fiction or in philosophy, without pretensions to being timeless discoveries.

RICHARD MASON

Royce, Josiah

American. *b:* 10 November 1855, Grass Valley, California. *d:* 14 September 1916, Cambridge, Massachusetts. *Cat:* Absolute idealist. *Ints:* Metaphysics. *Educ:* University of California, Berkeley, AB 1875; Universi-

ties of Leipzig and Göttingen, 1875–6; Johns Hopkins University, PhD 1878. *Infls:* Kant, Fichte, Hegel, Schopenhauer, Bradley, James and Peirce. *Appts:* 1878–82, Instructor in English, University of California, Berkeley; 1882–1916, Visiting Professor to Professor of Philosophy, Harvard University.

Main publications:

(1885) *The Religious Aspect of Philosophy*, Boston: Houghton Mifflin; reprinted, New York: Dover, 1955.
(1892) *The Spirit of Modern Philosophy*, Boston: Houghton Mifflin; reprinted, New York: Dover, 1983.
(1897) *The Conception of God*, New York: Macmillan.
(1899–1900) *The World and the Individual*, 2 vols, New York: Macmillan; reprinted, Magnolia, Mass.: Peter Smith, 1983.
(1908) *The Philosophy of Loyalty*, New York: Macmillan.
(1908) *Race Questions, Provincialism, and Other American Problems*, New York: Macmillan.
(1912) *The Sources of Religious Insight*, New York: Charles Scribner's Sons.
(1913) *The Problem of Christianity*, New York: Macmillan; reprinted, Chicago: University of Chicago Press, 1968.
(1914) *War and Insurance*, New York: Macmillan.
(1916) *The Hope of the Great Community*, New York: Macmillan.
(1919) *Lectures on Modern Idealism*, New Haven, CT: Yale University Press.

Secondary literature:

Clendenning, J. (1985) *The Life and Thought of Josiah Royce*, Madison: University of Wisconsin Press.
Marcel, G. (1945) *La Métaphysique de Royce*, Paris: Gallimard (English translation, *Royce's Metaphysics*, trans. V. and G. Ringer, Chicago: University of Chicago Press, 1956).
Oppenheim, F. M. (1980) *Royce's Voyage Down Under: A Journey of the Mind*, Lexington, Kentucky: University of Kentucky Press.
Smith, J. E. (1950) *Royce's Social Infinite*, New York: Library of Liberal Arts Press.

The son of pioneer parents, Josiah Royce brought to his philosophical career as the leading American exponent of absolute idealism the flair of a Westerner. Already a Harvard University professor of philosophy, Royce published a history focused on the first decade of the Americanization of California, *California from the Conquest in 1846 to the Second Vigilance Committee in San Francisco* (Boston: Houghton Mifflin, 1886). He exposed the chicanery of General John Charles Fremont, the principal figure in the American seizure of the Mexican province. Pursuing his analysis of American character as susceptible to false ideals, Royce also published a realistic Western novel, *The Feud of Oakfield Creek* (Boston: Houghton Mifflin, 1887). The novel depicts a feud between a San Francisco millionaire against a populist settler over the possession of land. Royce's philosophical idealism dawned early in his career. Kant and Hegel were his philosophical idols, and the problems of knowledge his earliest philosophical concerns. In Germany he attended the lectures of H. Lotze, and at Johns Hopkins he studied under G. S. Morris. The first major fruition of his idealism was *The Religious Aspect of Philosophy* (1885), a work which contains a unique argument for the existence of God as the Absolute Knower. The argument proceeds from the existence of error. Since truth consists in the correspondence of a judgement to its object, and since all judgements refer to the objects they intend, no judgement could be deemed false, so that error would not exist. But error, the discrepancy of a judgement with its real object, does exist. The possibility of error requires the supposition of further judgements transcending the error. Such further judgements culminate in an all-inclusive system of thought, or the Absolute Knower. Royce's argument for the absolute from the possibility of error persuaded few thinkers, although William **James** at the time fell under its spell. Major challenges, most notably in the debate arranged by George Holmes Howison at the University of California in the summer of 1895, later

published in *The Conception of God* (1997), confronted Royce with the objection that his absolutism swallowed up personality and moral responsibility. Royce's next approach to the absolute was *The World and the Individual* (1899–1900). Based on Royce's Gifford Lectures delivered at the University of Aberdeen, it identifies as the 'world knot' the double-barrelled question: What is an idea and how is an idea related to reality? Royce distinguished the internal meaning of an idea from its external meaning. The internal meaning is the purpose in the mind having the idea; the external meaning is the object to which the idea refers. In the first volume of *The World and the Individual* Royce distinguished four answers to the question, each generating a conception of being: realism, mysticism, critical rationalism and constructive idealism. As a result of Royce's dialectical examination, only the fourth—constructive idealism—is left standing as the sole conception that bridges the gap between idea and reality. The idealist conception regards the purpose in the individual mind as an expression of the same Will that expresses itself in the world. Idealism, according to Royce's argument, further guarantees the reality of finite individuals embraced in the Absolute Individual. To make his case Royce utilized conceptions derived from modern mathematics and mathematical logic, and in particular sought to respond to the absolutism of F. H. **Bradley**, who had denied the possibility of knowledge of the absolute. Thus the first volume contains, in addition to the lectures, a supplementary essay, 'The one, the many, and the Infinite'. Hence Royce was a pioneer in the use of mathematical logic in the formulation of philosophical argumentation. Bradley's positive influence on Royce is evident in Royce's use of the term 'experience' instead of the term 'thought' in his later philosophy. Meanwhile, Royce's colleague William James, with whom he had team-taught courses, was developing his own philosophy of radical empiricism, pragmatism and pluralism, and the debates continued on home ground. In addition, younger philosophers, such as Ralph Barton Perry, took issue with Royce's treatment of realism, and the movement of new realism was launched. Royce entered the fray. He insisted that his own conception of ideas as purposes was a form of pragmatism, which was tenable only if it was absolute. James's reduction of absolute idealism pragmatically to signifying merely that, since the world is conceived to be perfect, we may take 'moral holidays' had irritated the morally conscientious Royce. After all, one of Royce's arguments for personal immortality had pivoted on his acceptance of the Kantian idea that the finite individual self needs all eternity to fulfil his moral obligation. But Royce retorted in kind to James's strictures. He construed James's conception of truth to mean 'truth' is equivalent to the 'expedient', and he translated the oath of the witness in the jury box in court as follows: 'I swear to tell the expedient, the whole expedient, and nothing but the expedient, so help me future experience.' And he persisted in his dismissal of realism as an epistemology, charging that it placed an unbridgeable gulf between ideas and reality. But Royce's indulgence in polemics did not deter him from constructive philosophical work. In the wake of pragmatism, his thought turned practical. In *The Philosophy of Loyalty* (1908), he grounded morality, first, in the principle of loyalty as the commitment of the individual to a cause, and, ultimately, on the principle of loyalty to loyalty. The relation of the finite individual to the absolute persisted as Royce's most crucial philosophical problem. *The Problem of Christianity* (1913), esteemed to be Royce's greatest work, was his last major attempt to solve the problem. Borrowing from Charles **Peirce** the theory of interpretation as a triadic relation, he construed interpretation to be a cognitive social process distinct from perception and conception, and designated its three terms as (i) the consciousness being interpreted, (ii) the interpreting consciousness, and (iii) the consciousness to whom the interpretation is addressed. Individuals participating in interpretation are bound together to form a community, thereby exemplifying how many finite individuals can become one community. Royce pointed to Pauline Christianity as the exemplar of the principle of the community of interpretation. As individuals have the capacity to extend themselves to embrace common events in the past and common deeds in the future as their own, they are capable of forming communities of memory and of hope. Add to this capacity the principle of oyalty, or love, shaped by the Will to Interpret, and humankind is destined to form the invisible Church, the Community of Interpretation, the Beloved Community. In a basic sense, Royce's last major work transformed the absolute into a community. Royce was intellectually and emotionally shaken by the outbreak of the First World War. He responded, hastily, to propose a visionary scheme of international insurance to safeguard nations against war. When insurance experts criticized the proposal as impractical, he offered a revision that did not allay the criticisms.

Sources: DAB; Edwards; J. Clendenning (ed.) (1970) *The Letters of Josiah Royce*, Chicago: Univ. of Chicago Press; EAB.

ANDREW RECK

Russell, Bertrand Arthur William

British. *b:* 18 May 1872, Trelleck, Wales. *d:* 2 February 1970, Penrhyndeudraeth. *Cat:* Logical empiricist (with reservations). *Ints:* Mathematical logic; metaphysics; philosophy of mind; politics; philosophy of science; history of philosophy; (opposition to) religion. *Educ:* Trinity College, Cambridge, 1890–4. *Infls:* Hume, Peano, Moore and Wittgenstein. *Appts:* Fellow of Trinity College, Cambridge, 1895–1901 and 1944–70; College Lecturer, 1910–16; University of

Chicago, 1938–9; University of California at Los Angeles, 1939–40; many visiting appointments.

Main publications:

The McMaster University Edition of Russell's *Collected Papers* (London: Allen & Unwin, 1983–) will be the definitive edition.

See also Werner, M. (1981) *Bertrand Russell: A Bibliography of his Writings 1895–1976*, Munich: Saur, and Blackwell, K. and Juja, H. (eds) (1995) *A Bibliography of Bertrand Russell*, London: Routledge. In particular:

(1900) *A Critical Exposition of the Philosophy of Leibniz*, Cambridge: Cambridge University Press.

(1903) *The Principles of Mathematics*, Cambridge: Cambridge University Press; second edition, 1937.

(1905) 'On denoting', in *Mind* (reprinted in many collections).

(1910) *Philosophical Essays*, London: Longmans, Green.

(1910–13) (with A. N. Whitehead) *Principia Mathematica*, Cambridge: Cambridge University Press; second edition, 1925–7.

(1912) *The Problems of Philosophy* London: Williams & Norgate.

(1913) *The Theory of Knowledge*; in *Collected Papers*, vol. VII, ed. E. R. Eames and K. Blackwell, London: Allen & Unwin, 1984 (published posthumously).

(1914) *Our Knowledge of the External World as a Field for Scientific Method in Philosophy*, London: Open Court.

(1918) *The Philosophy of Logical Atomism* (lectures), in *Monist*, 1918–19.

(1919) *Introduction to Mathematical Philosophy*, London: Allen & Unwin.

(1921) *The Analysis of Mind* London: Allen & Unwin.

(1927) *The Analysis of Matter*, London: Kegan Paul.

(1940) *An Inquiry into Meaning and Truth*, London: Allen & Unwin.

(1945) *A History of Western Philosophy*, London: Allen & Unwin.

(1948) *Human Knowledge: Its Scope and Limits*, London: Allen & Unwin.

(1959) *My Philosophical Development*, London: Allen & Unwin.

(1967–9) *Autobiography*, London: Allen & Unwin.

Secondary literature:

Ayer, A. J. (1972) *Russell*, London: Fontana/Collins.

Blackwell, K. (1985) *The Spinozistic Ethics of Bertrand Russell*, London: Allen & Unwin.

Griffin, N. (1991) *Russell's Idealist Apprenticeship*, Oxford: Clarendon Press.

Hylton, P. (1990) *Russell, Idealism and the Emergence of Analytical Philosophy*, Oxford: Clarendon Press.

Jager, R. (1972) *The Development of Bertrand Russell's Philosophy*, London: Allen & Unwin.

Kilmister, C. (1984) *Russell*, Brighton: Harvester.

Monk, R. (1995) *Phantoms of the Dusk*, London: Cape (biography, vol. 1).

Pears, D. F. (1967) *Bertrand Russell and the British Tradition in Philosophy*, London: Fontana/Collins.

Ryan, A. (1988) *Bertrand Russell: A Political Life*, Harmondsworth: Allen Lane.

Savage, C. Wade and Anderson, C. A. (eds) (1989) *Rereading Russell: Essays in Bertrand Russell's Metaphysics*, Minneapolis: University of Minnesota Press.

Schilpp, P. A. (ed.) (1944) *The Philosophy of Bertrand Russell*, Evanston and Chicago: Northwestern University Press.

Russell summed up his work, not always without some reconstructive hindsight, in *My Philosophical Development* (1959) and in his *Autobiography* (1967–9). In 1895 he formed a plan to 'write one series of books on the philosophy of the sciences from pure mathematics to physiology, and another series of books on social questions. I hoped that the two series might ultimately meet in a synthesis at once scientific and practical' (1967–9, vol. 1, p. 125). The first part of this project was achieved, but not the final synthesis: most commentators agree that there is an unbridgeable gap between his writings on metaphysical or mathematical philosophy on one side and his works on morality, education, politics and his polemics against religion on the other. This latter part of his output (see Ryan 1988 for a full discussion) has been far less highly valued by later academic critics, although the proportion of his writing remaining in print must be testimony to its continuing popularity.

His long philosophical career fell into several phases.

(1) Until 1898, he was a Hegelian idealist (see Griffin 1991), a period he repudiated entirely.

(2) Then, he wrote: 'It was towards the end of 1898 that **Moore** and I rebelled against both Kant and Hegel. Moore led the way, but I followed closely in his footsteps' (1959, p. 54). Until around 1911 he was deeply engaged in the philosophy and foundations of mathematics, espousing varying forms of strongly realist metaphysics and epistemology.

(3) In 1911 he met **Wittgenstein**, first as his teacher and soon as a colleague. He had a period of atomism allied to forms of neutral monist ontology, with an increasing interest in language.

(4) From about 1927 to 1938 he spent much time away from narrowly defined philosophy, lecturing and writing on a huge range of popular subjects.

(5) Between 1938 and about 1950 he returned to academic philosophical work, making contributions to the philosophy of science.

(6) From 1950 to his death at the age of 98 in 1970, most of his energies went on extremely active political campaigning.

Russell said that his original interest in philosophy had two sources:

On the one hand, I was anxious to discover whether philosophy would provide any defence for anything that could be called religious belief, however vague; on the other hand, I wished to persuade myself that something could be known, in pure mathematics if not elsewhere.

(1959, p. 11)

It is impossible to summarize common or continuous views in his work; but there are some assumptions that do underlie it from 1898 onwards.

(1) He never moved away from an egocentric, Cartesian stance as the starting-point for philosophical questioning, and was therefore unable to shake off the set of traditional problems associated with the reliability of 'our' knowledge of 'the external world'. Here, he ended in a familiar *cul de sac*: 'the whole of what we perceive without inference belongs to our private world. In this respect, I agree with Berkeley. The starry heaven that we know in visual sensation is inside us. The external starry heaven that we believe in is inferred' (ibid., p. 27).

(2) He always maintained a reasoned confidence in what he was happy to collect under the title of *science*, accepting its results as data for philosophy, and preferring to clothe his philosophical writing in scientistic terminology ('analysis', 'atomism', 'incomplete symbols'). This preference may have been a reaction against the view of metaphysics as a consolatory branch of *belles lettres* which he castigated in his idealist predecessors.

(3) More important, he always maintained that philosophy, in analogy with 'science', could and should deliver substantive results: theories about what exists, what can be known, how we come to know it. This assumption in his work caused some of its most serious problems, and also set it apart in the most obvious way from both the early and the late thinking of Wittgenstein. Although he shared the early Wittgenstein's use of a language of analysis, a work such as *The Philosophy of Logical Atomism* (1918; very unlike Wittgenstein's *Tractatus*) was deeply ambiguous about the nature of the analytical enterprise, its objectives and the nature of its end-points. The status of his 'logical atoms' was entirely unclear. The whole project was presented as a 'scientific' investigation into what sort of things exist, and how the mechanism of perceptual knowledge is meant to work. Yet he understood that he was in what he himself believed to be the territories of physics and empirical psychology. Russell retained a desire for an edifice of philosophical theory which would somehow explain how the mechanism of

perception related to what can be known (or, sometimes, said). Here, his roots in the traditions of British empiricism are evident (see Pears, 1967), overlaid with an apparatus of modern logic and dressed in quasi-scientific language.

Russell's important contributions to philosophy began negatively, with his rejection of the idealism he had read in **Bradley** and heard from **McTaggart** (see Hylton 1990). His study of Leibniz (1900) gave an example for later analytical-historical studies in identifying a handful of crucial tenets in Leibniz, and then diagnosing the conflicts inherent in them. The same procedure was applied by Russell (and **Moore**) against idealism. There, the crucial tenet was claimed to be the 'dogma of internal relations': all individuals are necessarily related to each other, forming a single Whole. Russell argued for the existence of genuinely independent individuals and the entire truth of particular statements (see his *Philosophical Essays*, 1910). His leap from idealism to a world of separate facts raised problems about the ontological status of those facts, and the relations between a judging subject, a judgement and an object of judgement (see F. P. **Ramsey**, 'Facts and propositions', *Aristotelian Society Supplementary Volume*, 1927, for a clear discussion). Regardless of his difficulties, to him, pluralism was a necessary presupposition of 'analysis' (see *The Philosophy of Logical Atomism*, 1918, I).

Russell's ontological speculations were never resolved. By the time of *The Analysis of Mind* (1921) he had reached this view:

The stuff of which the world of our experience is composed is, in my belief, neither mind nor matter, but something more primitive than either. Both mind and matter seem to be composite, and the stuff of which they are compounded lies in a sense between the two, in a sense above them both, like a common ancestor.

(p. 11)

Both physics and psychology were built upon 'a neutral stuff' (p. 287). The mind itself was construed along Humeian lines, with 'a collection of events connected with each other by memory-chains' (p. 27) as a modernized version of Hume's *congeries* of ideas.

Russell's paper of 1905, 'On denoting', was the foundation of much twentieth-century philosophizing about language (F. P. Ramsey called it 'a paradigm of philosophy'). The overt question was the 'meaning' of expressions such as 'the common factor of 6 and 9' (or, more problematically, 'the integer between 2 and 3') or 'the King of France'. The question was forced on Russell by his assumption that the meaning of terms was what they stood for (following a model of naming). Such 'definite descriptions' plainly had meanings where, in some cases, they stood for nothing. The essential point of his theory, Russell wrote,

was that although 'the golden mountain' may be grammatically the subject of a significant proposition, such a proposition when rightly analysed no longer has such a susbject. The proposition 'the golden mountain does not exist' becomes 'the propositional function "x is golden and a mountain" is false for all values of x'.

(1959, p. 84)

Existence was understood in terms of truth: '"The author of *Waverley* exists" means "there is a value of c for which the propositional function 'x wrote *Waverley*' is always equivalent to 'x is c' is true"' (p. 85).

'On denoting' showed how a logical form could differ from obvious forms of common language. But it was not until 1918, Russell claimed later, that he first become interested in the definition of 'meaning' and in the relation of language to fact. 'Until then I had regarded language as "transparent" and had never examined what makes its relation to the non-linguistic world' (1959, p. 145). Although in his final period, after 1950, he tended to play down his earlier work on language (perhaps as a result of his scorn for what he considered as trivial, 'linguistic' philosophy), some of that work had been well ahead of its time. From 1921, for example, there is a passage that could have come from Wittgenstein twenty years later:

> Understanding words does not consist in knowing their dictionary definitions, or in being able to specify the objects to which they are appropriate. Understanding language is more like understanding cricket: it is a matter of habits, acquired in oneself and rightly presumed in others. To say that a word has a meaning is not to say that those who use the word correctly have ever thought out what the meaning is: the use of the word comes first, and the meaning is to be distilled out of it by observation and analysis. Moreover, the meaning of a word is not absolutely definite: there is always a greater or less degree of vagueness.
>
> (*The Analysis of Mind*, 1921, pp. 197–8)

... and more strongly still: 'For my part, I believe that, partly by means of the study of syntax, we can arrive at considerable knowledge concerning the structure of the world' (last words of *An Inquiry into Meaning and Truth*, 1940).

Russell's reputation is most unshakeable in logic and the philosophy of mathematics. His early search for a solid base of certainty for mathematical truth led him to the view that it was grounded in logic. His *logicism* was developed independently from the earlier work of **Frege**, and was expressed in notation he had learned from Giuseppe Peano in 1900. *The Principles of Mathematics* (1903) and the three volumes of *Principia Mathematica* (1910–13, written with A. N. **Whitehead**) remain as treasure-stores of painstaking logical argument: the foundation for modern, systematic logic (see Kilmister 1984). But the cracks in Russell's

project began to show as early as 1901, putting an end to his 'logical honeymoon', as he said (1959, p. 75). His interpretation of numbers as classes of classes was underminded by paradox: consider a class that is not a member of itself—is it a member of itself?—if yes, then no—if no, then yes. The theorizing required to avert this paradox cost Russell years of thought, and led to the development of important parts of the technical apparatus in *Principia Mathematica*. Later, after 1911, discussions with Wittgenstein convinced Russell that the logicist project was flawed in principle. He came to accept the view of the *Tractatus* that mathematical statements are vacuous tautologies, not truths about a realm of logico-mathematical entities.

In 1938, aged 66 and temporarily tired by two decades of political polemics, Russell returned to the academic teaching of philosophy. The results—*An Enquiry into Meaning and Truth* (1940) and *Human Knowledge* (1948)—contained valuable work on scientific method. He came to the view that inductive inference cannot be enough for 'science', and moved towards a surprisingly Kantian position that some 'principles of inference' must be presupposed: 'And whatever these principles of inference may be, they certainly cannot be logically deduced from facts of experience. Either, therefore, we know something independently of experience, or science is moonshine' (1948, p. 524). He ended by expressing his deeply ingrained empiricism in the broadest, most general terms:

> such inadequacies as we have seemed to find in empiricism have been discovered by strict adherence to a doctrine by which empiricist philosophy has been inspired: that all human knowledge is uncertain, inexact, and partial. To this doctrine we have not found any limitation whatever.
>
> (ibid., closing words)

Nothing has been said here about Russell's works on morality, politics and religion.

These were copious, forceful, elegant and full of wit, but he himself rarely saw them as original. He never shook off the radical, aristocratic, Victorian liberalism inherited from his parents. His attitude to religion was essentially that of an eighteenth-century rationalist.

An interesting angle on the tensions between Russell's many concerns is seen in his affection for Spinoza (see Blackwell 1985) and a Spinozistic strain that appears many times in his writing (most strikingly, at the end of *The Problems of Philosophy*, 1912). Passages such as this, on Spinoza, must have contained some element of would-be self-portraiture: 'The love of humanity is a background to all his thoughts, and prevents the coldness which his intellectualism might otherwise engender. It was through the union of the love of truth and the love of humanity, combined with an entire absence of self-seeking, that he achieved a nobility, both in life and in speculation, which has not been equalled by his predecessors or successors in the realm of philosophy' (review of Hale White and Stirling's translation of Spinoza's *Ethics*, *The Nation*, 12 November 1910, in *Collected Papers*, vol. VI, p. 254). Russell's repeated attempts at systematic philosophical theorizing maintain their interest more from the brilliance of his writing and the virtuosity of his logical talents than from the creation of any single positive set of views that could be encapsulated as *Russell's Philosophy*. (Indeed, it seems to have been fairly early in his career that he realized he was fated to change his mind so often that a lasting synthesis was unlikely.)

Russell is still the most widely read philosopher in the analytical tradition, as he might have wished: 'Philosophy proper deals with matters of interest to the general educated public, and loses much of its value if only a few professionals can understand what is said' (1948, p. 5). His popularity has had one important consequence: his writings may have brought more people to an interest

in philosophy than those of anyone else in the twentieth century, and this is not negligible. He himself came to judge his political campaigning against nuclear weapons as more valuable than theoretical philosophizing. Whatever one thinks of that, the example he set for the role of an intellectual in practical affairs has been hugely influential. (Here he resembles Noam **Chomsky**, who delivered the memorial lectures on Russell in Cambridge in 1970.)

The Principles of Mathematics (finished on the last day of the nineteenth century), written at great speed, with a passion of intellectual discovery, must remain a monument to Russell's great logical gifts. His place, with Frege, as a founder and builder of modern logic, must be untouchable.

His influence as a philosopher is less clear. Versions of logical empiricism similar to Russell's varied positions remained popular in academic philosophy in the USA for some time after the influence of Wittgenstein had obliterated them in Britain. Russell's analytical, quasi-scientific approach remained the dominant style in philosophy (but regrettably without his elegance and wit).

His relationship with Wittgenstein has been much debated. From 1911 to 1913 Russell's problems became Wittgenstein's problems. The extent of his intellectual generosity towards Wittgenstein was poorly acknowledged and has not been adequately recognized.

RICHARD MASON

Ryle, Gilbert

British. *b:* 19 August 1900, Brighton, England. *d:* 15 October 1976, Yorkshire (died while on holiday). *Cat:* Analytical philosopher. *Ints:* Epistemology; philosophy of mind; theory of meaning; Plato. *Educ:* Queen's College, Oxford. *Appts:* Taught at

Oxford; served with the Welsh Guards; Waynflete Professor of Metaphysical Philosophy, 1945; Editor of *Mind*, 1947.

Main publications:

(1931–2) 'Systematically misleading expressions', *Proceedings of the Aristotelian Society* 32.
(1933) *John Locke on the Human Understanding*, Oxford: Oxford University Press (lecture).
(1945) *Philosophical Arguments*, Oxford: Clarendon Press (inaugural lecture).
(1949) *The Concept of Mind*, London and New York: Hutchinson.
(1954) *Dilemmas*, Cambridge: Cambridge University Press.
(1962) *A Rational Animal*, London: Athlone Press (lecture).
(1966) *Plato's Progress*, Cambridge: Cambridge University Press.
(1971) *Collected Papers*, 2 vols (vol. 1: *Critical Esssays*; vol. 2: *Collected Essays, 1929–68*), London: Hutchinson; New York: Barnes & Noble.
(1979) *On Thinking*, ed. K. Kolenda, Oxford: Blackwell; New Jersey: Rowman & Littlefield.
(1993) *Aspects of Mind*, ed. Rene Meyer, Oxford: Blackwell.

Secondary literature:

Addis, Laird and Lewis, Douglas (1968) *Moore and Ryle: Two Ontologists*, University of Iowa Press.
Kolenda, K. (ed) (1972) *Studies in Philosophy: A Symposium on Gilbert Ryle*, Houston: Rice University.
Lyons, William (1980) *Gilbert Ryle: An Introduction to His Philosophy*, Brighton: Harvester Press.
Wood, Oscar P. and Pitcher, George (eds) (1960) *Ryle: A Collection of Critical Essays*, New York, Doubleday (good bibliography and autobiographical sketch).

Ryle's earliest philosophical interests focused on problems about philosophical method: what is characteristic of the sorts of questions that philosophers ask, and how are such questions to be satisfactorily answered? These concerns led him initially to a study of the work of recent and contemporary German philosophers, such as **Meinong**,

Brentano, Bolzano, **Husserl** and **Heidegger**, and it is with these authors that his first publications were concerned. But a distinctively Rylean answer to these problems began to emerge with the 1932 paper 'Systematically misleading expressions'. This argues that philosophical puzzles arise from a failure to notice that some expressions, often of ordinary language, are 'of such a syntactical form that [they] are improper to the fact recorded', and hence that the philosopher's job is 'the detection of the sources *in linguistic idioms* of recurrent misconceptions and absurd theories' (emphasis added). For example, just as 'Mr Baldwin is a statesman' picks out a subject and says that the subject has an attribute, so grammar would suggest that 'Mr Pickwick is a fiction' in a similar way picks out a subject and says that the subject has an attribute. But this suggestion, Ryle argues, is false. It is clear from the article that Ryle thinks that those who are misled by systematically misleading expressions are not the ordinary, unreflective users of them, but rather those (like philosophers) who theorize about them, and are hence led to postulate strange existents (like Mr Pickwick, or, more philosophically, Platonic forms, propositions, universals, etc.). What is less clear from the article is what makes an expression *non*-misleading, or 'proper' to the facts it records.

This conception of philosophy is extended, and given lengthy application, in Ryle's best-known work, *The Concept of Mind* (1949). The book is a prolonged attack on Cartesian dualism, which Ryle mockingly labels 'the official doctrine', or the dogma of the ghost in the machine. He argues that the Cartesian is guilty of a series of 'category mistakes'—in other words, that he has been misled by systematically misleading expressions. *Exactly* what a category is, is never made clear, but roughly it is a range of items of which the same sorts of things can be meaningfully asserted. Thus, in a cricket team, the bowler and the batsman belong to the same category, in that they are members of the team. But team spirit would belong to a different category, since it is not a further and ethereal member of the team but rather is a set of *relations between* the members, and relations between entities are not themselves a further entity of the same kind. Again, two citizens who pay taxes belong to the same category, but the average tax-payer belongs to a different one. Ryle argues that the Cartesian has failed to notice that our mental and physical concepts belong to different categories. Realizing that talk about the mind is not talk about a *physical* entity, the Cartesian concludes that it must be talk about a *non-physical* entity, failing to realize that it is not talk about an entity of any kind. In addition to, and perhaps as a consequence of, making this overarching category mistake, the dualist is then led into subsidiary errors of a similar kind, for example in confusing occurrences or episodes on the one hand, with dispositions, tendencies and capacities on the other.

Ryle's positive thesis, which assigns mentalistic talk to what he regards as the correct category, treats talk about the mind as talk about the way in which we behave. 'In describing the workings of a person's mind', he tells us, 'we are not describing a set of shadowy operations. We are describing the ways in which parts of his conduct are managed'. So to say that someone was painting thoughtfully would be to say *how* he was painting, not to say his painting was accompanied by a second invisible process of thinking. It is statements like this, and others with a similar content, which support the interpretation of Ryle as a logical behaviourist. But Ryle's account of specific mental concepts often falls short of his programmatic declarations. When talking about emotions and sensations, for example, he does not attempt to show that in describing someone as feeling a pang, we are 'describing the ways in which parts of his conduct are managed'. He argues instead that one can make mistakes about one's feelings and sensations because the description of them

often embodies a hypothesis about what caused them (for example, a chill *of disquiet*, a tug *of commiseration*) and this hypothesis can be mistaken. This may be true, but it does not establish the official behaviourist programme. Problems about the nature of the mind, and the recurrent temptation to think of our mental life as a set of operations performed in a private 'inner' theatre, continued to preoccupy Ryle in his later writings, and some of his subsequent reflections can be found in the second volume of his *Collected Papers* (1971) and in the two posthumous collections of material *On Thinking* (1979) and *Aspects of Mind* (1993).

It was not just in the field of mind that Ryle deployed his conception of philosophical methodology. In *Dilemmas* (1954), he sought to show that other philosophical puzzles (about fatalism, about infinity, about the contrast between common sense and science, etc.) arise out of a misunderstanding of how language operates, and can be solved by getting clear about the proper logic of everyday concepts. Part of his interest in Plato (revealed in a number of articles in volume 1 of the *Collected Papers*, and in *Plato's Progress*, 1966) derived from his ability to interpret Plato as engaging in the sort of logico-linguistic analysis which Ryle himself favoured. Without in any way founding a school of 'Ryleans', Ryle was an immensely influential philosopher. With Wittgenstein and Austin, although in a very different way from each of them, he was responsible for the linguistic method of philosophizing which dominated the middle decades of the century and which was known as linguistic philosophy. Although few philosophers would now endorse the behaviourism of *The Concept of Mind*, its insistence on a priori connections between mind and behaviour would still be widely accepted—for example, by functionalists among others. Even philosophers such as D. M. Armstrong and D. C. Dennett, who would count themselves among Ryle's critics, would acknowledge the influence on them of Ryle's thinking. If Ryle's writings now seem the products of an earlier era, it is because their considerable lessons have been so thoroughly absorbed into contemporary thinking.

Sources: Edwards; DNB; Turner; WW.

NICHOLAS EVERITT

Santayana, George (Jorge Augustin Nicolas Ruiz de S.)

Spanish. *b:* 16 December 1863, Madrid. *d:* 29 September 1952, Rome. *Cat:* Systematic philosopher. *Ints:* Metaphysics; epistemology; ethics; aesthetics; politics. *Educ:* Taken to America 1872; educated at Harvard. *Infls:* Plato, Aristotle and Spinoza. *Appts:* Member of Philosophy Department, Harvard, 1889–1912; an inheritance allowed him to relinquish his post in 1912, after which Santayana lived in Europe, based chiefly in Rome, and devoted himself to writing (he retained Spanish nationality all his life but wrote in English).

Main publications:

All published by Scribners (New York) and Constable (London). A collected edition of works up to 1940, the Triton Edition, was published by Scribners (14 volumes). A new complete works is currently being issued by the MIT Press.

(1896) *The Sense of Beauty.*
(1905–6) *The Life of Reason,* 5 vols.
(1910) *Three Philosophical Poets.*
(1913) *Winds of Doctrine.*
(1916) *Egotism in German Philosophy.*
(1923) *Scepticism and Animal Faith.*
(1927/30/38/40) *The Realms of Being.*
(1933) *Some Turns of Thought in Modern Philosophy.*
(1946) *The Idea of Christ in the Gospels.*
(1951) *Dominations and Powers.*

Secondary literature:

Ames, Van Meter (1965) *Proust and Santayana: The Aesthetic Way of Life,* New York: Russell & Russell.
Arnett, W. E. (1957) *Santayana and the Sense of Beauty,* Bloomington: Indiana University Press.
Butler, R. (1956) *The Mind of Santayana,* Chicago: Henry Regnery.
Cory, D. M. (1963) *Santanaya: The Later Years,* New York: Braziller.
Duron, J. (1949) *La Pensée de George Santayana,* Paris: Nizet.
Farré, L. (1953) *Vida y Pensamiento de Jorge Santayana,* Madrid: Verdad y Vida.
Lachs, J. (1988) *George Santayana,* Twayne Publishers.
Levinson, H. S. (1992) *Santayana: Pragmatism and the Spiritual Life,* University of North Carolina Press.
Munson, T. N. (1962) *The Essential Wisdom of George Santayana,* New York: Columbia University Press.
Schilpp, P.A. (ed.) (1940) *The Philosophy of George Santayana,* Evanston and Chicago: Northwestern University Press.
Sprigge, T. L. S. (1974) *Santayana,* London: Routledge.

Santayana is usually thought of as the author of *The Sense of Beauty* (1896) and of its central thesis, that beauty is pleasure taken to be a property of an object. It is a quirk of history that the creator of the system of the *Realms of Being* (1927–40), and of its predecessor *The Life of Reason* (1905–6), should be best known for a doctrine he does not refer to after his first book. One of the reasons for the comparative neglect of Santayana's works since his death has undoubtedly been his prose style: a poet, essayist and novelist as well as a philosopher, Santayana preferred to write in a prose which is mellifluous, metaphorical and often beautiful. His reputation as a prose stylist is unassailable, but his work did not find favour with those who believed that philosophy should be written as it was by William **James** or **Russell**.

The major work of the early part of Santayana's career is *The Life of Reason* (5 volumes), an evaluative survey of human institutions from the standpoint of ethical eudaemonism: happiness is the good for humankind, and is best secured by the harmonization of our various interests by the use of reason. Santayana surveys society, religion, art and science, estimating which, if any, of the forms of these institutions exhibited in history have promoted the rational life, and sketching alternative, ideal forms. These surveys are prefaced in the first volume, *Reason in Common Sense*, by an account of the birth of reason, the process whereby the immediate flux of experience is ordered by the mind. What emerges is the 'common-sense' world picture of a universe of physical objects and minds, with a concomitant development of self-consciousness, and a shift from instinctive action to the deliberate pursuit of ideals. Hence, Santayana says that his subject is progress. He sets out to answer the question: 'In which of its adventures would the human race, reviewing its whole experience, acknowledge a progress and a gain?' (Triton Edition, vol. III, p. 13).

The stress on progress and the dynamic reform of institutions gave this work considerable appeal in the USA, where elements of aestheticism and detachment in Santayana's earlier works had attracted adverse criticism. Interestingly, when free of the Harvard ambience (which he never liked), Santayana developed in the *Realms of Being* a system in which a refined aestheticism becomes prominent. The compatibility of this system with that of the *Life of Reason* is a central issue in Santayana studies.

Santayana prefaces the later system with *Scepticism and Animal Faith* (1923), in which its epistemological basis is set out. If knowledge is that which is beyond all doubt, then the only acceptable epistemology is a solipsism of the present moment. However, it is psychologically impossible to live by such a belief; we have an irresisitible urge ('animal faith') to believe in the independence of the external world, and therefore our worldview contains non-indubitable elements. Further, Santayana distinguishes between existence and being: to exist is to stand in external relations such that these relations are not deducible from the nature of the existent. Being is the ontological status attributable to, for example, definite qualities which do not happen to be part of the existing universe, for example a definite shade of colour. Santayana next proceeds to divide what there is into four irreducibly different categories, the four realms of being: essence, matter, truth and spirit.

An essence is a character or quality which has the ontological status of being, and the being of every essence is exhausted by its definition, not in words, 'but the character which distinguishes it from every other essence. Every essence is perfectly individual' (Triton Edition, vol. XIV, p. 19). All essences are universal and eternal, being individual, outside space and time, and standing in no external relations. The totality of all essences is the realm of essence and is infinite. Santayana insists that all essences are equally primary, although whether this can be true of the essence of pure being itself is a moot point. Some essences are manifested in existence; one mode of manifestation is to be imagined by a consciousness; another is embodiment in matter.

Matter is the only active principle among the realms of being. It is external to consciousness, spatial, temporal and mutable: all change and all existence (as distinct from being) is grounded in matter. It is the flux of matter which determines which essences are embodied, and accordingly determines the content of the realm of truth. Spirit (i.e. consciousness) is an epiphenomenon of matter. A central concept in this philosophy of nature is that of a trope, defined as the essence or form of an event. This notion is used by Santayana to define what he calls the psyche. Denying all causal efficacy to spirit, Santayana has to find a material agent to determine the course of life and both body and spirit, and this is the psyche, 'a system of tropes, inherited or acquired, displayed by living bodies in their growth and behaviour' (Triton Edition, vol. XIV, p. 324).

Santayana held a correspondence theory of truth: propositions are true if what they assert to be the case is the case, and the sum of all true propositions is the realm of truth. Further, Santayana contends that any fact has a complete description which constitutes the truth about it. Since such a description, however, would include a specification of all the relations of the fact, any complete description of any fact would be infinite. The realm of truth is that segment of the realm of essence which happens to be illustrated in existence.

The fourth realm of being is that of spirit or consciousness. Spirit and body are not two facts incongruously juxtaposed and mysteriously related: they are realizations of the same fact in incomparable realms of being. Spirit is a moral integration and dignity accruing to a body when the latter develops a certain degree of organization and responsiveness to distant things. It is incarnate by nature, not accident, and cannot exist disembodied. Santayana sometimes defines spirit as the inner light of attention, and attention is by definition transitive. An instance of awareness Santayana calls an intuition, and the object given in intuition is an essence. When an essence is taken to be a sign of something in the external world, our knowledge of the object is symbolic. When the essence is intuited for itself, our knowledge is said to be literal. Pure intuition Santayana considers to be the natural function of spirit, to which it tends whenever it can (which is, generally, very rarely). To experience essences in pure intuition is also to experience them aesthetically, and so the spiritual and aesthetic modes of life turn out to be identical.

In many respects, Santayana's claim for the unity of his earlier and later thought is defensible: many major positions remain unchanged, notably materialism and epiphenomenalism. There is room for a contemplative ethic in both systems, though it is true that it is hardly mentioned in *The Life of Reason*, whereas it is prominent in *The Realms of Being*.

ROBERT WILKINSON

Sartre, Jean-Paul

French. *b:* 1905, Paris. *d:* 1980, Paris. *Cat:* Existentialist. *Ints:* Phenomenology; ontology; psychology. *Educ:* École Normale Supérieure, 1924–8; research student at the Institut Français in Berlin and at Freiburg University, 1933–5. *Infls:* Literary influences: Descartes, Hegel, Husserl, Heidegger and Marx. Personal influence: Simone de Beauvoir. *Appts:* Taught philosophy at lycées in Paris and elsewhere.

Main publications:

(1936) 'La Transcendence de l'égo', in *Recherches Philosophiques* 6 (English translation, 'The transcendence of the ego', trans. F. Williams and R. Kirkpatrick, New York: Noonday Press, 1957).

(1936) *L'Imagination*, Paris: Alcan (English translation, *The Imagination*, trans. F. Williams, University of Michigan Press, 1962).

(1939) *Esquisse d'une théorie des émotions*, Paris: Hermann (English translation, *Sketch for a Theory of the Emotions*, trans. Philip Mairet, Methuen, 1962).

(1940) *L'Imaginaire: psychologie phénoménologique de l'imagination*, Paris: Gallimard (English translation, *The Psychology of Imagination*, New York: Bernard Frechtman, 1948).

(1943) *L'Être et le néant*, Paris: Gallimard (English translation, *Being and Nothingness*, trans. Hazel Barnes, London: Methuen, 1957).

(1960) *Critique de la raison dialectique*, part 1, Paris: Gallimard (English translation, *Critique of Dialectical Reason*, trans. Hazel Barnes, New York, 1964).

(1983) *Cahiers pour une morale*, Paris: Gallimard (English translation, *Notebooks for an Ethics*, trans. David Pellaner, Chicago: University of Chciago Press, 1992).

(1983) *Les Carnets de la drôle de guerre*, Paris: Gallimard (English translation, *War Diaries*, trans. Q. Hoare, London: Verso Books).

(1985) *Critique de la raison dialetique*, vol. 2 (incomplete), Paris: Gallimard.
(1989) *Vérité et existence*, Paris: Gallimard (English translation, *Truth and Existence*, trans. Ronald Aronson, Chicago: Chicago University Press, 1992).

Secondary literature:

Blackham, H. J. (1961) *Six Existentialist Thinkers*, London: Routledge & Kegan Paul.
Catalano, J. S. (1987) *Commentary on Jean-Paul Sartre's Critique of Dialectical Reason*, Chicago: University of Chicago Press.
Cranston, M. (1962) *Sartre*, Edinburgh: Oliver & Boyd.
Danto, A. C. (1975) *Sartre*, New York: Viking Press.
Howells, Christina (ed.) (1992) *The Cambridge Companion to Sartre*, Cambridge: Cambridge University Press.
Manser, A. (1967) *Sartre*, New York: Oxford University Press.
Murdoch, I. (1953) *Sartre, Romantic Rationalist*, Cambridge: Bowes & Bowes.
Warnock, M. (1972) *The Philosophy of Sartre*, London: Hutchinson.

Sartre was a leading exponent of atheistic existentialism, a novelist, playwright and critic as well as a philosopher. He was at one time a Communist, then a Marxist. In later life he developed his own style of Marxist sociology. During the Second World War he was a soldier and for nine months was a prisoner of war in Germany. After his release he worked in the Resistance Movement and when the war ended became editor of *Les Temps Moderne*. In 1964 he was awarded, but refused, the Nobel Prize for Literature. He became politically active after the 1968 May Revolt. His last major philosophical work, the *Critique of Dialectical Reason* (1960) was written, he maintained, to reconcile existentialism and Marxism. Concomitantly with his philosophical work he was producing novels, plays, criticism and political comment. His first novel, *Nausea* (1938), succeeds both as philosophy and novel. His trilogy of novels *Roads to Freedom* is regarded as a classic of twentieth-century literature.

Sartre's early work is influenced by and is also critical of **Husserl** and **Heidegger**. In *The Transcendence of the Ego* (1936) he uses a phenomenological method, derived from Husserl, to describe the structure of consciousness. At the same time he argues against Husserl's identification of the self with transcendental consciousness. In *The Imagination, The Psychology of the Imagination* and *Sketch for a Theory of the Emotions* (1936, 1940, 1939) he works at the borderline between philosophy and psychology. In the last of these he criticizes the theories of **James**, Janet and Dembo, rejects Freud's theory of the unconscious and develops his own view of emotion as a means of transforming the world.

Sartre's *Being and Nothingness* (1943) is a major document of existentialism. He describes it as 'an essay on phenomenological ontology'. Its primary question is: 'What is it like to be a human being?' Sartre's answer is that human reality consists of two modes of existence: of being and of nothingness. The human being exists both as an in-itself (*en-soi*), an object or thing, and as a for-itself (*pour-soi*), a consciousness. The existence of an in-itself is 'opaque to itself ... because it is filled with itself'. In contrast, the for-itself, or consciousness, has no such fullness of existence, because it is no-thing.

Sartre sometimes describes consciousness of things as a kind of nausea produced by a recognition of the contingency of their existence and the realization that this constitutes Absurdity. The realization generates a desire of the for-itself to exist with the fullness of being of an existing thing but without contingency or loss of consciousness. The desired embodying of consciousness is never possible: it can never become a thing and remain consciousness. The two regions of being are entirely distinct and the ideal of fusing them is 'an unrealizable totality which haunts the for-itself and constitutes its very being as a nothingness of being'. He says: 'It is this ideal which can be called God ... man fundamentally is the desire to be God.'

According to Sartre, consciousness, because it is nothingness, makes us aware of the possibility of choosing what we will be. This is the condition of human freedom. To perform an action a person must be able to stand back from participation in the world of existing things and so contemplate what does not exist. The choice of action is also a choice of oneself. In choosing oneself one does not choose to exist: existence is given and one has to exist in order to choose. From this analysis Sartre derives a famous slogan of existentialism: 'existence precedes and commands essence'. He maintains that there is no reason for choosing as one does. The choice is unjustified, groundless. This is the perpetual human reality.

'Bad faith' is an important concept in Sartrean existentialism. To act in bad faith is to turn away from the authentic choosing of oneself and to act in conformity with a stereotype or role. Sartre's most famous example is that of a waiter:

> Let us consider this waiter in the café. His movement is quick and forward, a little too precise, a little too rapid. He comes towards the patrons with a step a little too quick ... his voice, his eyes express an interest a little too solicitous for the order of the customer ... he gives himself the quickness and pitiless rapidity of things ... the waiter in the café plays with his condition in order to *realize* it.
>
> (1943, p. 59)

After the Second World War Sartre began a radical reconstruction of his ideas. He planned the *Critique of Dialectical Reason* (1960) in two volumes, the first to be a theoretical and abstract study, the second a treatment of history, but he completed only one volume. His aim was to establish an a priori foundation for dialectical thought which would justify Marx's transformation of the Hegelian dialectic by showing that rational human activity, or praxis, is necessarily dialectical. He saw Marxism as the dominant philosophy of the twentieth century and existentialism as one element in its structure. At the same time he criticizes Marxism's way of observing society as a whole within a dialectical framework and its neglect of the individual point of view. He therefore advocates the use of the dialectic from the agent's standpoint and argues that praxis, examined, shows itself to embody the dialectical procedures as a necessary condition of its activities: we unavoidably use it, he maintains, whenever we attempt to examine ourselves or society at large. This is the basis of the proposed interaction of Marxism and existentialism that will enable Marxism to take on 'a human dimension'.

Sartre has been criticized for the conception of total human freedom he expounded in *Being and Nothingness*, and especially for the implications of his account of the human being as a solitary individual who is detachable from historical and social contexts (see, for example, **Murdoch** 1953, chapter 7). In the *Critique* he repudiates much of that early position and admits limits to freedom.

Some of Sartre's philosophical writings have, in accordance with his wishes, been published posthumously; most significantly, *Notebooks for an Ethics* (1983), a work that goes some way to fulfilling the promise Sartre made at the end of *Being and Nothingness* to devote a subsequent work to ethical questions.

DIANÉ COLLINSON

Saussure, Ferdinand de

Swiss. *b:* 1857, Geneva. *d:* 1913, Geneva. *Cat:* Language theorist; semiotician. *Educ:* Universities of Geneva, Berlin and Leipzig. *Infls:* The neogrammarian school of linguistics. *Appts:* Teacher of languages, École Pratique des Hautes Études, Paris; Professor of Linguistics, University of Geneva.

Main publications:

(1878) *Mémoire sur le système primitif des voyelles dans les langues indo-europeennes*, Leipzig: publisher unknown.

(1916) *Cours de linguistique générale*, ed. Charles Bally, Albert Sechehaye and Albert Reidlinger, Paris: Payot (*Course in General Linguistics*, trans. Wade Baskin, London: Peter Owen, 1960).

Secondary literature:

Aarsleff, Hans (1982) *From Locke to Saussure: Essays on the Study of Language and Intellectual History*, London: Athlone Press.

Culler, Jonathan (1975) *Structuralist Poetics: Structuralism, Linguistics and the Study of Literature*, London: Routledge; Ithaca, NY: Cornell University Press.

——(1976) *Saussure*, London: Collins.

Holdcroft, David (1991) *Saussure: Signs, System, and Arbitrariness*, Cambridge: Cambridge University Press.

Koerner, E. F. K. (1973) *Ferdinand de Saussure: The Origin and Development of his Linguistic Thought in Western Studies of Language*, Braunschweig: Vieweg.

Starobinski, Jean (1979) *Words Upon Words: The Anagrams of Ferdinand de Saussure*, New Haven: Yale University Press.

Saussure is acknowledged to be the founder of modern linguistics, the thinker most responsible for reorganizing the discipline along scientific lines. Through his *Course in General Linguistics* (1916) he, had a major impact not just on linguistics but on cultural studies in general, the book providing the basis for the development of structuralism and semiology, the theory of signs. Saussure's earliest source of influence was the neogrammarian school of historical linguistics that he encountered at the University of Leipzig during his studies there, although he was ultimately to react against what was essentially a philologically oriented style of linguistics. The only book published by Saussure during his life was the early neogrammarian-influenced *Mémoire* (1878), a work of comparative philology which investigated the vowel system of early Indo-European languages, but his fame rests on the *Course*, published posthumously from student notes of his University of Geneva lecture series, 1907–11. Saussure's primary concern in the *Course* is to outline a methodology for linguistics, thus establishing the nature of the linguist's object of study and placing the subject on a scientific footing. What he is searching for in his enquiry is the underlying structures of language. It is this methodological bias which marks him out from previous schools of linguistics, which in the main had treated the subject historically. The linguistic model developed by Saussure has been adopted and refined by structuralist theorists such as Lévi-Strauss and Barthes, and through their work and that of their followers has attained a powerful cultural significance. Saussure's most important insight is probably his recognition that language is a system: a self-contained and self-regulating totality with its own set of rules and procedures, or grammar. Language as a system (*langue*), the primary object of Saussure's enquiry, is differentiated from language as a set of utterances (*parole*), with chess, another self-contained, self-regulating totality, being put forward as an analogy for how *langue* operates. The heart of Saussure's linguistics is the theory of the sign, an entity consisting of a signifier (a word, whether spoken or written) and a signified (the mental image or concept lying behind a word). When signifier and signified combine in an act of understanding, the word 'dog' and the concept of 'dog' for example, they form the sign. Language for Saussure is a system of signs bound together by grammatical conventions, and it constitutes the model for all other sign-systems within the general science of semiology. When we respond to a sign within a system, as to the colour showing on a traffic light, we do so according to our understanding of the grammar of the particular system. To say that the sign is conventional is to say that it is arbitrary—one word being as good as another to describe an object, as long as there is general agreement as to its use amongst the relevant language-users—and this has been one of the most contentious notions in Saussure, since it raises the spectre of radical instability of meaning. Saussure himself was unhappy with the implications of the notion and eventually settled for the rather unsatisfactory solution of 'relative' arbitrariness instead. The arbitrariness of the sign allows it to change over time, and Saussure distinguishes between language in its synchronic and dischronic forms. The former refers to language as a static totality complete with its constant element (its grammar), the latter to language in its evolutionary phases in time where change can occur, say in the meaning of a word. Saussure further distinguishes between syntagmatic and paradigmatic relations as regards words. When words are strung together in phrases or sentences, these grammatically organized sequences are called syntagms; when words are more loosely connected (as in the 'association of ideas' mode of thinking), then they are described as being in associative (or paradigmatic) relation. Value is seen to be system-bound and function-oriented for Saussure: the value of a word is a matter of its functional relationship to other words in its sequence.

Saussure also pursued a rather curious theory in later life that Latin poets had deliberately concealed anagrams of proper names in their work, although he never managed to produce any very hard evidence for his belief and published nothing on the topic. Saussure's work has proved to be a major source of inspiration both inside and outside the field of linguistics, and the *Course* can be considered one of the landmarks of twentieth-century intellectual history, particularly in the way that it establishes the credentials of language as the crucial site for debates about culture. In this respect Saussure is one of the major sources of what has been called the 'linguistic turn' in modern intellectual enquiry. Within linguistics itself Saussure's influence lives on in the development of structural linguistics—one of the dominant trends in the discipline—from the work of Jakobson and the Prague School (who influenced Lévi-Strauss in their turn) down to **Chomsky** and his transformational-generative grammar. In wider cultural context Saussure's linguistic theories have provided the basis for structuralism, with the terminology and various binary oppositions of the *Course* being taken over wholesale by structuralists and semiologists. Until the advent of poststructuralism the linguistic model developed by Saussure constituted one of the most powerful and influential analytical tools available to culture theorists, and Saussure's ideas have been enthusiastically propagated in fields as diverse as anthropology (Lévi-Strauss), fashion and advertising (Barthes) and even psychoanalysis (the post-Freudian French psychoanalyst Jacques **Lacan** has argued that the unconscious is structured like a language). The standard approach adopted by the structuralist in the analysis of any cultural phenomenon is derived straight from Saussurean methodology: it is to demarcate the boundaries of the system in question, then to set about classifying the operations of the system's grammar within synchronic and diachronic perspective. Even post-structuralism, which consciously seeks to undermine the assumptions of structuralist methodology, such as the commitment to deep structures and to metaphysical essences in general, owes a considerable debt to Saussure since it is his notion of the arbitrariness of the signifier that provides one of the starting points for the post-structuralist project. Derridean deconstruction, as a case in point, relentlessly emphasizes the signifier's arbitrariness in order to back up its claim that meaning is basically unstable, thus licensing some of the wilder flights of post-structuralist fantasy. **Derrida's** deployment of Saussure in the cause of poststructuralism has ensured that the latter figure remains a significant cultural force right through to the close of the twentieth century.

STUART SIM

Scheler, Max

German. **b:** 22 August 1874, Munich. **d:** 19 May 1928, Frankfurt. **Cat:** Phenomenologist. **Ints:** Value theory; epistemology; metaphysics; philosophy of religion; sociology of knowledge; philosophical anthropology. **Educ:** University of Jena. **Infls:** Husserl, Augustine, Pascal, Nietzsche and Bergson. **Appts:** 1899–1906, Lecturer, University of Jena; 1906–10, Lecturer, University of Munich; 1919–28, Professor of Philosophy and Sociology, University of Cologne; 1928, Professor of Philosophy, University of Frankfurt.

Main publications:

(1913) *Der Formalismus in der Ethik und die materiale Wertethik* (English translation, *Formalism in Ethics and Non-Formal Ethics of Value*, trans. M. S. Frings and R. L. Funk, Evanston: Northwestern University Press, 1973).
(1913) *Zur Phänomenologie und Theorie der Sympathiegefühle und von Liebne und Hass* (English translation, *The Nature of Sympathy*, trans. P. Heath, London: Routledge & Kegan Paul, 1954).
(1921) *Vom Ewigen im Menschen* (English translation, *On the Eternal in Man*, trans. B. Wall, London: SCM Press).
(1926) *Die Wissensformen und die Gesellschaft.*
(1928) *Die Stellung des Menschen im Kosmos.*
All included in:
(1954) *Gesammelte Werke*, Berne: A. Francke Verlag.

Secondary literature:

Frings, M. S. (1965) *Max Scheler*, Pittsburgh: Duquesne University Press.

——(ed.) (1974) *Max Scheler (1874–1928): Centennial Essays*, The Hague: Martinus Nijhoff.
Good, P. (ed.) (1975) *Max Scheler im Gegenwartsgeschehen der Philosophie*, Bern.
Perrin, R. (1991) *Max Scheler's Concept of the Person*, London: Macmillan.

The early years of Scheler's philosophical career were spent in Jena, which at that time was dominated by idealism of the neo-Kantian variety. However the study of **Husserl's** *Logical Investigations* converted him to phenomenology, which he interpreted as essentially realist in character. In 1906 he moved to Munich and joined an already flourishing circle of phenomenologists. But in 1910 he became a private scholar, having had to resign his position in Munich for personal reasons. This situation lasted until his appointment to a Chair in Cologne in 1919. At the beginning of the First World War he wrote his *The Genius of War and the German War*, in which, like many other intellectuals including Husserl, he saw something positive in war, a kind of spiritual regeneration. After the war, however, he adopted a pacifist position. For a time he was a committed Catholic. However, he never had any time for official Church philosophy, drawing inspiration from Augustine rather than Aquinas. He later distanced himself from Catholicism and even from theism. He died at the height of his powers in 1928, shortly after his move to Frankfurt. His friend and admirer, Martin **Heidegger**, announcing his death to his own students in Marburg, described Scheler as the most powerful force in contemporary philosophy.

Scheler was not a typical academic philosopher. He was an elemental force, a kind of philosophical volcano. The sheer profusion of his ideas and the lack of any clearly defined unity makes summary difficult. For a large part of his career he described himself as a phenomenologist. What attracted him about Husserl's *Logical Investigations* was the attack on psychologism and the defence of the possibility of the intuition of essences. He was deeply hostile to the idealistic form which Husserl's phenomenology subsequently assumed. Scheler's phenomenological realism is distinctive in the epistemological priority it gives to feeling and emotion over 'theoretical' modes of consciousness. Perhaps the best example of Scheler's phenomenology at work is his *Formalism in Ethics* (1913), the work for which he will probably be best remembered. In this work he defends what would nowadays be called a form of moral realism. It is partly a negative work, designed to demonstrate the inadequacies of the most influential attempt to combat subjectivism and relativism, viz. Kantian ethics, that 'colossus of steel and bronze' as Scheler calls it. The formalism and consequent emptiness of Kantian ethics rests on a failure to distinguish between *goods* as things that are desired and aimed for and *values*. Kant is absolutely right in thinking that ethics with its unconditional requirements on conduct cannot be based on goods. But it does not follow that it cannot be based on values. It is a mistake to suppose that what is a priori concerns form only. Values are a priori and moreover exhibit a hierarchical order which is itself a priori. There is clearly some affinity here with the intuitionism of **Moore** and Ross (Scheler was familiar with the former). But whereas the apprehension of value is something essentially intellectual for these British intuitionists, for Scheler values are disclosed in feelings. The denial of cognitive significance to feelings, he thinks, rest on the mistaken view that feelings are simply internal occurrences, lacking intentional structure. It would be interesting to investigate, from a Schelerian perspective, how far Hume's subjectivism rests on an inadequate understanding of the nature of feeling.

Scheler also applied phenomenology to notable effect in the field of religion. In his *On the Eternal in Man* (1921), written when he was still a professing Catholic, he describes the essential structures of religious consciousness. Such phenomenological description embraces both the 'object' of such consciousness, as intended, and the various forms of religious 'act' which make up such consciousness. There can be no proof (*Beweis*) of God's existence but there can be an *Aufweis*, in the sense of a bringing to see. In his later, less phenomenological and more metaphysical, work in this area God is depicted not as a preexisting entity but as something emergent in man in the course of a cosmic struggle between spirit (*Geist*) and urge (*Drang*), the two essential attributes of the primordial ground of being (*Urgrund des Seins*).

Other features of Scheler's thought which deserve mention are:

(1) His concept of personhood. A person is not a thing or substance, not even a nonphysical thing or substance. Rather a person is the 'executor', 'doer' (*Vollzieher*) of 'acts'. It does not exist as something behind its acts but *in* and *through* its acts. As such persons in their personhood can never be objectified.

(2) His treatment of the 'problem of other minds'. Rejecting both analogical inference and empathy as the basis of such knowledge, he claims that attention to the 'phenomenological facts' shows that we directly perceive the other person's joy in their laughter, their sorrow in their tears, and so on. We can only deny this on the basis of the presupposition that perception is simply a 'complex of physical sensations'.

(3) His conception of the sociology of knowledge, which investigates the connections between different kinds of knowledge and the value systems of different social groups. However, he insists that this does not amount to sociologism, which would have the same sceptical and relativistic consequences as the psychologism so effectively refuted by Husserl.

(4) His notion of philosophical anthropology. In his *Die Stellung des Menschen im Kosmos* (1928) he deals first with those elements which human beings share with animals: feeling-urge (*Gefühlsdrang*), in-

stinct, associative memory and organically bound practical intelligence. As regards these features human beings differ from animals only in degree. The *essential* difference is that human beings have spirit (*Geist*), animals do not. It is spirit which makes human beings open to the world (*weltoffen*) in the sense that they are able to objectify things and view them as they are rather than being wholly absorbed in an 'environment' (*Umwelt*) structured by their life needs.

PAUL GORNER

Schlick, Friedrich Albert Moritz

German. *b:* 14 April 1882, Berlin. *d:* 22 June 1936, Vienna. *Cat:* Physicist; philosopher physics. *Ints:* Epistemology. *Educ:* Berlin 1900–4, Heidelberg 1901, Lausanne 1902; PhD in Physics, Berlin, 1904; Habilitation, Rostock, 1911 (concept of truth). *Infls:* Helmholtz, Kirchhoff, Hilbert, Mach, Planck, Poincaré and Wittgenstein. *Appts:* Rostock 1911–21, Kiel 1921; Chair of the History and Theory of the Inductive Sciences, University of Vienna, 1921–36.

Main publications:

(1917) *Raum und Zeit in der moderne Physik*, Berlin: Springer (English translation, *Space and Time in Contemporary Physics*, Oxford: Clarendon, 1920).

(1918) *Allgemeine Erkenntnislehre*, Berlin: Springer; second edition, 1925 (English translation, *General Theory of Knowledge*, Blumberg, Vienna and New York: Springer, 1974).

(1921) (ed. with P. Hertz) H. von Helmholtz, *Schriften zur Erkenntnistheorie*, Berlin: Springer.

(1922) (with M. Rubner and E. Warburg) *Helmholtz als Physiker, Physiologe und Philosoph*, Karlsruhe: C. F. Müller.

(1925) 'Naturphilosophie', in M. Dessoir (ed.) *Lehrbuch der Philosophie*, Berlin, II, 397–492.

(1927) *Vom Sinn des Lebens*, Erlangen: Palm & Enke.

(1930) *Fragen der Ethik*, Vienna: Springer (English translation, *Problems of Ethics*, trans. Rynin, New York: Prentice-Hall, 1939).

(1934) *Les Énoncés scientifiques et la réalité du monde extérieure*, Paris: Hermann.

(1935) *Sur le fondement de la connaissance*, Paris: Hermann.

(1937) *L'École de Vienne et la philosophie traditionelle, Travaux du IXe Congrès International de Philosophie*, Paris: Hermann.

(1938) *Gesammelte Augsätze*, Vienna: Gerold & Co.

(1948) *Gesetz, Kausalität und Wahrscheinlichkeit*, Vienna: Gerold & Co.

(1948) *Grundzüge der Naturphilosophie*, Vienna: Gerold & Co (English translation, *Philosophy of Nature*, trans. von Zeppelin, New York: Philosophical Library, 1968).

(1952) *Natur und Kultur*, ed. J. Rauscher, Vienna: Stgt Humboldt Verlag.

(1979) *Philosophical Papers*, 2 vols, ed. Mulder and van de Velde Schlick, Vienna Circle Collection no. 11, Dordrecht: Reidel.

(1986) *Die Probleme der Philosophie in ihrem Zusammenhang*, ed. Mulder *et al.*, Hamburg: Suhrkamp (English translation, *The Problems of Philosophy in their Interconnection*, trans. Heath, Vienna Circle Collection, no. 18, Dordrecht: Reidel, 1987).

Secondary literature:

Ayer, A. J. (1970) *Logical Positivism*, London: Allen & Unwin.

Gadol, E. T. (1982) *Rationality and Science*, Vienna, Springer.

Haller, R. (ed.) (1982) *Schlick und Neurath ein Symposion*, Amsterdam: Rodopi.

Johnston, W. M. (1972) *The Austrian Mind*, Berkeley: University of California Press.

Juhos, B. (1967) 'Schlick, Moritz', in Paul Edwards (ed.) *Encyclopedia of Philosophy*, New York: Macmillan, VII: 319a–324b.

Kraft, V. (1950) *Der Wiener Kreis*, Vienna: Springer (English translation, *The Vienna Circle*, trans. A. Pap, New York: Philosophical Library, 1953).

Neurath, O. (1935) *Le Développement du Cercle de Vienne et l'avenir de l'empirisme logique*, Paris: Hermann.

Passmore, J. A. (1957) *A Hundred Years of Philosophy*; second edition, London: Duckworth, 1966.

Reichenbach, H. (1951) *The Rise of the Scientific Philosophy*, Berkeley and Los Angeles: University of California Press.

Ryckman, T. A. (1991) 'Conditio sine qua non. Zuordnung in the early epistemologies of Cassirer and Schlick', *Synthèse* 88: 57–95.

Waismann, F. and McGuinness, B. (eds) (1967) *Wittgenstein und der Wiener Kreis*, Oxford:

Blackwell (English translation, *Wittgenstein and the Vienna Circle*, trans. Schulte and McGuiness, Oxford: Blackwell, 1979).

Moritz Schlick was the key figure in the later development of the neo-positivist Vienna Circle. An early exponent of Einstein's relativity theory he was brought, at the suggestion of Hans Hahn, from Kiel to the Vienna Chair orginally created for Ernst Mach. At least initially, though, his work shows no trace of the verificationist doctrines usually associated with the Vienna Circle. Schlick's approach also differed from that of his associates in that there was little of their obvious left-wing and anti-clerical politics. Schlick's anti-metaphysical programme sought a more scientific and rigorous philosophy, depending on a logical analytic approach. In this, no doubt, he was one source of the anti-historical attitude that so marked off the neo-positivists from even their hero Mach among their predecessors. In his early work the general theory of knowledge was to be modelled on the abstract sciences, particularly physics and mathematics. It was to be purely discursive, consisting of the knowledge of the relations between things, not the acquaintance with things in themselves, which he regarded as metaphysical. Such purely propositional knowledge was to be attained by conjectural systems of concepts set up as signs to represent things, to symbolize them and their mutual relations, and be verified after the fact. Truth, not rejected by Schlick but regarded as easily obtainable compared with the more valuable generality of relations, is defined by the existence of unambiguous reference to the facts. In this discursive propositional system concepts were defined implicitly by their place in the system, and theory was thought of as a kind of net giving each concept and thus object its place. It thus functioned as a classification of reality.

It is hard to assign the detailed influences behind Schlick's work. He shows acquaintance with most of the empiricists and rationalists among his predecessors, in French and English as well as in German, including the nineteenth-century positivists and neo-Kantians. His system, however, has much in common with that of **Duhem** of the early 1890s, no doubt because of their mutual dependence on nineteenth-century physicists like Kirchhoff and acquaintance with highly formalized mathematical systems. It has also, with its strongly fallibilist tendency, much that would have been more acceptable to **Popper** than the later verificationist and probabilistic theories associated with neo-positivism. Its one feature in common with later neo-positivism is its insistence that analytic a priori and synthetic a posteriori are mutually exclusive, and on the principle of contradiction. The verifiability theory of meaning was very much a later development, possibly under the influence of the Wittgenstein of the *Tractatus*. It is difficult to see how Schlick could have acquiesced in anything like the doctrine, possibly misrepresented by **Ayer**, that meaningful sentences were logical constructions out of sense data. For if sense data are genuine sensations, signs could never be logical constructions of what they signify, and if not, it remains unclear how concepts and propositions do in fact represent the actual sensations.

Sources: Metzler; H. Feigl (1937) in *Erkenntnis* 7: 393–419; P. Frank (1949) *Modern Science and its Philosophy*, Cambridge, Mass.: Harvard UP; Ziegenfuss & Jung; NöB, 19: 120–8; DSB 1975: 177a–179b (bibliography).

R. N. D. MARTIN

Searle, J(ohn) R(ogers)

American. *b:* 1932, Denver. *Cat:* Analytic philosopher. *Ints:* Philosophy of language; philosophy of mind. *Educ:* Universities of Wisconsin and Oxford. *Infls:* Gottlob Frege, Ludwig Wittgenstein and J. L. Austin. *Appts:* 1959, Assistant Professor, 1964, Associate

Professor, 1967, Professor, University of California, Berkeley; visiting positions in Britain, Italy, Germany, Canada, Brazil, Norway and the USA; 1977, Member of the American Academy of Arts and Sciences.

Main publications:

(1958) 'Proper names', *Mind* 68.
(1964) 'How to derive "ought" from "is"', *Philosophical Review* 73.
(1969) *Speech Acts*, Cambridge: Cambridge University Press.
(1978) 'Prima facie obligations', in Joseph Raz (ed.), *Practical Reasoning*, Oxford: Oxford University Press.
(1979) *Expression and Meaning*, Cambridge: Cambridge University Press.
(1980) 'Minds, brains, and programs', *The Behavioral and Brain Sciences* 3.
(1983) *Intentionality*, Cambridge: Cambridge University Press.
(1984) *Minds, Brains and Science: The 1984 Reith Lectures*, London: British Broadcasting Corporation.
(1985) (with Daniel Vanderveken) *Foundations of Illocutionary Logic*, Cambridge: Cambridge University Press.
(1992) *The Rediscovery of the Mind*, Cambridge, Mass.: MIT Press.

Secondary literature:

Lepore, Ernest and van Gulick, Robert (eds) (1991) *John Searle and His Critics*, Oxford: Basil Blackwell.
Parret, Herman and Vershueren, Jef (eds) (1992) *Searle on Conversation*, Amsterdam Press and John Benjamins.

Searle has tried to develop a comprehensive theory of language and the mind. Following **Austin**, he held that all speech consists of 'speech acts' and speech acts have different levels. Uttering a sentence—referring and predicating—Searle called a 'propositional act'. But in performing a propositional act one may thereby perform a further act: *in* uttering it one may be, for instance, commanding, apologizing, or whatever. Such further acts Searle called 'illocutionary acts'. Much of Searle's early work was devoted to

clarifying the notions of propositional and illocutionary acts, and classifying the various sorts of illocutionary act.

A speech act is an action, and much of Searle's more recent work has been an attempt to forge an account of the mental—in particular to give an account of intentionality. His account places intentionality within the area of the biological: according to Searle, the mind is caused by and realized in the physical structure of the brain. Although he favours a naturalistic account he has resisted popular reductionist theories. Most famously, he has argued against the fashionable attempt to understand the mind as a computer program: in his famous 'Chinese room' argument, he argued that computer programs are specified in purely syntactical terms, and thus cannot capture the semantic dimension that is essential to many mental phenomena.

One of Searle's earliest, and most famous, articles ('How to derive "ought" from "is"') already used some of the techniques of speech-act theory, arguing that such linguistic practices as promising enabled one to derive, by normal logical means, evaluative conclusions form factual premises. Searle's work has, from the beginning, engendered considerable controversy—in the case of his rejection of computer models of the mind, from outside of the philosophical community. The conception of speech acts, however, has become part of common philosophical thought.

Sources: Personal communication.

ANTHONY ELLIS

Strawson, Peter Frederick

British. *b:* 23 November 1919, London. *Cat:* Analytical philosopher of logic and language. *Ints:* Epistemology; metaphysics. *Educ:* St John's College, Oxford. *Infls:* Analytical and Oxford philosophy, in particular H. P. Grice. *Appts:* 1946, Assistant Lecturer in

Philosophy, University College of North Wales; John Locke Scholar, University of Oxford; 1947–68, Lecturer in Philosophy (1947), Praelector (1948), Fellow (1948–68), Honorary Fellow (1979) of University College, Oxford; 1960, Fellow of the British Academy; 1966–87, Reader (1966–8), then Waynflete Professor of Metaphysical Philosophy (1968–87), University of Oxford; 1968–87, Fellow, then Honorary Fellow (1989), Magdalen College, Oxford; 1971, Honorary Member, American Academy of Arts and Sciences; 1977, Knighted; 1990, Member, Academia Europaea; several visiting appointments in the USA and Europe.

Main publications:

(1952) *Introduction to Logical Theory*, London: Methuen.

(1959) *Individuals: An Essay in Descriptive Metaphysics*, London: Methuen; new edition, London: Routledge, 1990.

(1966) *The Bounds of Sense: An Essay on Kant's 'Critique of Pure Reason'*; new edition, London: Routledge, 1990.

(1971) *Logico-Linguistic Papers*, London: Methuen.

(1974) *Freedom and Resentment, and Other Essays*, London: Methuen.

(1974) *Subject and Predicate in Logic and Grammar*, London: Methuen.

(1985) *Scepticism and Naturalism: Some Varieties. The Woodbridge Lectures 1983*, London: Methuen.

(1992) *Analysis and Metaphysics: An Introduction to Philosophy*, Oxford: Oxford University Press.

Secondary literature:

Corvi, Roberta (1979) *La filosofia di P. F. Strawson*, Scienze Filosofiche 24, Milan: Vita e Penserio.

Van Straaten, Z. (ed.) (1980) *Philosophical Subjects: Essays Presented to P. F. Strawson*, Oxford: Clarendon Press (includes select bibliography of Strawson's work to 1980).

The influence of analytical and ordinary language philosophy account for Strawson's interest in language, thought and their 'objects'. This interest appears already in 'Truth' (*Analysis*, 1949), which attacks the semantic theory of truth: 'true' does not describe semantic or other properties; rather, 'true' and 'false' are performative or expressive—to say a sentence is 'true' is to express agreement with it. This article prompted his controversy with J. L. **Austin**, a defender of the correspondence theory of truth: explaining truth as correspondence between statements and facts fails, argues Strawson, since facts are not something statements name or refer to—'facts are what statements (when true) state' (1971, p. 196).

Strawson's 1950 article 'On referring' (collected in 1971) attacks **Russell**'s 'theory of definite descriptions'. For Russell, a sentence such as 'The King of France is wise' is false, since, when analysed, it contains an assertion of existence (namely, 'There is a King of France'). Russell's analysis, Strawson argues, compounds the notions of referring to something and asserting its existence—'to refer is not to assert' (p. 15)—though in referring to something one may 'imply' (in the special sense Strawson reserves for this word) that it exists. Strawson argues that Russell fails to distinguish sentences (or expressions), their use and their utterance. Whereas for Russell a sentence is true, false or meaningless, Strawson maintains that a sentence is significant in virtue of conventions governing its use, irrespective of whether the sentence, when uttered, is about something. A sentence such as that concerning the King of France is meaningful but, if not used to refer to something, the question of its truth or falsity does not arise.

Interest in the relation between formal logic and ordinary language continues in *Introduction to Logical Theory* (1952), which partly aims 'to bring out some points of contrast and of contact between the behaviour of words in ordinary speech and the behaviour of symbols in a logical system' (p. iv). Formal logicians cannot, Strawson argues, give the exact, systematic logic of expressions of everyday speech, 'for these expressions have no exact and systematic logic' (p. 57). Formal logic is an 'idealized abstraction' revealing certain structural traits of ordinary language but omitting others. The notion of a gap between formal logic and ordinary language has drawn criticism (for example, **Quine** in *Mind*, 1953), but it motivates Strawson's criticisms of the formal semantics popularized by Donald **Davidson** (see 'On understanding the structure of one's language', in *Freedom and Resentment*, 1974).

Strawson's concerns also appear in *Individuals* (1959), the subtitle of which, however, marks a new interest in 'descriptive metaphysics'. This enterprise differs from 'revisionary metaphysics', in that while 'descriptive metaphysics is content to describe the actual structure of our thought about the world, revisionary metaphysics is concerned to produce a better structure' (p. 9), and from conceptual analysis in its scope and generality, since its aims 'to lay bare the most general features of our conceptual structure'. The book's first part maintains that material bodies are the basic particulars to which we refer and of which we predicate qualities, kinds, etc. Chapter 3, 'Persons', argues for the primitiveness of the concept of a person, 'a type of entity such that *both* predicates ascribing states of consciousness *and* predicates ascribing corporeal characteristics ... are equally applicable to a single individual of that single type' (p. 102). Making states of consciousness secondary in relation to the concept of a person enables Strawson to avoid traditional difficulties concerning the mind–body problem. The book's second part examines the distinction between logico-grammatical subjects and their predicates. Reflection on two traditional criteria for this distinction allows Strawson to view particulars as paradigm logical subjects and thus to explain 'the

traditional, persistent link in our philosophy between the particular–universal distinction and the subject–predicate (reference–predication) distinction' (p. 188). In arguing that a subject expression presupposes some empirical fact identifying a particular, Strawson comes to regard particulars as 'complete' and universals as 'incomplete', thus giving added depth to **Frege**'s notion of 'saturated' and 'unsaturated' sentence constituents.

The conclusions reached in *Individuals* form the basis for later works, notably *The Bounds of Sense* (1966) and *Subject and Predicate* (1974), but also underpin Strawson's examination of scepticism and naturalism in 1985, where he rejects philosophical scepticism and reductive naturalism by appeal to certain traits in ordinary ways of thinking and speaking. Certain essays in *Freedom and Resentment*, however, show Strawson's work in other areas of philosophy (notably ethics and aesthetics); and in his most recent publication (1992, published in France in 1985), based on introductory courses taught at Oxford, he examines the nature of philosophical practice (which turns out to be largely his own). In this work, he distances himself from ordinary language philosophy and reductive analytical philosophy, regarding philosophy as the attempt to understand the relations between concepts, an attempt that, while broadly 'analytical', does not aim to reduce such concepts to others more simple.

Sources: P. F. Strawson (1988) 'Ma philosophie: son développement, son thème central et sa nature générale', *RTP* 120: 437–52; WW; IWW; Burkhardt; Edwards.

STUART LEGGATT

Tarski, Alfred

Polish-American. *b:* 14 January 1902, Warsaw. *d:* 26 October 1983, Berkeley, California. *Cat:* Mathematician; logician; philosopher. *Ints:* The theory of truth; philosophy of language; logic; semantics; foundations of mathematics. **Educ:** University of Warsaw, PhD 1926 (supervised by Stanislaw Lesniewski). **Infls:** Lvov-Warsaw School, Stanislaw Lesniewski, Jan Łukasiewicz. **Appts:** 1922–5, Instructor in Logic, Polish Pedagogical Institute, Fical, Warsaw; 1925–39, Docent, and Adjunct Professor of Mathematics and Logic, University of Warsaw; 1939–41, Research Associate in Mathematics, Harvard University; 1941–2, Member, Institute for Advanced Study, Princeton; 1939–68, Lecturer, Associate Professor, then Professor (1946) at the University of California, Berkeley; 1968–83, Professor Emeritus, University of California, Berkeley.

Main publications:

(1933) *Projeci prwady w Jezykach nauk dedukcyjnych* [The Concept of Truth in the Languages of Deductive Sciences], Warsaw.

(1935) *O logice matematycanaj i metodsie dedukcjnaj*, Lvov (translated and expanded as *Introduction to Logic and the Methodology of Deductive Sciences*, New York: Oxford University Press, 1941).

(1935–6) 'Der Wahrheitsbegriff in den formalisierten Sprachen', *Studia Philosophica* 1: 261–405.

(1944) 'The semantic conception of truth and the foundations of semantics', *Journal of Philosophy and Phenomenological Research* 4: 341–75.

(1953) (with Andrzej Mostowski and Raphael M. Robinson) *Undecidable Theories*, Amsterdam: North-Holland.

(1956) (ed. and trans. J. H. Woodger) *Logic, Semantics, Metamathematics: Papers from 1923 to 1938*, Oxford: Clarendon Press.

(1973) (with R. M. Montague and D. S. Scott) *An Axiomatic Approach to Set Theory*, Amsterdam: North-Holland.

(1981) (ed. S. R. Grant and R. N. Mackenzie) *The Collected Works of Alfred Tarski*, 4 vols, University of California Press.

Secondary literature:

Barwise, J. and Etchemendy, J. (1987) *The Liar: An Essay on Truth and Circularity*, Oxford: Oxford University Press.

Black, Max (1948) 'The semantic definition of truth', *Analysis* 8: 49–63.

Carnap, Rudolf (1934) *Logical Syntax of Language*, Vienna, London: Kegan Paul and New York: Harcourt Brace, 1937.

Church, Alonzo (1979) 'A comparison of Russell's resolution of the semantical antinomies with that of Tarski', *Journal of Symbolic Logic* 41: 747–60.

Field, Hartry (1972) 'Tarski's theory of truth', *Journal of Philosophy* 69(13): 347–75.

Jordan, Zbigniew (1967) 'The development of mathematical logic in Poland between the two wars', in Storrs MacCall (ed.), *Polish Logic 1920–39*, Oxford: Clarendon Press.

Luschei, Eugene C. (1962) *The Logical Systems of Lesniewski*, Amsterdam: North-Holland.

Popper, Karl R. (1972) 'Philosophical comments on Tarski's theory of truth', in *Objective Knowledge: An Evolutionary Approach*, Oxford: Clarendon Press.

Quine, W. V. (1966) 'On an application of Tarski's theory of truth', in *Selected Logic Papers*, New York: Random House.

Wolenski, Jan (1993) 'Tarski as a philosopher', in Coniglione, F. (ed.) *Polish Scientific Philosophy*, Amsterdam: Rodopi.

Alfred Tarski made major contributions to logic and mathematical theory. Whle his own interests were predominantly mathematical, his work on metalogic and semantics has had the most direct impact on the development of analytical philosophy, although his earlier contributions on set theory are of interest to more logically orientated philosophers, as is his work on the concept of logical consequences which anticipated by more than a decade similar, but less well-known work by Karl **Popper** on deductive inference.

His most thorough exploration of the semantic issues was in his monograph-length paper (The Concept of Truth in Formalized Languages, first published in German, 1935–6). As the title implies, Tarski saw his task as one of providing a satisfactory account of truth for the specialized idioms of science and mathematics. The elements of Tarski's strategy were a) to characterize what he called adequacy conditions—the minimal conditions that should be met by any adequate theory of truth, and b) to provide a definition of truth which meets those conditions. The aim was to supply a definition of the term 'true sentence' which was both materially adequate and formally correct. He noted that although the notion of a true sentence in colloquial language seemed quite clear and intelligible, he considered that all previous attempts to characterize exactly what this really meant had been fruitless and vague. While owning himself to be puzzled by traditional disputes, he none the less thought that he was determining the core sense of the 'classical' or 'correspondence' notion, as opposed to other well-established notions, including the pragmatist notion of truth as utility.

For Tarski, any acceptable definition of truth should have as a consequence all instances of his T-schema: 'S is true if, and only if, p', for which one concrete example might be 'Snow is white' is true if, and only if, snow is white'. It is important to emphasize that Tarski's schema is not itself intended as a definition—that is the point of calling it a material adequacy condition—it serves to fix the extension of the predicate '... is true', the things to which it applies, namely the sentences of the given language. As regards formal correctness, this condition is intended to avoid the notorious paradoxes and antinomies, of which the Liar paradox is among the best known. These anomalies arises when i) a language contains its own semantics, i.e. the means of referring to its own expressions, and ii) when the standard logical laws apply. Tarski regarded i) as a conspicuous feature of natural languages, and in large measure it explains his pessimism about the possibility of applying formal methods to informal, as contrasted with formal, languages. Given that abandoning logical law was unthinkable, Tarski introduced his distinction between object-language and meta-language. By this means, he hoped to neutralize the antinomies. Thus, for a given language L, the prima facie paradoxical sentence 'This sentence is false in L' could not itself be a sentence of the object-language L, but only of its metalanguage L*. Moreover, for adequate discussion of semantics, the meta-language needed to be richer in expressive resources than the language it was used to discuss.

Tarski's reason for thinking that instances of the T-schema give only 'partial' definitions of truth is this: that only the totality of such T-sentences for a language could provide a complete definition, and given that the number of sentences in a language is potentially infinite, no such totality of T-sentences could be delivered. Tarski also required that no semantic terms (e.g. 'true') should be taken as primitive. In this he was influenced by his commitment to physicalism which could no more tolerate irreducible semantic concepts than it could tolerate irreducible mentalistic ones.

Tarski's theories have had a mixed reception among philosophers. From a technical point of view, Tarski's strategy only works for sentences whose logical forms can be represented in first-order logic, i.e. for sentences whose truth-values are determined by the truth-values of atomic sentences. But there are many meaningful sentences which do not readily lend themselves to such formalization, such as counterfactual conditionals and sentences involving modal notions like those of necessity and possibility.

Karl Popper enthusiastically embraced Tarski's work on truth as rehabilitating the traditional correspondence theory. Others have regarded his adequacy condition as a best neutral and at worse irrelevant to the debate concerning the merits of the correspondence notion as against those of the coherentists and the pragmatists. One complaint has been that Tarski's theory supplies no *criterion* of truth, although it was never part of his intention to provide such a criterion. Despite Tarski's own scepticism about the possibility of applying his formal methods to natural languages, there have been comprehensive attempts to exploit his ideas in providing theories of meaning for natural languages, of which two of the more notable examples are provided by the work of Donald **Davidson** and Richard Montague. Additionally, Hartry Field contributed amendments to the theory with a view to fulfilling Tarski's own physicalist aims. The debate between proponents of truth-conditional semantics and more informal approaches to the issue of meaning in natural languages owes a considerable debt to Tarski's pioneering work.

Sources: Edwards; Steven Givant (1986) 'Bibliography of Alfred Tarski', *JSL* 5: 913–41; Turner; Jan Wolenski (1989) *Logic and Philosophy in the Lvov-Warsaw School*, Norwell: Kluwer.

DENIS POLLARD

Tillich, Paul

German. **b:** 20 August 1886, Starzeddel, Prussia. **d:** 22 October 1965, Chicago, Illinois. **Cat:** Existentialist; theologian. **Ints:** Philosophy of religion. **Educ:** Universities of Berlin, Tübingen, Breslau and Halle-Wittenberg. **Infls:** Schelling and Martin Heidegger. **Appts:** University of Berlin, Privatdozent 1919–24; Universities of Marburg, Dresden and Leipzig, 1925–9; Professor of Philosophy, Frankfurt, 1929–33; Union Theological Seminary, 1933–55; Harvard, 1955–62; University of Chicago, 1962–5; ordained into the Evangelical Lutheran Church of the province of Brandenburg, 1912.

Main publications:

(1932) *The Religious Situation*, New York: Holt.
(1936) *The Interpretation of History*, New York: Scribners.
(1948) *The Protestant Era*, Chicago: Chicago University Press.
(1948) *The Shaking of the Foundations*, New York: Scribners.
(1951–63) *Systematic Theology*, 3 vols, Chicago: University of Chicago Press.
(1952) *The Courage To Be*, New Haven: Yale University Press.
(1954) *Love, Power, and Justice*, New York: Oxford University Press.
(1957) *Dynamics of Faith*, New York: Harper.
(1959) *Theology of Culture*, New York: Oxford University Press.

(1962) *Morality and Beyond*, New York: Harper & Row.
(1963) *Christianity and the Encounter of the World Religions*, New York: Columbia University Press.
(1965) *Ultimate Concern*, ed. D. M. Brown, New York: Harper & Row.

Secondary literature:

Alston, William P. (1961) 'Tillich's conception of a religious symbol', in Sidney Hook (ed.), *Religious Experience and Truth*, New York: SUNY Press.
Kegley, C. W. and Bretall, R. W. (eds) (1956) *The Theology of Paul Tillich*, New York: Macmillan (includes bibliography).
McKelway, A. J. (1964) *The Systematic Theology of Paul Tillich*, Richmond, Va.: John Knox Press.
Scharlemann, Robert P. (1969) *Reflection and Doubt in the Thought of Paul Tillich*, New Haven: Yale University Press.

Tillich burst onto the American scene in a time of contradictions, as a dialectical thinker wishing to do justice to basic but opposing points of view valid within a certain context but not assimilable to each other. His genius lay in bringing the opposed positions into juxtaposition so that they might enrich each other while remaining themselves. His witness was such that his European publications in article form were quickly translated and made into books which exercised wide influence in the American theological scene, and beyond.

He worked with four oppositions: (i) that between neo-Orthodoxy and Christian liberalism, where his religious existentialism added social relevance to the former and depth to the latter; (ii) Protestantism and Catholicism, where he endorsed the Protestant principle (forbidding identification of the divine with any human creation), while producing a system intelligible to Thomistically inclined scholars; (iii) philosophy and theology, where the former posed questions whose most fruitful answers were to be found in a theological 'method of correlation', bringing finite and infinite perspectives together; (iv) bourgeois capitalism and the Marxist challenge, where he said 'yes' to the 'prophetic, humanistic and realistic elements' in Marx and 'no' to the negative elements in the Soviet system (1936, section 11, part 1).

Exploring the 'symbolic' character of religious expression, Tillich argued that symbols point to the ultimate and 'participate' in the reality they signify. They also have life histories, coming into being, developing, becoming enfeebled, dying and being replaced by other symbols. 'Being itself' he believed to be a literal expression, apparently because it was, in his view, a self-validating concept.

Tillich defined religion as the object of ultimate concern. Movement from anxiety to courage is one of the routes to the ultimate. On this theme (1952) he discussed four stages of courage, which recapitulated stages of culture. The 'courage to be as a part' gives way to individuality, the 'courage to be as oneself'. This stage of life, and of the world, gives way to meaninglessness and the 'courage of despair'. Despair gives way to the 'courage to accept acceptance' and ordinary theism to 'the God above the God of theism'.

Sources: Reese.

WILLIAM REESE

Unamuno y Jugo, Miguel de

Spanish. *b:* 1864, Bilbao, Spain. *d:* 1935, Salamanca. *Cat:* Analyst of the human condition. *Ints:* Epistemology; ethics. *Infls:* Pascal and Kirkegaard. *Appts:* Spent almost all of his adult life, from 1891 onwards, at the University of Salamanca, first as Professor of Greek and then as Rector; this way of life was punctuated by six years of political exile (1924–30), enforced by the government of Primo de Rivera as a result of Unamuno's republicanism.

Main publications:

All in *Obras completas*, 16 vols, Madrid: Aguado, 1950–9:
(1895) *En torno al casticismo.*
(1905) *Vida de Don Quijote y Sancho.*
(1910) *Mi religión y otros ensayos breves.*
(1912) *Contra esta y aquello.*
(1913) *Del sentimiento trágico de la vida.*
(1931) *La agonía del Christianismo.*

Secondary literature:

Ferrater Mora, José (1957) *Unamuno, bosquejo de una filosofía*, second edition, Buenos Aires: Editorial Sudamericana.
Huertas-Jourda, José (1963) *The Existentialism of M. de Unamuno*, Gainsville: University of Florida Press.
Lacey, A. (1967) *Miguel de Unamuno: The Rhetoric of Existence*, The Hague: Mouton.
Marías, Julián (1943) *Miguel de Unamuno*, Madrid: Espasa-Calpe.
Meyer, François (1955) *L'ontologie de M. de Unamuno*, Paris: PUF.
Oromí, Miguel (1943) *El pensamiento filosófico de Miguel de Unamuno*, Madrid: Espasa-Calpe.
Rudd, Margaret Thomas (1963) *The Lone Heretic*, Austin: University of Texas Press.

Unamuno was perhaps not a philosopher in the sense in which **Russell** or **Wittgenstein** were, and was not concerned with either the construction of systems or the analysis of technical problems. Yet his thought, though unsystematic, has a reach and penetration which make it impossible not to classify it as philosophical. It centres around a number of profound themes: immortality, religion, the role of reason, human nature and the human predicament, and how to live in a world in which reason does not appear to cohere with or satisfy the deepest of human needs. Unamuno was also concerned with some specifically Spanish themes: the nature of the Spanish character, the place of Spain in Europe and the right form of government for his country. These concerns are expressed not only in Unamuno's primarily religious or philosophical works, but also in poetry and novels.

The basis of Unamuno's thought is his

view of human nature and the human predicament. He objects strongly to the conception of human nature espoused by academic philosophers, a conception which overemphasizes our rationality and the value of reason while at the same time ignoring the most important aspects of our situation. For Unamuno, a human being is not an entity whose primary and distinctively valuable attribute is the capacity for rational thought but rather an individual of flesh and blood (*de carne y hueso*, literally of flesh and bone), faced with the fact of mortality and agonizing internal conflicts—this stress on individuality, concreteness and *angst* is one of a number of elements in Unamuno's outlook which make it more akin to existentialism than any other. Consonant with this basic premise is his repeated attack on rationalism, especially in its scientific form. For reasons which will become clear, he regards reason as the faculty which leads us to despair, and rationalism falsifies the human condition by failing to deal adequately with our deepest needs. His attack on what he termed 'wretched logic' (*la cochina logica*) begins in his *Vida de Don Quijote y Sancho* (1905) and is a major theme of his most important philosophical work, *Del sentimiento trágico de la vida* (1912).

Reason leads us to despair, Unamuno argues, principally because its conclusions contradict the deepest of all human desires, the hunger for personal immortality (*el hambre de la inmortalidad personal*). Above all things, human beings wish to continue to be themselves indefinitely, though without the experience of pain. Moreover, our wish is not for an immortality of angelic contemplation or merging with an absolute but for the resurrection of the body, and for a life of perpetual action. The whole tendency of rational investigation is to indicate that this deepest of wishes is in fact frustrated, and there is therefore a profound tension at the heart of the human condition: 'to live is one thing and to understand is another ... there is between them such an opposition that we

can say that everything vital is anti-rational and everything rational anti-vital. And this is the basis of the tragic sense of life' (1913, ch. 2). Our deepest wish is to live forever, whilst our reason tells us we are faced with annihilation. This painful contradiction is the tragic sense of life, and never leaves us: human consciousness, Unamuno concludes, is therefore best characterized as a lifelong illness.

Granted that we have no belief in personal immortality, how is it appropriate for us to behave in this condition? Unamuno argues that an authentic life is possible, a life informed by adherence to an ideal based on a passage in Senancour's novel *Obermann* (1804): if annihilation is what is reserved for us, let us make it an injustice. We must strive to become fully ourselves, to make ourselves irreplaceable. We must fight destiny, even if we know we have no hope of victory, in a Quixotic manner. Our only 'practical solace' (*consuelo práctico*) for having been born is work—Unamuno notes that Adam and Eve were set to work *before* the Fall—and so in practical terms we must seek full personal realization and irreplaceability via our work. We must so work as to leave our mark on others, to dominate them: 'The true religious morality is at bottom aggressive, invasive' (1913, ch. 11) This 'domination', however, is not to be thought of as a crude political ascendancy or attaining of worldly power, but rather a making of ourselves unforgettable, and this can often be done as well passively as actively.

In the course of elaborating this outlook Unamuno develops a number of other ideas of philosophical interest. As might be expected, granted his view of human nature and the place of reason in it, Unamuno has an appropriate philosophy of belief. Our fundamental attitudes to life are not the consequence of rationally worked out beliefs, but spring instead from features of the personality which are not rational: 'It is not our ideas which make us optimists or pessimists, but our optimism or pessimism, derived as much from physiological or perhaps pathological origins, which makes our ideas' (1913, ch. 1). The tragic sense (*sentimiento*) of life is no exception: it is universal and prerational, though it can be corroborated by rational beliefs. Further, Unamuno's outlook leads him to a particular conception of the activity of philosophizing itself. Philosophy is not a detached, rational pastime nor an academic or scholastic discipline, but a way of coping with the human predicament: we live first, then philosophize (*primum vivere, deinde philosophari*). We philosophize either to resign ourselves to life, or to find some finality in it, or to amuse ourselves and distract ourselves from our griefs.

ROBERT WILKINSON

Weil, Simone

French. *b:* 1909, Paris. *d:* 1943, near Ashford, Kent, England. *Cat:* Moral and social philosopher; philosopher of religion. *Educ:* Collège Henri IV and École Normale Supérieure. *Infls:* Plato, Pythagoras and the Stoics, and Eastern philosophy; personal influences include Emile Chartier ('Alain') and the Dominican priest Father J. M. Perrin. *Appts:* After having received her agrégation, taught at different lycées; 1934–5, worked in a Renault factory in Paris, and for a short time in 1936 was in an anarchist brigade in the Spanish Civil War; came to London to join the Free French in 1942; contracted tuberculosis and, refusing to eat more than her compatriots under the Nazi occupation, died in a nursing home.

Main publications:

(1947) *La Pesanteur et la Grâce*, Paris: Plon (English translation, *Gravity and Grace*, London: Ark Paperbacks, 1987).

(1950) *L'Attente de Dieu*, Paris: Gallimard (English translation, *Waiting on God*, London: Routledge & Kegan Paul, 1951).
(1950) *L'Enracinement*, Paris: Gallimard (English translation, *The Need for Roots*, London: Ark Paperbacks, 1987).
(1951) *La Condition ouvrière*, Paris: Gallimard.
(1951) *Lettre à un religieux*, Paris: Gallimard.
(1955) *Oppression et liberté*, Paris: Gallimard (English translation, *Oppression and Liberty*, London: Ark Paperbacks, 1988).
(1988) *Oeuvres Complètes*, 4 vols, Paris: Gallimard.

Secondary literature:

Kempfner, G. (1960) *La Philosophie mystique de Simone Weil*, Paris: La Colombe.
McClellan, D. (1989) *Simone Weil: Utopian Pessimist*, London: Macmillan.
Winch, P. (1989) *Simone Weil: The Just Balance*, Cambridge: Cambridge University Press.

Simone Weil's work was wide-ranging and diffuse, but concentrated on two central areas: moral and social issues, and the religious life. In the former she embarked on a quest for a programme of social justice and enquired into the nature and possibility of human freedom. In the latter she was concerned with the spiritual, religious and mystical elements which, she believed, were interwoven with this earthly life.

The two facets of Weil's philosophy were linked by her conception of humanity. She considered that our situation in the universe is twofold: we have an inner sense of freedom and the belief that humanity is basically good, but these are constantly threatened with encroachment and annihilation from outside by the forces of necessity found in the natural laws which govern the universe.

The freedom and goodness of humanity are also under threat from immersion in a collectivist society. Human beings may believe that they will gain a sense of security from being a part of such a society, but the reality is that their individuality will be distorted or destroyed. Weil detected a strong collectivist and universalist tendency in contemporary society, but it is not a modern phenomenon: collectivism can also be found in various historical periods, including that of the Roman Empire, which Weil referred to as the 'great beast'.

In *La Condition ouvrière* (1951) she stated that modern industrial organizations in particular have an exploitative capitalist social structure which puts profit and production before human beings, and thus depersonalizes and dehumanizes them. Although she recognized that there can be no abolition of industrial organizations, she recommended that work must be reorganized, not as a bureaucratic 'hierarchy of functions' with its inevitable division of labour, but as an industrial democracy with workers having full consultation about their own working lives and conditions. Crucially Weil thought that such restructuring, in order to be complete, would have to be shot through with spiritual values and the workers' awareness of their own dignity and sense of responsibility towards each other.

The theme of responsibility and duty towards others is also taken up in *L'Enracinement* (1950). Weil considered that people cannot claim rights, but have rights conferred on them. They are, purely because of their status as human beings, the objects of the eternal and unconditional duties binding on all human agents. In this work, she developed the theme that people need to feel rooted in a community, for which the state is no substitute. If there is no cohesive social group to which people belong, as is the case with many industrial workers, there is a sense of dislocation and loss. Nevertheless, to have a sense of community does not fully satisfy human needs: people also have to be rooted in the spiritual realm.

Spiritual growth reaches its completion in what Weil regarded as the only true loss of self, that of the one-pointedness of mystical experience in which the self is emptied and becomes transparent to God. This state is attainable through rigorous spiritual self-discipline, like that outlined by St John of the Cross and prefigured or reflected in certain non-Christian philosophies, such as that of Plato and many varieties of Eastern thought.

KATHRYN PLANT

Whitehead, A(lfred) N(orth)

British. *b:* 15 February 1861, Ramsgate, England. *d:* 30 December 1947, Cambridge, Massachusetts. *Cat:* Mathematician; philosopher of science; process metaphysician. *Ints:* Philosophy of science. *Educ:* Trinity College, Cambridge, BA 1884, DSc 1905. *Infls:* Maxwell, Boole and Russell. *Appts:* 1884–1910, Fellow, Assistant Lecturer to Senior Lecturer, University of Cambridge; 1911–18, Lecturer in Applied Mathematics and Mechanics, University College, London; 1918–24, Chief Professor of Mathematics, Imperial College of Science and Technology, London, and Dean of the Faculty of Science, University of London (1918–22); 1924–37, Professor of Philosophy, Harvard; 1931, elected Fellow of the British Academy; 1945, awarded the Order of Merit by the British Crown.

Main publications:

(1910–13) (with Bertrand Russell) *Principia Mathematica*, 3 vols, Cambridge: Cambridge University Press.

(1919) *An Enquiry Concerning the Principles of Natural Knowledge*; second edition, Cambridge: Cambridge University Press, 1925.

(1920) *The Concept of Nature*, Cambridge: Cambridge University Press.

(1922) *The Principle of Relativity, with Applications to Physical Science*, Cambridge: Cambridge University Press.

(1925) *Science and the Modern World*, New York: Macmillan Co.; reprinted, New York: The Free Press, 1967.

(1926) *Religion in the Making*, New York: Macmillan Co.

(1927) *Symbolism: Its Meaning and Effect*, New York: Macmillan Co.; reprinted, New York: Fordham University Press, 1985.

(1928) *The Aims of Education and Other Essays*, New York: Macmillan Co.; reprinted, New York: The Free Press, 1967.

(1929) *The Function of Reason*, Princeton, NJ: Princeton University Press; reprinted, Boston: Beacon Press, 1958.

(1929) *Process and Reality: An Essay in Cosmology*, New York: Macmillan Co.; reprinted corrected edition, ed. D. R. Griffin and D. W. Sherburne, New York: The Free Press, 1967.

(1933) *Adventures of Ideas*, New York: Macmillan Co.; reprinted, New York: The Free Press, 1967.

(1934) *Nature and Life*, Chicago: University of Chicago Press.

(1938) *Modes of Thought*, New York: Macmillan Co.

Secondary literature:

Lowe, V. (1962) *Understanding Whitehead*, Baltimore: Johns Hopkins University Press.

——(1985) *Alfred North Whitehead: The Man and His Work, Vol. I: 1861–1910*, Baltimore: Johns Hopkins University Press.

——(1990) *Alfred North Whitehead: The Man and His Work, Vol. II: 1910–1947*, ed. J. B. Schneewind, Baltimore: Johns Hopkins University Press.

Schilpp, P. A. (ed.) (1941) *The Philosophy of Alfred North Whitehead*, Evanston: Northwestern University Press; second edition, New York: Tudor Publishing Co., 1951.

Sherburne, D. W. (1966) *A Key to Whitehead's 'Process and Reality'*, New York: Macmillan; reprinted, Chicago: University of Chicago Press, 1981.

Whitehead first achieved eminence in the field of mathematics. His fellowship dissertation was devoted to Maxwell's *Treatise on Electricity and Magnetism*. Becoming engrossed in the investigation of the various systems of symbolic reasoning allied to ordinary algebra, such as Hamilton's quaternions, Grassman's calculus of extension and Boole's symbolic logic, he authored (1898) *A Treatise on Universal Algebra, with Applications*, vol. 1 (Cambridge University Press). In 1903 he was elected a Fellow of the Royal Society in London. He next published (1903) *The Axioms of Projective Geometry* (Cambridge University Press) and (1907) *The Axioms of Descriptive Geometry* (Cambridge University Press).

Meanwhile, Whitehead had come to accept the logicist thesis that the foundations of mathematics rested in logic, a thesis favoured by Bertrand **Russell**, his former student at Cambridge who had switched to philosophy. In 1901 Whitehead and Russell began their famous collaboration, the former serving as the mathematician, the latter as the philosopher, to produce *Principia Mathematica*. Whitehead was to prepare a fourth volume on geometry, but never did so. The new matter in the second edition (1925) is solely Russell's. After resigning his lectureship at Cambridge and moving to London, Whitehead produced a popular, introductory text for the Home University Library of Modern Knowledge, *An Introduction to Mathematics* (London: Williams & Norgate, 1911). He also delivered several addresses and wrote numerous papers on education, published in *The Organisation of Thought, Educational and Scientific* (London: Williams & Norgate, 1917) and *The Rhythm of Education* (London: Christophers, 1922). This phase of his work culminated in *The Aims of Education and Other Essays* (1928). In London Whitehead's focus shifted to the philosophy of science. This shift, which allied him with the neo-realists G. E. **Moore**, C. D. Broad, T. P. Nunn and Bertrand Russell, also led to his philosophical break with Russell.

Whitehead's contributions to the philosophy of science, or of nature, are contained in several remarkable books. *An Enquiry Concerning the Principles of Natural Knowledge* (1919) unleashed Whitehead's realism. *The Concept of Nature* (1920) decried the bifurcation of nature into mind and nature, and, having adopted a realistic stance, portrayed nature as consisting of the passage of events, to be understood in terms of objects, including what Whitehead called 'eternal objects', recurrent universals akin to Plato's forms or Santayana's essences. In this work Whitehead also unveiled his method of extensive abstraction, a method to explain how mathematical entities such as points and lines are abstracted from concrete experience. *The Principle of Relativity, with Applications to Physical Science* (1922) was Whitehead's endeavour to offer a theory alternative to Einstein's. At Harvard Whitehead's philosophy took a speculative turn. In *Science and the Modern World* (1925) he showed how the categorial presuppositions formulated by the philosopher-scientists of the seventeenth century exhibited a cosmology which the romantic poets of the nineteenth century had rebelled against because of its devaluation of nature, and which the scientific discoveries of the late nineteenth and early twentieth centuries were overthrowing. Whitehead suggested nothing less than a revolution in philosophical cosmology, an overhaul of the basic categories of thought. *Science and the Modern World* was a popular success. It elucidated then arcane scientific theories such as relativity and quantum mechanics, associating these scientific notions with a whole range of human values, in history, literature, religion and civilization. It also introduced philosophical phrases that caught on in process philosophy, such as the fallacy of misplaced concreteness, the fallacy of simple location and the conception of God as the principle of concretion. *Religion in the Making* (1926) defined religion as that which the individual does in his own solitude to appreciate the novelty and to assuage the loss that incessant change or process entails. It further advanced process theology when it underscored the dynamic quality of religion as itself caught up in change. *Symbolism: Its Meaning and Effect* (1927) presented Whitehead's theory of conceptual meaning and of perceptual knowledge. This epistemology repudiated the theories of the contemporary heirs of David Hume. It recognized two sorts of perception, perception in the mode of presentational immediacy and perception in the mode of causal efficacy. Ready to present

a new system of philosophy, Whitehead seized the opportunity to do so in the Gifford Lectures he delivered at Edinburgh in 1928. The result was the most famous system of speculative philosophy in the English language in the twentieth century— *Process and Reality* (1929). Defining speculative philosophy as the endeavour to frame a consistent and coherent system of categories which would be comprehensive enough to interpret every item of experience, Whitehead proposed such a system, subject to subsequent revision. Among its nine categories of existence are the categories of actual entities, eternal objects, prehensions and nexus. An actual entity is an occasion of experience, identical with the simplest quantum event; it feels—i.e. prehends—all its past negatively and positively. It is lured, concresces or completes itself, then perishes, to be prehended by its successors. Ingredient in its constitution are eternal objects which ingress or are prehended by it. Actual entities form societies, or nexus; the human person, for example, is a society. Distinct from the categories of existence is the category of the ultimate: it is creativity, the one, and the many. Creativity is, however, not God: it is neither an actual entity nor a society of actualities, but rather the surge of activity or novelty, of flux ongoing in all actual entities. The idea of God is a notion derivative from the categories, categorial obligations and categorial explanations advanced by Whitehead. As the first accident of creativity, God, in his primordial and in his consequent natures, is the actual entity that guarantees the order of cosmos. *Process and Reality* has been grandly appreciated by some American philosophers, such as, F. S. C. Northrop, Paul Weiss and Charles **Hartshorne**, although others, like W. V. O. **Quine**, are more disposed to continue in the vein of the earlier works. Still it has endured as the mainspring of process theology. Noteworthy among Whitehead's last books is *Adventures of Ideas* (1933). It presents his philosophy of civilization, stressing the primary, creative role of general ideas. It also offers easy access to Whitehead's mature philosophy.

Sources: DNB 1941–50; Edwards.

ANDREW RECK

Wittgenstein, Ludwig Josef Johann

Austrian (naturalized British in 1939). **b:** 26 April 1889, Vienna. **d:** 29 April 1951, Cambridge, England. **Cat:** Logical atomist (developed form); later, *sui generis*. **Ints:** Language; philosophy of mind; logic; philosophy of mathematics; nature of philosophy. **Educ:** Technische Hochschule, Charlottenburg, 1906–8; University of Manchester, 1908–11; Trinity College, Cambridge 1911–13. **Infls:** In *Culture and Value* he listed Boltzmann, Hertz, Schopenhauer, Frege, Russell, Kraus, Loos, Weininger, Spengler and Sraffa; Brouwer might be added. **Appts:** Fellow of Trinity College, Cambridge, 1930–6; Professor of Philosophy and Fellow of Trinity College, Cambridge, 1939–47.

Main publications:

(1921) *Logisch-Philosophische Abhandlung* (the only major work published in his lifetime), in *Annalen der Naturphilosophie* vol. 14 (English translation, *Tractatus Logico-Philosophicus*, trans. D. F. Pears and B. F. McGuinness, London: Routledge & Kegan Paul, 1961).

Wittgenstein's principal works (with dates of composition), include:
(1914–16) *Notebooks 1914–16*; ed. G. E. M. Anscombe and G. H. von Wright, trans. G. E. M. Anscombe, Oxford: Blackwell, 1961.
(1929) 'A lecture on ethics'; in *Philosophical Review* 74, 1965 (in Klagge and Nordmann 1993).
(before 1933) 'Philosophy', sections 86–93 of the so-called *Big Typescript* (in Klagge and Nordmann 1993).
(1933–5) *The Blue and Brown Books*; Oxford: Blackwell, 1958.
(1931–48) 'Bemerkungen über Frazers *Golden Bough*'; ed. R. Rhees, in *Synthese* 17, 1967 (in Klagge and Nordmann 1993.

(1937–44) *Bermerkungen über die Grundlagen der Mathematik* (English translation, *Remarks on the Foundations of Mathematics*, ed. G. H. von Wright, R. Rhees and G. E. M. Anscombe, trans. G. E. M. Anscombe, Oxford: Blackwell, 1956).
(1938 and 1942–6) *Lectures and Conversations on Aesthetics, Psychology and Religious Belief*; ed. C. Barrett, Oxford: Blackwell, 1966.
(to 1949) *Philosophische Untersuchungen* (English translation, *Philosophical Investigations*, ed. G. E. M. Anscombe and R. Rhees, trans. G. E. M. Anscombe, Oxford: Blackwell, 1953).
(1949–51) *Über Gewissheit* (English translation, *On Certainity*, ed. G. E. M. Anscombe and G. H. von Wright, trans. G. E. M. Anscombe and D. Paul, Oxford: Blackwell, 1969).
(1914–51) *Vermischte Bermerkungen* (English translation, *Culture and Value*, ed. G. H. von Wright, trans. P. Winch, Oxford: Blackwell, 1980).

Other publications consist of correspondence, lecture notes by students and manuscripts by Wittgenstein varying in length from short notes to fully finished typescripts. Several important short writings are collected in J. Klagge and A. Nordmann (eds) (1993) *Ludwig Wittgenstein: Philosophical Occasions 1912–1951*, Indianapolis and Cambridge: Hackett.

Secondary literature:

Principal biographies in English:
McGuinness, B. F. (1988) *Wittgenstein: A Life*, vol. 1, London: Duckworth (to 1922).
Malcolm, N. (1958) *Ludwig Wittgenstein: A Memoir with a Biographical Sketch by George Henrik von Wright*, Oxford.
Monk, R. (1990) *Ludwig Wittgenstein: The Duty of Genius*, London: Cape.

Bibliographies:
Frongia, G. and McGuinness, B. F. (eds) (1990)*Wittgenstein: A Bibliographical Guide*, Oxford: Blackwell.
Shanker, V. A. and Shanker, S. G. (1986) *Ludwig Wittgenstein: Critical Assessments*, vol. 5, *A Wittgenstein Bibliography*, London: Croom Helm (lists 5,868 items).

Selected monographs and commentaries:
Anscombe, G. E. M. (1959) *An Introduction to Wittgenstein's Tractatus*, London: Hutchinson.
Black, M. (1964) *A Companion to Wittgenstein's Tractatus*, Cambridge.
Hacker, P. M. S. (1972) *Insight and Illusion*, Oxford; revised 1986.

——and Baker, G. P. (1980, 1986; 1990, 1995) *Wittgenstein: An Analytical Commentary on the Philosophical Investigations*: vol. 1, *Meaning and Understanding*; vol. 2, *Rules, Grammar and Necessity*; vol. 3, *Meaning and Mind*; vol. 4, *Mind and Will*, Oxford: Blackwell.

Hallett, G. (1977) *A Companion to Wittgenstein's Philosophical Investigations*, Ithaca, NY: Cornell University Press.

Kenny, A. (1973) *Wittgenstein*, Harmondsworth: Penguin.

Kerr, F. (1986) *Theology after Wittgenstein*, Oxford: Blackwell.

Kripke, S. A. (1982) *Wittgenstein on Rules and Private Language*, Oxford: Blackwell.

McGinn, C. (1984) *Wittgenstein on Meaning*, Oxford: Blackwell.

Malcolm, N. (1986) *Nothing is Hidden*, Oxford: Blackwell.

Pears, D. F. (1987–8) *The False Prison* , 2 vols, Oxford.

Wright, C. (1980) *Wittgenstein on the Philosophy of Mathematics*, London: Duckworth.

There are many collections of papers, including:

Block, I. (ed.) (1981) *Perspectives on the Philosophy of Wittgenstein*, Oxford: Blackwell.

Pitcher, G. (ed.) (1968) *Wittgenstein: The Philosophical Investigations*, London: Macmillan (contains many initial reviews and important early papers on Wittgenstein).

Phillips Griffiths, A. (ed.) (1991) *Wittgenstein: Centenary Essays*, Royal Institute of Philosophy Lectures vol. 28 (1989–90), Cambridge.

Shanker, V. A. and S. G. (eds) (1986) *Ludwig Wittgenstein: Critical Assessments*, 5 vols, London: Croom Helm.

Vesey, G. (ed.) (1974) *Understanding Wittgenstein*, Royal Institute of Philosophy Lectures vol. 7 (1972–3), London: Macmillan.

Wittgenstein has been the most influential twentieth-century philosopher in the English-speaking world. Interpretations of his work vary radically on almost every point, to the extent that it would be misleading to suggest that any neutral account can be given. Some knowledge of his life is needed to form a view of the two phases of his work—represented by his two masterpieces, the *Tractatus Logico-Philosophicus* and the *Philosophical Investigations*—and of the relationship between them. Opinions differ on the continuity or discontinuity of his development, from commentators who see a complete volte-face to those who detect enduring interests and attitudes.

In his youth Wittgenstein studied for six years as an engineer. He worked briefly, in the late 1920s, as an architect. Perhaps as a result, a practical, almost mechanical, approach to philosophy can sometimes be seen in his work, even in writing as abstract as his *Remarks on the Foundations of Mathematics* (see I, SS 119, 122; III, SS 21, 49, 51; V, S 51).

In 1911 he went to Trinity College, Cambridge, to study with **Russell**, on the advice of **Frege**. The themes which took life in his notebooks soon afterwards included some which had preoccupied Russell for many years: the nature and ingredients of a proposition; its relation to objects; logical truth. There was also a concern with the will, the self and the place of value which Wittgenstein may have brought from his early reading of Schopenhauer.

The *Tractatus Logico-Philosophicus* was composed during the Great War while Wittgenstein was serving in the Austrian army. (Few classics of philosophy could have been written in worse conditions.) He wrote of it in a letter to Ludwig von Ficker (1919): 'My work consists of two parts: of the one presented here, plus all that I have *not* written. And it is precisely this second part that is the important one. My book draws limits to the sphere of the ethical from the inside as it were' (P. Engelmann, *Letters from Ludwig Wittgenstein with a Memoir*, Oxford: Blackwell, 1967, p. 143). Despite the Russellian logical skeleton of the work—of great technical interest to later Anglo-American commentators—Wittgenstein's emphasis on the ethical aims of the *Tractatus* must be taken seriously. He believed (and continued to believe at least up to his 'Lecture on ethics' in 1929) that value stood outside what he thought of as 'the world': 'If there is any value that does have value, it must lie outside the whole sphere of what happens and is the case' (6.41).

He needed to fit together 'what happens and is the case' with what *can* be said about it, and to set that apart from what *cannot* be said—about 'the sense of the world' (6.41) and about 'the will in so far as it is the subject of ethical attributes' (6.423). *Saying* is possible. Saying—language—consists of 'the totality of propositions' (4.001). And 'only propositions have sense' (3.31). But: 'If the world had no substance, then whether a proposition had sense would depend on whether another proposition was true. In that case we could not sketch out any picture of the world (true or false)' (2.0211–12). But 'we' *can* do this... so the world does have a substance ... The argument is a Kantian, transcendental one, leading to a world of objects, pictured in language. 'A proposition is a picture of reality' (4.01/4.021) and 'The totality of true propositions is the whole of natural science ...' (4.11).

Wittgenstein relied on strong dichotomy: on one side was language consisting of articulated (3.141) propositions, in which everything sayable depended on (without necessarily being reducible to) the fact that elementary propositions can picture states of affairs; on the other side were the realms of the will, ethics and the mystical. Here, nothing could be *said*, though something might be *shown*. Logic and mathematics, which could not be seen as presenting facts about the world, were diagnosed as tautologies—the limiting case of the combination of signs (4.466). They were not—like attempts to *say* something about value or ethics—nonsensical (*unsinnig*). But they were empty of sense (*sinnlos*) because they *said* nothing. The contrast was between what was *said* and what was *shown*: 'Logical so-called propositions *show* [the] logical properties of language and therefore of [the] Universe, but *say* nothing' (*Notebooks 1914–16*, p. 107). Logic was 'not a body of doctrine but a mirror-image of the world' (6.13).

These views embodied radical implications for philosophy. It could not be a 'body of doctrine' or aim at 'philosophical propositions'. It could be an activity of elucidation—'the logical clarification of thoughts' (4.112). And what was written in the

Tractatus might well be elucidatory, but would have to be recognized as nonsensical itself: purporting to *say* what could only be *shown*. 'What we cannot speak about we must pass over in silence' (7).

After the *Tractatus* Wittgenstein underwent a decade of mental turmoil when he worked in rural Austria as an elementary teacher and as a gardener. He returned to philosophy in the late 1920s during the time when he was helping to design a house for his sister in Vienna. In 1928 he attended a lecture by Brouwer (on Mathematics, Science and Language). He joined discussions of the Vienna Circle. In 1929 he went back to Cambridge, where he was awarded a PhD for the *Tractatus* and where he began the teaching which was to have an enormous influence on philosophy during and after the rest of his life.

Wittgenstein was never a logical positivist. But the frequent misidentification of the 'objects' in the *Tractatus* with items of elementary experience may have led his thoughts towards the connections between linguistic sense and the empiricist notion of 'inner' mental experiences. This theme was central to much of his subsequent work. A less evident but equally significant breaking-point came in his early view of necessity as tautological. The crux appeared very early as a concern: 'A point cannot be red and green at the same time: at first sight there seems no need for this to be a logical impossibility' (*Notebooks 1914–16*, 16 August 1916; see also *Tractatus* 6.3751). Further thought on this in the 1930s led to a new understanding of modality.

A view of meaning was needed in Wittgenstein's early thinking to sustain his view of what was unsayable. In his middle and later years meaning moved to the centre of his interests in its own right. The *Blue Book* (1933–4) opened with the question 'What is the meaning of a word?' In the *Tractatus* (3.203) he had written: 'A name means an object. The object is its meaning ...'. This single, direct, essentialist link between language and reality was denied later, or diminished to a special case. Wittgenstein's attention moved towards the meaningfulness of gestures, questions, orders, proposals, guesses, greetings, wishes and so on. He catalogued cases where precision and determinacy were irrelevant to meaningfulness, and where the senses of common terms (for example, 'game') could be conveyed successfully when they could not be found to stand for anything in common. His interest in meaning in social contexts has often been seen as a form of holism—sense would be determined by an indefinitely wide range of linguistic, social and cultural conditions ('use in language', *Philosophical Investigations* I, S43). But more probably, having held an extremely clear-cut theory of meaning, he now wanted to deny that *any* theory could cover the sufficient or necessary conditions for meaning or meaningfulness. (See Anscombe, 'A theory of language?', in Block 1981.)

The most important area where this was applied was where words had been thought to stand for mental objects: 'red' somehow stands for my inner impression of redness; 'toothache' gets its sense for me because I have used it to stand for an ache in my tooth. Part I of the *Philosophical Investigations* is preoccupied with this theme. It comes to a focus in the passages known as the 'private language arguments' (SS242–309; or wider—see **Kripke** on this point). One strand in these arguments is a suggestion that an understanding of the sense of any term cannot depend on personal acquaintance with its reference (what it stands for). Someone who has never had toothache (seasickness, a hangover) uses 'seasickness' just as intelligibly as someone who has. Its meaning 'for' the user of the word, which seems essential, 'drops out of consideration as irrelevant' (I, S293). What matters is that the word is used in accordance with the rules of language, which have to be social, 'public', not 'private' inside the language-user. Otherwise the word could have no 'function'

(S260). Its use could have no 'criterion of correctness': 'whatever is going to seem right to me is right. That only means that here we can't talk about "right"' (S 258). 'The meaning of a word is not the experience (*Die Bedeutung ist nicht das Erlebnis*) one has in hearing or saying it, and the sense (*Sinn*) of a sentence is not a complex of such experiences' (ibid., II, p. vi).

This thinking was fatal to an empiricist account of meaning, where words acquired their meanings by standing for mental contents (ideas, sense data, impressions). The whole view of language as a 'vehicle of thought' (I, S329) changed radically. So did central elements in any philosophical psychology, such as the self and the will. The latter half of the *Philosophical Investigations*, Part I, and subsequent lectures in the 1940s worked through the consequences and ramifications.

Wittgenstein's *Remarks on the Foundations of Mathematics* is an incomplete and unrevised text which must be read with reservations. In it he stresses the need for practical use as a touchstone for mathematical theorizing: 'What can the concept "non-denumerable" be used for?', for instance (on Cantor, I, Appendix II, S2). He may have been influenced by Brouwer, and some have read him as a mathematical intuitionist, although the psychological basis of intuitionism cannot have appealed to him.

His work has had much influence in social anthropology, social theory and the philosophy of religion (Leach, Winch D. Z. Phillips). The denial of clear foundations for meaning in the form of determinate links between language and reality could be widened from language to social or religious practice. A search for justifications in terms of objective, factual truth might be replaced by legitimation in terms of social or cultural use.

Wittgenstein himself was extremely averse to any form of theorizing—linguistic, social, mathematical and so: 'We can only *describe* and say, human life is like that' ('Remarks on

Frazer', in Klagge and Nordmann 1993, p. 121). This applied equally in philosophy, although it is undeniable that he did present his own aetiology, diagnosis and prescription for philosophical problems. It should be enough to describe the actual use of language. 'Philosophical problems arise when language *goes on holiday*' (*Philosophical Investigations* I, S38). Like Kant, he believed that people have tendencies to think (speak) in ways which lead to erroneous, illusory or misleading questions. The answer, he believed, was to see the normal uses of language perspicuously, to get a clear oversight (*Übersicht*). The aim was '*complete* clarity. But this means that the philosophical problems *completely* disappear' (I, S133).

Wittgenstein's final period, in Part II of the *Philosophical Investigations*, in *On Certainty* and in his lectures of the 1940s, showed a new balance among his interests. His dislike of philosophical theory and his views on the philosophy of mind focused into a dislike of 'scientific' psychology. He had said earlier that 'What we are supplying are really remarks on the natural history of human beings' (I, S415). *On Certainty* applied this in the theory of knowledge. Epistemological *certainty* could have its origins neither in theoretical foundations (as in classical empiricism) nor in unsupported, intuitive common sense (as asserted by G. E. **Moore**). Instead, doubt, certainty, justification, evidence, knowledge and so on were associated with actual social practice, and that appeared to provide some kind of legitimation: 'Our knowledge forms an enormous system. And only within this system has a particular bit the value we give it' (S410); 'I would like to reserve the expression "I know" for the cases in which it is used in normal linguistic exchange' (S260). *On Certainty* is an unrevised text, dating from the last months of Wittgenstein's life. He might well have repudiated the appearance of unsophisticated holism and relativism that can be read into some of its less cautious passages.

Wittgenstein regarded his later philoso-phy as intrinsically unsystematic. His philosophical style was highly individual: aphoristic, full of questions, suggestions, jokes, snatches of dialogue, arguments with himself. Wittgenstein's writings, in terms of the volume of commentary on them, have had an immense influence. His work was at the centre of philosophical attention in the English-speaking world through at least the 1950s and 1960s, with its main school of study at Oxford. (It was also the subject of lurid debate, as, for example, engendered by **Gellner**'s *Words and Things* (1959).)

Wittgenstein advised his own students to give up philosophy and take up something useful instead, such as medicine or carpentry. To the extent that few did this (though some did) his successful influence may have been slight. He was equally unsuccessful in convincing his successors against the value of explanatory theory. Attempts to discover theories of meaning (or even reference) have continued unabated, in the face of the plain implication of the *Philosophical Investigations* that there can be no sufficent conditions for making sense. The growth of cognitive psychology and social theory also show how his thinking may have been disregarded.

There could be no single verdict on Wittgenstein. The *Tractatus*—as he probably intended it—stands at one pole of a certain type of metaphysics, presenting a clear, dogmatic account of what can be said and why. Some strands in his later thought appealed to writers associated with postmodernism: metaphysical explanation and justification were abolished, to be replaced only by a clear view of how things are, how language is used, how culture and society operate.

RICHARD MASON

Zhang Binglin (Chang Ping-lin)

Chinese. *b:* 1868, Yuhang, Zhejiang Province,

China. *d:* 1936, Suzhou. *Cat:* Historian of ancient Chinese philosophy; anti-Qing dynasty political leader. *Ints:* Textual criticism and philological studies, Zhuangzi, Buddhism and old text Confucianism. *Educ:* Studied the Chinese classics in Yuhang and the classics, philology and history with Yu Yue in Hangzhou. *Infls:* Zhuangzi, anti-Manchu scholars, Yu Yue and ancient philologists. *Appts:* 1896–8, staff member, *Current Affairs Journal*; 1898, staff member of Zhang Zhidong (Governor General of Hubei and Hunan Provinces); 1902–3, teacher of sinological studies, Patriotic Society school, Shanghai; 1906–8, Editor, the Tongmenghui journal *Minbao* (Tokyo); 1906–8, Leader, Restoration Society revolutionary party and other political groups; posts under Sun Zhongshan and Yuan Shikai; Editor, the journal *Huaguo*; Head, Zhangshi guoxue jiang yansuo private school, Suzhou; Editor, magazine *Zhiyan*.

Main publications:

(n.d.) *Answers to Questions on Philology.*
(n.d.) *Discussions of Chinese Classics*, Zhonghua Book Company.
(n.d.) *Interpretation of Jiwulun.*
(n.d.) *Interpretation of Zhuangzi.*
(n.d.) *Literature and History.*
(n.d.) *Liu Zizheng's Views on the Zuozhuan.*
(n.d.) *New Dialects.*
(n.d.) *Notes on the Spring and Autumn Annals and on Zuo's Commentary.*
(n.d.) *A Study of the Radicals in the Shuowen.*
(1906–11) articles in *Classical Studies Academic Journal.*
(1914) *Revised Views.*
(1914) *Selected Works of Zhang Taiyan.*
(1917–19) *Zhang's Works*, 24 vols.
(1933) *Second Series of Zhang's Works.*
(1939) *Catalogue of the Writings of Taiyan.*
(1939) *Third Series of Zhang's Works*, 3 vols.

Secondary literature:

Boorman, H. (ed.) (1970) *Biographical Dictionary of Republican China* New York and London: Columbia University Press.

Briere, O. (1956) *Fifty Years of Chinese Philosophy 1898–1950*, London: George Allen & Unwin Ltd.
Complete Chinese Encyclopedia (1987), Philosophy Volumes, Beijing: Chinese Encyclopedia Publications.
Weber, J. (1986) *Politics im Leben des Gelehrten Cheng Ping-lin 1869–1936*, Hamburg: MOAG.

Zhang Binglin, who was also known as Zhang Taiyan, was a major political figure acting to overthrow the Qing dynasty and an outstanding commentator on the Confucian classics and other ancient Chinese philosophy. He also developed his own philosophical system. His early political collaboration with Liang Qichao and Kang Youwei in the late 1890s ended over his rejection of Kang's devotion to maintaining the monarchy. In 1900 Zhang cut off his queue to display his unwillingness to cooperate with monarchists seeking reform within the framework of the Qing dynasty. Several times he was forced to seek safety in Taiwan and Japan, where he instigated the formation of anti-Manchu patriotic organizations imbued with a sense of Chinese history and a devotion to anti-Qing revolution. Upon his return to Shanghai in 1902 Zhang joined Cai Yuanbei and others in radical educational projects, which also provided a focus for secret revolutionary work. In this period he taught sinological studies at the Patriotic Society school. His anti-Qing articles in the newspaper *Subao* led to imprisonment in Shanghai, after which he returned to Japan to edit the journal *Minbao* for Sun Zhongshan's revolutionary party Tongmenghui. Zhang's growing discontent with Sun led to an unsuccessful attempt to remove Sun as head of the Tongmenghui. In 1910 Zhang was elected head of a rival revolutionary party, the Guangfuhui, or Restoration Society. After the 1911 revolution Zhang resigned from the Tongmenghui and formed parties and groupings challenging the Tongmenghui and its successor, the Guomindang, in the unstable politics of early Republican China.

Zhang served China's first Presidents, Sun Zhongshan and Yuan Shikai, but conflict with Yuan led to his house arrest from 1913 until Yuan's death in 1916. Zhang lectured abroad to overseas Chinese. Upon his return unsuccessful missions for Sun's Guangzhou government led to Zhang's retirement from political life in 1918.

Zhang's great strength as a scholar grew out of his training with Yu Yue in philology and textual criticism. Zhuangzi's views and daoist suspicion of civilization and the state led to early opposition to Confucianism, but he later became a leading commentator on the Confucian classics, supporting the traditional old text school of interpretation against Kang Youwei's advocacy of new text interpretation. He was especially devoted to *Zuo's Commentary on the Spring and Autumn Annals*. His interest in Buddhist writings led to influential studies comparing the daoist writings of Laozi and Zhuangzi with the Buddhist text *Jushe Weilun*. Buddhist, daoist and Western idealism influenced his mature systematic philosophy. He held that a single underchanging hidden principle underlies all perception and that subjective perceptions require no objective world to explain them. His analysis of perception, influenced by Kant, combined categories derived from rational thought and empirical representations. Although Zhang wrote several superb works in philology and linguistics, the most important for philosophical study is his *Discussions of Chinese Classics*, showing how linguistic knowledge is crucial to understanding classical texts. He used Indian, Western and ancient Chinese logic to develop a sophisticated theory of names. He was also interested in ancient Chinese legal and ethical codes as central to Chinese culture, with a special concern for rites of mourning. Zhang wrote traditional prose and poetry of great distinction. He strenuously opposed the vernacular movement begun by Hu Shi, but by the end of his life this movement had displaced Zhang's own style from the centre of literary life.

NICHOLAS BUNNIN

GUIDE TO SCHOOLS AND MOVEMENTS

This contains short descriptions and bibliographies concerning the major schools of philosophy mentioned in the entries. Names in bold indicate that there are individual entries for these philosophers, schools or movements.

Absolute Idealism

A form of **idealism** that stems from Schelling and Hegel and which includes **Hegelianism**, though it was developed outside Germany as much with reference to native philosophical controversy as to Hegel. Forms of absolute idealism were developed in England by **Bradley**, Joachim and Bosanquet and, in America, by **Royce**, Calkins and Blanshard. Absolute idealism regards the world of sense as only partially real. Human knowledge, or what passes as such, is highly fragmentary and partial. True knowledge is of propositions that perfectly cohere with one another. Whatever is real is an aspect of the eternal consciousness or Absolute Spirit. Absolute idealism had some tendency to pantheism and collectivism and was opposed by those wishing to emphasize individual persons in metaphysics (**personalists**) and in politics.

Bibliography

Cunningham, G. Watts (1993) *The Idealistic Argument in Recent British and American Philosophy*, Freeport, NY: Books for Libraries Press.
Joachim, H. H. (1906) *The Nature of Truth*, Oxford.
Metz, Rudolf (1938) *A Hundred Years of British Philosophy*, trans. J. W. Harvey, T. E. Jessop and H. Sturt, ed. J. H. Muirhead, London: Allen & Unwin. (Originally published in German, Heidelberg, 1934.)
Quinton, A. M. (1971–2) 'Absolute Idealism', *Proceedings of the British Academy* 57.
Randall Jr, John Herman (1967) 'F. H. Bradley and the working-out of absolute idealism', *Journal of the History of Philosophy* 5: 245–67.
Robinson, Daniel S. (1951) 'Philosophy today: absolute idealism', *Personalist* 32: 125–36.
Sprigge, T. L. S. (1983) *The Vindication of Absolute Idealism*, Edinburgh: Edinburgh University Press.

STUART BROWN

Analytical Philosophy

Analytical philosophers are those who believe that the main, or the only, task for philosophy is the 'analysis' of concepts and that philosophy should not attempt, or can attempt only with qualifications, to be 'synthetic', i.e. to make statements about the nature of reality. Though the modern analytical movement has tended to be opposed to traditional metaphysics, analysis has been conceived as a part of philosophy at least since Socrates. The modern movement began with **Frege**'s analytical work on the nature of mathematics and is characterized initially by an emphasis on logical analysis. **Russell**'s theory of descriptions, which sought to show how a referring expression like 'the present King of France' could have meaning even though no such person exists, was taken to be a paradigm of logical analysis. Among the other leading early figures were **Moore** and the early **Wittgenstein**. The **Vienna Circle**, especially **Carnap**, was influenced by this phase of analytical philosophy and in turn influenced it, for instance, through A. J. **Ayer**. Though Cambridge and Vienna are commonly regarded as the birthplaces, Justus Hartnack has claimed that analytical philosophy originated, largely independently, in **Uppsala**. Poland also developed its own tradition of analytical philosophy, associated with Twardowski and the **Lvov-Warsaw** Circle.

Analytical philosophy has developed in a number of ways. One development was through the influence of the later Wittgenstein, who, after his return to philosophy in the late 1920s, became increasingly doubtful about the practice of reductive analysis. Strictly speaking, he rejected analysis, but his later **linguistic philosophy** is commonly regarded as a development within the same tradition rather than a repudiation of it. Analytical philosophy took root in the highly pluralistic culture of America and, in so doing, was itself affected by other movements such as **pragmatism** and, as a result, became more diverse. Because of these and other developments, many of the tenets characteristic of early analytic philosophy have been questioned from within the tradition. Some, like **Quine**, have attacked the analytic-synthetic distinction. **Strawson**, though he sought to defend it, was willing to engage in what he termed 'descriptive metaphysics'. The place of logic in philosophy is no longer agreed. Many analytical philosophers since the 1970s have had broader sympathies with traditions, both present and past, to which their predecessors had been hostile.

A further broadening influence on analytical philosophy has been a burgeoning of interest in areas of philosophy which had previously been neglected. Whereas logic, language, epistemology and philosophy of science had seemed to be central areas, since the 1950s analytical philosophers have been working, for instance, in such areas as the following: aesthetics (Sibley, Wollheim and others), ethics (Stevenson, **Hare**, Foot and others), philosophy of education (Hirst and Peters), philosophy of history (Dray), philosophy of law (Dworkin and Hart), philosophy of religion (Alston, Mitchell and Swinburne, amongst others), philosophy of the social sciences (Winch) and political philosophy (G. A. Cohen).

Philosophy in the English-speaking world, as well as in Scandinavia, has remained broadly within this tradition, and its influence has continued to increase elsewhere. It has been introduced in Spanish, for instance, by Ferrater Mora, in German by Tugendhat and, in Portuguese by Hegenberg. In France commentary on Wittgenstein has been given by Jacques Bouveresse and on **Davidson** and Dennett by Pascal Engel.

Select Bibliography

Ammerman, Robert (ed.) (1965) *Classics of Analytic Philosophy*, New York: McGraw-Hill.

Antiseri, Dario (1975) *Filisofia Analitica: l'analisi del linguaggio nella Cambridge-Oxford Philosophy*, Rome: Citta Nuova.

Corrado, Michael (1975) *The Analytic Tradition in Philosophy. Background and Issues*, Chicago: American Library Association. (Contains bibliography.)

Ferrater Mora, José (1974) *Cambio de marcha in filosofia* [Shifting Gear in Philosophy], Madrid: Alianza Editorial.

Hartnack, Justus (1967) 'Scandinavian philosophy' in Paul Edwards (ed.) *Encyclopedia of Philosophy*, New York: Macmillan & Co.

Hylton, Peter Russell (1990) *Idealism and the Emergence of Analytic Philosophy*, Oxford: Clarendon Press.

Pap, Arthur (1949) *Elements of Analytic Philosophy*, New York: Macmillan.

Passmore, John (1988) *Recent Philosophers*, London: Duckworth.

Skolimowski, Henryk (1967) *Polish Analytical Philosophy. A Survey and Comparison with British Analytical Philosophy*, London: Routledge & Kegan Paul.

Urmson, J. O. (1956) *Philosophical Analysis*, Oxford: Oxford University Press.

Weitz, Morris (ed.) (1966) *Twentieth Century Philosophy: The Analytic Tradition*, New York: Free Press.

Williams, Bernard and Montefiore, Alan (1965) *British Analytical Philosophy*, London: Routledge & Kegan Paul.

STUART BROWN

Comtean Positivism

A movement that pursued the ideals and practices of the positivism inspired by Auguste Comte (1798–1875). According to Comte, the history of the sciences must pass through theological and metaphysical stages before arriving at the 'positive' stage, when scientists abandon claims to absolute truth in favour of the empirical study of the 'relations of succession and resemblance' between phenomena. The French Revolution, according to Comte, had taken French society from a theological to a metaphysical stage. What was needed was a positive sociology which, because properly scientific, would command consent and lead to a better society. Later on, Comte made positivism into a kind of secular religion, with holy days, a calendar of 'saints' and a catechism. Positivist Societies assembled in quasi-churches and engaged in a secular analogue of worship, a cult of reason.

Comte's positivism was very influential in France and in the twentieth century Lévy-Bruhl wrote an enthusiastic book about Comte. By the 1920s, however, according to Benrubi, French philosophy was more marked by reactions against an 'empiric positivism' (Benrubi, p. 13). Comte had a number of admirers in England, including J. S. Mill. A London Positivist Society was founded in 1877 though, from 1898–1916—most of the life of the movement in England—there were two independent Positivist groups in England. According to Metz, they 'displayed their greatest strength and vigour of growth' in the eighties and nineties. 'At the turn of the century a rapid process of decay set in which nothing could arrest, and under which the whole movement languished and slowly died away', (Metz p. 181). One of the groups, led by Frederic Harrison, remained more active and its journal *The Positivist Review* was published until 1925.

A number of Italian philosophers were influenced by Comtean positivism, including Ardigò, Marchesini, Martinetti, Rignano and Varisco. It was also influential in Latin America in the nineteenth century but, when its application failed to deliver political or economic improvements, there were reactions against it in the early twentieth century, which were an important starting-point for much original philosophical thought, notably with Caso and Vasconcelas in Mexico.

Bibliography

Benrubi, Isaac (1926) *Contemporary Thought of France*, trans. Ernest B. Dicker, London: Williams & Norgate.

Bridges, J. H. (ed.) (1915) *Illustrations of Positivism: A Selection of Articles from the 'Positivist Review' in Science, Philosophy, Religion and Politics*, London: Watts.

Charlton, D. G. (1963) *Secular Religions in France 1815–1870*, London: Oxford University Press.

Kent, W. (1932) *London for Heretics*, London: Watts. (Originally published in German, Heidelberg, 1934.)

Metz, Rudolf (1938) *A Hundred Years of Philosophy*, trans. J. W. Harvey, T. E Jessop and H. Sturt, ed. J. H. Muirhead, London: Allen & Unwin. (Originally published in German, Heidelberg, 1934.)

STUART BROWN AND
ROBERT WILKINSON

Critical Realism

This label was adopted by an influential group of American realists in 1920 to distinguish themselves from the **new realists** of a decade before. The group included D. Drake, A. O. Lovejoy, J. B. Pratt, A. K. Rogers, G. Santayana, R. W. Sellars and C. A. Strong. They opposed what they took to be the 'naive' realism of the new realists, who believed that physical objects were perceived directly. According to the critical realists the mind directly perceives only ideas or sense-data. They thus returned to the epistemological dualism of Descartes. Some, but not all, also accepted an ontological dualism of mind and body.

Outside America, Dawes Hicks adopted the term 'critical realism' to characterize his own position. (See also **Realism**.)

Bibliography

Primary:
Drake, D. and others (1920) *Essays in Critical Realism*, New York: Garden Press.
Kurtz, Paul (1967) *American Philosophy in the Twentieth Century: A Sourcebook*, New York: Macmillan.
Sellars, R. W. (1932) *A Philosophy of Physical Realism*, New York: Macmillan.
Secondary:
Harlow, V. E. (1931) *A Bibliography and Genetic Study of American Realism*, Oklahoma City: Harlow.
Montague, William. P. (1937) 'The story of American realism', *Philosophy* 12: 140–50, 155–61.
Passmore, John (1957) *A Hundred Years of Philosophy*, London: Duckworth, ch. 12.
STUART BROWN

Empiricism

Broadly, the doctrine that all knowledge of the world is based upon sense-experience. Empiricism has been particularly favoured in the twentieth century by both **Pragmatists** and **Logical Positivists**. William **James** referred to his theory of knowledge as 'radical empiricism' and both A. J. **Ayer** and Herbert Feigl styled their view 'logical empiricism'. Although empiricism was very influential in the first half of the century, especially amongst philosophers of science and those who were sceptical about the possibility of metaphysics, it later became subject to radical criticism from philosophers such as **Quine**, **Wittgenstein** and **Feyerabend**.

Bibliography

Anderson, John (1962) *Studies in Empirical Philosophy*, Sydney: Angus & Robertson.
Ayer, A. J. (1940) *Foundations of Empirical Knowledge*, London: Macmillan.
Feyerabend, Paul K. (1965) 'Problems of empiricism', in R. G. Colodny (ed.) *Beyond the Edge of Certainty*, Englewood Cliffs, NJ: Prentice-Hall.
Jørgenson, Jørgen (1951) *The Development of Logical Empiricism*, Chicago: University of Chicago Press.
Morick, Harold (ed.) (1972) *Challenges of Empiricism*, Belmont, CA: Wadsworth, and London: Methuen, 1980.
Quine, W. Van O. (1936) 'Two dogmas of empiricism', in *From a Logical Point of View*, London: Gollancz; second edition 1946.

STUART BROWN

Evolutionary Philosophers

Not so much a school as a variety of philosophers who have given evolution, particularly Darwin's theory, a central place in their system. These have sometimes been **naturalistic**, as was Haeckel's, and sometimes agnostic, as was Spencer's. But others have sought to accommodate Darwin's scientific work within a metaphysical or evaluative framework that was more sympathetic to religion. Some, like C. Lloyd Morgan, interpreted the idea of evolution in a non-mechanistic and non-reductionist way, leaving room for theism. Others, like Teilhard de Chardin, have accommodated evolution within a pantheistic system.

Bibliography

Primary:
Boodin, John Elof (1923) *Cosmic Evolution*.
Bergson, Henri (1907) *L'Evolution creatrice*, Paris.
Goudge, Thomas A. (1961) *The Ascent of Life: A Philosophical Study of Evolution*, London: Allen & Unwin.
Hobhouse, L. T. (1901) *Mind in Evolution*, London.
Morgan, C. Lloyd (1923) *Emergent Evolution*, London.
Noble, E. (1926) *Purposive Evolution*, London.
Sellars, Roy Wood (1922) *Evolutionary Naturalism*, Chicago: Open Court.

Secondary:
Dotterer, Ray H. (1950) 'Early philosophies of evolution', in V. T. A. Ferm (ed.) *A History of Philosophical Systems*, Freeport, NY: Books for Libraries Press, pp. 365–73.
MacDougall, W. (1923) *Modern Materialism and Emergent Evolution*, London, 1923.
Stow, Persons (ed.) (1950) *Evolutionary Thought in America*, New Haven, CT: Yale University Press.
STUART BROWN

Existentialism

The term 'existentialism' is usually taken to refer to a broad movement, of which **Heidegger** and **Sartre** are often regarded as the two main exponents. Other thinkers frequently labelled 'existentialist' are Kierkegaard, **Jaspers**, **Marcel**, Buber and, in her earlier writings, Simone de Beauvoir. It has also been claimed that such temporally remote figures as St Augustine and Pascal are amongst the intellectual ancestors of existentialism. The movement reached its zenith in the immediate postwar period in France, but began to decline by the 1960s.

A general concern of existentialism is to give an account of what it is like to exist as a human being in the world. There is no complete unanimity on what this account must contain: both the atheism of Sartre and the religious thought of Marcel and Buber are incorporated within existentialist thought. Nevertheless, certain more explicit features of this bald statement can be formulated. Epistemologically, it is denied that there can be an absolutely objective description of the world as it is without the intervention of human interests and actions. The world is a 'given' and there is no epistemological scepticism about its existence; it has to be described in relation to ourselves. There is no fixed essence to which beings have to conform in order to qualify as human beings; we are what we decide to be.

Human consciousness has a different mode of being from that of physical objects. A human being exists not only as a thing (a body) but also as 'no-thing'; that is, as a consciousness, or emptiness, that is the condition for choosing what one will do and be. We cannot choose whether or not to choose; even if we think we can refuse to make a choice, that in itself is a choice.

The issues of freedom and choice are of crucial importance in existentialism. Sartre thinks that authentic choices are completely undetermined. If we act to fulfil the requirements of a social role—if, for example, a waiter carries out what he thinks are the preset duties of his job, or unrequited lovers behave as they think they ought to do—then we are guilty of choosing in bad faith. If we make our decisions merely by reference to an external moral code or set of procedures, then we are, similarly, not arriving at authentic choices. Buber disagrees with Sartre over what it is to choose: he maintains that values which have been discovered, not invented, can be adopted for one's life (Cooper 1990: 173).

Many existentialists consider that there are two approaches to the world. For Sartre, we can erroneously consider ourselves to be determined objects, no different in the way we exist from the fixed, familiar, solid physical objects that surround us. When we become aware that our existence is not like that of physical objects, we are thereby dislocated from the material world and slide into an authentic perspective which is fluid and *angst*-ridden. For Buber, there is no feeling of *angst* or dislocation. Any of our experiences are capable of transporting us from the humdrum, everyday, causally-governed I-It world-perspective in which only part of our being is engaged, to the atemporal and acausal I-Thou world of freedom, dialogue and the reclamation of the wholeness of our human existence.

It is often claimed that existentialism is concerned with key or crisis experiences. Existentialist themes are thus suitable for inclusion in literary works, as has happened with Sartre's philosophical novel *La Nausée* and with many of his plays, including *Les Mains Sales.*

According to David Cooper (1990: viii), existentialism has had an influence on later philosophers such as Richard **Rorty**. It is in the mainstream of twentieth-century philosophical thought and contributes significantly to the replacement of the Cartesian inheritance which has dominated philosophy for the last three centuries.

Bibliography

Primary:
The primary sources for existentialism are to be found under the individual headings of the various existentialist thinkers. Publication details of Sartre's novel and play are as follows:

Sartre, J.-P. (1938) *La Nausée*, Paris: Gallimard (English translation, *Nausea*, London: Penguin, 1976).

——(1948) *Les Mains Sales*, Paris: Gallimard (English translation, *Crime Passionnel*, London: Methuen, 1961).

Secondary:
Cooper, David E. (1990) *Existentialism*, Oxford: Blackwell.

Kaufmann, W. (ed.) (1975) *Existentialism from Dostoievsky to Sartre*, New York: New American Library.

Macquarrie, J. (1973) *Existentialism: An Introduction, Guide and Assessment*, London: Penguin.

Olafson, F. A. (1967) *Principles and Persons: An Ethical Interpretation of Existentialism*, Baltimore: Johns Hopkins University Press.

Solomon, R. C. (1972) *From Rationalism to Existentialism*, New York: University Press of America.

——(1987) *From Hegel to Existentialism*, Oxford: Oxford University Press.

Sprigge, T. L. S. (1984) *Theories of Existence*, London: Penguin.

Warnock, M. (1970) *Existentialism*, Oxford: Oxford University Press.

KATHRYN PLANT

Frankfurt School

This term was initially used to refer to the 'Critical Theorists' associated with the Institut für Sozialforschung [Institute for Social Research], after it was re-established in Frankfurt am Main after the Second World War; it has now come to be used to cover 'critical theory' as a whole, from its beginnings in the 1920s to its present state as a dispersed but still active philosophical tradition.

The Institut für Sozialforschung was established as a private foundation in 1923 to develop interdisciplinary Marxist research, and when Max Horkheimer succeeded the historian Carl Grünberg as Director in 1930 he inaugurated the conception of a distinctive 'critical theory'. The Institute provided a base or looser forms of support for many of the most brilliant neo-Marxist thinkers of the twentieth century. Although the rise of Nazism meant that it had to move, first to Geneva and Paris, and then, in 1934, to New York, its work survived all these vicissitudes and its journal, the *Zeitschrift für Sozialforschung*, published from 1932 to 1941 (the last three parts in English), remains one of the richest intellectual documents of the period.

As well as Max Horkheimer, Theodor **Adorno** and Herbert **Marcuse**, those associated with the Institute included Walter **Benjamin**, the historian Franz Borkenau, Horkheimer's close associate the economist Friedrich Pollock and two other economists, Henryk Grossman and Arkady Gurland, the psychologists Bruno Bettelheim and Erich Fromm, the political and legal theorists Otto Kirchheimer and Franz Neumann, the Sinologist Karl Wittfogel and the literary theorist Leo Lowenthal. Felix J. Weil, the founder of the Institute, also published two literature surveys in the journal, whose articles and book reviews spanned an enormous range of material.

The distinctive Frankfurt School perspective is, however, essentially that of Adorno, Horkheimer and Marcuse. It is a flexible neo-Marxism oriented around an increasingly negative philosophy of history epitomized by Adorno and Horkheimer's *Dialectic of Enlightenment*, which they wrote at the height of the Second World War, arguing that the Enlightenment critique of myth and domination itself contributes to new forms of domination. Helmut Dubiel has aptly characterized their perspective as a response to three critical challenges: those of fascism, Stalinism and managerial capitalism, whose perceived similarities and apparent invincibility pushed the Frankfurt thinkers into a position of permanent and increasingly desperate opposition.

A second generation of postwar critical theorists, notably Jürgen **Habermas**, Karl-Otto Apel, Albrecht Wellmer and, for a time, Alfred Schmidt, pursued the perspectives of the Frankfurt School in a more orthodox academic context, aiming to integrate the individual social sciences with philosophy in a constructive synthesis closer to the original intentions of Critical Theory than to its postwar development. More recently, a number of philosophers and sociologists who worked with Habermas in the 1970s such as Claus Offe, Axel Honneth, and Klaus Eder are continuing the project of critical theory into the nineties.

Bibliography

Primary:
The Institute's collective publications include the following (as well as various histories listed in Jay 1973).
(1936) *Studien über Autorität und Familie*, Paris: Felix Alcan.
(1956) *Soziologische Exkurse*, Frankfurt: Europäische Verlagsanstalt (English translation, *Aspects of Sociology*, trans. John Viertel, London: Heinemann, 1973).
Secondary:
Bottomore, Tom (1984) *The Frankfurt School*, London: Tavistock.
Dubiel, Helmut (1978) *Wissenschaftsorganisation und politische Erfahrung. Studien zur frühen Kritischen Theorie*, Frankfurt: Suhrkamp
(English translation, *Science and Politics. Studies in the Development of Critical Theory*, Cambridge, Mass.: MIT Press, 1985).
Held, David (1980) *Introduction to Critical Theory: Horkheimer to Habermas*, London: Hutchinson.
Honneth, Axel and Wellmer, Albrecht (eds) (1986) *Die Frankfurter Schule und die Folgen*, Berlin: De Gruyter.
Jay, Martin (1973) *The Dialectical Imagination. A History of the Frankfurt School and the Institute of Social Research*, 1923–1950, London: Heinemann. (Includes substantial bibliography.)
Wiggershaus, Rolf (1987) *Die Frankfurter Schule*, Munich: Hanser (English translation, *The Frankfurt School*, trans. Michel Robertson, Cambridge: Polity, 1993).

WILLIAM OUTHWAITE

Hegelianism

A form of **absolute idealism**, associated with the influence of the German philosopher, G. W. F. Hegel (1770–1831). Hegelianism was important throughout the Western World in the nineteenth century and its influence was carried into the twentieth century — for instance, by Edward Caird in Britain and W. T. Harris in America. Hegelians elsewhere included Bolland in the Netherlands. Native forms of absolute idealism, more tenuously linked to Hegel, were developed in England by **Bradley** and Bosanquet, in Italy by **Croce** and **Gentile** and, in America, by **Royce** and Blanshard. Though Hegel was a *bête noire* to analytical philosophers and his influence in the English-speaking world was very low in the middle decades of the century, study of his work has burgeoned since the 1970s.

Bibliography

De Guibert, Bernard (1949) 'Hegelianism in France', *Modern Schoolman* 26: 173–7.
Findlay, J. N. (1956) 'Some merits of Hegelianism', *Proceedings of the Aristotelian Society* 56: 1–24.
Haldar, H. (1927) *Neo-Hegelianism*, London.

Levy, Heinrich (1927) *Die Hegel-Renaissance in der deutschen Philosophie*, Charlottenburg.

McTaggart, John Ellis (1901) *Studies in Hegelian Cosmology*, Cambridge.

Metz, Rudolf (1938) *A Hundred Years of British Philosophy*, trans. J. W. Harvey, T. E. Jessop and H. Sturt, ed. J. H. Muirhead, London: Allen & Unwin. (Originally published in German, Heidelberg, 1934.)

STUART BROWN

Hermeneutics

Hermeneutics, the art and methodology of interpretation originated in Ancient Greece, became an adjunct to theology under Christianity and achieved prominence in the last century as a methodology of the human studies which challenged the predominance of positivism. Recently it became fashionable among Western intellectuals, particularly because it figured in the philosophies of **Heidegger** and **Gadamer**.

Interpreting the law, religious texts and literature is as old as the investigation of nature. Because life and liberty can depend on getting the law right, salvation on correctly reading the divine message, and cultural coherence on reasonable agreement about literature, hermeneutics arose to meet the need for methodical and veridical interpretation. The primary subject matter of hermeneutics are texts but by the nineteenth century — mainly through the work of Schleiermacher and **Dilthey** — meaningful phenomena such as speech, physical expressions, actions, rituals or conventions, were included as text-like because in them human experience is interpreted and communicated. So their study–unlike that of mute nature–requires a hermeneutic approach. Understanding a person's worries or the institutions of a society is more like interpreting a poem or legal text than like explaining chemical changes.

The range of hermeneutics has been further extended — first in Dilthey's Philosophy of life, and more recently in contemporary, continental philosophy — by stressing that interpretation is a pervasive and characteristic feature of human life which finds its systematic consummation as a Hermeneutic Philosophy.

The traditional, but continually refined methodology of interpretation starts by recognizing as its aim the grasping of the meaning of individual entities. The relation between parts and whole, both the internal structure of a text (or something text-like) and its wider context become focal, resulting in the Hermeneutic Circle in which the meaning of the parts determine that of the whole, while the latter, in turn, determines the former (a sentence and its words, a poet's whole output and one of his poems, are examples). As a consequence there is here no fixed starting point for cognition and this has been treated as a challenge to the search for certain foundations associated with traditional epistemology.

This does not, however, dispense with epistemological issues. Even if certainty eludes us, as it does in other cognitive enterprises, and there are, notoriously, subjective elements in much interpreting, truth, or at least a distinction between better and worse, remains the goal. To ground such judgements requires spelling out the presuppositions of a hermeneutic approach.

One is that there are common, basic features of humanity. There would be no basis for interpretation if we could not assume — in spite of variety and historical change — that others purposively are capable of reasoning and emotionally respond much like us.

The second presupposition is Vico's principle that man can understand what man has made. The two presuppositions are, obviously, interdependent. A common nature makes the human world familiar and our capacity to decode its manifestations confirms and defines the range of that communality.

Hermeneutics as the methodical exploration of meaning is distinct from other forms of cognition and uses presuppositions and processes all of its own; this does not exclude, however, sharing some presuppositions and procedures with other cognitive approaches.

Bibliography

Dilthey, W. (1976) 'The development of hermeneutics', in H. P. Rickman (ed.) *Dilthey: Selected Writings*, Cambridge: Cambridge University Press. (The original German version appeared in vol. 5 of his Collected Works.)

Gadamer, H. G. (1975) *Truth and Method*, trans. Terren Bruden and John Cumming, London: Sheed & Ward.

Habermas, Jürgen (1968) *Knowledge and Human Interest*, trans. J. Shapiro Heinmann, Evanston, Ill.: Northwestern University Press.

Palmer, R. E. (1969) *Hermeneutics*, Evanston, Ill.: Northwestern University Press.

Ricoeur, Paul (1981) *Hermeneutics and the Human Sciences*, ed. and trans. John B. Thompson, Cambridge: Cambridge University Press.

H. P. RICKMAN

Idealism

In the late seventeenth century the term 'idealist' was used by Leibniz to refer to a philosopher who gave priority to the human mind, who attached a lesser importance to the senses and who opposed **materialism**. He referred to Plato as 'the greatest of the idealists', associating the Greek philosopher with doubts about the existence of a material world. This last aspect impressed Kant, and as a result of his influence, idealism came to be most commonly contrasted with **realism**. Kant sought to mediate and, in his way, overcome the dispute between realists and idealists. But he acknowledged his was a form of idealism (as well as a form of realism) and he greatly influenced the German idealist tradition which, especially through Hegel, held a dominant position in

Western philosophy at the beginning of the twentieth century.

Hegelianism was represented in the early twentieth century by Edward Caird in Britain and W. T. Harris in America. Native forms of **absolute idealism** were developed in England by **Bradley** and Bosanquet and, in America, by **Royce**. Absolute idealism was, however, being opposed from the beginning of the century and indeed before by **pragmatism**, **personalism** (or personal idealism) and **realism**. The influence of idealism waned considerably during the first half of the century, though there were indications of a revival in the 1980s and 1990s.

Bibliography

Primary:

Foster, John (1982) *The Case for Idealism*, London: Routledge & Kegan Paul.

Rescher, Nicholas (1982) *Conceptual Idealism*, Washington, DC: University Press of America.

Sprigge, T. L. S. (1983) *The Vindication of Absolute Idealism*, Edinburgh: Edinburgh University Press.

Walker, R. C. S. (1989) *The Coherence Theory of Truth: Realism, Anti-Realism, Idealism*, London: Routledge.

Secondary:

Coates, P. and Hutto, D. (eds) (forthcoming) *Current Issues in Idealism*, Bristol: Thoemmes Press.

Cunningham, G. Watts (1933) *The Idealistic Argument in Recent British and American Philosophy*, Freeport, NY: Books for Libraries Press.

Dasgupta, Surendranath (1962) *Indian Idealism*, Cambridge: Cambridge University Press.

Ewing, A. C. (1945) *Idealism: A Critical Survey*, London: Methuen.

Howie, John and Burford, Thomas (eds) (1975) *Contemporary Studies in Philosophical Idealism*, Boston, Mass.: Stark & Co.

Metz, Rudolf (1938) *A Hundred Years of British Philosophy*, trans. J. W. Harvey, T. E. Jessop and H. Sturt, ed. J. H. Muirhead, London: Allen & Unwin. (Originally published in German, Heidelberg, 1934.)

Milne, Alan (1962) *The Social Philosophy of English Idealism*, London: Allen & Unwin.

Muirhead, J. H. (1931) *The Platonic Tradition in Anglo-Saxon Philosophy. Studies in the History of Idealism in England and America*, London: Allen & Unwin.

Quinton, A. M. (1971–2) 'Absolute idealism', *Proceedings of the British Academy* 57.

Vesey, Godfrey (ed.) (1982) *Idealism. Past and Present*, Cambridge: Cambridge University Press.

STUART BROWN

Intuitionism

In mathematics intuitionism names a system propounded by L. E. J. Brouwer (1881–1966) that identifies truth with being known to be true. Its claim is that in mathematics a statement is true only if there is proof of it and that a mathematical entity exists only if a constructive existence proof can be given for it. According to Brouwer, mathematics is not reducible to logic in the way propounded by **Frege** and **Russell**. Mathematical intuitionism rejects the law of double negation, the law of the excluded middle and classical *reductio*.

In ethics intuitionism is the view that moral truths are known by intuition, that is, known directly rather than inferred. G. E. **Moore** (1873–1958) was a major proponent of this view, holding that goodness was a non-natural and non-analysable property that could be apprehended by a faculty of 'intuition'.

Bibliography

Dummett, Michael (1977) *Elements of Intuitionism*, Oxford: Oxford University Press.

Heyting, A. (1966) *Intuitionism*, second edition, Amsterdam: North-Holland.

Hudson, W. D. (1967) *Ethical Intuitionism*, London: Macmillan.

Parkinson, G. H. R. (1988) *An Encyclopaedia of Philosophy*, London: Routledge.

DIANÉ COLLINSON

Legal Positivism

The term 'positivism' is used in a special sense in connection with the law, for instance to deny that there are any rights (such as supposed 'natural rights') except those granted by the 'positive' laws of particular countries. Legal positivism goes back at least to the eighteenth century and is associated, for instance, with Jeremy Bentham. It is represented in the twentieth century by, amongst others, Hans Kelsen. Although legal positivists are not necessarily positivists in a broader sense, legal positivism is a consequence of **Logical Positivism** insofar as statements about 'natural rights' can be regarded as metaphysical and therefore, on that doctrine, meaningless. Some of those associated with logical positivism, such as the founder of the **Uppsala School**, Axel Hägerström, are known also for being legal positivists.

Bibliography

Detmold, M. J. (1984) *The Unity of Law and Morality: A Refutation of Legal Positivism*, London: Routledge & Kegan Paul.

MacCormick, Neil (1986) *An Institutional Theory of Law: New Approaches to Legal Positivism*, Dordrecht: Reidel.

Shuman, Samuel I. (1963) *Legal Positivism: Its Scope and Limitations*, Detroit: Wayne State University Press.

STUART BROWN

Linguistic Philosophy

Influenced in varying degree by the later **Wittgenstein**, a number of mostly Oxford or Cambridge philosophers, including **Ryle**, **Austin** and Wisdom began to practice philosophy as though its problems could be solved, or dissolved, through careful attention to details of language. Ryle's influential *Concept of Mind* sought to show, by looking at mental verbs, adverbs and adjectives, how the Cartesian 'ghost in the machine' was a myth. Austin drew attention to some of the other uses of language than to state facts. Wisdom sought to develop an idea of Wittgenstein's that philosophy was in some respects like psychotherapy. Linguistic philosophy has been influential throughout the English-speaking world, for instance, in the work of Bouwsma and **Searle** in America, and Scandinavia, through the work of von Wright and Hartnack and others.

Linguistic philosophy may be regarded as a development within **analytical philosophy**, which also focuses on language. But those who are usually called 'linguistic philosophers' reject the idea of a logical language and stress the study of ordinary language.

Bibliography

Chappell, V. C. (ed.) (1964) *Ordinary Language*, Englewood Cliffs, NJ: Prentice-Hall, 1964.
Rorty, Richard (ed.) (1967) *The Linguistic Turn: Recent Essays in Philosophical Method*, Chicago: Chicago University Press. (Contains good bibliography.)
Waismann, Friedrich (ed. Rom Harré) (1965) *The Principles of Linguistic Philosophy*, London: Macmillan.

STUART BROWN

Logical Positivism

The term 'Logical Positivism' was used originally to refer to the standpoint of a group of philosophers, scientists and philosophers who became known as the **Vienna Circle**. The chief tenets of logical positivism were that: (1) the only genuine propositions (that are strictly true or false about the world) are those that are verifiable by the methods of science; (2) the supposed propositions of ethics, metaphysics and theology are not verifiable and so are not strictly 'meaningful'; (3) the propositions of logic and mathematics are meaningful but their

truth is discovered by analysis and not by experiment or observation; (4) the business of philosophy is not to engage in metaphysics or other attempted assertions about what is the case—it is, rather, to engage in analysis.

Although logical positivism belongs within the broad movement known as **positivism** and can be thought of as having precursors in the eighteenth century Enlightenment and in the nineteenth century movement associated with Comte, it is a distinctively twentieth century development, reflecting a new emphasis on logic and language. It is presaged in **Wittgenstein's** *Tractatus Logico-Philosophicus* (1921) but properly derives from the **Vienna Circle** and associated groups in Berlin (to which **Hempel** and von Mises were attached), **Lvov** and **Uppsala**. It became one of the most influential movements in philosophy in the middle decades of the century. After the rise of Nazism, many of the leading figures of the movement, including **Carnap** and Hempel, emigrated to the United States. Logical positivism was also influential in Scandinavia, in Sweden as the legacy of the Uppsala School, in Finland through the advocacy of Kaila and in Denmark because of Jørgensen. In England the movement had one of its most eloquent representatives in A. J. **Ayer**, whose critique of ethical and religious propositions continued to influence philosophical debate long after the Second World War, as in the writings by R. M. **Hare** on ethics and in the critique by A. G. N. Flew of theological assertions.

Although logical positivism was very influential it had never been free of difficulties. It had never been possible to state the all-important principle of verifiability accurately enough so that it drew the line between the propositions of science, on the one hand, and those of metaphysics etc. on the other, in the 'right' place. The credibility of the principle was undermined by repeated failure to draw this line satisfactorily or to explain the status of the principle itself.

Leading philosophers who had at one time been sympathetic to logical positivism moved to new positions. W. Van O. **Quine**, for instance, argued that the distinction between analytic and synthetic propositions assumed in much empiricist writing was not tenable. In the 1960s there was a broad reaction against scientism in the West. The scientistic orientation of the logical positivists had been repugnant to some philosophers such as Wittgenstein all along. By the late 1960s logical positivism was no longer directly influential in Western intellectual culture, though it had influenced the development of **analytical philosophy**.

Bibliography

Primary:

Ayer, A. J. (1936) *Language, Truth and Logic*, London: Gollancz; second edition 1946.

——(ed.) (1959) *Logical Positivism*, Glencoe, Ill.: Free Press, and London: Allen & Unwin. (This work has an extensive bibliography.)

Feigl, H. and Blumberg, A. (1931) 'Logical positivism, a new movement in European philosophy', *Journal of Philosophy*.

Reichenbach, Hans (1951) *The Rise of Scientific Philosophy*, Berkeley and Los Angeles: University of California Press.

Secondary:

Coffa, J. Alberto (1991) *The Semantic Tradition from Kant to Carnap: To the Vienna Station*, Cambridge: Cambridge University Press.

Friedman, Michael (1991) 'The re-evaluation of logical positivism', *Journal of Philosophy* 10.

Gower, Barry (ed.) (1987) *Logical Positivism in Perspective*, Totowa: Barnes & Noble.

Hanfling, Oswald (1981) *Logical Positivism*, Oxford: Blackwell.

Jørgenson, Jørgen (1951) *The Development of Logical Empiricism*, Chicago: University of Chicago Press (Encyclopedia of Unified Science Series).

Quine, W. Van O. (1936) 'Two dogmas of empiricism', in *From a Logical Point of View*, London: Gollancz; second edition 1946.

Rescher, Nicholas (ed.) (1985) *The Heritage of Logical Positivism*, New York: Lanham.

STUART BROWN

Lvov-Warsaw School

Also known as 'the Warsaw Circle', this school of logical analysis had affinities with the **Vienna Circle**. Though they developed independently there were many contacts between the two groups. But, according to Z. Jordan, other philosophers such as **Russell**, **Frege**, Hume, Leibniz, Mill, Spencer, Bolzano, Brentano, **James**, Poincaré, Duhem, Mach, Hilbert, Einstein, **Husserl**, Bridgman, **Whitehead** and Weyl were 'equally influential' (Jordan 1945, p. 32). The School's central preoccupation was with logic and language. They sought in a logical language 'a more perfect medium than ordinary speech'. Negatively they distrusted 'abstract speculation of an illusive and deceptive clarity'. Some, like Ajdukiewicz, were closer to **Logical Positivism**, but others, like Kotarbiski, Łukasiewicz and **Tarski**, though favouring logic without metaphysics, held less extreme views than the **Vienna Circle**. In general the Polish philosophers avoided the ambitious programmatic ventures of the Austrians.

Bibliography

Coniglione, Francesco (ed.) (1993) *Philosophy and Determinism in Polish Scientific Philosophy*, Amsterdam: Rodopi.

Jordan, Z. (1945) *On the Development of Mathematical Logic and of Logical Positivism in Poland between the Two Wars*, London: Oxford University Press.

Skolimowski, Henryk (1967) *Polish Analytical Philosophy: A Survey and Comparison with British Analytical Philosophy*, New York: Humanities Press.

Woleenski, Jan (1984) *Logic and Philosophy in the Lvov-Warsaw School*, Dordrecht: Kluwer Academic.

STUART BROWN

Marxism

Although probably best known as a socio-political theory (the source of Communism, for example), Marxism is at base a philosophical theory whose roots lie in **Hegelian** idealism and its notion of the dialectic. Whereas Hegel postulated a 'World Spirit' gradually attaining self-realization through a process of dialectical progression, the Marxist dialectic is firmly located at the material level—thus the concept of dialectical materialism on which Marxism is structured. When applied to history by Marx (see *The Communist Manifesto*) the theory of dialectical materialism yields a picture of class struggle being waged over time, with each form of society (or 'thesis') generating its own contradiction (or 'antithesis'), until a new synthesis is achieved, setting off the dialectical process on yet another cycle. From such a perspective medieval society is superseded by bourgeois society, which in its turn is to be superseded by a new, classless, socialist society—the 'dictatorship of the proletariat', where the working class takes over control of society's means of production, thereby extending the cycle of class struggle.

Marx saw society as consisting of an economic base and cultural superstructure, with the base as dominant. The nature of a society's cultural superstructure (its various institutions, legal, political, educational, and so forth) was held to be largely determined by the nature of its economic base and the means of production this entailed. Marx explores the nature of the economic base of a capitalist society, and the type of social being that proceeds from it, in his major work, *Capital*. The main impact of capitalist economics, it is contended, is to alienate workers from their labour, a phenomenon later referred to by Marxist theorists as reification—the transformation of labour and worker into commodities to be bought and sold on the open market. Marx thus bequeaths to his followers a philosophical theory which has a definite socio-political agenda—to change the world, rather than merely to interpret it.

In the twentieth century Marxism has been an extremely influential theory, not just politically (as in the establishment of several Marxist political systems such as the USSR and the Chinese People's Republic), but also philosophically and aesthetically. There have been various schools within Marxism, among the most important of which have been the Soviet and the Western; the former (**Lenin**, Stalin *et al.*) primarily concerned with the practical political issue of constructing a new socialist state, and the latter (**Lukács**, the **Frankfurt School** *et al.*) generally characterized as more interested in aesthetic and academic philosophical matters. (Maoism represents yet another variant, an adaptation of Marxist thought to the very different social conditions of a peasant-dominated Eastern society.) Marxism's impact on aesthetic debate has been considerable, with the controversy between supporters of realism and modernism mirroring a longer-running historical debate about the proper social role of art and the artist.

In the late twentieth century the decline of Marxism as an international political force has severely eroded its philosophical and aesthetic authority. For **postmodernists**, for example, Marxism has become a paradigm case of an outmoded 'grand narrative', or universal theory.

Bibliography

Anderson, Perry (1976) *Considerations on Western Marxism*, London: NLB.

McLellan, David (1973) *Karl Marx: His Life and Thought*, Basingstoke: Macmillan.

Marx, Karl (1867) *Das Kapital*, Hamburg: Meissner & Behre (English translation, *Capital*, vol. I, trans. Eden and Cedar Paul, London: Dent, 1960).

——and Engels, Friedrich (1848) *Manifest der Kommunistischen Partei*, London: Communist League (English translation, *The Communist*

Manifesto, ed. Frederic L. Bender, New York and London: Norton, 1988).

STUART SIM

Materialism

In metaphysics, the view that the world is fundamentally material and that mental phenomena are a function of or are reducible to physical phenomena. Materialism and **idealism** are diametrically opposed in metaphysics and there is a long history to this opposition in Chinese and Indian philosophy, as well as in European. **Marxism** involves what is known as 'dialectical materialism', which has been influential not only in the former Soviet Union and in China, but also, though to a much lesser degree, in Japan and Latin America. Materialists in the western world characteristically adopt what they term 'scientific **realism**'. Philosophical materialism has had influential advocates in both the United States (R. W. Sellars) and Australia (J. J. C. Smart and D. M. Armstrong and is now vigorously debated in books and journals throughout the English-speaking world.

Bibliography

Armstrong, D. M. (1968) *A Materialist Theory of Mind*, London: Routledge & Kegan Paul; second edition, 1993.

Bunge, Mario (1981) *Scientific Materialism*, Dordrecht: Reidel.

Churchland, Paul M. (1981) 'Eliminative materialism and propositional attitudes', *Journal of Philosophy* 78: 67–90.

Feyerabend, Paul K. (1963) 'Materialism and the mind–body problem', *Review of Metaphysics* 17: 49–66.

Lund, David H. (1994) *Perception, Mind and Personal Identity: A Critique of Materialism*, Lanham, MD: University Press of America.

McGill, V. J., Farber and Sellars (1949) *Philosophy for the Future: The Quest of Modern Materialism*, New York.

McGinn, Colin (1980) 'Philosophical materialism', *Synthese* 44: 173–206.

Madell, Geoffrey (1988) *Mind and Materialism*, Edinburgh: Edinburgh University Press.

O'Connor, John (ed.) (1969) *Modern Materialism: Readings on Mind–Body Identity*, New York: Harcourt, Brace & World.

Robinson, Howard (1982) *Matter and Sense: A Critique of Contemporary Materialism*, Cambridge: Cambridge University Press.

Sellars, R. W. (1950) 'The new materialism', in V. T. A. Ferm (ed.) *A History of Philosophical Systems*, Freeport, NY: Books for Libraries Press, pp. 418–28.

Smart, J. J. C. (1963) *Philosophy and Scientific Realism*, New York: Humanities Press.

STUART BROWN

Munich Circle

The Munich Circle (based at the University of Munich) marks a significant moment in the development of phenomenology in the first half of the twentieth century. The origin of the circle owed much to Theodor Lipps (1851–1914), for the early members of the circle were his students who had been holding regular meetings (since 1901) for the purposes of discussing his (Lipps's) descriptive psychology—see his *Grundtatsachen des Seelebens* (1883). The group called itself Akademisch-Psychologischer Verein, and it was at one of its meetings that Lipps chose to defend his psychologism against **Husserl**'s recent onslaught on it in *Logische Untersuchungen* (1901). Husserl had argued that, contrary to Lipps's claim, psychologism could not act as a foundation for logic; for to suggest that the psychology of knowledge can furnish such a foundation is to leave open the avenue to scepticism and, with it, the destruction of knowledge, and of any sense of truth and falsehood. Despite his vigorous defence of his position, Lipps was horrified to witness the speed with which his students progressively embraced the new discipline of **phenomenology**, especially in its Husserlian formulation in the *Logische Untersuchungen*, in addition to their interest in Husserlian aesthetics and the general issue of value. What was clear to these students, but opaque to Lipps, was that here was a radical approach to the question of the foundation of science which did not depend on psychologism, **positivism** or **naturalism**.

Intoxicated by Husserl's new discipline of phenomenology, the members of the circle began to travel between Munich and Göttingen, where Husserl was teaching at the time. This meant that some members of the Munich Circle were also members of the Göttingen Circle.

The members of the Munich Circle whose energy and scholarship solidified the phenomenological approach to philosophy in the following years were: Adolf Reinach (before his departure for Göttingen, where he founded another phenomenological circle), Theodor Conrad, Moritz Geiger, Aloys Fischer, August Gallinger, Ernst von Aster, Hans Cornelius, Dietrich von Hilde-brand and, from 1906, Max **Scheler**. Those who belonged to the Munich and the Göttingen Circles were: Wilhelm Schapp, Kurt Stavenhagen, Hedwig Conrad-Martius, Dietrich von Hilde-brand, Jean Hering, Edith Stein, Fritz Kaufmann, Alexander Koyré and Roman **Ingarden**.

Select Bibliography

Boring, E. G. (1950) *A History of Experimental Psychology*, second edition, New York: Appleton-Century-Crofts.

Geiger, Moritz (1913) 'Beiträge zur Phänomenologie des ästhetischen Genusses', *Jahrbuch für Philosophie und Phänomenologische Forschung* 1, Halle: Niemeyer, pp. 567–684.

Ingarden, Roman (1957) 'Über die gegenwärtigen Aufgaben der Phänomenologie' *Archivio di Filosofia*, pp. 229–42.

Spiegelberg, A. (1971) *The Phenomenological Movement: A Historical Introduction*, The Hague: Martinus Nijhoff.

SEBASTIEN ODIARI

Naturalism

This term has many meanings and there are not only different kinds of naturalism — ethical, epistemological and aesthetic, for instance — but varieties within these. None the less, when the term is used out of context and without qualification, it most commonly refers to a perspective according to which it is not necessary to invoke any supernatural causes in order to explain phenomena. **Materialism** is one form of naturalism, but a naturalist need not be a materialist. **Santayana** was a major influence on American naturalism in the early twentieth century, for instance on Morris Cohen and Woodbridge; **Dewey**, R. W. Sellars, Ernest Nagel and Sidney Hook were also leading naturalists.

Ethical naturalism is another common form of naturalism, according to which actions that are right or wrong are so in virtue of possessing some (natural) property. **Utilitarianism** is one kind of naturalistic ethics.

Bibliography

Fenner, D. E. W. (1993) 'Varieties of aesthetic naturalism', *American Philosophical Quarterly* 30: 353–62.

Ferm, Vergilius (1950) 'Varieties of naturalism', in V. T. A. Ferm (ed.) *A History of Philosophical Systems*, Freeport, NY: Books for Libraries Press, pp. 429–41.

Franklin, R. L. (1973) 'Recent work on ethical naturalism', *American Philosophical Quarterly* 7: 55–95.

Krikorian, Y. H. (ed.) (1944) *Naturalism and the Human Spirit*, New York: Columbia University Press.

Kurtz, Paul (1990) *Philosophical Essays in Pragmatic Naturalism*, Buffalo, NY: Prometheus.

Munro, James (1960) '"Naturalism" in philosophy and aesthetics', *Journal of Aesthetics and Art Criticism* 19: 133–8.

Pettit, Philip (1992) 'The nature of naturalism— II', *Proceedings of the Aristotelian Society, Supplementary Volume* 66: 245–66.

Pratt, J. B. (1939) *Naturalism*, New Haven, CT: Yale University Press.

Scott, Jr, Robert B. (1980) 'Five types of ethical naturalism', *American Philosophical Quarterly* 17: 261–70

Sellars, R. W. (1970) 'Realism, naturalism and humanism', in G. P. Adams and W. P. Montague (eds), *Contemporary American Philosophy*, vol. 2, 1930.

Stroud, Barry (1977) 'Transcendental arguments and epistemological naturalism', *Philosophical Studies* 31: 105–15.

Wagner, S. J. and Warner, R. (eds) (1993) *Naturalism: A Critical Appraisal*, Notre Dame: Notre Dame University Press.

STUART BROWN

Neo-Kantians

The so-called 'Neo-Kantians' did not so much form one unified movement as they represented many, often quite different, reactions to the philosophical positions prevalent in Germany around the middle of the nineteenth century, and especially to Hegelian Idealism and the many different forms of **Naturalism**, Monism and **Materialism** found in Büchner, Haeckel, Vogt and others. During this period, characterized by an 'anarchy of conviction' (**Dilthey**), the 'return to Kant' seemed to be a promising strategy to many. Yet, there appears to be no clearly identifiable philosophical tendency common to all. The term *Neukantianismus* has been in use since about 1875. Though it was at that time not unusual to talk of *Jungkantianer* (young Kantians) or of a 'new criticism', the characterization of the new approach to philosophy as 'neo-Kantianism' took hold.

Otto Liebmann, who formulated the motto 'Back to Kant' in 1865, is usually regarded as the first representative of this movement. Others who were important for the beginnings of Neo-Kantianism were Eduard Zeller (1814–1908), Hermann von Helmholtz (1821–94), and Friedrich Albert Lange (1828–75), who are sometimes taken to characterize the 'early' or 'physiological'

Neo-Kantianism. Their view is contrasted with the 'metaphysical' or 'realistic' views of Liebmann, Alois Riehl (1844–1924), Enrich Adickes (1866–1928), Friedrich Paulsen (1864–1908), and Max Wundt (1879–1963), for instance. A late representative of this persuasion is Heinz Heimsoeth (1886–1975). The two most important philosophical traditions identifiable within Neo-Kantianism are the so-called 'Marburg School' and the 'Southwest German', 'Baden' or 'Heidelberg School'. Also important was the so-called 'Göttingen' or 'Neo-Friesian' school.

The most important philosophers of the Marburg school were Hermann Cohen (1842–1918), Paul Natorp (1854–1924), and Ernst **Cassirer** (1874–1945). Also significant were Rudolf Stammler (1856–1938), Karl Vorländer (1860–1928), and Arthur Buchenau (1879–1946). Cohen's and Natorp's thought was close to the metaphysical school, but Cohen placed a greater emphasis on 'the fact of science' and epistemological considerations. Indeed, philosophy for him was nothing but a 'theory of the principles of science and therewith of all culture'. Opposed to any form of Psychologism, Cohen opted for a very Platonic interpretation of Kant. Cassirer, who was Natorp's most important student, placed more emphasis on culture than his teachers. In doing so, he came close to the views of the Baden school. The philosophers of this form of Neo-Kantianism had placed greater emphasis on the investigation of values and their role in the humanities from the very beginning. The most important members of this school were Wilhelm Windelband (1848–1915) and Heinrich Rickert (1863–1936). Others were Jonas Cohn (1869–1947), Emil Lask (1875–1915) and Bruno Bauch (1877–1942). The Göttingen school was characterized by the thought of Leonard Nelson (1882–1927) who, to a large extent, followed Jakob Friedrich Fries (1773–1843). Reacting especially to the Marburg school, Nelson placed greater emphasis on psychology, while at the same time denying that he was advocating

Psychologism. Nelson was not as influential as his colleagues in Marburg and Baden, though Rudolf Otto (1869–1937) was to some extent indebted to him.

Bibliography

Adair-Toteff, Christopher (1994) 'The neo-Kantian Raum controversy', *British Journal of the History of Philosophy* 2: 131–48.

Beck, Lewis White (1967) 'Neo-Kantianism', in Paul Edwards (ed.) *The Encyclopedia of Philosophy*, New York: Macmillan.

Dussort, Henri (1963) *L'école de Marbourg*, Paris: Presses universitaires de France.

Finnis, J. M. (1987) 'Legal enforcement of "Duties of oneself": Kant vs. Neo-Kantians', *Columbia Law Review* 87: 433ff.

Köhnke, Klaus-Christian (1992) *The Rise of Neo-Kantianism: German Academic Philosophy between Idealism and Positivism*, New York: Cambridge University Press. (Originally published in German as *Entstehung und Aufstieg des Neukantianismus*, Frankfurt am Main: Suhrkamp, 1986.)

Lehmann, Gerhard (1963) 'Kant im Spätidealismus und die Anfänge der neukantischen Bewegung', *Zeitschrift für philosophische Forschung* 23: 438–56.

Ollig, Hans-Ludwig (ed.) (1982) *Neukantianismus. Texte der Marburger und der Südwestdeutschen Schule, ihre Vorläufer und Kritiker*, Stuttgart: Reclam Verlag.

——(ed.) (1987) *Materialien zur Neukantianismus-Diskussion*, Darmstadt: Wissenschaftliche Buchgesellschaft.

Piché, Claude (1991) 'Kants dritte Kritik und die Genese des badischen Neukantianismus', *Akten des siebenten internationalen Kant-Kongresses, kurfürstliches Schloss zu Mainz, 1990*, II(2), ed. Gerhard Funke, Bonn and Berlin: Bouvier Verlag, pp. 615–28.

Willey, Th. E. (1978) *Back to Kant. The Revival of Kantianism in German Social and Historic Thought, 1860–1914*, Detroit.

MANFRED KUEHN

Neoscholasticism

The name given to a philosophical movement which began in the middle of the nineteenth century and which, though it has tended to focus narrowly on the thought of Thomas Aquinas, can be regarded as a revival and continuation of scholastic philosophy in general. Scholasticism, as it came to be called during the Renaissance, originated in the Aristotelian revival of the twelfth century, and flourished in the thirteenth and fourteenth centuries. After a period in the doldrums it was revived in the sixteenth and seventeenth centuries by Cajetan, John of St Thomas, and Francisco Suárez, in what is known as the 'second scholasticism'. It then declined once more, and was virtually moribund until a revival of interest in Thomas Aquinas took place within the Catholic Church in the early and mid-nineteenth century. Despite initial hostility within that Church, important centres of a revived scholasticism had been established in Rome and Louvain by the end of the century, and a number of influential journals consolidated the revival. Initially, in Louvain at any rate, neoscholastics were committed to a belief in a *philosophia perennis*, and to the view that, in the entire history of European thought, Aquinas had come closest to expounding such a philosophy. However, study of the sometimes radical differences among the great medieval philosophers showed that the quest for a *philosophia perennis* was not part of the scholastic tradition, and throughout the present century neoscholasticism itself has manifested substantial internal divisions. What all neoscholastics share is, firstly, a commitment to some form of realism, both epistemological and, in particular, the objective reality of values; secondly, a commitment to metaphysics as the foundational philosophical science; and thirdly, a belief that earlier scholastic philosophers approached philosophical issues in broadly the right kind of way. The dominant trend in neoscholasticism at present is 'transcendental Thomism', which derives from a confrontation and partial synthesis of some elements of Thomism with Kant (Bernard **Lonergan**, Emerich Coreth, Joseph Maréchal) and **Heidegger** (Johannes Lotz).

Bibliography

John, Helen James (1966) *The Thomist Spectrum*, New York: Fordham University Press.

McCool, Gerald A. (1989) *Nineteenth-Century Scholasticism*, New York: Fordham University Press.

——(1989) *From Unity to Pluralism*, New York: Fordham University Press.

Van Riet, Georges (1965) *Thomistic Epistemology*, 2 vols, St Louis and London: Herder.

HUGH BREDIN

New Realism

The 'New Realists' were a group of six American philosophers (E. B. Holt, W. T. Marvin, W. P. Montague, R. B. Perry, W. T. Pitkin and E. G. Spaulding) who produced a series of programmatic articles in 1910 and shortly thereafter. In these articles they opposed the idealist doctrine of internal relations. They asserted the independence of the known from the knower in the case of at least some objects—physical things, minds or mathematical entities. To avoid either an idealistic or a materialist theory of the mind, some—particularly Holt—adopted a neutral monism.

In England, **Moore** and **Russell** have a good deal in common with these New Realists, as had Alexander, and are sometimes grouped with them. (See also **Critical Realism** and **Realism**.)

Bibliography

Primary:

Holt, Edwin B. *et al.* (1910) 'The program and first platform of six realists', *Journal of Philosophy, Psychology and Scientific Methods* 7: 393–401.

—— (1912) *The New Realism: Cooperative Studies in Philosophy*, New York: Macmillan.

Secondary:

Boman, L. (1955) *Criticism and Construction in the Philosophy of the American New Realism*, Stockholm: Alquist & Wittsell.

Metz, Rudolf (1938) *A Hundred Years of British Philosophy*, trans. J. W. Harvey, T. E. Jessop and H. Sturt, ed. J. H. Muirhead, London: Allen & Unwin, pp. 530–704. (Originally published in German, Heidelberg, 1934.)

Passmore, John (1957) *A Hundred Years of Philosophy*, London: Duckworth, ch. 11.

STUART BROWN

Personalism

The term has its origins in the nineteenth century in the view of Schleiermacher and others that God is a person and not as conceived in systems of pantheism and **Absolute Idealism**. Its use in the earlier part of the twentieth century, when a number of philosophers claimed the title, is more focused on individual human persons as fundamental and irreducible realities. **Maritain**, Mounier and Stefanini defended a Christian or Catholic 'personalism' against naturalistic and **materialistic** philosophies. For similar reasons some absolute idealists, including Caird, Calkins and Green are associated with personalism. But, to a large extent, those who called themselves 'personalists' were reacting against the then prevalent tradition of absolute idealism. Many were themselves inclined to **idealism**, such as Brightman, Carr, Howison, Rashdall and Webb, and rejected the tendency of **Hegelian** idealism to monism and pantheism, which they took to deny ultimate reality to individual persons. But some personalists were **realists**, as were Pringle-Pattison and Pratt. The **pragmatist** Schiller adopted the word for himself. Macmurray's personalism was partly a reaction to broader cultural influences which tended to depersonalize people as well as to mechanistic and reductionist trends in philosophy. The same is true to a large extent of the Mexican personalist, Antonio Caso.

Personalism under Howison and Bowne, became an established school at the University of Boston, as it did also at the University of Southern California. The journal *The Personalist* was founded in 1919 but was renamed *The Pacific Philosophical Quarterly* in 1980.

Bibliography

Primary:
Bowne, Borden Parker (1908) *Personalism*, Norwood, Mass.: Plimpton Press.
Knudson, A. C. (1949) *The Philosophy of Personalism*, Boston, Mass.: Boston University Press.
Macmurray, J. (1961) *Persons in Relation*, London: Faber.
Sturt, H. (ed.) (1902) *Personal Idealism*, London: Macmillan.
Secondary:
Brightman, E. S. (1950) 'Personalism (including personal idealism)', in V. T. A. Ferm (ed.) *A History of Philosophical Systems*, Freeport, NY: Books for Libraries Press.
Deats, Paul and Robb, Carol (1986) *The Boston Personalist Tradition in Philosophy, Social Ethics, and Theology*, Macon, GA: Mercer University Press.
Lavely, John H. (1967) 'Personalism', in Paul Edwards (ed.) *Encyclopedia of Philosophy*, New York: Macmillan & Co.
Metz, Rudolf (1938) *A Hundred Years of British Philosophy*, trans. J. W. Harvey, T. E. Jessop and H. Sturt, ed. J. H. Muirhead, London: Allen & Unwin, pp. 380–98. (Originally published in German, Heidelberg, 1934.)
Passmore, John (1957) *A Hundred Years of Philosophy*, London: Duckworth, ch. 4.

STUART BROWN

Phenomenology

What unites the various things that have been called phenomenology is more a matter of family resemblance than doctrines held in common. The following kinds of phenomenology may be distinguished.

Realist phenomenology
This owed its inspiration to **Husserl**'s *Logical Investigations*. It is characterized by a rich ontology which rejects the **empiricist** restriction of what there is to the physical and the mental. There are physical entities and mental entities but there are also numbers, states of affairs, logical laws, institutions, works of art and so on. Following the slogan 'To the things themselves!' entities of all ontological types are to be taken as they present themselves to consciousness and not as some theory or system says they must be. Everything has its 'what', its essence. Phenomenology is the study of essences and relations between essences by means of a kind of non-sensory seeing or intuition (*Wesensschau*). The truths which such phenomenology lays bare are a priori. The a priori is not merely formal but can pertain to literally anything, e.g. there are a priori truths about sensation. Moreover the *necessity* which characterizes a priori truths has nothing to do with how we think or even how we must think but is purely objective. Although considerable emphasis is given to the intentionality of consciousness—its being 'of' or 'about' something, its directedness-toward something—and intentional experiences constitute much of the subject-matter of phenomenology, this is not because it is thought that somehow things other than consciousness depend for their existence and character on consciousness. Rather the failure to recognize intentionality is blamed for attempts to reduce material objects to sensations, logic to psychology, values to feelings.

Transcendental phenomenology
Despite having been the inspiration for realist phenomenology Husserl's phenomenology developed into a form of **idealism**. For transcendental phenomenology consciousness or subjectivity is the exclusive theme. Objects of consciousness figure in phenomenological description but as purely intentional objects, i.e. objects *qua* objects of consciousness. From motives which are partly Cartesian and partly Kantian a procedure is adopted for arriving at *pure* consciousness. This is not an item in the

world but that for which there is a world. The operation which enables the phenomenologist to enter the transcendental dimension of pure consciousness is the phenomenological or transcendental reduction. This is a way of *reflecting* on consciousness, as opposed to being absorbed by the world and items in the world, which involves the suspending or putting out of action of all beliefs regarding the real existence and real nature of all objects of consciousness (including the world as a whole). Intentionality is no longer conceived as the way in which a conscious subject relates itself to a pre-existing reality but as the medium in which what counts as real is constituted. Transcendental phenomenology is the description of the essential structures of the constitution (constituting) of the world in transcendental subjectivity.

Hermeneutic phenomenology

This is how **Heidegger** describes his own form of phenomenology. Phenomenology is the method of ontology, the study of the Being (*Sein*) of beings (what is, *Seiendes*). A necessary preliminary to the question of the meaning of Being as such is the ontology of the being which asks the question about Being. To say that Being is the proper subject-matter of phenomenology suggests that Heidegger is engaged in something totally different from transcendental phenomenology, for which the subject-matter is transcendental consciousness. However the difference is not as great as it first seems. Being is not some great abstraction but that which makes it possible for beings to show themselves or be encountered. *Dasein* (Heidegger's term for human being) is unique inasmuch as its Being involves an understanding of Being, that of itself and that of what is not itself. Phenomenology is hermeneutic in the sense that it consists in the *interpretation*, the conceptual unfolding (*Auslegung*) of *Dasein*'s understanding of Being. The being with the understanding of Being is not a transcendental ego outside the

world but a being whose Being is Being-in-the-world. However this is not a crude reverting to pre-Kantian naiveté. *Dasein* is not in the world in the sense of one thing being located in a much bigger thing. It is not a *subject* which unlike the transcendental subject is not outside the world. Rather the conception of *Dasein* as Being-in-the-world represents an attempt to overcome the subject-object dichotomy. What Heidegger means by 'world' is a structure of significance. This is not something over and against *Dasein* but part and parcel of what *Dasein* is. Reversing the customary order, theoretical modes of intentionality, comportment to beings, are seen as grounded in practical modes. Being-in-the-world is not itself an instance of intentionality, but a condition of the possibility of intentionality.

Existential phenomenology

This is best exemplified by **Merleau-Ponty**. Towards the end of his philosophical career Husserl introduced the idea of the *Lebenswelt* (life-world), the world of lived experience. The properties and structures attributed by the natural sciences to the 'objective' world are themselves the product of a process of idealization and mathematization of 'life-wordly' structures. The task of philosophy is not to down-grade the life-world as 'mere appearance' but to remove from it the 'garment of ideas' which science has thrown over it. Largely through the influence of Merleau-Ponty many phenomenologists came to see the description of the life-world and the exposure of the 'prejudice' of the idea of an objective world of wholly determinate entities as phenomenology's principal task. What makes such phenomenology existential as opposed to transcendental is that the consciousness of the life-world it seeks to describe is that of the concrete, situated, historical, engaged body-subject in the world rather than that of a transcendental ego. It involves a 'reduction' in the sense of the suspension or putting out of action of the objective sciences but not a genuinely transcendental reduction. Unlike Husserl, Merleau-Ponty does not see the laying bare of the life-world as merely a stage on the way to world-constituting transcendental subjectivity.

Bibliography

Primary:
Husserl, E. (1990) *Logische Untersuchungen*, Halle; second edition, 1913 (English translation, *Logical Investigations*, trans. J. N. Findlay, London: Routledge & Kegan Paul, 1970).
——(1913) *Ideen zu einer reinen Phänomenologie und phänomenologischen Philosophie*, Halle (English translation, *Ideas: General Introduction to Pure Phenomenology*, trans. W. R. Boyce Gibson, London: Allen & Unwin, 1958).
——(1949) *Cartesianische Meditationen*, The Hague (English translation, *Cartesian Meditations*, trans. Dorion Cairns, The Hague: Martinus Nijhoff, 1969).
——(1962) *Die Krisis der europäischen Wissenschaften und die transzendentale Phänomenologie*, The Hague (English translation, *The Crisis of European Sciences and Transcendental Phenomenology*, trans. David Carr, Evanston: Northwestern University Press, 1970).
Heidegger, M. (1927) *Sein und Zeit*, Halle (English translation, *Being and Time*, trans. John Macquarrie and Edward Robinson, Oxford: Basil Blackwell, 1962).
——(1976) *Grundprobleme der Phänomenologie*, Frankfurt (English translation, *The Basic Problems of Phenomenology*, trans. Albert Hofstadter, Bloomington: Indiana University Press, 1982).
——(1979) *Prolegomena zur Geschichte des Zeitbegriffs*, Frankfurt (English translation, *History of the Concept of Time Prolegomena*, trans. Theodore Kisiel, Bloomington: Indiana University Press, 1985).
Merleau-Ponty, M. (1945) *Phénoménologie de la Perception*, Paris (English translation, *Phenomenology of Perception*, trans. Colin Smith, London: Routledge & Kegan Paul, 1962).**Secondary:**
Howard. M., Howarth, J. and Keat, R. (1991) *Understanding Phenomenology*, Oxford: Basil Blackwell.
Pivcevic, E. (1970) *Husserl and Phenomenology*, London: Hutchinson University Library.
Spiegelberg, H. (1960) *The Phenomenological Movement*, The Hague.

PAUL GORNER

Philosophical Anthropology

This movement can be traced back to the eighteenth century—particularly to Kant—and it has precursors in the early part of the twentieth century, including **Dilthey** and **Husserl**. It flourished in Germany in the 1920s and 1930s, when Max **Scheler** and Helmut Plessner were key figures. It has since spread elsewhere and has attracted attention in the English-speaking world. The movement can be characterized as a reaction against the overly scientistic, mechanistic or reductionist studies of human nature characteristic of Darwinian, Freudian and other approaches. Modern science is often seen by those who associate themselves with philosophical anthropology as in a state of crisis (sometimes as reflecting a crisis in Modern European society). With its emphasis on not treating humans as mere scientific objects but as free beings, it has affinities with certain other movements, such as **Existentialism** and **Phenomenology**. Amongst those most commonly associated with philosophical anthropology are Ludwig Binswanger, Martin Buber, Ernst **Cassirer**, Arnold Gehlen, R. D. Lang, Michael Polanyi and Werner Sombart. But the breath of the movement makes a consensus about its history unlikely. It has been developed in a number of discipline areas, including biology, psychology and theology, in different ways. Those who describe themselves as engaging in 'philosophical anthropology' define themselves in various ways and they construct and associate themselves with different histories.

Bibliography

Primary:
Agassi, Joseph (1977) *Towards a Rational Philosophical Anthropology*, The Hague: Martinus Nijhoff.
Cassirer, Ernst (1963) *An Essay on Man*, New Haven, CT: Yale University Press.

Haeffner, G. (trans. E. Watkins) (1990) *The Human Situation: A Philosophical Anthropology*, Notre Dame: Notre Dame University Press.

Holbrook, David (1988) *Further Studies in Philosophical Anthropology*, Aldershot: Avebury.

Landmann, Michael (1955) *Philosophische Anthropologie*, Berlin (English translation, *Philosophical Anthropology*, trans. D. J. Parent, Philadelphia: Westminster Press, 1974).

Rescher, Nicholas (1990) *Human Interests: Reflections on Philosophical Anthropology*, Stanford: Stanford University Press.

Secondary:

Lenfers, Dietmar (1989) *The Marvel of Human Being: A Student Manual of Philosophical Anthropology*, Dublin: Dominican.

Pappe, H. O. (1961) 'On philosophical anthropology', *Australasian Journal of Philosophy* 39: 47–64.

——(1967) 'Philosophical anthropology', in Paul Edwards (ed.) *Encyclopedia of Philosophy*, New York: Macmillan & Co.

Wein, H. (1957) 'Trends in philosophical anthropology in post-war Germany', *Philosophy of Science*: 46–56.

STUART BROWN

Positivism

Broadly, any view that accords to science a monopoly of knowledge about the universe. Positivism is characteristically anti-metaphysical and commonly anti-religious. The term was introduced by Claude-Henri Saint-Simon (1760–1825) and popularized by his follower, Auguste Comte (1789–1857). **Comtean Positivism** was not only a philosophy but a substitute religion—a religion of humanity, with its equivalents of churches and worship. It was less professionally academic than the **Logical Positivism** of the **Vienna Circle**, some of whose members rejected the term 'positivism' because of its associations with the older movement and preferred the phrase 'logical **empiricism**'. Against this, however, one member, Victor Kraft, argued in favour of accepting the label 'positivist': 'The Vienna Circle shares with traditional positivism, after all, the restriction of all positive knowledge.'

Bibliography

Frankel, Charles (1950) 'Positivism', in V. T. A. Ferm (ed.) *A History of Philosophical Systems*, Freeport, NY: Books for Libraries Press, pp. 329–39.

Kolakowski, Leszek (1968) *Positivist Philosophy from Hume to the Vienna Circle*, trans. N. Guterman, New York: Doubleday, and Harmondsworth: Penguin Books, 1972.

Kraft, Victor (1953) *The Vienna Circle: The Origin of Neo-Positivism*, trans. A. Pap, New York: Philosophical Library.

STUART BROWN

Post-Marxism

Post-Marxism can be defined in two main ways: first, as an attempt to reformulate Marxist thought in the light of recent theoretical and social developments that challenge many of the assumptions and categories of classical **Marxism**; secondly, as a *rejection* of Marxist doctrine in favour of one or other of these recent theoretical developments. One way of signalling the difference is Ernesto Laclau and Chantal Mouffe's distinction between being 'post-*Marxist*' or '*post*-Marxist'. To be the former is, with Laclau and Mouffe, to be committed to finding space within Marxism for a whole new range of social protest movements—feminism, anti-institutional ecology, ethnic, national, and sexual minorities, for example—as well as for the techniques of **post-structuralism** and **postmodernism**. It is also to challenge the validity of many classical Marxist assumptions such as the central position of the working class in bringing about social change, and the notions of hegemony and historical necessity. The new Marxism aims at a pluralistic approach to politics.

Post-Marxism, on the other hand, implies

a definite break with, and move beyond, the Marxist cause and its concerns. A case in point would be the many French intellectuals whose faith in Marxist theory was shaken by the actions of the French Communist Party during the 1968 Paris *événements*, when the Party was widely felt to have colluded with the state in defusing a revolutionary situation. Thinkers such as Jean-François **Lyotard** and Jean Baudrillard subsequently rejected Marxism, turning instead to postmodernism in its various guises. *Post-Marxism* is more of an attitude — of disillusionment in the main — towards Marxism than a specific system of thought in its own right.

Bibliography

Laclau, Ernesto and Mouffe, Chantal (1985) *Hegemony and Socialist Strategy: Towards a Radical Democratic Politics*, London: Verso.
——and——(1987) 'Post-Marxism without apologies', *New Left Review*, 166.
Lyotard, Jean-François (1974) *Economie libidinale*, Paris: Minuit (English translation, *Libidinal Economy*, trans. Iain Hamilton Grant, London: Athlone Press, 1993).
Smart, Barry (1992) *Modern Conditions, Postmodern Controversies*, London: Routledge.

STUART SIM

Postmodernism

Postmodernism is a movement which began in the 1970s. Its chief exponents include Jean-François **Lyotard**, Jean Baudrillard, Gilles Deleuze and Félix Guattari. It is found in philosophy, culture and the arts, and claims **Nietzsche** amongst its philosophical ancestors.

Whilst no clear definition of postmodernism can be given, it includes an examination of the social and cultural tendencies which have dominated advanced capitalist societies since the late 1950s and is characterized by dislocation and fragmentation; a concern with images, the superficial and the ephemeral; and a rejection of the traditional philosophical search for an underlying unity, reality, order and coherence to all phenomena. The movement is a successor to and a critique of **modernism**, a term which Lyotard (1979, 1984, p. xxiii) uses 'to designate any science that ... make[s] an explicit appeal to some grand narrative'. Such narratives are alleged to be comprehensive accounts of a teleological process which will ultimately realize some hitherto idealized state of affairs. The two accounts for which Lyotard reserves his main attack are that of emancipation, which stems from the Enlightenment and the French Revolution, and that of speculation, which stems from the **Hegelian** tradition and its ideal of the complete synthesis of knowledge. All grand narratives and the consensual collusion or acquiescence upon which they were founded have collapsed, and the question of justification or 'legitimization' of any enterprise which was permitted by their assumption has once more become acute.

Lyotard maintains that due to the computerization of the past three decades, the nature of knowledge itself has changed. Any information which cannot be rendered into a form suitable for being stored in a databank is marginalized. Knowledge is legitimized not by an appeal to its truth, or its ability to represent accurately what is objectively the case. Instead, there is an appeal to its efficiency: minimization of input or maximization of output or both are the goals to be achieved.

To replace grand narratives there are language-games, which are relative, restricted and incommensurable. Each language-game is governed by its own set of rules and is played by those who contract in, whether implicitly or explicitly. There is no self-legitimation of language-games, which are arbitrary and thus replaceable. They are always placed against an opponent, whether other people or language as it is traditionally used.

Postmodernism also advocates the view that time is dislocated. On the 'grand narrative' approach, time is regarded as a constant, uniform, objective, one-directional flow which is split into past, present and future. The present is considered as the link between past and future, and the temporal process is reflected in the tenses of verbs. According to postmodernism, there is no objective reality governing the structure of language: what is traditionally thought of as being in the past or the future can be recalled or inscribed into what is traditionally regarded as the present. With the rejection of 'grand narrative' time, there is a temporal fragmentation into a series of perpetual and dislocated presents which are not to be contrasted with the past or the future.

Novels which 'play' with the temporal process, such as James Joyce's *Finnegans Wake*, are in this respect to be regarded as postmodern, as are all avant-garde works of art which are presentations of dislocated or fragmented time, space or meaning, whether or not they are from the postwar period. A play such as Samuel Beckett's *Waiting for Godot* is held to be a repudiation of the modernist expectation that there is any overall, comprehensive meaning to be found within the text itself, or to be legitimately provided by any unregenerately modernist member of the audience. The avant-garde is on the margins of art, and is kept there by those who collude in or create the arbitrary rules of art criticism. The view that there is no objective reality behind the series of ephemeral images which are presented to us reaches its most extreme in statements such as Baudrillard's, that the Gulf War did not take place; instead, the West was confronted with fragmentary television images which presented, but did not represent, American 'smart bombs' taking out Iraqi emplacements.

Some aspects of the postmodernist programme are of more interest or use than others. The avant-garde in art can lead the audience, viewer or critic to think about and possibly to revise the expectations or principles on which their approach to art is based, but not all consensually founded beliefs are arbitrary and replaceable, and emancipation and the relief of suffering are worthy goals even if they can never be fully realized.

Select Bibliography

Primary:
Lyotard, J.-F. (1979) *La Condition Postmoderne*, Paris: Editions de Minuit (English translation, *The Postmodern Condition*, trans. G. Bennington and B. Massumi, Manchester: Manchester University Press, 1984).
Secondary:
Fekete, J. (ed.) (1987) *Life after Postmodernism: Essays on Value and Culture*, Manchester: Manchester University Press.
Jameson, F. (1990) *Postmodernism, or the Cultural Logic of Late Capitalism*, Durham, NC: Duke University Press.
Norris, C. (1990) *What's Wrong with Postmodernism? Critical Theory and the Ends of Postmodernism*, Baltimore: Johns Hopkins University Press.
Sarup, M. (1988) *An Introductory Guide to Post-structuralism and Postmodernism*, Hemel Hempstead: Harvester Wheatsheaf.
Silverman, H. J. (ed.) (1990) *Postmodernism—Philosophy and the Arts*, London: Routledge.
——and Welton, D. (eds) (1988) *Postmodernism and Continental Philosophy*, Albany: State University of New York Press.

KATHRYN PLANT

Post-structuralism

Post-structuralism is a movement within philosophical and literary criticism. It emerged from and was hostile to **structuralism**, which laid claim to scientific objectivity, detachment and comprehensiveness. Its main exponents are Jacques **Derrida**, Jacques **Lacan**, Julia **Kristeva**, Jean-François **Lyotard** and, in his later writings, Roland Barthes. It has trends in common with **postmodernism** and includes deconstruction within its scope. It began in France in the late 1960s, quickly spreading to other parts of Europe and North America.

As a movement, it is characterized by being anti-traditional, anti-metaphysical and anti-ideological. At its most philosophically respectable, it claims that many or all philosophical writings in the Western tradition inadvertently undermine themselves by not being able to sustain the assumptions on which they are based. One example of this is found in Derrida's critique of Lévi-Strauss, where Derrida claims that there is an underlying contradiction between the assertions that the taboo on incest is natural, but nevertheless has to be enforced by social sanctions. Another illustration comes from Rousseau's *Emile*: it is asserted that the psychological nature of women is different from that of men, but that women should not (not cannot) follow the same interests and occupations as men.

According to post-structuralist thought, there is no stability of meaning or, in Derrida's terminology, no 'metaphysics of presence' in language. This position goes against the view of **Saussure** that the meanings of words can be anchored down by those of other words which occur in the same sentence or phrase. The post-structuralist argument is that a word cannot be thus fixed in meaning, because that of other words is equally unstable.

Allied to this position is the broad view that the meaning of a literary text is also indeterminate. This assertion can be understood in one of two ways: that instead of there being just one definitive and authoritative interpretation of a literary work, there can be multiple meanings; or that a text can take any interpretation whatsoever. The more moderate claim can be useful because it allows new approaches in literary criticism.

Post-structuralism casts doubt upon the status of the subject as a persisting entity, as such an entity would be a fixed and permanent structure.

Advantage is taken by some of the North American post-structuralists, and by Derri-

da himself, of the inclusion of word-association by Saussure in his work on linguistics. Such association escapes from the allegedly public nature and rule-governedness of language, and is held up as a prime example of liberation and creativity. Derrida's article 'Shibboleth' (Hartman and Budick (eds) 1986) contains the word-associations 'shibboleth', 'circumcision', 'anniversaries', 'rings' 'constellations', and is interspersed with words in German; no doubt to take advantage of the Saussurean assertion that the division between natural languages is not clear-cut but arbitrary.

What is most useful in the post-structuralist programme are the secondary commentaries on the works of previous thinkers and the new perspectives on literary texts. If these aspects alone were retained from post-structuralism, it would become a less radical and more respectable philosophical and literary movement.

Select Bibliography

Derrida, J. (1986) 'Shibboleth', in G. Hartman and S. Budick (eds) *Midrash and Literature*, New Haven: Yale University Press.

Dews, P. (1987) *Logics of Disintegration: Post-Structuralist Thought and the Claims of Critical Theory*, London: Verso.

Easthope, A. (1988) *British Post-Structuralism*, London: Routledge.

Merquior, J. (1986) *From Prague to Paris: A Critique of Structuralist and Post-Structuralist Thought*, London: Verso.

Sarup, M. (1988) *An Introductory Guide to Post-structuralism and Postmodernism*, Hemel Hempstead: Harvester Wheatsheaf.

Weedon, C. (1987) *Feminist Practice and Post-Structuralist Theory*, Oxford: Blackwell.

KATHRYN PLANT

Pragmatism

Pragmatism originated in the 1860s out of discussions among a number of thinkers in science, mathematics, law, psychology, and philosophy, all influenced by Darwin's theory of evolution, aiming at attaining a scientific philosophy in which questions could be settled as decisively as in the sciences. The term 'pragmatic' was adopted from Kant's *Critique of Pure Reason*, where it is used to designate a type of judgement about which there can be no objective certainty but about which one is practically certain, as shown by one's willingness to bet on it. **Peirce** credited the British psychologist and philosopher Alexander Bain with the key definition of belief as 'that on which one is prepared to act'. Although pragmatism is not a philosophy of opportunism and is not incompatible with adhering to certain principles, it is centrally concerned with what 'works' for the purposes at hand, and the idea of the practical is central to the pragmatic philosophy, even though pragmatism's conception of the practical is itself a disputed matter.

One thinker, otherwise little known, who played an important role in the development of pragmatism was Chauncey Wright, a scientist and mathematician who constantly emphasized the importance of the Darwinian theory and attempted in his brief life to work out an evolutionary account of consciousness. The actual founder of pragmatism was Charles Sanders Peirce. Peirce conceived of pragmatism as a method for the clarification of ideas, and used it to clarify the ideas of meaning, truth, and reality. Peirce thought of inquiry as originating in doubt, uncertainty, an unsatisfactory feeling from which we struggle to free ourselves, which in turn stimulates inquiry or thought, aimed at eliminating the irritation of doubt by producing in its place belief, which Peirce characterized as a satisfactory feeling marked in our natures as a habit of action. To have a belief is to have a habit of acting in a certain way under certain conditions. The idea is that the meaning of an abstract conception is to be found in our conception of its practical or sensible effects under various hypothetical conditions.

Peirce arrived at his conception of truth by applying the pragmatic criterion; thus he held that the truth is that opinion upon which inquiry converges if carried on long enough, so that the truth is the opinion fated to be accepted as the ultimate outcome of inquiry. Thus, instead of defining inquiry as a process aiming at truth, Peirce defined truth as the outcome of inquiry, inquiry carried on in a certain way and with certain safeguards, such as those that characterize scientific procedures. Reality, he claimed, is what it is independently of what anyone thinks about it, so reality is the object of a true belief.

Peirce's conception was adopted and modified by William **James**. Applying the pragmatic theory of meaning to the concept of truth, James was led to the view that the truth of an idea is to be found in its working; it is true if it satisfies, is verifiable and verified in experience. Peirce was bothered by this modification of his original idea, and renamed his doctrine 'pragmatic*ism*', a term 'ugly enough to be safe from kidnappers'. What troubled Peirce was that James appeared to allow subjective elements into the equation: if believing that a certain idea is true would lead one to act in a way different from the way one would behave if one believed it false, then on James's view the idea would be said to have meaning, for it makes a difference in conduct and concrete life. For Peirce this importation of belief into the criterion of meaning was not applicable in the requisite way to scientific inquiry. On James's view, since reality is malleable and subject to change in accordance with human desires, so therefore is truth. This Peirce could not accept. However, while Peirce's writings were generally ignored, James's treatment of it made pragmatism famous as well as controversial.

James made pragmatism famous. John **Dewey** applied it to all areas of life, especially though not solely to education. Dewey held that an idea is true if it satisfies the conditions of the problem it was developed to solve. Dewey conceived of all ideas as hypotheses, tentative solutions to problems, true to the extent that they satisfy the conditions of the problem. Dewey's model of inquiry is the biological one of what an organism does when it is hungry: hunger is a dissatisfied state from which the organism struggles to free itself by engaging in food seeking activities; the activity of finding and eating food satisfies the conditions of the problem, and thinking, on Dewey's view, arises only out of problematic or indeterminate situations. Although the indeterminate situation becomes determinate through inquiry, determinacy is not a permanent condition; the solution of one problem leads to new problems, and the meaning of life, knowing, and inquiry are to be found in action. Dewey generalized this model to cover social and moral problems as well as scientific inquiry. On Dewey's view, called 'instrumentalism', all social thinking is a form of social inquiry involving experimentation, which requires active modification of the environment. The situation consisting in the organism in constant interaction with the environment changes as the relation between the organism and the environment changes, and the aim is to exercise intelligent control over the indeterminate situation to bring it to a satisfactory termination. Thus ideas, thinking, mind are instrumental to reconstruction of the indeterminate situation, and inquiry and knowing occur for the sake of adaptation to and modification of the environment. Dewey came to hold that the traditional problems of epistemology and large numbers of other traditional philosophical questions arise out of confusions generated by tradition, failure to question unexamined presuppositions, and failure to take adequate account of the biological basis of human life.

Both James and Dewey held that mind developed in the process of evolution as a means of enabling creatures who developed minds to adapt to and modify their environments. George Herbert Mead held views very like Dewey's. However, he carried this evolutionist and pragmatic view of mind further than the other pragmatists, and developed an original theory of the origin of language and intelligence and the self out of the interactions among different organisms and the gestures in which they engage in this interaction. This led to an original and very difficult metaphysics and a theory of social psychology remarkable for its originality and fruitfulness.

C. I. Lewis developed a 'conceptualistic pragmatism', a pragmatic theory of the a priori. Whereas Dewey regarded the distinction between analytic and empirical truths as an 'untenable dualism' merely marking the different roles each play in inquiry, Lewis advanced the idea that a priori ideas can be justified and modified on pragmatic grounds. It is the a priori element in knowledge, Lewis held, which is pragmatic, not the empirical. F. C. S. Schiller had quite a different perspective, not that of a logician. Though not one of the originators of pragmatism, he was a British ally very sympathetic to some ideas of William James, especially James's idea of the will to believe. He called his philosophy humanism, and it has come to be called pragmatic humanism. He played an important role in British philosophy as a critic of the absolute idealism of **Bradley** and Bosanquet, a role enhanced by his special rhetorical gifts.

All told, the most important pragmatists were Peirce, James, and Dewey. In recent years some of their key ideas have been accepted, modified, and applied in different ways by such contemporary philosophers as W. V. O. **Quine**, Donald **Davidson**, and Richard **Rorty**. So, after a period of desuetude in the middle part of the twentieth century, pragmatism, in a somewhat different guise, is very much alive and again at the centre of philosophical discussion.

Bibliography

Abel, Reuben (1966) *Humanistic Pragmatism: The Philosophy of F. C. S. Schiller*, New York: The Free Press.

Dewey, John (1920) *Reconstruction in Philosophy*, Boston, Mass.: The Beacon Press, revised edition, 1948.

Fisch, Max H. (1986) *Peirce, Semeiotic, and Pragmatism*, Bloomington: Indiana University Press.

James, William (1907) *Pragmatism*, New York: Longmans, Green and Co.

——(1909) *The Meaning of Truth: A Sequel to 'Pragmatism'*, New York: Longmans, Green and Co.

Madden, Edward H. (1963) *Chauncey Wright and the Foundations of Pragmatism*, Seattle: University of Washington Press.

Mead, George Herbert (1934) *Mind, Self and Society*, Chicago: University of Chicago Press.

——(1964) *Selected Writings*, ed. Andrew J. Reck, Chicago: University of Chicago Press.

Murphy, Arthur E. (1993) 'Pragmatism and the context of rationality', *Transactions of the C. S. Peirce Society* 29(2, 3 and 4): 123–78, 331–68, 687–722.

Peirce, C. S. (1934) *Collected Papers*, vol. V, *Pragmatism and Pragmaticism*, Cambridge, Mass.: Harvard University Press.

Sleeper, Ralph W. (1986) *The Necessity of Pragmatism*, New Haven, CT: Yale University Press.

Thayer, H. S. (1981) *Meaning and Action: A Critical History of Pragmatism*, Indianapolis: Hackett Publishing Company, second edition.

——(ed.) (1982) *Pragmatism: The Classic Writings*, Indianapolis: Hackett Publishing Company.

Wiener, Philip P. (1949) *Evolution and the Founders of Pragmatism*, Cambridge, Mass.: Harvard University Press.

MARCUS SINGER

Process Philosophy

A metaphysical philosophy that postulates process rather than substance as fundamental. This movement has been dominated by **Whitehead**, though **Hartshorne** has also been influential in the latter part of the century. The journal *Process Studies* was founded in 1971.

Bibliography

Brown, Delwin, *et al.* (eds) (1971) *Process Philosophy and Christian Thought*, Indianapolis: Bobbs-Merrill.

Lucas, George (1989) *The Rehabilitation of Whitehead: An Analytic and Historical Assessment of the Process of Philosophy*, Albany, NY: SUNY Press.

Moreland, J. P. (1988) 'An enduring self: the Achilles' heel of process philosophy', *Process Studies* 17: 193–9.

Neville, Robert C. (1974) *The Cosmology of Freedom*, New Haven, CT: Yale University Press.

——(1987) 'Contributions and limitations of process philosophy', *Process Studies* 16: 283–98.

Reck, Andrew J. (1975) 'Process philosophy, a categorical analysis', *Tulane Studies in Philosophy* 24: 58–91

Sibley, Jack R. and Gunter, Pete A. Y. (eds) (1978) *Process Philosophy: Basic Writings*, Washington, DC: University Press of America.

STUART BROWN

Realism

Controversies connected with 'realism' are deeply embedded in philosophy and, in the West, date back at least to Plato and Aristotle, each of whom was a prototype for one kind of realist. Plato opposed the view that moral values are dependent on social convention and his theory of forms represents one kind of moral realism. Plato's 'realism' has tended to be associated with belief in the existence of abstract entities generally and especially about mathematical objects. Realism in mathematics has been a common, though controversial position, and was espoused by **Frege**, amongst others.

Although a realist about abstract objects, Plato tended to deny the reality of the objects of the senses and, for this reason, is associated with **idealism**. In this respect Aristotle differed from him and Aristotle's realism about the objects of the senses remains hugely influential, for instance, in the Scholastic tradition. Even when **absolute idealism** dominated in British and American universities, early in the twentieth century, Aristotle always provided an alternative. Twentieth-century realism has not only these connections with the distant past but also with other realisms, such as that of the Scottish Common Sense School. It is thus a word of great historical complexity and no general statement can do justice to the choice of the term 'realist' by twentieth-century philosophers as a whole. Realism has been opposed not only to idealism, but to subjectivism, relativism, constructivism and phenomenalism. The opposition to idealism, however, was of particular importance earlier in the century.

The realist revolt against absolute idealism dates back at least to **Russell** and **Moore** in the 1890s. It was characterized by an espousal of pluralism, external relations, a correspondence theory of truth and a belief in realities independent of a mind. In America there were different schools of realism such as **New Realism** and **Critical Realism** and these terms are also extended to thinkers with similar views elsewhere.

Among the persistent problems about realism has been, how to accommodate it within an **empiricist** epistemology. Those who have favoured an empiricist epistemology of science have been inclined to deny the reality of theoretical entities. Against this there have been those who have called themselves 'scientific realists', such as W. Sellars, who have wished to assert the reality of all the entities spoken of in science, including those that are not observable.

Many philosophers in the 1980s and 1990s, reacting against a previously common subjectivism in ethics or various forms of pervasive relativism, have sought to defend ethical realism.

Bibliography

Primary:
Bhaskar, Roy (1975) *A Realist Theory of Science*, Leeds: Leeds Books.
Devitt, Michael (1984) *Realism and Truth*, Oxford: Blackwell.
Moore, G. E. (1903) 'The refutation of idealism', *Mind* New Series 7.

Putnam, Hilary (1982) 'Three kinds of scientific realism', *Philosophical Quarterly* 32: 195–200.
Wild, John (1948) *Introduction to Realistic Philosophy*, New York: Harper & Bros.
Wright, Crispin (1992) *Truth and Objectivity*, Cambridge, Mass.: Harvard University Press.
Secondary:
Bowman, Lars (1955) *Criticism and Construction in the Philosophy of American New Realism*, Stockholm: Almqvist & Wiksell.
——(1967) 'British and American realism, 1900–1930', *Monist* 51: 159–304.
Dummett, Michael (1982) 'Realism', *Synthese* 52: 55–112.
Feyerabend, Paul (1964) 'Realism and instrumentalism', in Mario Bunge (ed.) *The Critical Approach to Science and Philosophy*, New York: Free Press.
Harlow, Victor (1931) *A Bibliography and Genetic Study of American Realism*, Oklahoma City: Harlow Publishing Co.
Passmore, John (1985) *Recent Philosophers*, London: Duckworth, ch. 5.
Perry, Ralph Barton (1926) *Philosophy of the Recent Past*, part V, New York: Scribner's.
Schneider, Herbert (1946) *A History of American Philosophy*, New York: Columbia University Press, pp. 571–2.
——(1964) *Sources of Contemporary Realism in America*, Indiana: Bobbs-Merrill.

STUART BROWN

Semiology

Semiology, or 'the science of signs', is largely derived from the work of the linguist Ferdinand de **Saussure**, one of the major sources of inspiration behind **structuralism**, a movement that can fairly claim to be the home of semiological analysis. For Saussure, language was a system and, crucially, a system of conventionally-agreed signs that elicited a predictable response from the individual. The study of language was essentially the study of the relations between its various signs, that is, of the internal grammar of the linguistic system. Language became the model for how all sign systems worked, with Saussure predicting the development of a more general discipline called 'semiology' (after the Greek word for sign, *semeion*) that would study such systems.

Semiological analysis is a matter of analysing the grammatical relations between signs within a given system. Claude Lévi-Strauss thus treats a group of South American Indian myths as a self-contained system, where the signs in question are manipulated around in each individual myth in the manner of variations on a theme. The group in effect constitutes a genre with its own common underlying grammar.

Roland Barthes' work contains some of the most sustained examples of semiological analysis in the structuralist literature, with its detailed researches into such phenomena as advertising and fashion. In each case Barthes's concern is to identify the semiological codes involved in the system and how the audience responds to these. Literature and film equally go to make up sign systems for structuralist analysis, with the analyst setting out to identify and describe the grammar applying within an individual text, or across literary or cinematic genres (detective thrillers, westerns, etc.).

Bibliography

Barthes, Roland (1957) *Mythologies*, Paris: Seuil (English translation, *Mythologies*, trans. Annette Lavers, London: Jonathan Cape, 1972).

Culler, Jonathan (1983) *Structuralist Poetics: Structuralism, Linguistics and the Study of Literature*, London: Routledge & Kegan Paul.

Lévi-Strauss, Claude (1964) *Mythologiques I: Le cru et le cuit*, Paris: Plon (English translation, *The Raw and the Cooked: Introduction to a Science of Mythology, I*, trans. John and Doreen Weightman, New York: Harper & Row, 1969).

Saussure, Ferdinand de (1916) *Cours de linguistique générale*, ed. Charles Bally, Albert Sechehaye and Albert Reidlinger, Paris: Payot (English translation, *Course in General Linguistics*, trans. Wade Baskin, London: Peter Owen, 1960).

STUART SIM

Structuralism

Structuralism is a methodology originally used in the social sciences and later adapted to the treatment of literary texts and, more broadly, all artworks. Its first major exponent was Ferdinand de **Saussure**, whose theoretical work in linguistics is the common ancestor of all later structuralist analyses. Saussure himself gave the impetus to later structuralist work by his statement that all aspects of social life could be treated by the methodology that he had adopted for linguistics.

The structuralist approach is what Saussure calls 'static' or 'synchronic': that is, it is ahistorical. It takes a cross-section of its subject-matter and provides an analysis of the way in which all parts of a self-regulating system function together to form a consistent and coherent whole. Such elements have meaning or significance or function only by comparison with other elements, and from their place within the total system. For Saussure, the meaning of a word, or what he calls a 'sign', is partly determined by contrast with the other words in the context of which it occurs. Structuralist methodology is also intended to be purely descriptive: it takes as its raw data only actually-occurring social phenomena, which it does not evaluate or judge.

One important distinction made by Saussure was that between the deeper level of *langue*, or the rules and procedures operative within a natural language, and the surface level of *parole*, or the strings of words generated within and limited by those rules and procedures. A two-tier division was similarly adopted by later comparative structuralists: Lévi-Strauss, for example, thought that particular myths were exemplifications of a deeper underlying structure or pattern common to all myths, and claimed that his discoveries in this area could be used for a further structuralist study of how all human minds operate. Structuralism links all individual examples of social phenomena to their underlying structure, and this means that their authors or origins are not taken into consideration in any way.

If used properly, structuralist analyses can be useful, although limited. One criticism levelled against the methodology is that it simply assumes that the phenomena studies are coherent wholes: neither in Lévi-Strauss's treatment of myth, nor in Edmund Leach's study of Genesis, is there any attempt to disprove the competing hypothesis that the subject-matter is a loose collection of narrative from different sources. Another objection is that, by the improper use of the methodology, what is alleged to be the underlying structure of particular exemplifications is simply imposed and not discovered.

Structuralism has had a powerful influence on many disciplines throughout most of the twentieth century, but in the last three decades it has been displaced by **post-structuralism**, its hostile descendant.

Bibliography

Works on structuralism by individual authors include:
Barthes, R. (1990) *S/Z*, trans. R. Miller, Oxford: Blackwell.
Leach, E. (1969) *Genesis as Myth*, London: Jonathan Cape.
Lévi-Strauss, C. (1969) *The Raw and the Cooked*, London: Jonathan Cape.
Saussure, F. de (1974) *Course in General Linguistics*, London: Fontana.

General works on structuralism include:
Piaget, J. (1971) *Structuralism*, London: Routledge.
Sturrock, J. (ed.) (1979) *Structuralism and Since*, Oxford: Oxford University Press.

KATHRYN PLANT

Uppsala School

The Uppsala School was, according to Wedberg, 'the first unequivocally naturalistic academic school in philosophy' in Sweden.

Academic philosophy there had previously been strongly idealistic. The new positivistic movement was founded by Axel Hägerström and Adolf Phalén and flourished in the period 1910–40. Justus Hartnack has claimed that **analytical philosophy** can be said to have originated, largely independently, in three places: Cambridge, Uppsala and Vienna. The Uppsala School shared with the **Vienna Circle** a strong bias against metaphysics, as well as the view that moral utterances have no truth value. It shared with the Cambridge analysts such as **Moore** and **Russell** both their emphasis on conceptual analysis and a strong commitment to **realism** in reaction to the previously dominant **idealism**.

The Uppsala School was in some respects continued in the period after the Second World War by Konrad Marc-Wogau, Ingemar Hedenius and others. These, however, were more influenced by the Vienna Circle and by Anglo-American analytical philosophy than by Hägerström and Phalén.

Bibliography

Hartnack, Justus (1967) 'Scandinavian philosophy', in Paul Edwards (ed.) *Encyclopedia of Philosophy*, New York: Macmillan & Co.
Sandin, Robert T. (1962) 'The founding of the Uppsala School', *Journal of the History of Ideas* 23: 496–512.
Wedberg, Anders (1980) 'Sweden', in John R. Burr (ed.) *Handbook of World Philosophy: Contemporary Developments Since 1945*, London: Aldwych Press, pp. 173–90.

STUART BROWN

Utilitarianism

Utilitarianism is a normative ethical doctrine springing from largely nineteenth-century foundations and deriving from the view that happiness is the greatest good. It judges the morality of acts by their consequences. The best known version of the Principle of Utility is that formulated by John Stuart Mill (1806–73): 'The creed which accepts as the foundation of morals, Utility, or the greatest Happiness Principle holds that actions are right in proportion as they tend to promote happiness, wrong in their proportion as they tend to produce the reverse of happiness' (*Utilitarianism*, ch. 1).

Jeremy Bentham (1748–1832) is widely regarded as the founder of modern Utilitarianism although its general principle was enunciated earlier by Helvetius, Hutcheson and Hume. Bentham maintained that only pleasure is intrinsically good and pain intrinsically bad, and that the amount of pleasure or pain produced is the determining factor in judging the morality of an action.

J. S. Mill refined Bentham's morally vulnerable claim that it is the *quantity* of pleasure or pain that counts by distinguishing between 'higher' and 'lower' pleasures, but in allowing that some pleasures are better than others this doctrine invited the criticism that in cases of two actions producing equal amounts of pleasure something other than pleasure determines their moral values. Mill also placed emphasis on personal liberty and the individual conscience rather than on the mechanical calculation of pleasures and the social and legislative sanctions favoured by Bentham. A significant flaw in Mill's defence of happiness as the supreme good is his failure effectively to meet the criticism that there is a general conviction that on many occasions the bringing about of a just state of affairs over-rides the aim of creating the maximum of happiness.

Utilitarian doctrine was criticized and developed by Henry Sidgwick (1833–1900) who in *The Methods of Ethics* (1874) rejected psychological hedonism and argued that moral principles may be known intuitively. G. E. **Moore**, in chapter 3 of his *Principia Ethica* (1903), likewise rejected psychological hedonism and also argued that Utilitarianism was guilty of committing the naturalistic fallacy, that is, of deducing moral judge-

ments from statements of fact. His own view was that good is a non-natural property that is known intuitively and that an action is right if its consequences would be better than any other alternative and possible action.

In the latter half of the twentieth century much discussion has focused on the relative merits of rule-utilitarianism, which holds that right actions are those that conform to rules general observance of which would maximize happiness, and act-utilitarianism, which holds that the right action is the particular one that maximizes happiness in a situation. Both forms of utilitarianism are vulnerable to the criticism that they do not adequately satisfy intuited principles concerning justice and equity. Another influential view is that developed by J. J. C. Smart who has argued that there is no proof of the truth or falsity of utilitarianism but that it embodies a certain attitude that is apt to appeal to the generality of people and that offers guidance for the conduct of the moral life. A comparable approach has been elaborated by R. M. **Hare**, resulting in a doctrine of 'preference utilitarianism' that avoids many of the difficulties connected with the estimation of pleasures and pains and in which the morally right act is the one that provides people with what they would prefer to have and prevents them from having what they prefer not to have.

Utilitarianism has been stringently criticized by Bernard Williams who has maintained that it disregards the kind of significance life actually has for mature persons who, he points out, shape their lives meaningfully by means of projects the importance of which is not recognized by a doctrine that seeks simply to satisfy as many preferences as possible, taking no account of their differing values.

Bibliography

Primary:
Bentham, Jeremy (1789) *Introduction to the Principles of Morals and Legislation*, London.
Mill, J. S. (1861) *Utilitarianism*, London.

Moore, G. E. (1903) *Principia Ethica*, Cambridge: Cambridge University Press.

Sidgwick. H. (1874) *The Methods of Ethics*, London: Macmillan.

Warnock, M. (ed.) (1962) *Utilitarianism*, London: Fontana/Collins. (Contains Mill's *Utilitarianism*, his *On Liberty*, and the first five chapters of Bentham's *Introduction to the Principles of Morals and Legislation*.)

Secondary:

Hare, R. M. (1981) *Moral Thinking*, Oxford: Clarendon Press.

Lyons, D. (1965) *The Forms and Limits of Utilitarianism*, Oxford: Oxford University Press.

Quinton, A. (1973) *Utilitarian Ethics*, London: Macmillan.

Sen, A. K. and Williams, B. A. O. (eds) (1982) *Utilitarianism and Beyond*, Cambridge: Cambridge University Press.

Smart, J. J. C. and Williams, B. A. O. (1973) *Utilitarianism: For and Against*, Cambridge: Cambridge University Press.

DIANÉ COLLINSON

Vienna Circle

The name adopted by a group of **Logical Positivists** in Vienna who were led by Moritz **Schlick**. The leading philosophers in the group were Rudolf **Carnap**, Otto Neurath, Herbert Feigl, Friedrich Waismann, Edgar Zilsel and Victor Kraft. Amongst the prominent scientists and mathematicians were Phillip Frank, Karl Menger, Kurt **Gödel** and Hans Hahn. Both Ludwig **Wittgenstein** and Karl **Popper** knew members of the Circle, though they distanced themselves from its ideas. A. J. **Ayer** was associated with the Circle as a young man and became one of the most able advocates of its point of view in the English-speaking world. The group published a manifesto in 1929 stating its 'scientific outlook' (*wissenschaftliche Weltauffassung*). It also organized an international congress in Prague, followed by others in the 1930s at Königsberg, Copenhagen, Prague, Paris and Cambridge. By these means alliances were formed with similar groups in Berlin, **Uppsala** and Warsaw (see

Lvov-Warsaw School). The Vienna Circle had fellow-travellers throughout the world, particularly in the USA (Ernest Nagel, Charles Morris and W. V. O. **Quine**) and in Britain (Susan Stebbing and Richard Braithwaite). Its international influence was consolidated through editorial control of the journal *Erkenntnis*, which Carnap and Hans Reichenbach made the principal publication of the Logical Positivism movement.

The Circle was broken up by the rise of Nazism in the German-speaking world. Its influence remained none the less considerable in other countries. In the USA, where Carnap had emigrated, an ambitious series of brochures entitled the *International Encyclopedia of Unified Science* was planned. This series was eventually completed, though some of the numbers in it (**Kuhn**'s *Structure of Scientific Revolutions*, for instance) were remote in spirit from logical positivism. In the English-speaking world generally the influence of the Vienna Circle was considerable, though diluted, because of the way logical positivism affected **Analytical Philosophy**. In Scandinavia the influence has also continued, particularly through the **Uppsala School**.

Bibliography

Ayer, A. J. (1956) 'The Vienna Circle', in Gilbert Ryle, *et al. The Revolution in Philosophy*, London: Macmillan.

——(1959) 'History of the Logical Positivism movement', in A. J. Ayer (ed.) *Logical Positivism*, Glencoe, Ill.: Free Press, and London: Allen & Unwin, pp. 3–10.

Kraft, Victor (1950) *Der Wiener Kreis, Der Ursprung des Neopositivismus*, Vienna (English translation, *The Vienna Circle: The Origin of Neo-Positivism*, trans. A. Pap, New York: Philosophical Library, 1953).

Neurath, Otto (1935) *Le développment du Cercle de Vienne et l'avenir de l'empiricisme logique*, Paris: Hermann.

——, Carnap, R. and Hahn, H. (1929) *Wissenschaftliche Weltauffassung: Der Wiener Kreis*, Vienna: Wolf.

Smith, Barry (1987) 'Austrian origins of logical positivism', in Barry Gower (ed.) *Logical Posi-*

tivism in Perspective, Totowa, NJ: Barnes & Noble.

Übel, Thomas E. (ed.) (1991) *Rediscovering the Forgotten Vienna Circle*, Dordrecht: Kluwer Academic Publishers.

STUART BROWN

Vitalism

This term and some close variants have been used to describe some quite different types of philosophy in the twentieth century.

One of the major types of usage is in the philosophy of biology, where vitalism is used to denote the view that life is a property of organisms which is irreducible to physio-chemical processes, a view held, for example, by Driesch and von Uexküll. These thinkers maintain that, whilst there are close links between the organic and inorganic proper-ties of organisms, no reduction of the former to the latter is possible. Organisms exhibit principles or modes of being entirely distinct in kind from the non-organic. Vitalism in this sense is to be differentiated from the views of biologists like J. S. Haldane and von Bertalanffy, who preferred to think of themselves as 'organicists', maintaining that many organic processes can be reduced to

inorganic ones, but denying that the inor-ganic can be identified with the mechanical.

The second important usage of this term is in the compound 'ratio-vitalism', adopted by **Ortega y Gasset** to describe his own philosophy, and consequently very influen-tial in the Hispanic language communities. Ortega differentiates his view from the usage in the philosophy of biology described above; from epistemologies which regard knowledge as a biological process (e.g. Avenarius); and from epistemologies claim-ing the possibility of a non-rational grasp of ultimate reality (e.g. **Bergson**). Ratio-vitalism is the view that (a) reason is the only means to knowledge, but (b) insists that reason must be regarded as a property of a living subject, thinking the system in question.

Bibliography

Edwards, Paul (ed.) (1967) *Encyclopedia of Philo-sophy*, New York: Macmillan & Co.

Ferrater Mora, José (1984) *Diccionario de Filoso-fía*, Madrid: Alianza Editorial, fifth edition.

Nagel, E. (1961) *The Structure of Science*, London: Routledge & Kegan Paul.

Ortega y Gasset, José (1924) *Ni vitalismo ni racionalismo*, also in *Obras Completas* III.

Schlick, M. (1949) *Philosophy of Nature*, New York: Philosophical Library.

Toulmin, S. and Goodfield, J. (1962) *The Archi-tecture of Matter*, London: Hutchinson.

ROBERT WILKINSON